The Back Channel

A MEMOIR OF AMERICAN
DIPLOMACY AND
THE CASE FOR ITS RENEWAL

William J. Burns

RANDOM HOUSE

New York

Published in the United States by Random House, an imprint and division of Penguin Random House LLC, New York.

RANDOM HOUSE and the HOUSE colophon are registered trademarks of Penguin Random House LLC.

Library of Congress Cataloging-in-Publication Data
Names: Burns, William J. (William Joseph), author.
Title: The back channel: a memoir of American diplomacy and the case for its renewal / by William J. Burns.
Description: First edition. | New York: Random House, [2019] | Includes bibliographical references and index.
Identifiers: LCCN 2018042715 | ISBN 9780525508861 | ISBN 9780525508878 (ebook)
Subjects: LCSH: Burns, William J. (William Joseph) | Diplomats—United States—Biography. | United States—Foreign relations—1945–1989. | United States—Foreign relations—1989–
Classification: LCC E840.8.B857 A3 2019 | DDC 327.2092 [B]—dc23
LC record available at https://lccn.loc.gov/2018042715

Printed in the United States of America on acid-free paper

randomhousebooks.com

2 4 6 8 9 7 5 3 1

First Edition

Book design by Debbie Glasserman

For Lisa,
who has enriched my life
beyond measure, and made
everything possible

Contents

The Back Channel

Prologue

I REMEMBER CLEARLY the moment when I saw American diplomacy and power at their peak. I was seated behind Secretary of State James Baker at the opening of the Madrid Peace Conference in the autumn of 1991, feeling numb from exhaustion and excitement. Around a huge T-shaped table in the Spanish royal palace sat a collection of international leaders and—breaking a decades-long taboo—representatives of Israel, the Palestinians, and key Arab states. At the head of the table, alongside President George H. W. Bush, was Soviet president Mikhail Gorbachev. He was visibly tired and distracted, the leader of a faded superpower two months away from collapse. They were all united less by shared conviction about Arab-Israeli peace than by shared respect for American influence—fresh off the spectacular defeat of Saddam Hussein, the bloodless triumph of the Cold War, the reunification of Germany, and the reordering of Europe.

For a young American diplomat, Madrid was a heady moment. It was a dramatic illustration of how diplomacy could achieve what had seemed unthinkable. For the first time, Arabs and Israelis gathered in the same room, and agreed to the same terms for negotiations. With that, the door for the resolution of a conflict that had roiled the region and the world for more than four decades cracked open. They sat down together, against their instincts, because we asked, at a moment when well-framed U.S. requests were not easily ignored. It marked a time of uncontested American primacy in a world no longer bound by Cold War rivalry—when history seemed to flow inexorably in America's direction, the power of its ideas driving the rest of the world in a slow but irresistible surge toward democracy and free markets.

On that day in Madrid, global currents all seemed to run toward a period of prolonged American dominance. The liberal order that the United States had built and led after World War II would soon draw into its embrace the former Soviet empire, as well as the post-colonial world for which we had competed. Great power rivalry had rarely seemed so quiescent. Russia was flat on its back, China was still turned inward, and the United States and its key European and Asian allies faced few regional threats and even fewer economic rivals.

Globalization was gathering pace, with the American economy propelling greater openness in trade and investment. With only a single website and eleven million cellphones in use around the world, the promise of the information revolution was tantalizing, as was that of remarkable medical and scientific breakthroughs. The reality that a profoundly important era of human progress was unfolding only reinforced a sense of permanence for the nascent Pax Americana.

The question at the time was not whether America should seize the unipolar moment, but how and to what end. Should the United States use its unmatched strength to extend American global dominance? Or, rather than unilaterally draw and dominate the contours of a new world order, should it instead lead with diplomacy to shape an order in which old rivals had a place, and emerging powers had a stake?

* * *

ONE YEAR LATER, after President Bush had lost his bid for reelection, I was tasked with writing a transition memo to the incoming

Clinton administration and Secretary of State Warren Christopher. In it, I tried to capture the paradox for American statecraft. The memo began by welcoming the new administration to "a world in the midst of revolutionary transition, in which you will have both an historic opportunity to shape a new international order and a sobering collection of problems to contend with."

While "for the first time in fifty years we do not face a global military adversary," I wrote, "it is certainly conceivable that a return to authoritarianism in Russia or an aggressively hostile China could revive such a global threat." I argued that "alongside the globalization of the world economy, the international political system is tilting schizophrenically toward greater fragmentation." Ideological competition was not over—it was simply reshaped:

> The collapse of Communism represents an historic triumph for democracy and free markets, but it has not ended history or brought us to the brink of ideological uniformity. A great wave of democratic institution-building is taking place, driven by a surging post-Communist interest in the political and economic empowerment of individuals. But democratic societies that fail to produce the fruits of economic reform quickly, or fail to accommodate pressures for ethnic self-expression, may slide back into other "isms," including nationalism or religious extremism or some combination of the two. In much of the world, including parts of it that are very important strategically for us, Islamic conservatism remains a potent alternative to democracy as an organizing principle.[1]

The memo highlighted a number of other growing problems, from climate change to the AIDS epidemic and continued fragility in the Balkans. There were as many challenges as there were holes in my analysis. I couldn't yet grasp the pace and significance of China's rise, the intensity of Russia's resurgence, or the anger and frustration seething beneath so many authoritarian Arab societies. What was

easier to see was the potential for diplomacy to harness unprecedented military, political, and economic advantage to promote American interests and help make the world more peaceful and prosperous.

The potential for American diplomacy seems far less evident today.
The global order that emerged at the end of the Cold War has shifted
dramatically. Great power rivalry is back: China is systematically modernizing its military and is poised to overtake the United States as the
world's biggest economy, slowly extending its reach in Asia and across
the Eurasian supercontinent; Russia is providing graphic evidence
that declining powers can be at least as disruptive as rising ones, increasingly convinced that the pathway to revival of its great power status runs through the erosion of an American-led order.

Regional orders that seemed stable shortly after the end of the
Cold War are now collapsing, none more so than in the region for
which the Madrid Conference once held so much hope. The implosion of the Arab state system is the sharpest illustration of the risks of
emerging vacuums and the dissipation of American influence. With
tactical agility and a willingness to play rough, Vladimir Putin has
reasserted a Russian role in the region that seemed unimaginable in
that palace in Madrid, where Gorbachev's beleaguered presence was
more a political convenience for the United States than a mark of
Moscow's clout. A half-century-long American moment in the Middle East—inherited from the British, boosted by Desert Storm and
Madrid, and badly damaged by the Iraq War in 2003—is now disap-
pearing.

Meanwhile, a quarter century of convergence toward a Western
model is giving way to a new form of globalization, featuring a new
diversity of actors and the fragmentation of global power, capital, and
concepts of governance. There is much that is positive in all of these
trends. Hundreds of millions of people have risen out of poverty and
into the middle class; unprecedented progress has been made in
health and life expectancy; human society is more connected than
ever before, with half the population of the globe now enjoying access

to the Internet, and more than nine billion digital wireless devices in use.

In the United States and much of Europe, however, the backlash against globalization has been building. Donald Trump's election and Britain's decision to exit the European Union both reflected a deep popular unease, a growing anxiety that the dislocations of a globalized economy are not worth the benefits, that globalization not only doesn't lift all boats, but homogenizes political culture and obscures national identity. Those impulses, harnessed with demagogic flair by President Trump and European nationalists, have aggravated political polarization and incapacitated governance. Fewer than 20 percent of Americans now express confidence in government, half the figure in 1991. Gridlock is the default position in Washington and bipartisan compromise a distant memory.

The value of American leadership is no longer a given—at home or abroad. Fatigue with international intervention after nearly two decades at war has fed a desire to free the United States from the constraints of old alliances and partnerships and reduce commitments overseas that seem to carry unfair security burdens and economic disadvantage. The disconnect has grown between a disillusioned American public and the conceits of a Washington establishment often undisciplined in its policy choices and inattentive to the need to explain plainly the practical value of American leadership in the world.

Donald Trump didn't invent all of these trends and troubles, but he has fed them and made them worse. His erratic leadership has left America and its diplomats dangerously adrift, at a moment of profound transformation in the international order.

My own story helps shed light on how this came to pass, and how America's role has evolved. I hope it helps illuminate the back channels of my profession, and drags the argument for diplomacy into the light of public debate. I hope it also shows why the sidelining of diplomacy is so tragic, and why its restoration is so important. My goal is not to offer an elegy for American diplomacy but a reminder of its significance, and of the wider value of public service, amid the mistrust and disparagement so willfully sown by so many.

Long before Trump's election, my diplomatic apprenticeship exposed me to the best—and worst—of American statecraft and its practitioners, from the early rituals of my first overseas tour to a junior role in a Reagan White House recovering from the self-inflicted wound of the Iran-Contra affair. I saw adept American diplomacy under Bush and Baker and marveled at the skill with which they harnessed America's extraordinary leverage to shape a post–Cold War order. In Boris Yeltsin's Russia, I learned the limits of American agency when it is arrayed against the powerful forces of history. As ambassador in Jordan, I was reminded that American leadership could make a profound difference, especially to a partner undergoing a precarious and consequential leadership transition.

During the post–9/11 years, I led an embattled Bureau of Near Eastern Affairs in Washington as the inversion of the roles of force and diplomacy intensified. The casting aside of the Bush 41 administration's unique mix of caution and daring, in favor of a disastrous mix of militancy and hubris, fumbled an historic chance to reset America's role in the world. Rather than successfully shaping a new order, we compounded regional dysfunctions and undercut our influence.

The underlying challenge for the rest of my diplomatic career—including as ambassador in Putin's Russia and the most senior career American diplomat from the end of the Bush 43 administration through most of Obama's presidency—was how to adjust to a world in which American dominance was fading, in part due to structural forces, and in part due to our own grievous missteps. From reimagining and realigning relationships with emerging global rivals like Russia and China and partners like India, to navigating the turbulent waters of the Arab Spring and direct diplomacy with adversaries like Iran, those years made clear to me that the tests awaiting the next generation of diplomats will be even more formidable.

In the age of Trump, America is diminished, the president's worldview smaller and meaner, the world full of difficult currents. The enlightened self-interest at the heart of seventy years of American foreign policy is disdained, and the zero-sum joys of mercantilism and unilateralism are ascendant. Seen from the Trump White House, the United States has become hostage to the international order it created, and liberation is overdue.

Trump's worldview is the antithesis of Baker and Bush 41, who combined humility, an affirmative sense of the possibilities of American leadership, and diplomatic skill at a moment of unparalleled influence. The clock can't be turned back to that moment, of course; today's world is more complicated, crowded, and competitive. We are no longer the dominant power, but we can be the pivotal power for many years to come—best positioned among our friends and rivals to assemble and drive the coalitions and initiatives we need to answer the tests of our time.

The task will be to use what remains of the historic window of American preeminence to shape a new international order, one that accommodates new players and their ambitions while promoting our own interests. Neither unthinking retrenchment nor the muscular reassertion of old convictions will be effective prescriptions in the years ahead. The United States will have neither the singular unifying purpose of competition with the Soviet Union nor the singular unrivaled position of strength we enjoyed for nearly two decades after the end of the Cold War.

We will not be able to safeguard our values and interests on our own, or by big sticks alone. It will require persuading our partners as well as our adversaries of their stake in such an order. Only diplomacy can deliver on that.

* * *

SHORT OF WAR, diplomacy is the main instrument we employ to manage foreign relations, reduce external risks, and exploit opportunities to advance our security and prosperity. It is among the oldest of professions, but it is also among the most misunderstood, and the most unsatisfying to describe. It is by nature an unheroic, quiet endeavor, less swaggering than unrelenting, often unfolding in back channels out of sight and out of mind. Its successes are rarely celebrated, its failures almost always scrutinized. Even as visible and accomplished a practitioner as Henry Kissinger has called diplomacy "the patient accumulation of partial successes"—hardly the stuff of bumper stickers.[2]

A diplomat serves many roles: a translator of the world to Washington and Washington to the world; an early-warning radar for troubles and opportunities; a builder—and fixer—of relations; a maker, driver, and executor of policy; a protector of citizens abroad and promoter of their economic interests; an integrator of military, intelligence, and economic tools of statecraft; an organizer, convener, negotiator, communicator, and strategist.

Diplomatic engagement is not a favor to an adversary, but a means of reconnaissance and communication. It is a way to better understand trends, assess motivations, convey determination, and avoid inadvertent collisions. It is a method of maneuvering for future gain, a means of gaining wider support by demonstrating our willingness to engage and exposing the intransigence of rivals or foes.

The central function of diplomats is to try to manage the world's inevitable disorders and crises. Our embassy in Pakistan worked tirelessly in 2005–6 to organize the largest relief operation since the Berlin Airlift, in the wake of an earthquake that killed more than eighty thousand Pakistanis. In 2008–9, American diplomacy was at the heart of an international effort to stop an epidemic of piracy off the coast of East Africa. Senior American diplomats brought together the U.S. military, international relief organizations, and African governments to cope with the Ebola crisis in 2014. All of those efforts required substantial international cooperation. None could have been

accomplished by the United States alone—but none could have succeeded without American diplomatic leadership.

Diplomacy is also essential to the promotion of a level playing
field for American businesses abroad, to help open doors to the 95
percent of the world's consumers who live outside our borders, create
more jobs at home, and attract more foreign investment. Diplomats
manage visas for more than a million foreign students in the United
States, who generate about $40 billion every year for the American
economy, and for the tourists whose visits produce another $200 bil-
lion annually. Diplomats help American citizens in difficulty overseas, whose predicaments run the gamut from lost passports to
long-term imprisonment. They connect America to foreign societies,
run educational exchange programs, engage with people outside of
government, and try to cut through misunderstanding, mistrust, and
misrepresentation of American realities.

Diplomacy is a human enterprise, rooted in interactions between
people. Americans are often tempted to believe that the world re-
volves around us, our problems, and our analysis. As I learned the
hard way, other people and other societies have their own realities,
which are not always hospitable to ours. That does not mean that we
have to accept or indulge those perspectives, but understanding them
is the starting point for sensible diplomacy.

The process by which American diplomacy is implemented is also
all too human, full of the moments of clarity and courage, as well as
shortsightedness and clumsiness, that characterize any other human
endeavor. Policymakers and diplomats are often compelled to make
decisions under unforgiving time pressures, with inevitably incomplete information. That is hard to grasp from outside the arena, where
those realities can seem simpler and clearer than they do inside.

Diplomacy and the world it seeks to navigate have certainly
evolved in the nearly four decades since I joined the Foreign Service.
Nonstate actors—from the benign, like the Gates Foundation, to the

malign, like al-Qaeda—have steadily eroded what was once the near monopoly on power enjoyed by states and governments. The addition of cyberspace to the global commons, and advances in artificial intelligence, synthetic biology, and other technological domains, have added a new dimension to international competition, outpacing the capacity of governments to devise rules of the road. Global challenges like climate change and resource scarcity are no longer vague "emerging threats" but present-day crises. In American policymaking, there has been a growing tendency to centralize control and even execution in the White House, and to overrely on military force while allowing diplomatic muscles to atrophy, with dramatic military interventions squeezing diplomats to the margins.

* * *

AMERICAN DIPLOMACY IS adrift at a moment in history in which it means more than ever to our role as the pivotal power in world affairs. It will take a generation to reverse the underinvestment, overreach, and strategic and operational flailing of recent decades, not to mention the active sabotage of recent years under President Trump. The reconstruction of American diplomacy will require renewed investment in the fundamentals of the craft—the core qualities and roles that have always been the essence of what is required of effective diplomats: smart policy judgment, language skills, and a sure feel for the foreign landscapes in which they serve and the domestic priorities they represent. It will also require a more strategic adaptation than we've mustered during the course of my career, one that ensures we are positioned to tackle the consequential tests of tomorrow and not just the policy fads of today. Most important, it will require a new compact with the American people—leveling with them about the purpose and limits of American engagement abroad, and demonstrating that domestic renewal is at the heart of our strategy and priorities. Effective diplomacy begins at home, but it ends there, too—in better jobs, more prosperity, a healthier climate, and greater security.

What I learned all those years ago in that splendid hall in Madrid, and time and again throughout my long career, is that diplomacy is one of our nation's biggest assets and best-kept secrets. However battered and belittled in the age of Trump, it has never been a more necessary tool of first resort for American influence. Its rebirth is crucial to a new strategy for a new century, one that is full of great peril and even greater promise for America.

1

Apprenticeship:
The Education of a Diplomat

MY FIRST DIPLOMATIC mission was an utter failure. The most junior officer in our embassy in Jordan in 1983, I eagerly volunteered for what at the time seemed like a straightforward assignment: to drive a supply truck from Amman to Baghdad. It all seemed to me like an excellent adventure, a chance to see the thinly populated, rock-strewn desert of eastern Jordan, and visit Iraq, then in the midst of a brutal war with Iran.

The senior administrative officer at Embassy Amman was a griz-zled veteran renowned for his ability to get things done, if not for his willingness to explain exactly how he accomplished them. He assured me the skids had been greased at the Iraqi border: Getting across would be no problem. The seven-hour drive to the border went uneventfully. Then, at the little Iraqi town of Rutba, adventure met Saddam Hussein–era reality. The skids, it turned out, had not been greased. An unamused security official rejected my paperwork and ordered me to remain in the truck while he consulted with his supe-riors in Baghdad.

I spent a cold, sleepless night in the cab of the truck, incapable (in that pre-cellphone age) of communicating my predicament to my colleagues in Amman or Baghdad, and increasingly worried that my diplomatic career would not survive its first year. At first light, an Iraqi officer informed me that I'd be proceeding to Baghdad under police escort. He allowed me one brief phone call from the local post office to the on-duty Marine security guard at Embassy Amman. I explained what had happened, and he was able to convey to my colleagues in Baghdad the circumstances of my delay.

With a dour policeman who introduced himself as Abu Ahmed beside me, I began the long drive through many of the dusty towns of Anbar Province that America's Iraq wars would make all too well known—Ramadi, Fallujah, Abu Ghraib. My travel partner had an unnerving habit of idly spinning the chamber on his revolver as we drove along the rutted highway. At one point he pulled out a popular regional tabloid with the cast of *Charlie's Angels* on the cover. "Do all American women look like this?" he asked.

As the late afternoon sun was beginning to fade, we stopped for gas and tea at a ramshackle rest stop run by two of his brothers, just outside Fallujah, his hometown. As we sipped our tea, sitting on wobbly plastic chairs, Abu Ahmed's nieces and nephews appeared to see the exotic American. I've always wondered what happened to them over the tumultuous decades that followed.

Abu Ahmed and I, weary and running out of things to talk about, finally arrived at a large police compound on the northwestern outskirts of Baghdad in early evening. I was relieved to see an American colleague waiting for me; I was less relieved to learn that the Iraqis refused to accept our customs documents and insisted on confiscating the truck and its cargo. There was nothing particularly sensitive in the truck, but losing a dozen computers, portable phones, and other office and communication equipment was an expensive proposition for a State Department always strapped for resources. We protested, but got nowhere.

My colleague made clear that he'd take this up with the Foreign

Ministry, which elicited barely a shrug from the police. Now separated from the truck and released by the police, I went back to our modest diplomatic facility and told my story over a few beers. The next day, I flew back to Amman. As far as I know, neither our truck nor our equipment was ever returned.

* * *

A LIFE IN diplomacy seems more natural in retrospect than it did when I was stumbling along from Amman to Baghdad all those years ago, learning my first lesson in professional humility. But public service was already in my blood. I grew up as an Army brat, the product of an itinerant military childhood that took my family from one end of the United States to the other, with a dozen moves and three high schools by the time I was seventeen.

My father and namesake, William F. Burns, fought in Vietnam in the 1960s and eventually became a two-star general and the director of the U.S. Arms Control and Disarmament Agency. He was an exemplary leader, thoughtful and exacting, someone whose high standards and model of public service I always wanted to approach. "Nothing can make you prouder," he once wrote to me, "than serving your country with honor." His was a generation accustomed to taking American leadership in the world seriously; he knew firsthand the dangers of ill-considered military conflicts, and what diplomacy could achieve in high-stakes negotiations. My mother, Peggy, was the devoted heart of our family. Her love and selflessness made all those cross-country moves manageable, and held us all together. Like my dad, she grew up in Philadelphia. They met in the chaste confines of a Catholic high school dance—with nuns wielding rulers to enforce "six inches for the Holy Spirit" between them—and built a happy life shaped by faith, family, and hard work.

Making our close-knit Irish Catholic family whole were my three brothers: Jack, Bob, and Mark. As in many Army families, constantly bouncing from post to post, we became one another's best friends. We shared a love of sports across seasons and places, and looked out for one another on all those first days in new schools.

My upbringing bore little resemblance to the caricature of the cosmopolitan, blue-blooded foreign service officer. Through the years, however, a few useful diplomatic qualities began to emerge in faint outline. Because we moved so often, I became adaptable, constantly (and sometimes painfully) adjusting to new environments. I grew curious about new places and people, increasingly accustomed to trying to put myself in their shoes and understand their perspectives and predispositions. I developed a detachment about people and events, an ability to stand back and observe and empathize, but also a reluctance—born of many departures—to get too close or too invested. I also came to know my own country well, with a feel for its physical expanse and beauty, as well as its diversity and bustling possibility. I grew up with not only an abiding respect for the American military and the rhythms of Army life, but a vaguely formed interest of my own in public service.

In 1973, I went to La Salle College on an academic scholarship, my dreams of a basketball scholarship long since surrendered to the hard realities of limited talent. A small liberal arts school run by the Christian Brothers in a rough neighborhood in North Philadelphia, La Salle offered a valuable education inside and outside the classroom. It was then a school with lots of first-generation college students, mostly commuters, who worked hard to earn their tuition, took nothing for granted, and prided themselves on puncturing pretension. La Salle, like Philadelphia in the 1970s, was not for the faint of heart.

The summer after my freshman year, I spent three months in Egypt with one of my best high school friends, Conrad Eilts, and his family. Conrad's father, Hermann F. Eilts, had become the American ambassador to Egypt when the United States restored diplomatic relations after the October 1973 war. An astute diplomat of the old school, Eilts was full of initiative and had a sure grasp of the region.

For a raw and untutored eighteen-year-old, that summer in Egypt was a revelation. It was my first time outside the United States since I was a preschooler at an Army post in Germany. It was also my first time in the Arab world, and I was entranced by the scents and sounds, the commotion of the souk, and the rich intonations of Arabic. Conrad and I roamed across Cairo, then mostly barren of tourists and bursting with street life and the endless cacophony of its traffic. One night after midnight, we eluded narcoleptic Ministry of Antiquities security guards and a pack of wild dogs and scrambled in pitch darkness partway up the Great Pyramid of Cheops in Giza, looking out across Cairo's skyline until dawn began to break. We traveled to Luxor and Abu Simbel in Upper Egypt, and to the Siwa Oasis in the Western Desert, not far from the great World War II battlefield at El Alamein. It was the kind of adventure I could only dream about during previous summers bagging groceries in the Army commissary.

Later that summer, we went with Ambassador Eilts to visit President Anwar Sadat at his retreat in Mersa Matruh, on the Mediterranean coast west of Alexandria. While the ambassador met in private with Sadat, we swam in the warm blue sea, surrounded by the president's massive bodyguards. We then had a casual lunch on the veranda of Sadat's modest seaside home, with the president and his family all still in their swimsuits. Sadat was the picture of relaxation, puffing on his pipe and describing in his deep baritone his hopes for further steps toward peace with Israel. It was my first taste of the Middle East, and of American diplomacy, and I was already getting hooked.

During my senior year at La Salle, I won a Marshall Scholarship to study for three years at Oxford University. No one from La Salle had ever won a Marshall before, and I had applied with no expectations and minimal effort. Established by the British government in the early 1950s to commemorate the generosity of the Marshall Plan, the program gave thirty Americans each year a chance to study in the United Kingdom. The Marshall opened my eyes to a new, and initially intimidating, world of possibility. I felt out of my depth, surrounded by what seemed to me to be more worldly Ivy Leaguers, and out of place on Oxford's storied quadrangles.

From my base at St. John's College, I pursued a master's degree, and eventually a doctorate, in international relations. My supervisor in the master's program was an Australian academic named Hedley Bull. With a dry, self-deprecating wit and considerable patience for unformed young minds like mine, Bull was a superb intellectual guide. History was the key to understanding international relations, he insisted, and leaders most often erred when they thought they were immune to its lessons. His book *The Anarchical Society* remains as clear and compelling a framework for thinking about international order as I have ever read. Bull's thesis was straightforward: Even in a Hobbesian world, sovereign states have a self-interest in developing rules and institutions to help shape their interactions and enhance their chances for security and prosperity.

"You Americans," Bull told me at one of our weekly tutorials, "tend to be impatient about the world's imperfections, and convinced that every problem has a solution."

I asked what was so wrong with that.

"Nothing, really," he said. "I admire American ingenuity. But diplomacy is more often about managing problems than solving them."

I wrote my doctoral dissertation on the use of economic aid as an instrument of American policy toward Egypt in the Nasser era. The core argument was that economic assistance could reinforce areas of shared purpose, but it rarely had much effectiveness as a "stick" to alter fundamentally policies where no such common ground existed. Withdrawing aid for the Aswan Dam project, or American food aid, would not compel Egypt to abandon ties with the Soviets; it would more likely harden Egyptian defiance. Hardly a groundbreaking insight, but one that successive U.S. administrations would have to learn and relearn.

Beyond academics, Oxford was rarely dull. Grittier than its dreaming college spires might suggest, it was caught up in all the early turmoil of Margaret Thatcher's Britain, with angry labor unrest at the Cowley motor works on the eastern edge of town, and protests in support of Provisional Irish Republican Army hunger strikers on a square across from St. John's. I played on the university basketball team, and traveled widely around Europe and the Middle East during long vacation periods. Those years were a chance to see my own country through the eyes of others, and I soon discovered a genuine sense of pride and satisfaction in trying to explain America to them. That was not easy in the late 1970s, with Vietnam and Watergate still weighing heavily on American society and our image abroad.

Shortly after Iranian militants took American diplomats hostage in Tehran in November 1979, I took the train down to London to sit for the written portion of the Foreign Service exam at the old U.S. embassy on Grosvenor Square. A fellow American graduate student at Oxford had mentioned casually that fall that he planned to take the test, and encouraged me to come along. I wasn't yet convinced that diplomacy was the profession for me, nor was I sure that the State Department would think I had much to offer as a diplomat. But my experience in Cairo several years before, my admiration for my father's public service, and my curiosity about other societies and life abroad all made me want to give it a try. To my relief, the exam was straightforward—a combination of general knowledge questions, American civics, and geography 101.

I was thrilled to pass and later to navigate successfully the more nerve-racking oral exam with a trio of grim-faced officials. "What's the biggest challenge in American foreign policy today?" one asked. "I think it's us," I replied. Then, channeling my inner Hedley Bull, I explained, "After Vietnam, we have to do a better job of understanding which problems we can solve, and which we can manage." I cited Jimmy Carter's success in the Panama Canal Treaty and in the Camp David negotiations with Egypt and Israel as examples of the former, and grinding Cold War competition with the Soviets as an illustration of the latter. The examiners looked a little bored, and more than a

little skeptical, but a few weeks later I got a formal letter of acceptance.

* * *

IN EARLY JANUARY 1982, I showed up to Foreign Service orientation in a dreary office building across the Potomac River from the
State Department. I was seated alphabetically next to Lisa Carty—
a tall, lovely New Yorker whose easygoing charm, kindness, and good
humor soon captivated me. Lisa and I fell in love at a pace wholly out
of character with our two relatively careful personalities, and would
be married two years later.

The Foreign Service of the early 1980s was still a relatively small,
somewhat insular institution, with about 5,500 officers staffing some
230 embassies and consulates overseas and a variety of Washington
positions. Its "pale, male, Yale" reputation was well earned. At the
time, nine out of ten foreign service officers were white, and fewer
than one in four were women. It had only been a decade since married women and women with children were allowed into the service
and since annual performance reviews stopped evaluating the "host-
ess skills" of wives. Homosexuality was no longer a basis for denial of
employment, but it wasn't until 1995 that President Clinton banned
the government from denying security clearances on grounds of sex-
ual orientation.

Alexander Haig was secretary of state, the first of ten secretaries
under whom I would serve. President Reagan had launched a massive military modernization program, part of an effort to reassert
American purpose and influence in the wake of the Soviet invasion of
Afghanistan in 1979 and the Iranian Revolution that same year. Conflicts in Central America transfixed official Washington, part of a
wider contest with a Soviet Union that no one imagined was already
in the last decade of its existence. Meanwhile, China's economic transformation was quietly gathering momentum, with Deng Xiaoping's
reforms producing double-digit growth. It was a moment of turbu-

lence and uncertainty across the globe—and a genuinely exciting time for a twenty-five-year-old just embarking on a diplomatic life.

The training course for new FSOs, known in bureaucratic jargon as "A-100," was about seven weeks long, though at times it felt interminable. It featured a procession of enervating speakers describing their islands in the great American policymaking archipelago, and offering primers on how embassies functioned and the foreign policy process worked.

By the end of the training period, I had learned more about administrative rules and regulations than I had about the nuances of diplomatic tradecraft. I was struck, however, by the expansive mandate of the profession. On any given day in any given country, diplomats were keeping a watchful eye on American citizens living and working in the country, encouraging local citizens to come visit and study in the United States, and building a wide range of contacts inside and outside government to explain and inform American policy.

Our class of entering officers was a wonderful, eclectic mix. Lisa and I were among the youngest in the group. The average age was thirty-two, with a former Jesuit priest in his mid-fifties at the far end of the actuarial scale. There were former Peace Corps volunteers and military veterans, a couple of high school teachers, and at least one failed rock musician.

With a princely annual salary of $21,000, an intriguing professional future, and a budding romance, I couldn't have been more content. In the last week of the A-100 course, we were given our first assignments. Mine was Amman, Jordan. I was delighted, given my exciting foray into the Arab world several years before, and the inevitable policy swirl of the region. Lisa had volunteered to go to Burkina Faso, which reflected her lifelong passion for development issues and made her very popular in the class, since no one else was too enthusiastic about the lifestyle awaiting them in Ouagadougou. In the perverse wisdom of the State Department, Lisa was assigned instead to Singapore. We dreaded our impending separation but knew it would be a fact of life in the Foreign Service. We got engaged before Lisa departed for Asia in late spring, leaving me to fend for myself for six months as an Arabic-language student in Washington.

Before I left for the Middle East, I wrote to Albert Hourani, the chief examiner for my Oxford doctorate and a brilliant scholar of the Arab world, to tell him where I had been posted. He replied warmly, noting that he had always found Jordan "a little quiet and unremarkable culturally, but interesting politically." He added that he had just agreed to provide academic supervision to King Hussein's oldest son, Prince Abdullah, who would be at Oxford in the coming year. While Hourani's note didn't make much of an impression on me at the time, Jordan and Abdullah would play a large part in the career I was just beginning.

* * *

AMMAN WAS DUSTY and nondescript in the early 1980s, a city of about a million people sprawled across a series of rocky hills and valleys on the central Jordanian plateau. When I arrived, King Hussein had been on the throne for thirty years, and had survived numerous assassination attempts. Jordan occupied a precarious perch in the region, surrounded by conflicts and sitting atop simmering tensions between the stubborn, clannish East Bank minority that dominated Jordanian politics and a Palestinian-origin majority harboring no shortage of resentments. Starved of natural resources, Jordan was heavily dependent on outside financial help and remittances from the Gulf.

As an introduction to Middle East politics and diplomacy, Jordan was especially well situated, at the crossroads of most of the major problems in the region—from the Lebanese civil war in the north, to the Iran-Iraq conflict in the east, and the Israeli-Palestinian dispute in the west. The American embassy itself was just the right size for a new FSO, big and central enough to provide exposure to a whole range of issues and professional challenges, but not so big that a junior officer would easily get lost in the machinery.

Dick Viets was the ambassador, a skilled and sophisticated diplomat, straight out of central casting with his white mane and ever-present pipe. Unlike most U.S. ambassadors in the Arab world, Viets had served in Israel, and had wide experience outside the Middle East, including in South Asia and as an aide to Henry Kissinger. He had a close and effective relationship with King Hussein, and a willingness to speak his mind to Washington. Viets's deputy, Ed Djerejian, and political counselor, Jim Collins, became lifelong mentors.

I spent my first year in Amman in the consular section, as was customary for new officers, no matter what their later specialties might be. My first boss was Lincoln Benedicto, who had spent time before the Foreign Service as a youth counselor in some of Philadelphia's toughest neighborhoods. He was a good manager with a razor-sharp sense for people who were trying to game the system, whether visa applicants or Americans down on their luck overseas. The Jordanian employees who staffed the consular section were a huge asset, an early demonstration for me of the critical role that foreign service nationals play at American diplomatic posts around the world. They were our trusted eyes and ears, patient guides, and the one thread of continuity of knowledge, expertise, and contacts as officers came and went.

I was not a stellar visa officer. I spent too much time practicing my Arabic in interviews with Bedouin sheikhs, and not enough time processing the endless stream of paperwork and visa applications that came with the job. I never particularly enjoyed my quarterly visits to the few young Americans imprisoned for drug offenses; Jordanian prisons were hard places, and there wasn't much I could do other than talk and try to offer a little bit of hope. My consular responsibilities gave me chances to travel outside Amman, however, and I eagerly sought out tasks that would get me on the road.

I persuaded Lincoln to let me spend two weeks with the Howeitat tribe in southern Jordan, ostensibly to improve my Arabic. By the early 1980s, the Bedouin spent more time in small pickup trucks than on camelback, although camels were still the ornery heart of their daily existence. Smuggling everything from cigarettes to televisions back and forth across the Saudi border was a primary, if not publicly advertised, income stream. I was kept at a polite remove from those activities, and spent most of my time testing the patience of local tribesmen with my grammatically challenged Arabic. Nearly every member of the Howeitat I encountered claimed to have played a prominent role in the filming of David Lean's *Lawrence of Arabia* two decades before. Set in the stark beauty of Wadi Rum and the Jordanian desert beyond the tiny port of Aqaba, the movie starred Peter O'Toole as Lawrence and Anthony Quinn as the great Howeitat tribal leader Auda Abu Tayi. The Howeitat were not quite as cinematic in person as the Anthony Quinn version, but my brief experience in their midst opened my eyes to the ways in which tradition and modernity were colliding across the Arab world, setting off disruptions that continue to reverberate.

In the summer of 1983, I moved to the political section, the part of the embassy charged with analyzing Jordan's domestic situation and foreign policy, and building contacts with key officials and political players. We were busy but happy, dealing with a steady stream of Washington visitors, keeping up with an active ambassador, and grappling with lots of interesting regional and domestic issues. Donald Rumsfeld, briefly the Reagan administration's Middle East envoy, swept through Amman a couple times that year, supremely confident but unfettered by much knowledge of the region. The wider regional landscape remained perilous, with the bombing of our embassy in Beirut in the spring of 1983 a terrible reminder of the increasing risks that American diplomats faced. The horrific attack on the U.S. Marine barracks in Beirut that October, in which 241 Marines were killed, reinforced the challenge.

Amman was hardly immune from those threats. In addition to periodic assassinations and attacks against Jordanian targets, our embassy warehouse was bombed, and a small car bomb was set off one weekday afternoon in the parking lot of the InterContinental Hotel across the street from the embassy. When I walked over afterward with one of our security officers to talk to the Jordanian police and intelligence officials who were investigating, a second car bomb was discovered, and fortunately defused. It had been set to go off some time after the first one, precisely to hit the crowd of officials and onlookers who would naturally gather. It was the first, but not the last, time that I was luckier than I was smart.

That set of events produced understandable alarm. The embassy was an old, cramped stone building, on one of Amman's main streets. With no obvious alternative locations in the short term, the decision was made to put up a sandbag wall in front of the building, two stories tall and six feet thick. The barrier was reassuring, if unphotogenic—until it collapsed after one of Jordan's rare rainstorms, transforming the entrance into a man-made beach.

My responsibilities in the political section were mainly to cover domestic politics, and to try to expand the embassy's relationships beyond our traditional palace and political elite sources. I worked methodically at that task, talking discreetly to Islamist politicians and Palestinian activists in Jordan's refugee camps. I wrote profiles of next-generation leaders and explored the politics of some of the major towns and cities, including Zarqa, the sprawling urban area just east of Amman, in which disenfranchised Palestinians and disgruntled East Bankers mixed uneasily (and from which Abu Musab al-Zarqawi, the founder of al-Qaeda in Iraq, would later emerge). In the spring of 1984, I covered the first parliamentary elections in nearly two decades—a cautious effort by King Hussein to let off some of the political steam that was building as economic conditions stagnated.

Toward the end of my tenure in the political section, I wrote a cable in which I tried to distill what I had learned and what worried me about the future of Jordan and the wider Arab world. Entitled "The Changing Face of Jordanian Politics," the cable began by noting that "the traditional system of power relationships which has underpinned the Hashemite regime for decades is beginning to buckle under increasing demographic, social, economic and political pressures."[1] By the end of the 1980s, 75 percent of Jordan's population would be under the age of thirty. Well over half would be living in the urban stew of Amman and Zarqa, largely cut off from their social and political roots in Palestine and elsewhere on the East Bank. The educational system had its flaws, but remained one of the best in the Arab world; when combined with decreasing economic opportunities, the resultant expectations gap could prove combustible.

"As material gains become more difficult for a growing number of Jordanians to obtain," I observed, "and as traditional social and political ties begin to fray, disaffected citizens are likely to turn increasingly to the political system for redress of their grievances. What they will probably find is a generally anachronistic and unresponsive structure, riddled with corruption, the preserve of a powerful but steadily diminishing proportion of the population intent upon shielding its power and wealth from interlopers. It is a system based on the fading realities of a bygone era, a time when East Bank tribal balance was the stuff of which political stability was made."

King Hussein's intuitive skill and personal grip on the imaginations of most Jordanians were significant brakes on serious instability. But the broad challenge, not just for Jordan but for the rest of the Arab world, was that meeting the demands for dignity and opportunity of the next generation, and the one beyond that, would eventually require greater agility and commitment to modernize creaky economic and political systems. Jordan under King Hussein and later King Abdullah would be better placed than most to cope, but it was not hard to anticipate many of the pressures that would eventually bubble over.

* * *

LATE IN THE summer of 1984, I returned to Washington for my next assignment. Lisa and I had been married earlier that year, and it was far easier for us both to find jobs in Washington than at a single overseas post. In what is a rite of passage for new officers learning the byzantine ways of the State Department bureaucracy, I took on a position as a staff assistant in the Bureau of Near East and South Asian Affairs. Lisa took a similar position in the Bureau of International Organization Affairs.

The Near East Bureau, or NEA, was in that era a proud, intense, and slightly inbred place. As one senior colleague put it to me on my first day on the job, it was a place where "three simultaneous wars are considered average." It was known as the "Mother Bureau" for its reputation for skillfully shepherding Arabists along their career paths, and for setting the standard among State's other regional bureaus for professionalism under pressure. Led by Assistant Secretary of State Dick Murphy, the bureau worked at a frantic pace, coping with constant crises in the region and congressional scrutiny at home. Murphy was a consummate gentleman and a wise professional, steeped in the perils and personalities of the Arab world.

My partner in the staff assistants' office during most of that year was David Satterfield. I always felt a little inadequate around David, who had immense facility in the arcane policy issues that bedeviled the bureau, bottomless energy, and a capacity to speak in crisp, precise talking points about any issue at any time. Our role in those low-tech days was basically to serve as the organizational hub for the bureau's policy work. We conveyed taskings from the secretary's office, reviewed and filtered the cables coming in from overseas posts, and made sure that Murphy was well prepared for his relentless schedule of meetings and trips. One of us would come in every morning at six to prepare a one- or two-page summary of overnight developments for Murphy's use in Secretary of State George Shultz's daily staff meeting. Given NEA's pace, we'd rarely get out of the office before nine or ten at night.

One of us would also accompany Murphy on his frequent overseas trips—shuttling between capitals, cultivating relationships, managing crises, and pushing large policy rocks up steep hills. The Middle East had its share of Sisyphean tasks. The bitter aftermath of the Israeli invasion of Lebanon a couple years earlier still consumed much of NEA's attention. Meanwhile, the grueling conflict between Iran and Iraq dragged on, with Washington quietly putting its thumb on the scale to support Saddam's Iraq. The familiar struggle to revive Arab-Israeli peace talks remained a priority, although as was so often the case it was a function more of aspiration than on-the-ground realities.

George Shultz's reliance on professionals like Dick Murphy, along with his own impressive integrity and intellect, won him many admirers in the department. Shultz was a firm believer in the importance of "tending the garden" in diplomacy, and expected Murphy to spend considerable time on the road, even when particular policy goals were so obviously elusive. One evening in the fall of 1984, I was walking with Murphy along the long wood-paneled corridor that runs down the middle of the seventh floor of the State Department, where the office of the secretary is located. Shultz appeared in the hallway outside his office as we walked past, and asked Murphy when he was heading back to the Middle East. Murphy replied that he had a number of commitments in Washington, including upcoming congressional testimony, and wasn't sure when he'd travel next. Shultz smiled and said, "I hope you can get back out there soon. It's important to keep stirring the pot."

The result of that conversation was a marathon trip, which stretched from North Africa to South Asia, and kept us on the road for nearly five weeks. My role was a mix of logistician and policy aide. Much of the trip involved shuttling between Israel, Lebanon, and Syria, as Murphy tried to broker a deal that would allow Israeli forces to withdraw from Lebanon, with Syrian forces not advancing southward beyond their positions in the Beqaa Valley. It was fascinating to watch him try to move the immovable Syrian president, Hafez al-Assad, who loved to filibuster with long soliloquies on Syrian history since the Crusades. Lebanese politicians, with deep-rooted survival instincts and an endless capacity for backbiting, were maddeningly entertaining. Israel's national unity government was frequently paralytic, with its two leaders and rotating prime ministers, Shimon Peres and Yitzhak Shamir, almost as suspicious of each other as they were of their Arab neighbors.

Nevertheless, Murphy somehow managed to maneuver the parties toward a slightly more stable disposition of forces, with the Israelis pulling back by the early summer of 1985 to a several-mile-wide "security zone" along Lebanon's southern border. Murphy's formula was equal parts persistence and ingenuity, steadily pressing for small practical steps, using American leverage carefully, and always conscious that this was another problem to be managed before it could ever be solved. As I was learning, diplomatic triumphs are almost always at the margins.

On that trip and several subsequent efforts over the next few months, Murphy worked hard to restart Arab-Israeli talks. Negotiations never materialized. Yasser Arafat was as hard to pin down as ever; King Hussein lost whatever patience he had for Palestinian machinations; and the Israeli side was immobile, with Shamir uninterested in negotiations over territory with anyone, and Peres interested only in negotiations with Hussein, without the headaches of Palestinian representatives and their desire for an independent state.

Iraq, then five years into its horrific war with Iran, was a particularly memorable stop. Tariq Aziz, Saddam's urbane and faintly menacing foreign minister, hosted Murphy for a long lunch of masgouf, the famous Iraqi fish dish. Aziz's security detail cleared a well-known restaurant on the Tigris of its patrons for the afternoon. Seated at an outdoor table overlooking the river, we could see Iraqi guards fanning out around the building, pistols drawn. The restaurant staff affected an air of normalcy, exchanging whispers about who these evidently important foreigners were. Puffing on a big Cuban cigar, Aziz professed great optimism about Iraq's prospects on the battlefield, and waxed poetic about the future of U.S.-Iraqi relations. Murphy was unimpressed. As down-to-earth as Aziz was full of mobster charm, Murphy smiled as we walked out of the restaurant and said, "He kind of reminds you of Al Capone, doesn't he?" I learned a lot about diplomacy from Dick Murphy, although I had no idea then that fifteen years later I'd wind up sitting in his office, not just emptying his outbox.

Near the end of my assignment, I was asked by Deputy Secretary John Whitehead's chief of staff if I'd be interested in becoming one of Whitehead's two special assistants. He thought my experience in NEA would serve me well in the stressful world of the seventh floor, where the department's senior leadership wrestled with the problems that couldn't be solved at lower levels. I spent the next year trying not to prove him wrong.

Whitehead had just become George Shultz's deputy, after a remarkable career that had taken him from the U.S. Navy and the D-Day invasion to the top of Goldman Sachs. Self-assured and thoroughly decent, Whitehead shared Shultz's faith in the State Department, although he was always a bit bemused by the difficulty of getting things done quickly, or at least as quickly as he had become accustomed to at Goldman.

My first day on Whitehead's staff was very nearly my last. He was an avid art collector, and had placed an original Degas ballerina miniature on the edge of his large desk. On my first morning, I walked in quietly and put a folder in the inbox, only to accidentally knock the Degas off the desk and onto the floor. Fortunately, the oriental carpet was thick, the ballerina bounced undamaged, and the deputy secretary resumed his reading with only a mild grimace in my direction.

The rest of my tour went more smoothly. My new position gave me a wide perspective on how the department worked, across the whole range of policy issues and bureaus. Whitehead took a special interest in economic issues, and played an important role in helping to open up East European economies as the Cold War was ending and the Soviet bloc was crumbling. I accompanied him on a variety of trips, from Europe to the Middle East and Africa. He helped manage the difficult aftermath of the *Achille Lauro* attack in the fall of 1985, when Palestinian terrorists murdered a wheelchair-bound American on a hijacked Italian cruise ship. He also took the lead in mobilizing European support for sanctions against Libya in the spring of 1986, after Muammar al-Qaddafi's agents struck a disco in West Berlin and killed several U.S. servicemen. Although himself a skeptic about the efficacy of economic sanctions, Whitehead was a skillful advocate, and his efforts in the mid-1980s laid the groundwork for a sanctions regime that two decades later helped persuade Qaddafi to abandon terrorism.

* * *

MY RUN OF professional good fortune continued in the summer of 1986, when I was assigned to the National Security Council's Near East and South Asia directorate, a four-person office covering Morocco to Bangladesh.

My new office was in room 361½ in the Old Executive Office Building, the elaborate structure next to the White House, which until World War II had housed the entire staffs of the State, War, and Navy departments. Whenever I got a little too full of myself, walking with my White House badge along the long, high-ceilinged corridors of the building or across West Executive Avenue for meetings in the White House, my ego would come right down to earth when I returned to my office. Room 361½ was a converted women's bathroom, the size of a walk-in closet, with exposed plumbing along the walls and a scent that served as a persistent reminder of the room's previous function.

My boss was Dennis Ross, a smart, even-tempered thirty-eight-year-old Californian with an academic background in Soviet and Middle East studies. The Reagan administration was still scarred by

its grim experience in Lebanon a few years before, groping unsuccess-
fully with various formulas for restarting Arab-Israeli negotiations,
and anxious about revolutionary Iran. We were all stretched thin in
the summer and fall of 1986, on an NSC staff whose core dysfunction
was quickly apparent even to a young and inexperienced diplomat
like me.

The modern NSC had grown out of the experience of the Kennedy
administration, when McGeorge Bundy led twenty or so political appointees and career professionals from State, Defense, and the intelligence community, organized in small regional and functional offices.
The main tasks of the NSC staff, then as now, involved staffing the
president for his foreign policy engagements; coordinating the preparation of options for presidential decision with the key cabinet agencies and ensuring that their views were clear, timely, and unfiltered;
and carefully monitoring implementation. The role of the national
security advisor and the NSC staff grew substantially under Richard
Nixon, who drew on the brilliance and ruthless bureaucratic agility of
Henry Kissinger to remake relations with China and the Soviet
Union, with the White House staff serving not only as coordinator
but also chief policy operator.

Ronald Reagan entered office in January 1981 committed to diminishing the role and reach of the NSC staff and reducing the tension between the NSC staff and cabinet principals that had continued
during the Carter administration. Reagan went through national security advisors at a rapid clip. John Poindexter, a Navy admiral, became Reagan's fourth NSC chief in four years at the end of 1985. A
decent man with a nuclear engineer's exacting intellect, Poindexter
was badly miscast in the role. Uncomfortable dealing with Congress
and the media, without personal or political connections to the president, not held in high regard by the leaderships of State, Defense, or
the CIA, he inherited a staff with some bad habits and explosive
secrets—which his own uncertain instincts and detached style proceeded to make worse.

The most dangerous of those secrets was a bizarre scheme that had begun earlier in 1985 as a clandestine effort by the NSC staff, working through a motley collection of Iranian and Israeli middlemen, to trade U.S. arms to Iran in exchange for the release of Americans held hostage in Lebanon. Poindexter's predecessor, Bud McFarlane, had championed the initiative, despite the long-standing U.S. policy against making concessions to terrorists. Beyond his interest in the return of American hostages, McFarlane saw the potential for a strategic opening to Iran, and contacts with "moderates" in Tehran. In May 1986, still engaged in the enterprise despite having handed over his post as national security advisor to Poindexter, McFarlane made a secret trip to Tehran with a small NSC staff team, in an unmarked Boeing 707 full of arms. The whole episode was the stuff of dark comedy, with McFarlane and his colleagues bearing a cake in the shape of a key to highlight their interest in an opening to Iran. No senior Iranians, let alone "moderates," emerged to meet McFarlane. Tehran did, however, buy the arms. It also eventually engineered the release of several American hostages by their Hezbollah captors in Lebanon.

What turned this strange story into a full-blown scandal that nearly brought down the Reagan presidency was a further twist. Led by Oliver North, a Marine lieutenant colonel in the NSC staff's political-military office, the White House had secretly diverted the proceeds of the arms sales to support the anti-Communist Contra forces in Nicaragua. Since Congress had formally forbidden the administration from funding the Contras, this was an illegal—and stunningly reckless—maneuver. Predictably, news of the arms-for-hostages effort leaked out in a Lebanese newspaper story in November 1986, and the Contra connection was soon exposed. Poindexter and North were gone by the end of the month.

As the Iran-Contra scandal unfolded, the NSC staff and the entire White House were in deep disarray. The president seemed stunned and adrift. Seeking a way out, he tasked a commission headed by

Senator John Tower of Texas to investigate the role the NSC staff had played in the scandal and recommend reforms. The Tower Commission Report, issued in February 1987, was sharply critical of the president's hands-off leadership style and the failings of the NSC, and advocated a long list of remedies. Frank Carlucci, a former career diplomat who had served as deputy director of the CIA and deputy secretary of defense, returned to government as Poindexter's successor. He brought as his deputy Colin Powell, a charismatic forty-nine-year-old Army general. Powell and Carlucci employed the Tower Commission Report as their "owner's manual," and quickly set about overhauling the staff and its structure.

Two-thirds of my colleagues on the NSC staff were soon transferred or fired. An experienced senior diplomat, Bob Oakley, was appointed head of the Near East–South Asia office, with Dennis staying on as his deputy and me remaining at the bottom of the organizational chart. Carlucci and Powell streamlined the overall NSC staff, installed a general counsel to ensure rigorous legal and ethical compliance, and insisted on strict accountability. They worked hard to rebuild trust with Secretary Shultz and Secretary of Defense Caspar Weinberger, restored the NSC staff to its nonoperational, coordinating role, and set up a disciplined system of interagency meetings, built around a Senior Review Group of cabinet principals, which Carlucci chaired, and a Policy Review Group of their deputies, led by Powell. Together with White House chiefs of staff Howard Baker and Ken Duberstein, Carlucci and Powell helped save the Reagan presidency, rebuild public and congressional trust in the White House, and support a renewed diplomatic push by Shultz that produced some significant late Cold War gains.

Powell made a particularly strong impression on me, as effective and natural a leader as I had ever encountered. Having grown up in the world of the military, I knew the significance of "command presence," and Powell personified the concept. Straightforward, demanding, and well organized, he was also warm and good-humored, with a ready smile and easy charm. His Policy Review Group meetings were precise and collegial. The departmental deputies never lacked for opportunities to lay out their views, but Powell made sure each session had a clear beginning, middle, and end—with a crisp statement of objectives, orderly discussion of options, and a concise summation of conclusions or recommendations to principals. For many meetings on Middle East issues, I'd write the talking points that Powell could draw on to guide the conversation. He always made them much more compelling.

Much of my work in 1987–88 revolved around the Persian Gulf, where the Iran-Iraq War ground on, and where our Gulf Arab allies remained deeply unsettled by the revelation of secret American overtures to a regime in Tehran that they despised and feared. The Gulf Arabs had still not recovered from the shock of the Iranian Revolution and all the uncertainties about American reliability that flowed from it. Every Iranian tactical advance in the war with Iraq sparked new worries.

Desperate to ward off the Iranians, the Iraqis had begun to attack Iranian oil tankers in the Gulf, trying to chip away at the resources that fueled the war effort. Since most Iraqi oil was exported by pipeline, and since it was hardly in Iran's interest to try to close the Strait of Hormuz on which its own oil exports depended, Tehran retaliated by striking the tankers of Saddam's Gulf Arab allies, especially Kuwait and Saudi Arabia. The resultant "tanker war" added a new theater to the conflict, and Iran's acquisition of Chinese-origin Silkworm antiship missiles threatened a rapid escalation. Late in 1986, the Kuwaitis approached both the United States and the Soviets for help in protecting their tankers, explicitly requesting that the United States "reflag" Kuwaiti-owned tankers—putting them under U.S. flag so that they would fall under the protection of the American Navy.

That touched off a series of complicated deliberations within the Reagan administration about how to respond. I joined Bob Oakley in weeks of Policy Review Group meetings, now chaired by John Negroponte. An accomplished diplomat, Negroponte succeeded Powell as deputy national security advisor in late 1987, when Powell took Carlucci's place and Carlucci moved to the Pentagon to replace Weinberger as secretary of defense. There were obvious downsides to agreeing to reflagging, not least the danger of getting sucked into the tanker war. Neither State nor the Navy were wildly enthusiastic about the prospect. As Weinberger was departing, however, he had registered with Reagan his strong concern that ceding the opportunity to the Soviets would be a major setback for American interests. Moreover, the White House was anxious to rebuild credibility and trust with the Gulf Arabs, and to send a post-Iran-Contra signal of American resolve. The president formally announced U.S. willingness to reflag in May 1987, just after the Iraqis had "inadvertently" fired a missile at the USS *Stark*, killing thirty-seven Navy personnel. While the intelligence was murky, I've never been convinced that the attack on the *Stark* was entirely an accident, given Saddam's interest in drawing the United States in and breaking the murderous stalemate with Iran.

The reflagging operation was conceived as a relatively low-key exercise, but that quickly proved wishful thinking. The Navy had only a handful of ships in the Gulf at the time, and had to make some major adjustments. It was short on minesweepers, and we had to drum up support from a number of European allies. The reflagging itself required endless legal gymnastics and interagency coordination. By late July, however, the United States was able to begin protecting eleven Kuwaiti tankers, now under U.S. flag, in convoys moving in and out of the Gulf. It didn't take long, however, for other crises to emerge. In September, a U.S. helicopter fired on an Iranian vessel caught laying mines. The following month, the Iranians fired missiles at a U.S.-flagged tanker in Kuwaiti waters, and U.S. Navy destroyers shelled an Iranian offshore platform in response.

There was no letup in the first half of 1988, and I remember many late nights and early mornings in the White House Situation Room monitoring the latest collision. In April, the USS *Samuel B. Roberts* struck an Iranian mine, and ten sailors were injured. Two Iranian oil platforms and a number of Iranian naval vessels were destroyed in retaliation. Finally, in July, the USS *Vincennes* mistakenly shot down an Iranian civilian plane, killing 290 passengers and crew. It was a terrible tragedy, but reflected the mounting risks of conflict in the crowded waters and skies of the Gulf. In August, the Iranians finally agreed to a UN-brokered cease-fire with Iraq.

As tensions in the Gulf began to ease, my own role at NSC shifted unexpectedly. Dennis Ross left to serve as Vice President Bush's chief foreign policy advisor in his 1988 presidential election campaign. Bob Oakley became our ambassador to Pakistan after the tragic death of his predecessor, Arnie Raphel. I assumed that Colin Powell would bring in a senior official to run the Near East office for the last six months of the administration, and was genuinely surprised when he asked me to take on the role of senior director and chief of the office. At thirty-two, and barely into the middle ranks of the Foreign Service, I was very junior for such a promotion. I went over to see Powell in his West Wing office and explained that I was appreciative of his confidence but thought he should find someone more experienced. I had even brought a few names to suggest. "I wouldn't have asked you to do this if I wasn't convinced that you could," Powell replied evenly. I understood immediately that there was only one right answer, swallowed my self-doubt, and replied that I'd do my best to honor his trust. I walked back to the Old Executive Office Building unsure of how I'd handle the responsibility, but buoyed by his vote of confidence.

The remaining months of the Reagan administration were a blur. More crises inevitably erupted. In December 1988, a terrorist bomb brought down Pan Am Flight 103 over Lockerbie, Scotland. All 259 passengers and crew were killed, along with 11 people in Lockerbie who were struck by debris. Initial suspicions focused on the Iranians, seeking revenge for the *Vincennes* shoot-down, or a Syrian-based Palestinian terror group. But the investigation eventually pointed toward Libyan responsibility, setting off another tortured chapter in relations with Qaddafi, and eventually in my own professional life.

A final episode in the Reagan administration's efforts to promote Arab-Israeli peace occupied much of my last months at the NSC staff. Throughout the first half of 1988, against the unsettling backdrop of mounting violence in the West Bank, Secretary Shultz and Dick Murphy had labored doggedly to launch negotiations. The idea was that Jordan could represent Palestinian interests, and that there would be an "interlock" in the process whereby talks on the final status of the West Bank and Gaza would proceed even as discussions of transitional arrangements unfolded. The Shamir government in Israel was resistant—unwilling to concede much in the face of Palestinian violence. King Hussein was wary of exposing Jordan to more regional criticism and distrustful that Arafat would ever cede negotiating responsibility to Jordan. In July 1988, his frustration complete, the king publicly relinquished Jordanian legal and administrative ties to the West Bank, stating bluntly that the PLO now bore sole responsibility for negotiating Palestinian interests.

Since the mid-1970s, the United States had insisted that it would deal directly with the PLO only if it met three conditions: acceptance of UN Security Council Resolution 242 and the land-for-peace formula for resolution of the conflict; an end to violence; and recognition of Israel's right to exist. As King Hussein cut his ties to the West Bank, and nervous that new leaders might emerge that he could not control, Arafat began to probe the possibility of opening a dialogue with the United States. One private diplomatic track was opened by a Palestinian American activist close to the PLO chairman, and another initiative was championed by the Swedish foreign minister. A complicated dance ensued, with Arafat taking a series of steps that came close to the three American conditions, but didn't quite meet them. The White House largely deferred to Shultz, who was adamant that the criteria could not be compromised. I stayed in close touch with Dick Murphy and his deputy, Dan Kurtzer, as they tried to nudge the intermediaries toward the finish line, and kept Powell carefully informed.

Not long after Vice President Bush's sweeping victory in the presidential election in November, a significant complication developed. Arafat applied for a visa to come to the United Nations in New York at the end of the month. I thought there were powerful arguments to grant the visa, given U.S. obligations as host of the UN. But Secretary Shultz remained deeply concerned about PLO involvement in terrorism, and was determined to show Arafat that he would not bend until the three conditions for U.S. dialogue were met. The president and Powell deferred to Shultz, and Arafat was denied a visa. As Shultz anticipated, the denial did not slow PLO interest in opening a direct dialogue, and may have convinced Arafat that he couldn't cut any corners.

By early December, Arafat was edging close to the mark. I joined Powell and Shultz and a few other aides for a meeting with President Reagan in the Oval Office to discuss next steps. Shultz argued persuasively that it was important to take yes for an answer if Arafat met the terms. This would be a service to President Bush, who would inherit a dialogue with the Palestinians, and not have to sacrifice any early political capital to bring it about. President Reagan readily agreed. "Let's just make sure they stick to their end of the bargain," he said.

On December 14, Arafat made a public statement in Geneva that matched the American criteria, and our ambassador in Tunis was authorized to begin a direct dialogue with PLO representatives. While we were still a long way from serious peace negotiations, it was a useful step forward. Both President Reagan's foreign policy legacy and his place in history looked immeasurably better in December 1988 than they had two years before.

As the inauguration of President Bush approached in January 1989 and I prepared to return to the State Department after two and a half intense years at the White House, I realized how fortunate I had been, and how much I had learned. I wrote in my last personnel evaluation at the NSC staff that I now understood "how the policy process should work, and how it shouldn't." I had also begun to learn that the profession of a diplomat was only partially that of diplomacy; you had to know how to navigate politics and policymaking as well. My apprenticeship as a diplomat had been unusually rich and varied over less than seven years, with experience in an exceptional embassy and tours with two strong public servants at senior levels of the department, followed by a roller-coaster ride at the NSC staff that took me from the bizarre lows of Iran-Contra to heady responsibilities under Colin Powell. Now I was about to launch into a new and even more fascinating chapter, returning to the State Department as the Cold War ended and the world was transformed.

2

The Baker Years: Shaping Order

THE OLD CAUCASUS spa town of Kislovodsk was in terminal decline, much like the Soviet Union itself. It was late April 1991, and Secretary Baker and the rest of us in his bone-tired delegation had just arrived from Damascus. With Baker scheduled to meet with Soviet foreign minister Aleksandr Bessmertnykh the next morning, we stumbled around in the evening gloom to find our rooms in the official guesthouse, long past its glory days as a haven for the party elite. My room was lit by a single overhead bulb. The handle on the toilet came off when I tried to flush it, and what trickled out of the faucet had the same sulfurous smell and reddish tint as the mineral waters for which the town was famous. It wasn't a particularly alluring setting, but I hadn't slept in twenty-four hours and longed to collapse in the bed, rusty springs and all.

First I had to deliver a set of briefing points to the secretary. I walked down to his suite, which was bigger and better lit than the other rooms, although with similarly understated décor. The State Department security agent stationed outside the door knocked and let me in. Baker was sitting at a desk reading press clips, still in his crisp white dress shirt and characteristic green tie. He smiled wearily and motioned me to sit down. The secretary's stamina and focus on preparation were legendary, but he was exhausted. A day before, he had spent nine hours in a diplomatic cage fight with Syrian president Assad. Nearly motionless as he sat in his overstuffed armchair, Assad had relished the endurance contest with Baker, spinning out long monologues about Syria's history and regional intrigues, and ordering enough tea to overwhelm even the hardiest bladders. Unintimidated and undefeated in Damascus, Baker was nevertheless worn out.

He glanced at the paper I handed him. The range of issues that he was going to discuss with Bessmertnykh would have been hard to imagine at the outset of Baker's tenure two years before. There were points on Germany's peaceful reunification in the fall of 1990, and background notes on the Soviet Union's increasingly uncertain future, with hardliners battling reformers, Gorbachev beset by independence-minded republics, and the economy in free fall. Historic negotiations were under way to lock in conventional and nuclear arms reductions. And in the Middle East, Baker was seeking to capitalize on the military triumph over Saddam Hussein and produce an Arab-Israeli peace conference, ideally with Soviet co-sponsorship.

Looking up from the memo and across the tattered furnishings of his suite, Baker asked, "Have you ever seen anything like this?" I assured him I hadn't, and started to tell him all about my new handleless toilet. "That's not what I meant," he said, unable to restrain his laughter. "I'm talking about the *world*. Have you ever seen so many things changing so damn fast?" Embarrassed, I acknowledged that I hadn't. "This sure is quite a time," he said. "I bet you won't see anything like it for as long as you stay in the Foreign Service."

He was right. For all the exceptional people and complicated challenges I have since encountered, the intersection of skilled public servants and transformative events that I witnessed in the Baker years at the State Department remains special. The end of the Cold War, the peaceful disintegration of the Soviet Union, and the successful reversal of Iraqi aggression marked a new era in international order.

President George H. W. Bush was well suited for the unprecedented changes unfolding around him, drawing on his eight years in the White House as vice president, his tenure as CIA director, and his life in the diplomatic arena, first as ambassador to the United Nations and then as envoy to China. Jim Baker was his closest friend, a wily political player, a former White House chief of staff and secretary of the treasury. Brent Scowcroft became the model for future national security advisors, forging a close bond with President Bush, managing the policy process with fairness and efficiency, and displaying consistently sound judgment and personal integrity. Dick Cheney was a strong leader at the Pentagon, well versed in national security issues as well as the dark arts of Washington politics. Colin Powell had become chairman of the Joint Chiefs of Staff, bringing with him not only a stellar record of military service but also his successful tenure as Reagan's national security advisor.

Their combination of policy skill and political acumen served our country well when the tectonic plates of geopolitics began moving in dramatic and unexpected ways. This was a team that had its inevitable imperfections and blind spots, and its share of misjudgments and disagreements, but as a group they were as steady and sound as any I ever saw. At one of those rare hinge points in history, they were realistic about the potency as well as the limits of American influence. They realized that American dominance could lead to hubris and overreach, but they had a largely affirmative view of how American leadership could shape and manage international currents, if not control them. Theirs was an example that I never forgot, and that every successive administration tried to reach.

* * *

I OWED MY entry onto the fringes of Baker's circle to my old boss, Dennis Ross. After the campaign, in which he served as Bush's foreign policy advisor, Dennis chose to go with Baker to the State Department. He judged, correctly, that the secretary's tight relationship with the president would make him the key player in American diplomacy. As director of the Policy Planning Staff, Dennis was given responsibility for two critical issues, the Soviet Union and the Middle East. Sitting on the steps of the Old Executive Office Building one sunny late November afternoon, he asked if I'd join him as his principal deputy. I accepted—uncertain about another professional leap for which I felt unprepared.

Jim Baker ran the State Department through a tight, close-knit group, working out of a string of offices along the seventh floor's "mahogany row." At one end of the wood-paneled hallway sat Deputy Secretary Larry Eagleburger, a rumpled, blunt-spoken, chain-smoking Foreign Service veteran, sometimes bursting at the seams of his aspirationally sized pinstriped suits. Baker relied on Eagleburger to manage the building and help ensure harmonious coordination with Brent Scowcroft, Eagleburger's longtime friend and colleague under Henry Kissinger. At the other end sat Bob Zoellick, who served as counselor, and later undersecretary for economic affairs. Still only in his mid-thirties, Bob was brilliant, creative, and incredibly disciplined. He was precisely the kind of talent Baker needed by his side at a moment when the shelf life of conventional wisdom often seemed to be measured in days, not years.

Sitting in an office with a connecting door to the secretary's suite was Margaret Tutwiler. Though she was nominally assistant secretary for public affairs and department spokesperson, Margaret's actual role was far more expansive. She had served under Baker in the Reagan White House and at Treasury, and was fiercely protective of his image and political flanks. Beneath her Southern graciousness, Margaret was tough as nails, with exceptional instincts about people. Just beyond her office was Bob Kimmitt's set of offices as undersecretary for political affairs, the number three job in the department. Kimmitt's roots with Baker also went back to the Reagan White House. A

West Point graduate and Vietnam veteran, Kimmitt had a quick mind and immense organizational ability. He oversaw the department's regional bureaus, and played a crucial role in managing the day-to-day policy process. Between Kimmitt and Zoellick sat Dennis and me, a few corridors removed from the rest of the Policy Planning Staff.

Baker had mastered the politics of foreign policymaking. He knew how to maneuver people and bureaucracies, and his feel for the international landscape was intuitive and pragmatic. He was a superb problem-solver, and made no pretense of being a national security intellectual or grand strategist. He was cautious by nature, and always attuned to the risks of unforeseen second- and third-order consequences. He was unchained by ideology and open to alternative views and challenges to convention. He was as good a negotiator as I ever saw, always thoroughly prepared, conscious of his leverage, sensitive to the needs and limits of those on the other side of the table, and with a lethal sense of when to close the deal.

Baker deftly used his closest advisors to run the institution and supply the innovation and imagination he sought, with just the right touch on the reins to draw on the strengths of each of them. He could rely on Zoellick and Ross for ideas and strategy; Eagleburger and Kimmitt to get things done and steer the bureaucracy; and Tutwiler to watch his back and avoid political landmines. While Baker's early, closed style produced predictable grumbling at State, it evolved considerably over time. The accelerating pace of events and his own growing appreciation of the skills of career personnel encouraged him to rely on a wider circle. Career professionals were drawn in and exhilarated by Baker's clout and success, which put State at the center of American diplomacy at a time of massive global change.

I had always been intrigued by the Policy Planning Staff, which had been launched in 1947 by Secretary George Marshall, and whose first director was George Kennan, the Foreign Service legend and architect of the Cold War strategy of containment. Marshall's charge to Kennan and the five staff members he assembled was to "develop

long-term programs for the achievement of U.S. foreign policy objectives." He added one laconic bit of advice: "Avoid trivia."[1] Kennan and
his colleagues played a pivotal role in devising the Marshall Plan, and
in laying the early foundations for American policy during the Cold
War. After Marshall left State in 1949, Kennan grew disenchanted
with both what he saw to be the militarization of his original concept
of containment and Dean Acheson's less sympathetic view of Policy
Planning's bureaucratic prerogatives. His influence waning, he soon
left the department for a sabbatical at Princeton.

The role of Policy Planning varied widely in significance after
Kennan. Subsequent directors often struggled to sustain the attention of secretaries of state, and to find an effective balance between
long-term strategy and the operational challenges that preoccupy the
secretary and the rest of the department on any given day. Successful
Planning Staffs, such as Kissinger's, did both.

Baker's Policy Planning Staff was as consequential as Kissinger's
or Marshall's. Baker treated it as his own mini–National Security
Council staff, relying on us for ambitious initiatives as the Cold War
was ending, speechwriting, tactical support on his travels, and the
briefing papers and talking points and press statements that fueled
the diplomatic machine. His relatively insular style, as well as the
drama and scope of world events, gave Policy Planning a huge (and
daunting) opportunity to shape strategies and decisions.

We eventually grew to thirty-one staff members, drawn from career ranks at State, the Pentagon, and CIA, as well as an eclectic group
from outside government. I served as Dennis's principal deputy and
alter ego, doing my best to help lead and manage the staff, and frequently traveling with Baker. The staff was full of stars—scholars like
John Ikenberry and Frank Fukuyama, whose article on "The End of
History" was about to catapult him to fame; FSOs like Russia hand
Tom Graham, the always irreverent Bill Brownfield, and my good
friend Dan Kurtzer; and civil servants like Aaron Miller, another close
friend and Middle East specialist, and Bob Einhorn, one of the gov-

ernment's premier arms control experts. We had gifted political appointees, like Andrew Carpendale, Walter Kansteiner, and John Hannah; talented if overworked speechwriters; and young interns like Derek Chollet, one of the most promising foreign policy minds of his generation.

It was a remarkable group, and a heady time. Our connection to Baker and privileged status in the department did not endear us much to the rest of the institution, so I spent a fair amount of energy trying to build a collegial reputation for our team. Still, it was no surprise when Tom Friedman, then the *New York Times* correspondent at the State Department, wrote in the fall of 1989 that we were viewed by many in the department as "a group of still-wet-behind-the-ears whippersnappers with too much authority for their tender years."[2]

* * *

WET BEHIND THE ears or not, nothing would have prepared us for the events of 1989.

Having served as central players throughout the Reagan administration, President Bush and Secretary Baker were intimately familiar with their inheritance. They knew that Central America would remain a major source of partisan strife and a potential drain on the Bush administration's foreign policy capital on the Hill. They were more optimistic about Asia, and at least initially encouraged by the trajectory of relations with China. Japan's economic boom was real, but its threat to our own economy was grossly exaggerated. The vast expanse from Afghanistan to Morocco seemed more settled than it had been in some time: The last Soviet troops departed Afghanistan on the eve of President Bush's inauguration in January 1989, the Iran-Iraq War was over, and threats to shipping and access to Gulf oil had receded. The beginning of dialogue with the PLO seemed to offer a modest new opening on the Arab-Israeli peace front, even as violence continued between Palestinians and Israelis in the West Bank and Gaza.

The central drama, however, was unfolding in the Soviet Union.

Mikhail Gorbachev was still trying to reform Soviet rule, aiming to reverse a perilous economic decline while preserving Communist Party rule at home and Soviet influence abroad. He faced mounting problems: economic decay; food shortages; a hostile old guard in the party; growing ethnic unrest and separatist sentiment in non-Russian republics; restive allies in Eastern Europe; and an increasingly disillusioned public. And yet few expected the imminent demise of the Soviet bloc, let alone the Soviet Union itself.

Reagan, the old Cold Warrior, had seemed in his later years in office to understand the desperation in Gorbachev's maneuvers and the terminal rot in the Soviet system. But Bush, Baker, Scowcroft, and their colleagues remained skeptical. They entered office determined not to be hoodwinked by Gorbachev. If he failed, it was not apparent that the Soviet Union would fail; it seemed more likely that hardliners would supplant him and restore the hard edge of the Cold War.

Bush and Baker took a careful approach to managing relations with Gorbachev during the first half of 1989. At the president's direction, Brent Scowcroft and his deputy, Bob Gates, launched a long interagency review of our policy toward the Soviet Union. As the review proceeded, Gates called for a "conscious pause" in U.S.-Soviet diplomacy. "A lot has happened in the relationship in an ad hoc way," Gates wrote. "We've been making policy—or trying to—in response to what the Soviets are doing, rather than with a sense of strategy about what we should be doing."[3] Baker was careful in his first meeting with his Soviet counterpart, Eduard Shevardnadze, that March in Vienna, and in conversations with Shevardnadze and Gorbachev in Moscow in May. He made clear to both that the Bush administration appreciated the sweep and potential of the changes they were attempting, but also emphasized that neither he nor the president appreciated being cornered by bold public proposals or acts of "one-upmanship" designed to portray Washington as the recalcitrant party. For Scowcroft and Gates, as well as for Cheney, the jury was still out on Gorbachev. As Scowcroft later put it, "Were we once again mistaking a tactical shift in the Soviet Union for a fundamental transformation of the relationship?"[4]

My colleagues and I in Policy Planning played an active role in the internal review process, but grew restive with its methodical pace, especially as events in the former Soviet bloc gathered speed in the spring of 1989. Free elections took place in the Soviet Union for the Congress of People's Deputies, giving fiery new figures like Boris Yeltsin a nationally televised platform to press for faster changes. Elections in June in Poland swept Solidarity into power, forming the first non-Communist government in postwar Eastern Europe. Later that month, Hungary removed the barbed wire along its border with Austria, and two hundred thousand Hungarians attended the reburial of Imre Nagy, the officially rehabilitated leader of the 1956 revolution. True to his "Sinatra Doctrine" of nonintervention in the political evolution of Eastern Europe, Gorbachev let the Poles and Hungarians do things their way.

By the fall of 1989, the pace of change convinced Baker that the United States could no longer afford to take the wary, risk-averse approach favored by the Pentagon and NSC staff. Their argument was essentially that the administration should hold out for Gorbachev to make more concessions as his position weakened. Baker, however, advocated a more activist policy—a systematic effort to shape a rapidly changing European landscape and lock in strategic advantages in partnership with Gorbachev and Shevardnadze. Beginning in early September, we sent Baker a series of papers that outlined alternative scenarios for the USSR if Gorbachev's reform efforts collapsed. They ranged from the gradual crumbling of the Soviet system to a military coup and authoritarian modernization, but they all underscored the urgency of the moment and the value of doing all we could to support constructive change. In a conversation in his office that autumn, Baker told us that "history won't forgive us if we miss this opportunity because we were too passive or not creative enough." With Baker's careful prodding, President Bush was coming around to this view too.

In late September, Baker hosted Shevardnadze and a large Soviet delegation for several days of talks near his modest ranch in Jackson Hole, Wyoming. The setting was spectacular, with the Tetons looming above the lodge where the talks took place, and the Snake River running nearby. Shevardnadze clearly appreciated Baker's informal hospitality and their budding friendship.

Eduard Shevardnadze was a fascinating figure, a product of the Soviet system who saw its flaws in cold relief and had the courage to try to do something about them. A proud native of Georgia, he understood the forces of nationalism bubbling within the Soviet Union better than most senior leaders. He was also unflinching in his diagnosis of the paralytic Soviet economy, and far more realistic in his assessment of the dangers of a conservative reaction against reform than Gorbachev, the ebullient optimist. On the wider international stage, Shevardnadze understood that rapidly declining Soviet leverage required an effort to build a new relationship with the United States, as a way of both stabilizing the situation at home and preserving as much of the Soviet Union's global role as possible. In Baker, Shevardnadze found a similarly pragmatic partner.

There was tangible progress on a number of issues at Jackson Hole. Shevardnadze made clear that the Soviets would no longer link significant reductions in nuclear arms to the future of missile defense, a major breakthrough that would lead eventually to the Strategic Arms Reduction Treaty in 1991, the largest and most significant arms control treaty ever negotiated. Logjams were broken on bilateral agreements on nuclear testing and chemical weapons. And the Soviet foreign minister said flatly that arms shipments to Nicaragua would cease, and that Moscow would press the Cubans to stop their shipments too.

Shevardnadze also impressed Baker with his candor on the domestic challenges that Gorbachev faced. Rather than give formulaic responses when Baker raised American concerns about possible Soviet use of force against protestors in the Baltic states or striking coal miners in Russia, Shevardnadze was blunt about the unreconstructed views of some in the Soviet leadership, and the risks of violence. He resisted Baker's suggestion that Gorbachev begin to "cut loose" the Baltic states, explaining his worries about the chain reaction that might cause in other parts of the USSR. The overall directness and depth of their conversations solidified Baker's activist inclination, and helped prepare the ground for Bush's summit meeting with Gorbachev in Malta that December.

Baker went on to lay out the administration's evolving approach in a series of speeches and public statements in October. He argued that perestroika's success would be determined by the Soviets themselves, but that it created an historic opportunity for a new relationship with the United States based on greater "points of mutual advantage." Advances in arms control and resolution of regional conflicts were obvious examples; Baker also offered technical assistance in support of Soviet economic reforms, and painted a wider picture of "a Europe whole and free."

Meanwhile, it was hard to keep track of events in Eastern Europe. On November 9, a bungled attempt to relax restrictions on travel to the West resulted in the fall of the Berlin Wall. As Dennis Ross and I sat in his office that Thursday afternoon watching the riveting CNN footage of Berliners hammering chunks out of the wall, we could see that the world we had known was changing—we just could have never predicted how much, how far, or how fast. Within weeks, popular movements toppled autocrats in Bulgaria, Czechoslovakia, and Romania. We tried to think ahead, and in a subsequent Policy Planning paper laid out a series of initiatives aimed at "consolidating the revolutions of 1989 in Eastern Europe."[5] Noting that "the post-communist reconstruction of Eastern Europe is no less challenging than the post-Nazi reconstruction of Western Europe," we pressed for concrete programs of technical and economic support, in cooperation with our European allies, and without provoking the Soviets.

By the time Gorbachev and Bush had their shipboard summit in stormy Mediterranean seas off Malta a month after the fall of the wall, the Soviet empire was no more. Gorbachev was matter-of-fact, telling Bush that they were "simply doomed to dialogue, coordination and cooperation. There is no other choice."[6] Building on the Jackson Hole discussions, they agreed to major nuclear and conventional forces cuts. Most interestingly, they signaled the possibility of a re-united, democratic Germany—a reality that had seemed unimagin-able for the better part of four decades.

Nowhere was Baker's diplomatic agility and foresight more evi-dent than in the rapid sequence of events that led, in less than a year, from the tearing down of the Berlin Wall to Germany's formal reuni-fication, within NATO, in October 1990. In discussions in Policy Planning in mid-November 1989, Frank Fukuyama proposed that Baker take the initiative and frame a series of principles on German reunification. In a subsequent memo to the secretary, Frank stressed several basic points: Germans—not outside powers—should deter-mine their own future; reunification should occur in the context of Germany's continued commitment to NATO, taking into account the legal role and responsibility of the four Allied powers (France, the United Kingdom, the United States, and the Soviet Union); the pro-cess should be gradual, peaceful, and step-by-step; and the Helsinki Act provisions on the inviolability of borders should apply. These early American principles helped set the tone and shape of the subse-quent diplomatic process. They also helped Baker address Germany's determination to make its own choices about its future; the early skepticism of the French and British about any rapid move to reuni-fication; and the obvious worries of the Soviets about the strategic consequences of a united Germany. Shaping the principles of policy debate, I learned, is often the first step toward winning it.

Baker also had to overcome more cautious sentiments within the White House and other parts of the administration. One paper from the European Affairs Bureau at State counseled Baker to avoid being "stampeded" into premature diplomatic initiatives. Zoellick and Ross strongly disagreed. For several years, Zoellick kept the memo on his desk and used it to remind me, only partly in jest, of the overly cautious mindset of the Foreign Service. Baker hardly needed to be persuaded. Given the breathtaking pace of change in 1989, he had no interest in sitting on the sidelines.

We spent much of the Christmas holiday working to devise a framework that would translate Fukuyama's principles into a practical process. The memo that resulted outlined a "Two Plus Four" process, in which West Germany and East Germany would shape internal arrangements, and the four Allied powers would help guide external arrangements. Dennis sent it to Baker in late January 1990, and the secretary quickly realized the utility of the concept—the first part addressed the needs of the Germans (and the concerns of some in the administration), and the second addressed those of the Soviets, French, and British. With President Bush's support, Baker sold the concept to German chancellor Helmut Kohl and foreign minister Hans-Dietrich Genscher in early February, agreeing to use Two Plus Four negotiations to press for rapid German unification and full NATO membership, while reassuring the Soviets that NATO would not be extended any farther to the east, and would be transformed to reflect the end of the Cold War and potential partnership with the Soviet Union.

In meetings a few days later with Shevardnadze and Gorbachev in Moscow, Baker won their initial support, and began the effort to ease their resistance to membership of a unified Germany in NATO. Baker maintained that Soviet interests would be more secure with a united Germany wrapped up in NATO, rather than a Germany untied to NATO and perhaps eventually with its own nuclear weapons. He also said that there would be no extension of NATO's jurisdiction or forces "one inch to the east" of the borders of a reunified Germany. The Russians took him at his word and would feel betrayed by NATO enlargement in the years that followed, even though the pledge was never formalized and was made before the breakup of the Soviet Union. It was an episode that would be relitigated for many years to come.

The Two Plus Four approach was broadly blessed at a meeting of foreign ministers in Ottawa in mid-February and announced by Baker and Genscher. In May, Gorbachev conceded to Bush that Germany should be able to choose its own alliance arrangements. Increasingly beleaguered by unrest and economic stagnation at home, with violence and mounting separatist movements in the Baltics and the South Caucasus, Gorbachev had dwindling leverage. Bush provided him with a series of informal assurances about the nonthreatening evolution of NATO, reinforcing Baker's earlier commitments. In July, Kohl and Gorbachev announced a sweeping agreement on German reunification, within NATO. On October 3, 1990, the new, united Germany formally emerged.

* * *

GIVEN THE HISTORIC drama unfolding in Europe, it was not surprising that Middle East policy had taken a backseat during Bush's first eighteen months in office. That all changed at the beginning of August 1990, when Saddam Hussein invaded Kuwait.

All of us in the administration underestimated Saddam's sense of both risk and opportunity. He had ruined Iraq's economy during eight years of war with Iran, which left the urban infrastructure in a shambles, produced a war debt of more than $100 billion, and cost half a million Iraqi lives. Neither Kuwait nor Saudi Arabia had any interest in writing off his debt or in conspiring to raise oil prices. Despite his brutally repressive grip, Saddam worried that a bleak economic outlook would make Iraqis restive. At the same time, he saw opportunity in popular trends in the region. It wasn't hard to cloak himself as a militant Arab nationalist, first the defender of the Arab world against Persian theocrats, and now the champion of Arabs oppressed by corrupt rulers beholden to the Americans and soft on Israel. Moreover, he assumed the end of the Cold War meant Washington would have less incentive to intervene in the Middle East, and could be warned off with a sufficient display of strength.

America's Arab partners were not much more astute about Saddam. President Hosni Mubarak, King Hussein, and King Fahd all had encouraged Bush to reach out to the Iraqi dictator. With the end of the Iran-Iraq War, their view was that Saddam would naturally turn his attention to domestic recovery and modernization. Iraq would remain a bulwark against revolutionary Iran, and a complicated neighbor, but not a short-term threat. During his first year in office, Bush cautiously probed the possibilities with Baghdad. The United States extended credit guarantees for Iraqi grain purchases, and Baker met with his Iraqi counterpart, the wily Tariq Aziz. But by the spring of 1990, the secretary had begun to take a harder view, especially after Saddam made a vituperative speech threatening to "burn Israel." Ross told Baker that it was an "illusion" to think that Saddam could be a reliable partner.

Meanwhile, Saddam resurrected a long-standing border dispute with the Kuwaitis, and accused them of waging "economic warfare." By midsummer, he had begun to mass troops on the Kuwaiti border. The allure of Kuwait for Saddam was obvious. Its annual GDP was nearly half the size of Iraq's; with its oil fields, Saddam could control more than 10 percent of global oil supply and quickly be in a position to write off his war debt. The risks seemed modest—the Kuwaiti military would be no match for his combat-hardened forces.

Mubarak and other Arab leaders continued to assure Bush that Saddam was just bluffing and seeking to improve his hand in negotiations with the Kuwaitis over their border dispute. When Saddam unexpectedly summoned U.S. ambassador April Glaspie for a meeting on July 25, she reiterated formal American policy: The United States did not take a position on the merits of Iraqi-Kuwaiti territorial differences, but did certainly take the position that they had to be resolved peacefully. Afterward, in her cable to Washington, Glaspie concluded that the United States had "fully caught Saddam's attention" and that he had committed to opening negotiations with Kuwait soon.[7] She was widely criticized later for not being emphatic enough with Saddam about the consequences of the use of force, but that was unfair. No one expected Saddam to launch a full-scale invasion, and President Bush sent a letter to Saddam on July 28 that was not much tougher in tone or substance than Glaspie's exchange.

Undeterred, Saddam sent his military across the border into Kuwait on August 2, occupied the entire country within two days, and immediately declared Kuwait to be Iraq's "nineteenth province." Baker had been in Siberia the day before, meeting Shevardnadze. He shared with Shevardnadze intelligence reports of the Iraqi military buildup, as well as his mounting concern, but Shevardnadze was as dismissive of the chances of an actual invasion as Arab leaders were. Baker then flew on to Mongolia for a previously scheduled visit, and was there when the Iraqi attack began. Ross advised him to travel directly to Moscow and issue a joint statement with Shevardnadze condemning Saddam's aggression. Nothing would carry more diplomatic impact, or symbolize more vividly how much U.S.-Soviet relations had changed. On August 3, barely twenty-four hours after the invasion began, Shevardnadze and Baker stood together at Vnukovo Airport outside the Soviet capital and denounced the attack. As Baker later wrote, that moment really did mark the end of the Cold War.

On August 4, Policy Planning made a first attempt to try to frame what was at stake. Entitled "The First Post–Cold War Crisis," our note read, "Saddam believes that the end of the Cold War has fundamentally changed the basic strategic calculations of both superpowers. Their main purpose for competition in Southwest Asia has been reduced and with it the priority they will place on preserving their cold war alliances. Part of the reason for the shift in Soviet and American policy, Saddam figures, is the dramatically increased cost of power projection and active involvement in regional conflicts. Saddam, like Khomeini ten years ago, is convinced that the myth of American power is far greater in the Middle East than its practical bite, and that if confronted with real costs, Washington will not stay the course."[8]

Our paper continued, "Saddam is also banking on what he believes is a fundamental trend in Arab attitudes and politics. The process of change in Eastern Europe has excited many Arab intellectuals and the economic frustrations of boom and bust oil revenues along with urbanization has provided Islamist and nationalist demagogues with a ready mass base. Saddam is appealing to nationalist radical symbols, partly to outflank the Islamist radicals, and is playing to a widespread mass inclination to blame the U.S. for their political and economic troubles. His calculation is that any Arab regime that has to depend on the U.S. for protection is vulnerable to internal insurrection."

Our prescription was straightforward. We needed to defend Saudi Arabia, and then reverse Saddam's aggression. In a second, more detailed memo two weeks later, we underscored the argument: "With all that is now at stake in the Gulf, we cannot afford to settle for an outcome less than complete Iraqi withdrawal from Kuwait and restoration of Kuwait's legitimate government."[9] The paper laid out a two-step approach: First, bring maximum multilateral political and economic pressure to bear on Saddam; then follow up with a sustained program of containment to deny him any escape from the domestic consequences of having failed in Kuwait and capitulated to the Iranians.

If Saddam did not back down, the second purpose of our diplomacy would be to serve as a foundation for international support for military action against Iraq. Being perceived to have exhausted all reasonable nonmilitary options would be critical to building and maintaining such support. Inability to pressure Saddam to withdraw by means short of force would not be a "failure" of diplomacy—it would rather be the shrewdest kind of diplomacy, creating the basis for an international coalition that could achieve Iraqi withdrawal from Kuwait and manage the aftermath.

The dilemma we faced, however, was that we did not have much time, since Saddam was cleverly exploiting potential fissures in the international consensus. President Bush had succinctly laid out the American bottom line in a statement to the press soon after Saddam's invasion: The occupation of Kuwait, he said, "will not stand." He and his team then moved to accomplish that goal, with a skill and drive as fine as any example I saw in government. Dick Cheney flew to Saudi Arabia, where he announced a military operation to defend the Saudis, dubbed Operation Desert Shield. Colin Powell and his commander in the field, General Norman Schwarzkopf, began mobilizing U.S. forces for deployment in the region. Brent Scowcroft and Bob Gates managed an impressive interagency process and pushed the strategy forward. Secretary Baker coordinated with Scowcroft, Cheney, and Powell on building a massive international coalition, attracting military and financial contributions, marshaling economic pressure on Saddam, and creating a powerful diplomatic foundation for action. At the United Nations, Ambassador Tom Pickering expertly set in motion a series of Security Council resolutions, first condemning the Iraqi attack, then putting in place economic sanctions unprecedented in their scope, which would eventually cut off nearly all of Iraq's exports and external sources of revenue.

I joined Baker on his September "tin cup" mission, covering nine countries in eleven days. He ultimately secured more than $50 billion in contributions, essentially defraying the entire cost of the U.S. military operation. Baker's style was no-nonsense. He had a checklist of what he needed, and a rapidly growing U.S. military deployment in the Gulf to underline his credibility. In Jeddah, King Fahd dispensed with typical Arab indirection and told Baker the Saudis would provide whatever he wanted. The Kuwaiti amir, huddled with his family and government in Saudi exile, was just as receptive. The Turks immediately shut down the pipeline through which much of Iraqi oil exports flowed, and Baker arranged a substantial World Bank loan to help cushion the effects on Ankara. In Egypt, President Mubarak pledged to send Egyptian troops to join the coalition. While their military value was negligible, the symbolic power of Arab contingents alongside U.S. forces was considerable.

Baker also visited Damascus on that trip, beginning a series of encounters with the cunning and ruthless Hafez al-Assad, Syria's president since 1971. Unsentimental about Saddam, a rival of many years from the same rough school of Arab leadership, Assad was impressed by the display of raw American power unfolding in the Gulf. Assad indicated a receptiveness to joining the coalition, and was clearly intrigued by Baker. He was even more intrigued by the prospect of sticking it to Saddam.

In Bonn, Kohl and Genscher, already in political debt to Bush and Baker for their support for German reunification, promised financial support. Baker joined Bush in Helsinki for another summit with Gorbachev. The Soviet leader, struggling increasingly with the challenge of holding the USSR together, saw the value of using his relationship with Bush to preserve a central diplomatic role despite the Soviet Union's waning international prestige.

In November, I accompanied Baker on an even longer trip. This one covered twelve countries on three continents over eighteen days. Its principal aim was to shore up support for a decisive Security Council resolution to authorize the use of force if Saddam did not withdraw fully and unconditionally from Kuwait. Traveling on Baker's aircraft, which had been Lyndon Johnson's Air Force One, was always an intense experience.

Baker had a small private cabin up front, with a tiny desk and a couch on which he could barely stretch out. The rest of his senior staff sat in the adjacent cabin, which featured a horseshoe of couches around a large table, and the oversized chair that Johnson had often used when meeting with his aides. The pace was frenetic, with short sessions with Baker to review what had just transpired in the last stop and plan for the next one, and the rest of the flight spent making calls to Washington, preparing talking points for upcoming meetings, and drafting short reports for Baker to send to the president. Sleep was rare.

In the next cabin sat an overworked administrative team and diplomatic security detail, juggling all the constantly shifting logistics. At the back of the plane sat the State Department press corps—a particularly accomplished group, including Pulitzer Prize winners like Tom Friedman and *The Washington Post*'s David Hoffman. Baker and Margaret Tutwiler were masters at managing the press, respectful of their role and expertise. They knew that the relationship was a two-way street, and often tested ideas and formulas in off-the-record sessions on the plane. The department press corps, in turn, knew that Baker was a formidable figure at the heart of history in the making, and treated him with the same respect he showed them.

By the end of that grueling trip, Baker had secured substantial support for what became UN Security Council Resolution 678, passed on November 29, authorizing the use of "all necessary means" to force Saddam out of Kuwait if he did not withdraw by January 15, 1991. The Soviets joined the United States and ten other countries voting in favor of the resolution. The Chinese abstained, uneasy about the use of force and miffed that Baker had not visited Beijing. Cuba and Yemen voted against. Baker, who had spent several hours in Sanaa trying to woo Yemeni president Ali Abdullah Saleh, warned that this would be "the most expensive vote the Yemenis ever cast." He wasn't kidding. When Saleh declined to support the resolution, the State Department moved quickly to slash assistance to Yemen by 90 percent.

Saddam immediately rejected the UNSC ultimatum, but agreed to a meeting in early January in Geneva between Tariq Aziz and Baker, a last chance to end the crisis peacefully. I had never seen so much drama and anxiety surrounding a single meeting, and haven't since. War was imminent, with more than half a million coalition troops now assembled near the Kuwaiti border, the most impressive and powerful international coalition since World War II.

There were worries about significant casualties, especially given the potential for use of chemical weapons by Saddam, who had deployed them in the past against the Iranians and his own Kurdish population. There were also fears that Saddam would choose the moment in Geneva to have Aziz offer a partial withdrawal while retaining control of the disputed oil fields along the border. That would be unacceptable under the terms of the Security Council resolutions, but it could undermine congressional support and throw a wrench into the coalition, likely causing the Soviets and others to press for a further pause on military action. The coalition we had worked so hard to build could easily unravel.

Baker's preparations for the meeting were characteristically exhaustive. His talking points were the product of extensive consultation in Washington. I spent nearly the entire plane ride to Geneva working with Dennis on the final version. Baker never read such points verbatim, but given the gravity of the moment, he planned to stick closely to the script. He had virtually memorized his terse introductory remarks, which ended with him warning that he hoped Aziz understood that this was the "last, best chance for peace." Even his handshake with Aziz across the table at the start of the meeting had been well thought through; he was determined not to offer the conventional diplomatic smile, and kept a grim expression for the cameras. Aziz, usually full of bravado, looked tense.

Baker was carrying a long letter from Bush to Saddam, which among other things made clear that the United States would reserve the right to use any weapons in its arsenal if the Iraqis resorted to chemical weapons or any other weapons of mass destruction. Baker summarized the contents of the letter, but Aziz refused to take it or read it, perhaps unsure of how Saddam would react if he brought such an ultimatum home. After the meeting ended, with no sign of flexibility from the Iraqis, Baker addressed the biggest assemblage of international media I had ever seen. "Regrettably," he began, "in over six hours of talks, I heard nothing today that suggested to me any

Iraqi flexibility whatsoever on complying with the UN Security Council resolutions." War was coming.

On January 12, Congress voted to authorize the use of force. Thanks in large part to the international support that Bush and Baker had mobilized, Saddam's stubborn brutality and intransigence, and polling showing the support of two out of three Americans, skeptical American legislators had come around. On January 16, just after the deadline set by the UN Security Council had expired, the United States launched a massive air attack on Baghdad. I watched it on television at home that evening with Lisa, still uncertain about where this would all lead, but confident in the U.S. military, and proud of all that Bush and Baker had achieved in a classic model of diplomatic coalition-building.

While an overwhelming display of U.S. technological superiority, the air campaign still had its anxious moments. Coalition forces made a high priority of eliminating Iraq's Scud missile capability, amid fears that Saddam would launch warheads loaded with chemical weapons. Inevitably, some Iraqi missiles struck Israel, which Saddam wanted desperately to bait into retaliation, thus expanding the conflict into an Arab-Israeli war and threatening Arab support for the coalition. Bush and Baker had worked closely with Israeli prime minister Yitzhak Shamir to defend against Scud attacks, and to avoid walking into the trap that Saddam was trying to set. Larry Eagleburger made several trips to Israel to urge restraint. I accompanied him on one of those missions and admired the gruff ease with which he connected with Shamir and other senior Israelis—and watched with amusement when he removed his gas mask during missile raid alarms to take alternating puffs from his cigarette and asthma inhaler.

Showing political courage, Shamir did not respond to the missile attacks, trusting that the Americans would quickly crush the Iraqi military. The subsequent ground operation in late February lasted barely one hundred hours. Saddam's forces were routed, expelled from Kuwait, and fleeing headlong back into Iraq when President Bush ended hostilities. Bush's decision, unanimously supported by his chief advisors, reflected remarkable discipline. It was certainly tempting to continue to pummel the Iraqi military, chase them all the way to Baghdad, and perhaps bring down Saddam's regime. Bush and Baker knew, however, that the coalition mandate, codified by the UN Security Council, was to push the Iraqis out of Kuwait and restore the legitimate government there. Reaching beyond that goal ran the risk of disintegrating the coalition, with all the collateral damage that might do to shaping post–Cold War order. As Baker put it to a few of us in a conversation in his office after he returned from the White House on February 27, the last day of the ground operation, "Sometimes the most important test of leadership is *not* to do something, even when it looks really damn easy. Overreaching is what gets people in trouble."

Despite the focus on the immediate military and diplomatic priorities, we had tried to help Baker think ahead about the long-term opportunities and risks that would undoubtedly emerge after Saddam was forced to withdraw from Kuwait. On the Gulf itself, we argued in a November 1990 paper that a freestanding balance of power among Iraq, Iran, and the Gulf Cooperation Council states was implausible after the crisis.[10] We'd have to contain Saddam, and continue to provide support to the Saudis and their Gulf Arab partners. A little too hopefully, we suggested that "this crisis may increase the opportunity to improve U.S.-Iranian relations." In another piece, we highlighted the wider U.S. regional stake "in quietly encouraging our friends to recognize that broader political participation and greater economic openness are important if the Arab world is to share in the progress sweeping other parts of the world." We proposed an Arab regional development bank as one way to stimulate change. And we laid special emphasis on the potential for renewing Arab-Israeli negotiations, with Saddam's brand of radical Arab nationalism discredited and our own regional and global influence virtually un-challenged. Though wary of all the pitfalls, Baker was intrigued by what might be possible on that front.

* * *

ON THE WALL outside his office in Houston, former secretary Baker keeps several rows of framed newspaper cartoons. They depict, with varying degrees of cynicism, his relentless pursuit of a breakthrough on Middle East peace following the Gulf War, over nine trips to the region from March to October 1991—a reminder of how many people doubted that he could succeed, and of how improbable the whole ef-fort seemed.

Faced with the monumental demands of dealing with the Soviet Union and Europe at the end of the Cold War, Baker avoided getting drawn into Arab-Israeli issues. In the Middle East, he saw few op-portunities and lots of headaches. He had little patience for the end-less arguments about peace process theology. His early experience with Prime Minister Shamir, a stubborn Israeli nationalist deeply suspicious of anything that might weaken Israel's grip on the West Bank and Gaza, had been unhappy. In May 1989, Baker had told the annual American Israel Public Affairs Committee (AIPAC) confer-ence in Washington that "now is the time to lay aside, once and for all, the unrealistic vision of a greater Israel." Shamir was not amused. When Shamir's protégé, then–deputy foreign minister Bibi Netan-yahu, accused the administration of "lies and distortions," it was Ba-ker's turn to be unamused. He banned Netanyahu from the State Department for the next eighteen months.

The Arabs did not do much to endear themselves to Baker, either. The U.S. dialogue with the PLO opened at the end of the Reagan administration had been stilted and unproductive. When a radical Palestinian faction staged an unsuccessful attack along the Israeli coast near Tel Aviv in May 1990, Baker was irate at Arafat's refusal to condemn the raid, or even distance himself from the Palestinian group that was responsible. Shortly thereafter, Bush and Baker suspended the dialogue indefinitely. Baker told my colleague Aaron Miller, "If I had another life, I'd want to be a Middle East specialist just like you, because it would mean guaranteed permanent employment." Beneath the sarcasm, Baker's lack of interest in getting dragged into interminable problems was unambiguous. He hated being "diddled," and the Middle East seemed overrun with diddlers.

After the Gulf War in the spring of 1991, however, Baker saw an opening. The defeat of Saddam Hussein boosted Arab moderates. Mubarak felt more secure. The Saudis and the Gulf Arabs owed the Bush administration their survival. Assad was sobered by the steep decline of his Soviet patrons, and impressed by American military and diplomatic prowess. A connoisseur of power, he understood that the ground was shifting in the region. King Hussein of Jordan was anxious to get back in good graces with Bush and Baker after staying aloof from the Desert Storm coalition. Arafat's sympathy for Saddam left him in similarly difficult circumstances, cut off from Arab financial support and worried that he was losing touch with Palestinians in the West Bank and Gaza who were engaged in a fitful uprising against Israeli occupation. His leverage was decreasing too.

Yitzhak Shamir was uneasy about the outcome of the war. On the one hand, Saddam's ability to threaten Israel had been dealt a massive blow. On the other, however, Shamir was anxious about where newfound ties with key Arab states might take the U.S. administration. Gorbachev was increasingly consumed with the collapsing Soviet Union, and had little alternative to cooperating with Washington on the Middle East, so long as Soviet pride of place was preserved. All of this added up to a moment of diplomatic opportunity that was exceedingly rare in the Middle East. As Dennis Ross argued to Baker, "We've just seen an earthquake. We have to move before the earth resettles, because it will, and it never takes long."

There was also an element of pride and competitiveness in Baker's thinking. Crucial as his role had been in constructing the Desert

Storm coalition, the war was naturally a moment for presidential leadership. President Bush was center stage, the full might of the American military beside him. Now Baker had before him a chance to win the peace, to show what American diplomacy could accomplish in the wake of sweeping military successes. For the consummate problem-solver, what bigger challenge was there than Arab-Israeli peace?

Baker was not especially interested in the arcane details of Arab-Israeli issues, or the history and culture of the region. He had an enormously retentive mind for what he needed to know to navigate a negotiation and bridge differences, and a gift for managing complicated personalities. He lowballed public expectations, always convinced that it was better to underpromise and overdeliver. His refrain to those of us immersed in his peacemaking effort was that we had to "crawl before we walk, and walk before we run." Baker's near-term goal was not to secure a comprehensive peace agreement, but rather to use the leverage that the United States had, before it evaporated, and set in motion a process that would for the first time bring the Israelis and all the Arab parties into direct negotiations with one another, within a framework that might sustain the process and perhaps even eventually produce substantive accords.

He had in mind a two-track approach, tilted more to the Israeli insistence on separate bilateral talks with each of their Arab adversaries than the historic Arab argument for an international conference that could impose binding outcomes on the parties. In a nod to Arab and international opinion, the process would start with a meeting of all the parties, which would simply launch talks rather than prescribe their end states. Then there would be a set of individual negotiations: Syrian-Israeli, Lebanese-Israeli, and talks between Israel and a delegation of Jordanians and Palestinians not formally connected to the PLO. The conference would launch a second track, engaging all the parties as well as key global players on wider regional challenges like water, environment, and economic development. Consistent with discussions with Gorbachev in the run-up to the war, the Soviets would nominally co-sponsor the initial conference and the ensuing process.

Given his earlier frustrations with Shamir, Baker realized that the key was to create a structure so attuned to Israeli concerns that the prime minister couldn't back out. Baker had to persuade the Syrians to temper their animosity toward Israel, and cajole the Palestinians into swallowing hard and accepting conditions for their participation that they resented deeply.

Baker set out on the first of his post–Gulf War trips just after President Bush's triumphal address to a joint session of Congress on the evening of March 6. His broad aim was to outline his concept for reviving Arab-Israeli negotiations, and his tactical goal was to harvest the debt owed the United States for the defeat of Saddam, especially by the Gulf Arabs, and show Shamir that the Arabs were prepared to engage him directly.

The scene when we landed in Kuwait City on the early afternoon of March 9 was unforgettable. The airport's main terminal was pockmarked by shellfire, with broken glass and rubble everywhere. When we helicoptered north to see some of the damage done by the Iraqis in their scorched-earth withdrawal, the sky turned black. Saddam's forces had set fire to five hundred Kuwaiti oil wells, and billowing dark smoke was everywhere, the air thick with soot and flames shooting upward across the apocalyptic horizon.

The rest of the trip was modestly encouraging. In Cairo, Hosni Mubarak was exuberant about the way in which Bush and the coalition had humbled Saddam. "Jim," he boomed across his spacious office, "I don't think Shamir will change, but this is your best chance." Shamir himself was cautious, especially about the proposed opening conference, and insistent that Palestinian representatives had to be part of a joint delegation with Jordan and unconnected to the PLO. The secretary had a useful introductory discussion with a group of ten Palestinians from the West Bank and Gaza, led by Feisal Husseini, a well-respected member of a prominent East Jerusalem family, and Hanan Ashrawi, a Ramallah academic whose emergence as a secular, nonviolent female leader fluent in the language of the street as well as diplomacy made a strong impression. Baker stopped in Damascus to see Assad again, and found him wary but ready to engage. In Moscow, the Soviets told the secretary that they were quite interested in co-sponsorship of the process; Baker made clear in return that Moscow would need to first restore full diplomatic relations with Israel.

That first trip demonstrated Baker's skill in managing both regional personalities and his own personnel. On the latter, he relied on a tight Middle East team who accompanied him throughout his 1991 shuttle diplomacy. Dennis Ross was Baker's senior advisor, and then there were three more junior aides: Dan Kurtzer, Aaron Miller, and me. We churned out massive quantities of talking points for Baker's meetings, strategy papers for his shuttles, public statements, and cables. It was Margaret Tutwiler who coined the term "food processors" to describe our endless churn. It probably didn't do much for our street credibility as hard-nosed diplomats when the phrase made it into a *Washington Post* profile of our work later that fall, but it certainly captured the grinding rhythm of serious diplomatic enterprises.

Baker understood from the outset that building personal trust with a complicated and often intractable set of regional players would be critical. The three most crucial to the effort were Shamir, Assad, and the Palestinians. In constructing a process largely to the Israeli prime minister's specifications, Baker worked assiduously to win the confidence of the ever-suspicious Shamir. They were an unlikely pair—the smooth, artful Texas patrician whittling away methodically at the reservations of the hardline Israeli political veteran, whose soft-spoken demeanor belied a steely resistance to compromise and an abiding mistrust of anyone who might try to lure him down that path. But they developed a genuine, if sometimes grudging, mutual respect, without which the Madrid Peace Conference would never have happened.

Delivering Hafez al-Assad and Palestinian representatives to the negotiating table, on terms that Shamir could stomach, was the key to cutting off his diplomatic routes of escape. Baker spent dozens of hours with Assad in 1991. Their meetings were tests of stamina, will, and ingenuity, with Assad filibustering and probing constantly for weaknesses in Baker's arguments or assurances. Alternately tough and empathetic, sometimes raising his voice in exasperation or threatening to abandon his peacemaking effort, Baker clearly established himself in Assad's eyes as a formidable and worthy negotiating partner. Assad regularly stretched Baker's patience to the breaking point, but came to trust the secretary's commitment and pragmatic disposition.

The same proved true of the Palestinians with whom Baker wrestled over those eight roller-coaster months. Husseini, Ashrawi, and their colleagues were caught in a vise. Their options tightly limited by Israeli occupation, they were further constrained by their political subordination to the PLO leadership in Tunisia, popular suspicions in the West Bank and Gaza, and the difficult parameters that Baker insisted upon for Palestinian representation in negotiations. They had no easy choices, but they came to trust Baker enough to take the chance that once engaged in direct negotiations, even if nominally part of a joint delegation with the Jordanians, they could translate their weak hand into tangible progress toward self-determination.

With Shamir, Assad, and the Palestinians, Baker was ecumenical in his candor. In one of the many pungent Texas expressions that he introduced into the Middle East political lexicon, he threatened to "leave a dead cat on the doorstep" of any party that balked at the diplomatic possibility he was offering. As the months wore on, their worries about being blamed by Baker for failure grew, even as their suspicions about one another remained intense. None of them were eager to call his bluff.

Baker made two more trips to the region in April. The first included a stop along the Turkish border with Iraq, where hundreds of thousands of Kurdish refugees were camped, fleeing Saddam's post-war repression and sorely in need of assistance and protection. That sea of humanity made a powerful impression on all of us, and Baker reinforced the inclination of President Bush to do more to help. The scenes from his April talks with the Arabs and Israelis on that trip were less spectacular, but similarly worrisome. Shamir still took issue with any form of United Nations participation in the peace confer-ence that Baker was proposing, and questioned whether UN Security Council Resolution 242, which had shortly after the 1967 war set out the basic formula of land for peace, should be the basis for negotia-tions. Assad, on the other hand, insisted on a clear UN role to provide "international legitimacy," a continuing role for the conference as the two tracks of negotiations unfolded, and a provision that the U.S. and Soviet co-sponsors would be expected to "guarantee" outcomes.

The Palestinians still maintained that they should be able to de-termine their own representatives, balking at Baker's position that they had to be part of a joint Jordanian-Palestinian delegation, and not include members either formally affiliated with the PLO or resi-dent in East Jerusalem. Although King Hussein, anxious to get back in American good graces, pledged full Jordanian support for the pro-cess, and Mubarak remained a stalwart backer, the Saudis had begun to slide back into their familiar risk-averse, pre–Desert Storm posi-tion, and dragged their feet on whether they'd participate in the con-ference and the follow-on multilateral track negotiations. Baker left his last set of discussions, which included both the nine-hour "blad-der diplomacy" episode with Assad and an equally frustrating stop in Jerusalem, increasingly concerned about whether the process would ever get off the ground.

In several more trips in late spring and summer, Baker steadily chipped away at the remaining resistance. There were predictable fits and starts in trying to persuade the Gulf Arabs to deliver on their commitments. When the Saudis pulled up short of making an ex-pected announcement of their participation at one point, Baker pounded his hand on his desk and said in exasperation, "Those guys could fuck up a two-car funeral."

Slowly but surely, the parties were coming around. In May, the Saudis agreed to attend the conference, an historic first. We found a recipe for the conference structure that Shamir and Assad both reluctantly accepted, with a UN observer role. Assad was impressed by Baker's offer of a U.S. security guarantee of whatever Israeli-Syrian border was negotiated, complete with the possibility of American forces on the Golan Heights. Assad indicated formally in a letter to Bush in July that he would participate. Finally, the Palestinians agreed to attend under the terms that Baker had outlined.

Baker returned to the region for an eighth time in October. He had scheduled a meeting in Jerusalem on the afternoon of October 18 with the new Soviet foreign minister, Boris Pankin, after which we planned to issue the invitations to the peace conference. The parties were still nervous and important details still unresolved. The Palestinians, in particular, were having difficulty producing the list of fourteen names for their part of the joint delegation that they had promised, so that Baker could make sure they met the agreed criteria.

Baker met with Husseini, Ashrawi, and several of their colleagues at the very un–Middle Eastern hour of 7:45 that morning at the old U.S. Consulate General facility on Nablus Road in East Jerusalem. He was unhappy about the last-minute snag, and tired of the wrangling. Baker understood how hard it was for the Palestinians to navigate their own leadership in Tunis, and he put on a masterful performance that morning. He implored Husseini and Ashrawi to pull themselves together for one final push across the goal line. He was direct about the choice the Palestinians faced. The only way they could regain control over the West Bank and Gaza was through negotiations with the Israelis, and if the deck was stacked against them in procedural terms, that was still the best they could hope for. Arafat had made a major mistake taking sides with Saddam, and this was the price. The United States was not going to deliver an outcome for the Palestinians; they'd have to work hard through negotiations, but the Bush administration would ensure a fair process. As he gathered the Palestinian delegation around him at the end of the meeting, he gave them one final pep talk. "Lots of people like to say that you never miss an opportunity to miss an opportunity," Baker said. "Show them that they're wrong."

By midafternoon, however, the Palestinians were still struggling. It was clear that they weren't going to give Baker any more than seven names that day, and it was uncertain that they could agree on the remaining seven. The dead cat was not far from their doorstep.

The mood in Baker's suite at the King David Hotel was tense. Foreign Minister Pankin sat forlornly at one end of the living room, with little to say or do but wait for Baker to make his next move. Tired and disappointed, Baker said he was inclined to postpone the conference. Margaret Tutwiler started preparing a short statement to inform the horde of reporters gathered on the first floor of the hotel.

Baker had always encouraged Dan, Aaron, and me to speak up, especially when we had dissenting views. The three of us quickly huddled in Baker's cramped walk-in closet, and decided to make a case to move ahead with the invitation. With Pankin and his aides looking on passively, every bit the disoriented representatives of a fallen superpower, Dan laid out our concerns to Baker. It was true that there was no guarantee that the Palestinians would produce the required names, and there was a real risk if a premature invitation led to embarrassment. On the other hand, there was at least as big a risk that the momentum Baker had built in recent months would stall. The other parties were perfectly capable of throwing more wrenches into the works, and the whole effort could collapse. Aaron and I seconded Dan's recommendation that we take the plunge. Baker listened carefully, and said he wanted to think about it for a few minutes. He consulted with Pankin, as much for the sake of form as anything else, and then opted to issue the invitation. The Palestinians soon got their act together and came up with the remaining names.

The Madrid Peace Conference opened less than two weeks later, on the morning of October 30. There was no shortage of drama in the air; I still recall how angry Baker looked when Syrian foreign minister Farouk al-Sharaa, in a move that was gratuitously nasty even by the standards of the Assad regime, paused in a rebuttal to hold up a 1947 British Mandate wanted poster of Shamir, who had fought for Israel's independence as a member of the notorious Stern Gang. Usually the picture of self-control, Baker looked at that moment as if he wanted to throw his gavel across the room at Sharaa.

There were a number of other fits and starts over the next few days, but eventually each of the bilateral negotiations got under way, and the multilateral talks with a wider group of regional and international players started not long thereafter. Through all the ups and downs, we never lost sight of just how extraordinary it was to gather all these players and personalities and get them to agree to what each had for so long insisted was nonnegotiable.

The election of Yitzhak Rabin and a Labor government in Israel the following June led to the secret Oslo talks between the Israelis and Palestinians, a direct outgrowth of what Baker had launched in Madrid. I suspect Baker could have brokered a Syrian-Israeli agreement, had there been a second Bush 41 term, and perhaps a permanent-status Israeli-Palestinian deal. His skills, weight within the administration, relationships with all the key players in the region, and proven ability to deliver could not be easily replicated. He seemed like the right peacemaker at the right time.

* * *

THE REST OF the world was hardly quiescent while the Middle East absorbed so much American diplomatic energy. With the Cold War over, and the old bipolar international order crumbling, all sorts of new centrifugal forces were at work. As we put it in a Policy Planning Staff memo to Baker in the summer of 1991, the Soviet Union's "external empire" had disintegrated in 1989, and now its "internal empire" was beginning to as well.

The Soviet Union proved far more brittle than many of us had assumed. On August 19, 1991, a motley group of Soviet conservatives staged a putsch against Gorbachev, putting him under house arrest in Crimea. The Soviet vice president, Gennady Yanayev, appeared on state television and with hands trembling and voice unsteady declared that a new committee of which he was the deeply unconvincing head had taken charge of the country. Boris Yeltsin, the recently elected president of the Russian Federation, courageously faced down the coup plotters in Moscow, with the backing of significant elements of the Soviet military. As the coup attempt unfolded, Baker was on vacation in Wyoming, and Dennis and his family were in New Hampshire. Back in Washington, my colleagues and I tried to understand what had happened, and where it might lead. Andrew Carpendale and John Hannah drafted two papers for Baker, the first analyzing the coup and its implications, and the second laying out a framework for dealing with the likely fragmentation of the Soviet Union.

It was clear that Gorbachev, despite surviving the coup, was a desperately weakened leader. Yeltsin was the man of the hour. The failed putsch had stripped bare the fecklessness of the conservative opposition, opening the way for radical democratic and market reform and a range of independence movements. Our memo suggested that the only way Gorbachev could stay afloat politically was to become the champion of truly ambitious structural reform, and the only way the Soviet center could hold the union together was as the driver of meaningful political and economic change, in a much more loosely federated system. Both, we predicted, were quite unlikely.

The more prescriptive paper laid out a set of principles to help govern American policy toward the issue of a potential breakup of the Soviet Union, similar to what we had provided Baker on German reunification in 1990. On their face, the five principles we suggested were not controversial: peaceful self-determination; respect for existing borders without unilateral modifications; respect for democracy and rule of law; respect for human rights, especially minority rights; and adherence to international law and obligations. Nevertheless, as we had found on German reunification, clear policy guidelines were critical to shape our approach and the tactical choices before us.

Baker outlined the five principles at a White House press briefing in early September, and then traveled to Moscow to get a firsthand sense of the situation. The makeshift barricades around the Russian White House were still in place. Baker saw both Gorbachev and Yeltsin, who each professed to be optimistic about their political futures. The secretary came away skeptical that Gorbachev could survive politically, and persuaded that the challenge for the Bush administration was to help make the crash of the Soviet Union as bloodless as possible.

By late December, the Soviet Union had ceased to exist. After a poignant visit with Baker in Moscow and a last telephone call as leader of the Soviet Union with President Bush, Gorbachev resigned on December 25 and his country was no more. I went again with Baker to Moscow in January for the opening of the Middle East multilateral talks. That was a surreal experience, with the Russian tricolor now flying over the Kremlin, and Yeltsin's new, independent Russian government effectively inheriting the role of co-sponsor.

In February, I joined Baker's trip to a number of the other newly independent former Soviet states. We landed in a Yerevan that was almost totally dark as night fell, the Armenian power system failing and electricity shortages the norm. Baku was nearly as dismal, with rusting gas and oil pipes littering the roadside on the way in from the bedraggled airport. The Central Asian states were brighter, but just as poor. President Islam Karimov in Uzbekistan whipped out a small laminated card containing Baker's "five principles" for dealing with the process of post-Soviet independence, which he said he always kept in his coat pocket. Baker enjoyed Karimov's hospitality in Tashkent and especially in exotic Samarkand. On the plane afterward, however, he expressed his lack of faith in Karimov's democratic conversion, noting that "that guy pays about as much attention to those principles as I do to Uzbek music."

At Baker's urging, the Bush administration tried to be systematic about supporting the new independent states. The United States rapidly established embassies in each capital and set up substantial programs of humanitarian assistance, market economic advice, and defense conversion. It also launched the Nunn-Lugar program, to help ensure the safety and security of Soviet nuclear weapons, which were now spread at least temporarily across four sovereign states.

Other troubles were always bubbling up. In the latter part of the Bush administration, Yugoslavia began to splinter. Serbian forces laid siege to Sarajevo, Bosnia's capital, in the spring of 1992, and concerns mounted in European capitals as well as in Washington. In June, based on a strategy memo that Dennis and Andrew Carpendale had helped put together, the secretary recommended to the White House a robust plan to build diplomatic and economic pressure on the Serbs, and potentially even to deploy a multilateral force to break the siege and ensure that relief supplies got through. Brent Scowcroft supported Baker. Cheney and Powell were less enthusiastic. The Serbs momentarily backed down before the U.S. initiative got off the ground, and humanitarian supplies flowed into Sarajevo. The worst, however, was yet to come. The Bush administration, with a presidential reelection campaign in full swing and poll numbers dropping from their post–Desert Storm peak, was not eager to take risks in the Balkans, and content to let the Europeans take the lead. Its failure to act more forcefully only made the choices of the next administration more complicated.

In late summer, Baker moved to the White House to lead the president's floundering campaign and serve as chief of staff. Dennis went with Baker. Larry Eagleburger became acting secretary of state, and asked me to serve as acting director of Policy Planning. Sitting in George Kennan's old seat and still only thirty-six, I felt an uneasy pride.

One of our main preoccupations over the next six months was trying to think through the contours of an American strategy for managing post–Cold War order. We had begun this effort with a paper for Baker in late April 1992, entitled a little too expectantly, "Foreign Policy in the Second Bush Administration: An Overview."[11] In it, we cited the accomplishments of Bush's team, noting, "You and the President have much to be proud of in foreign policy. The end of the Cold War, a united Germany in NATO, peace in Central America, Desert Storm, and the first negotiations between Israel and all its Arab neighbors in forty-three years are singular achievements. But they amount to an unfinished agenda. Historians will ultimately judge you by how well you use the second term to translate those first-term successes into a coherent and enduring legacy. Above all, you will be judged by how well you have handled the two main consequences of the Cold War: the transformation of the former Soviet empire, and the victorious though fraying alliance of the U.S., Europe and Japan."

The memo emphasized that the starting point for a successful strategy had to include an updated set of assumptions about the international landscape beyond the Cold War. With no global security rival to counterbalance, we were left with an increasingly regional security agenda. "We have a long-term stake in stability in at least three key regions—Europe, East Asia and the Persian Gulf," I argued. "The end of the Cold War and the defeat of Iraq remove the immediate threat of a hostile power dominating one of those regions. What we face instead is the challenge of providing reassurance in a period of uncertainty, marked particularly by geopolitical upheaval and ethnic rivalry in Eastern Europe and the former Soviet Union, ambiguity about the post–Cold War military roles of Germany and Japan, and the unclear path of post-revolutionary Iran." I stressed the crucial significance of strengthening our international economic competitiveness as the foundation of our foreign policy.

Another assumption was that "the system of nation-states that developed during the Cold War, and the elites who governed those states, are caught in a swirl of both centralizing and decentralizing forces. The result is not the obsolescence of the nation-state, which still remains the central actor in international relations, but rather the transformation of the particular system of nation-states that we've grown accustomed to over the last half-century." I continued that "from the disintegrated Soviet empire to the Balkans, to much of Africa and the Middle East, what is happening is that traditional elites who have either excluded significant national or ethnic groups from power or failed to deliver political or economic goods are under attack. . . . The consequences of this political proliferation, and the crisis of legitimacy at its core, are uncertain ones for the U.S. On the one hand, there are enormous possibilities for nurturing democratic values and institutions, creating an international environment that could become more benign than ever for Americans. On the other hand, however, the search for legitimacy and national self-expression will often be a violent process—and it may lead to answers that meet local tests of legitimacy that aren't very democratic, like conservative Islamic regimes or nationalist authoritarian ones."

Defining our new leadership role would not be easy. America's powerful position, I wrote, did not "imply American dominance of a unipolar world. Power, especially economic power, is too diffuse for so simple a construct. We need to be mindful of the dangers of hubris and the deep suspicions of many governments . . . about American unilateralism." At the same time, I pointed out that "the reality remains that the United States, at least for the transitional period in history following the Cold War, occupies a unique position at the intersection of a diverse international system, remaining both a critical balancer in security sub-systems from Europe to Asia, and the only major player with a foot in each of three key economic sub-systems (the Americas, Europe and Asia). In short, while multilateralism may be one of the hallmarks of a post–Cold War order, it will have to be shaped largely by American leadership."

In November, Bill Clinton defeated Bush, whose foreign policy achievements were overshadowed by mounting popular appetite for change and a thirst for post–Cold War domestic renewal. As part of the transition process, we crystallized our views in a paper Eagleburger shared with incoming secretary of state Warren Christopher in January 1993. It was entitled "Parting Thoughts: U.S. Foreign Policy in the Years Ahead."[12] We had refined our thinking quite a bit from the earlier drafts—and the notion of describing an agenda for a second Bush term was obviously long buried. Much of the analysis of the international environment was similar to what we had laid out before, but we highlighted both the advent of new transnational threats and the challenge of building domestic support for active American leadership. "A variety of new transnational threats has appeared," I wrote, "particularly environmental degradation, drugs and the spread of deadly diseases like AIDS. Such dangers demand collective action rather than purely national responses. They also require an aggressive, new international scientific agenda, in which American leadership will be critical."

The thrust of our paper was careful and realistic. We tried to take into account likely domestic constraints. We were mindful of traditional security risks and the danger of regional hegemons emerging. We also saw a shifting global landscape, where security had to be defined in broader terms and new threats had to be considered. We stressed the importance of leading by example and building coalitions of countries around our central role. We were not persuaded that the demise of the Soviet Union and the end of the Cold War meant that the United States could take a detached view of the world, but we were also careful in our recognition of the perils of overreach and failing to connect ends to means. Ours was a strategy that accepted limits, but also reflected confidence in the capacity of the United States to at least manage problems, if not solve them. It was very much the worldview of Jim Baker, and many of the lessons we tried to articulate haven't lost their relevance today, more than a quarter century later.

3

Yeltsin's Russia:
The Limits of Agency

IT WAS BARELY forty miles from Sleptsovskaya, a tiny Ingush border town overflowing with refugees, to the Chechen capital of Grozny. But in the late spring of 1995, it felt as if you were crossing from civilization, albeit in its tattered post-Soviet form, to a grim, darkened world in which civilization had lost its place. The main road ran alongside the Sunzha River east into Chechnya, full of ruts and potholes, with heavily mined fields on either side. I was riding with an embassy colleague in an old Soviet ambulance in search of a missing American humanitarian assistance expert named Fred Cuny. This was our first foray into Grozny, soon after the Chechen rebel leader, Dzhokhar Dudayev, and his forces had retreated south into the hills.

Our route was a kaleidoscope of reemerging normalcy and wartime brutality. Civilian traffic had returned, and roadside stands peddled everything from soft drinks and vodka to small arms and ammunition. Russian military vehicles rolled down the middle of the two-lane highway, scattering everything in their path, ridden by Russian troops who looked more like gang members than professional soldiers. Wearing bandannas, reflector sunglasses, and sleeveless T-shirts, and equipped with bandoliers and big knives in their belts, they tried hard to look intimidating. Some checkpoints along the way were manned by teenage conscripts notorious for shooting first and asking questions later, especially after darkness settled. Others were the preserve of *kontraktniki*, contract soldiers hardened by fighting in Afghanistan or more recent conflicts on Russia's former Soviet periphery. And then there were the OMON, the Ministry of Interior troops, cold-eyed and clad in black.

As we drove past the burned-out remains of houses and shops in Samashki, it was not hard to imagine the horrors of the night a few weeks before, when OMON soldiers swept into town and massacred more than two hundred Chechens, mostly women, children, and elderly men. Reportedly drunk and eager for revenge after their own losses in the Chechen campaign, OMON troops burned down homes with flamethrowers and threw grenades into crowded basements.

When we drove into Grozny itself, the scale of the devastation only grew. Forty square blocks in the center of the city had been leveled by Russian bombing in January and February—a campaign that left thousands dead. It was a scene that resembled a smaller version of Dresden 1945, or Stalingrad 1943.

Our brief trip gave us a glimpse of the terrible realities of that first Chechen war of the 1990s, which was in many ways a continuation of struggles between Russians and Chechens that went back nearly three centuries. It was also a glimpse of how far Russia had fallen since the collapse of the Soviet Union; here were the ill-fed and ill-trained remnants of the Red Army, once reputed to be capable of reaching the English Channel in forty-eight hours, now unable to suppress a local rebellion in an isolated part of Russia. And here was Boris Yeltsin, who had so courageously defied hardliners in August 1991 and buried the Communist system for good, exposed as an infirm and isolated leader unable to restore order and rebuild the Russian state. This was post-Soviet Russia at its low point, deeply humiliated and thrashing about, the promise of its post-Communist transition still not extinguished, but beginning to flicker.

It was no coincidence that Vladimir Putin would ride a ruthlessly successful prosecution of the second Chechen war several years later to become Yeltsin's unlikely successor. If you wanted to understand the grievances, mistrust, and smoldering aggressiveness of Putin's Russia, you first had to appreciate the sense of humiliation, wounded pride, and disorder that was often inescapable in Yeltsin's.

* * *

AS THE GEORGE H. W. BUSH administration wound down, I had been in Washington for eight years, and was well aware of how fortunate I had been. While it typically took at least two decades to rise to the ranks of the Senior Foreign Service, I had been promoted across that threshold in less than a decade. I was not interested in skipping more rungs on the career ladder. I wanted to refine my craft and get back overseas.

What I really wanted to do was work in what seemed to me to be the most interesting place an American diplomat could serve in the early 1990s: Russia. When the job of minister-counselor for political affairs in Moscow opened up, I leapt at the chance. Lisa was less than enthusiastic; she loved adventures, but this one would involve more professional sacrifices for her, and cold and dark was not the atmosphere she had aspired to as an Asia specialist. Ultimately, she came around to the idea. Part of the allure for both of us was the opportunity to spend a year at the old U.S. Army Russian Institute in Garmisch, at the foot of the Alps in Bavaria, where I would complete advanced Russian-language training. Now with two wonderful young daughters, Lizzy and Sarah, we also wanted a chance to decompress as a family. We arrived in Germany in the summer of 1993, and proceeded to spend as close to an idyllic year as we had in the Foreign Service.

I was the only diplomat among the group of U.S. Army officers studying Russian in Garmisch. Our instructors were all Russian émigrés. Some had been at the institute since the 1950s; others had come in the wave of Soviet Jewish emigration in the 1970s; a few younger teachers had arrived since the breakup of the Soviet Union. I loved the richness of the Russian language, and learned quickly. Lisa took introductory Russian with a class of special forces soldiers, and to this day has an alarmingly strong grasp of arcane military terminology in Russian. We took weekend trips around Europe, and went hiking and skiing whenever we could. In the late spring of 1994, I spent a couple weeks living with a working-class Russian family in St. Petersburg. It improved my vocabulary considerably—and opened up whole new vistas in Russian profanity, thanks to the family's ne'er-do-well eighteen-year-old son, an aspiring but not overly talented rock musician.

We arrived in Moscow in mid-July. I had read voraciously about the embassy's colorful history, enthralled by the stories of George Kennan and Chip Bohlen reporting from a Moscow transfixed by fear of Stalin's purges. A ramshackle mustard-colored building on the Garden Ring, the embassy was not far from the Moscow River and the Foreign Ministry. It had served as the U.S. chancery since the early 1950s, increasingly a firetrap and the target of massive bugging attempts. An electrical fire in 1991 had done considerable damage to the building. The spectacle of Russian intelligence agents rushing to the scene, thinly disguised as firefighters, had left an even more lasting impression.

A new embassy building, later discovered to have been bugged by the Russian construction crew, lay vacant and partially completed down the block from the old chancery. Directly in front of the main entrance stood an Orthodox church, so jammed with listening and monitoring equipment that it was known in the embassy community as "Our Lady of Telemetry," or alternatively, "Our Lady of Immaculate Reception." Across a busy street to the west was the Russian White

House, which still bore scars from the failed coup attempt against Yeltsin nine months before.

The American embassy was led by Ambassador Tom Pickering, a veteran of six previous ambassadorial posts, and the most capable professional diplomat for whom I ever worked. He was insatiably curious about every aspect of diplomatic work. He knew more about the widgets in the embassy boiler room than most of our technicians, and was an adroit problem-solver across the whole range of issues, from the plight of American citizens who had run afoul of Russian law to the delicate high policy work of managing relations with Yeltsin. Pickering's lack of Russian-language skills always frustrated him, but he was so quick (and his interpreter so good) that it never seemed too much of an impediment.

Pickering never met an instruction from Washington that he didn't want to first shape himself. He never wanted to be a diplomatic postman, simply waiting for orders from headquarters. His view was that he was the president's representative on the ground, paid not just to report on events but also to offer his best policy ideas and solutions, and sometimes to act first and ask for forgiveness later. Pickering's one weakness, as far as I could tell, was a need for speed on Russia's often menacing roads. Riding in the backseat of his armored limousine, impatient to get places and do things, he would offer running advice to his long-suffering driver about how to race in the wrong direction down one-way streets or maneuver through the reckless world of Moscow traffic.

There is no playbook or operating manual in the Foreign Service, and the absence of diplomatic doctrine, or even systematic case studies, has been a long-standing weakness of the State Department. Throughout my own formative years, good mentors mattered most of all—accomplished diplomats from whom I could draw essential lessons about negotiating and leadership. Experience was passed from generation to generation, and I never had a better role model than Tom Pickering.

In Russia, Pickering ran what was then one of the biggest American diplomatic missions in the world, including the embassy in Moscow and consulates in St. Petersburg, Yekaterinburg, and Vladivostok. Unlike almost all our other diplomatic posts, we had only a handful of locals working in our embassy and consulates in the summer of 1994, with roles from drivers and mechanics to consular clerks and assistants played by Americans. The Soviet government had refused to allow Russians to work for the U.S. mission after the spying and bugging crises of the mid-1980s, and Pickering was just beginning the process of rehiring them.

Pickering led a "country team," comprising the senior representatives of some twenty different U.S. agencies working at the embassy. State composed less than half of the total staff, with the remaining positions filled by Defense, Treasury, Commerce, Agriculture, and the intelligence community, among many others. I've always thought that the country team is the most effective example of interagency coordination in the U.S. government, at least from the point of view of the State Department. A strong ambassador, like Pickering, could not only ensure efficient implementation of policy through careful coordination among agencies in the field, but also shape policy formulation in Washington by working with the senior agency representatives at post.

As the president's representative, he had authority over other agencies in Russia, and more interagency clout than more senior officials in the State Department. Pickering used this wisely. He never had to wave around his presidential appointment letter to command the respect of other agency officials on his country team. His experience and attentiveness to their agendas won their loyalty, and he repeatedly demonstrated that he could help them advance their departmental goals through his own energy and access to senior Russian officials. In return, they gave him transparency and followed his lead. It's a credit to Pickering's leadership, and a mark of the strength of his country team, that I don't ever recall him being surprised by an action of intelligence or law enforcement representatives at the embassy, or anyone else. He didn't micromanage their affairs, but he set a clear policy direction and exercised his broad authority skillfully.

Ambassador Pickering's deputy chief of mission was Dick Miles, a wise, deeply experienced Russia hand. Down-to-earth, with excellent Russian-language skills, Dick had common sense and a talent for connecting with people across Russian society that proved to be huge assets for the embassy, and a strong example for the rest of us. As head of the political section, I was nominally the number three officer in the mission. Largely because of the frequency of Pickering's travels, I would spend half my nearly two years in Moscow as acting deputy chief of mission, and several weeks as chargé, when both Pickering and Miles were away.

We had twenty-seven officers in the political section, by far the biggest of any in the Foreign Service, as well as four administrative assistants, and two Russian nationals, who arranged appointments and translated documents in an office separated from the parts of the embassy where classified work was done. Our job was to provide ground truths, a granular sense of political and economic realities in Russia, so that policymakers in Washington could weigh them against all the other considerations overflowing their inboxes. We roamed widely across Russia's eleven time zones, trying to convey to Washington as clear an understanding as we could of the unfolding drama of a Russia struggling to absorb simultaneously three immense historical transformations: the collapse of Communism and the tumultuous transition to market economics and democracy; the collapse of the Soviet bloc and the security it had provided to historically insecure Russians; and the collapse of the Soviet Union itself, and with it a Russian empire built gradually over several centuries. Any one of those would have been difficult to manage; all three together were profoundly disorienting.

Travel in Russia in that chaotic time was always memorable. I spent one frigid afternoon talking to coal miners a thousand feet underground in Kemerovo, a fast-fading city in Siberia. In Vladivostok, then the murky heart of Russia's "wild east," I talked to a couple of local mafia pretenders, expansive in their description of new "business possibilities," none of which sounded much like the new market models that Western advisors were earnestly promoting in Moscow and St. Petersburg. Departing on one wintry trip to the North Caucasus, I watched in amazement as a technician for Air Dagestan, one of Aeroflot's countless dodgy post-Soviet spin-offs, went to work de-icing the wings of the battered old Ilyushin aircraft with a blowtorch. It wasn't much more reassuring to climb into the plane and walk past the cockpit, where the rheumy-eyed pilot was putting away a half-empty bottle of vodka.

Moscow had its own unique charms in the mid-1990s. I remember heading off one morning for an appointment in the Moscow mayor's office. As I walked toward the entrance, I noticed a number of Russians in suits lying spread-eagled in the snow, with a group of armed, uniformed men wearing black ski masks standing over them. It turned out that the men in ski masks were members of President Yeltsin's presidential guards, led by Yeltsin's increasingly powerful former bodyguard, Aleksandr Korzhakov. They were paying a courtesy call on executives of the Most Group, run by one of Russia's wealthiest oligarchs, Vladimir Gusinsky, whose offices were a few floors below the mayor's. Gusinsky had run afoul of Korzhakov, and this was how gentle reminders were conveyed in Moscow in 1994.

Moscow's lawlessness produced plenty of scary moments. One weekday afternoon in the early fall of 1995, someone fired a rocket-propelled grenade into the sixth floor of the chancery in broad daylight. The round pierced the wall and detonated in a copying machine, sending metal fragments and glass in all directions. Miraculously, no one was in the copying room at the time, and no one was injured or killed. The authorities rounded up a number of the usual suspects, but the culprit was never identified. It was symptomatic of life in Moscow in that era that it didn't seem wildly out of the ordinary for someone to have an RPG in the center of the city in the middle of the day.

*　*　*

BY THE SUMMER of 1994, Boris Yeltsin was a wounded figure, his limitations as a leader growing more and more apparent. Despite the sustained efforts of Bill Clinton and his administration to cultivate relations with the new Russia and accommodate the post-traumatic stress of the post-Soviet world, the limitations of U.S.-Russian partnership were also laid bare.

In his rivalry with Mikhail Gorbachev, Yeltsin had been the heroic destroyer of the old, calcified Soviet system. But he faltered in the next phase, the construction of an open political and economic system out of the rubble of Communism. At first, he gave full rein to a group of young reformers led by his first prime minister, Yegor Gaidar. Self-styled "kamikaze pilots," they rushed to reform, acutely conscious of the gravitational forces of impossibly high popular expectations, the hard realities of economic change, and the inevitable counterreaction of conservative factions. Hardship was the dominant feature on their landscape. Industrial production in Russia had fallen by half since 1989. Agricultural production was dropping too. At least 30 percent of the population lived below the poverty line, and massive inflation had wiped out the meager savings of a pensioner generation that had endured the trials of the Great Patriotic War (World War II) and postwar recovery. The public health system had collapsed, and contagious diseases like tuberculosis and diphtheria were reemerging. Nevertheless, Yeltsin and his small band of reformers pushed ahead. A massive and unwieldy "voucher program," theoretically offering shares in state-owned companies to individual citizens, resulted in the privatization of some 70 percent of the economy by the end of 1994. Somewhat predictably, the process was monopolized by a tiny minority, a new class of oligarchs who were as ruthless as they were entrepreneurial.

As reform spawned political resistance, Yeltsin seemed adrift. When the Duma's reactionary leadership challenged the constitutional basis of his rule in the fall of 1993, Yeltsin resorted to the use of force, relying on loyal military units to rout his opponents. While he believed he had no choice, the cost was high, politically and personally. New parliamentary elections at the end of the year boosted the rabid nationalist party of Vladimir Zhirinovsky, as well as a reemergent Communist Party. Lonely and overwhelmed, Yeltsin retreated steadily from day-to-day government business, drinking heavily to ease physical and political pain.

In December 1994, on the eve of a visit by Vice President Al Gore to Moscow, I tried to capture Russia's domestic predicament in a cable to Washington.[1] "Winter in Russia is not a time for optimists, and in some respects the popular mood here mirrors the descending gloom." Yeltsin's foreign policy sought to mask national weakness and reassert Russian prerogatives. "Born of a mood of national regret over the loss of superpower status and an equally acute sense that the West is taking advantage of Russia's weakness," I wrote, assertive policies abroad had become one of the few themes that united Russians amid continued bickering over domestic issues. Yeltsin was determined to reaffirm Russia's great power status and independent interests in Russia's so-called Near Abroad, the neighboring post-Soviet republics of Eurasia.

Stressing the attachment of Yeltsin and the country's political elite to Russia's sphere of influence in the former Soviet space, I emphasized mounting Russian concern about expansion of NATO. I noted that Yeltsin's tough public statements in the fall of 1994 about NATO expansion "were an unsubtle reminder of Russian angst about neglect of its interests in the process of restructuring European security institutions."

The cable concluded that "the honeymoon in American relations with the new Russia that blossomed in the immediate aftermath of the breakup of the Soviet Union is now long past." Russia had embarked on a long journey of redefinition, which would inevitably prove frustrating and perplexing as personalities shifted and policies collided, but that continued to hold potential for effective post–Cold War relations between us. It was critical, in my view, to "prioritize better among the many concerns on our agenda with the Russians. Two years ago, we could pretty much have it our way on a whole range of issues, so long as we paid some minimal deference to Russian sensibilities. That is no longer the case."

I visited a retired Soviet diplomat late one afternoon that winter in his modest apartment in central Moscow. He was a widower, alone with his memories and photographs of foreign postings across the Cold War. As we slowly drained a bottle of vodka, the snow falling silently outside his sitting room window, he reminisced about his career. He was not especially nostalgic about the Soviet system, and acknowledged its many weaknesses and cruelties. "We brought this upon ourselves," he said. "We've lost our way." It might take another generation for Russia to recover its confidence and purpose, but he had no doubt that it would. It would be a mistake to leave the impression with Russians that we had taken advantage of them when they were down on their luck. "Remember Churchill," he said. "In victory, magnanimity. You won't regret it."

The embassy urged caution on NATO enlargement. Before thinking seriously about extending offers of formal NATO membership to Poland and other Central European states, we recommended considering other forms of cooperation with former Warsaw Pact members, and perhaps a new "treaty relationship" between NATO and Russia. We underscored the utility of including Russia in the new "Contact Group" on Bosnia, which gathered together key European and American diplomats to resolve a conflict spinning out of control in the former Yugoslavia. Russia had limited weight on Balkan diplomacy, but engaging it systematically reduced its temptation to be a spoiler, and was a smart investment for the day when it would add more muscle to its assertiveness. Another good example was the inclusion of Russia in meetings of the "G-7"—the principal players in the post–Cold War West. The emergence of the "G-8" helped anchor a weak and floundering Russia in the respect and status that came with regular dealings with the G-7 countries.

President Clinton was quick to appreciate what was at stake. In a speech in April 1993, he noted, "The danger is clear if Russia's reforms turn sour—if it reverts to authoritarianism or disintegrates into chaos. The world cannot afford the strife of the former Yugoslavia replicated in a nation as big as Russia."[2] Clinton and Yeltsin developed a surprisingly close personal relationship, despite their differences in age and political culture, and despite all the storms in U.S.-Russian relations in the 1990s. Both big, hearty men blessed with natural political gifts if not born into political privilege, they helped navigate a complicated and uncertain era. Strobe Talbott, an accomplished Russian specialist and Clinton's former Oxford roommate, dubbed the president "the U.S. government's principal Russia hand."[3] Clinton made a high priority of managing Russia and its erratic president. As the head of a new bureau in the State Department overseeing policy toward Russia and the other former Soviet states, Talbott became the day-to-day manager of the relationship.

Talbott and his Russian counterpart, Deputy Foreign Minister Georgiy Mamedov, understood how to steer through their own bureaucracies and politics, and had a solid appreciation of each other's political limitations. Together, they constructed an elaborate architecture of cooperative U.S.-Russian mechanisms aimed at cementing an image of partnership between at least nominal equals. At the core was the Gore-Chernomyrdin Commission, led by Vice President Gore and Prime Minister Viktor Chernomyrdin, which was set up to organize relations between the two governments more systematically. Following its inaugural session in Washington in September 1993, the commission met twice yearly, home and away. Eventually growing to include eight different subcommittees, each co-led by an American cabinet officer or agency head along with his Russian counterpart, the commission fostered cooperation across a wide range of areas, from the environment to outer space. Gore and Chernomyrdin also developed an effective relationship. They were an unlikely duo, the ambitious young Tennessee politician with a penchant for technical detail, and the gray, sometimes inarticulate apparatchik. Nevertheless, their informal conversations on the margins of the commission meetings were often productive, and Chernomyrdin developed a reputation in the West for efficiency, at least by the low-bar standards of the old Soviet system.

For all the mechanisms and the high-level attention and visits, Russia's post-Soviet transition was proving a long and painful slog. As his health deteriorated and his political clout and attention span grew more attenuated, Yeltsin was anxious for an opportunity to show people that he was still capable of decisive and effective action, a political step around which Russians could unite. Reasserting Moscow's authority over Russia's increasingly disconnected regions was one obvious possibility, and the most obstreperous and defiant region of all, Chechnya, was a tempting target. With a rebellious history and an especially dark and forbidding presence in the Russian psyche, Chechnya seemed to Yeltsin to be overdue for the application of a strong hand. As tensions built in 1994, the embassy highlighted the danger signs on the horizon: "Yeltsin is by no means out of the woods on political arrangements with the regions—a serious misstep on Chechnya, to cite the most obvious trouble spot, could cause the unraveling of much of what has been achieved."[4] The serious misstep was not long in coming.

* * *

THROUGHOUT THE YEARS I served in Russia, I was always fascinated by the North Caucasus. At one time or another, I traveled to each of its five autonomous republics, which had been gradually swallowed up in the advance of Russian imperial power in the nineteenth century. With the snowcapped peaks of the Caucasus Mountains looming off in the south, there was a wildness and beauty to the terrain unlike anything else I saw across Russia's huge expanse. Mostly Muslim and mostly poor, the North Caucasus was one of the few parts of the Russian Federation in which populations were still growing. And like mountain peoples everywhere, they had a defiant streak.

Most defiant of all, at least in the eyes of suspicious Russians, were the Chechens. For nearly fifty years in the nineteenth century they had waged a guerrilla war against imperial Russia. During World War II, wary that the Chechens might side with the invading Nazis, Stalin brutally deported nearly the entire population—some four hundred thousand men, women, and children—to Kazakhstan. They returned more than a decade after the war, with a whole new set of historical grievances. When the Soviet Union collapsed, with Moscow distracted and struggling with reform, Chechnya grew increasingly restive and isolated—ripe for the reckless ambition of its first elected president, Dzhokhar Dudayev, a recently retired Soviet air force general. Erratic and self-important, Dudayev alternated between declarations of Chechnya's quasi-independence and protestations that he remained a "Russian patriot"; more mob boss than revolutionary, he manipulated Chechen clan politics and set up a variety of criminal rackets.

The truth, however, was that Chechnya's lawlessness differed only in degree from what was going on across much of Russia in the early 1990s. In many tangible respects, Chechnya remained a part of the Russian Federation, its borders open and its oil and gas flowing freely out of the republic, its meager pensions paid out of the Russian budget. Dudayev himself gradually lost popularity in Chechnya. While his thugs enriched themselves, local government services atrophied. Dudayev's openly rebellious behavior grated on Yeltsin, a deeply irritating reminder of his inability to assert his grip. Similarly proud, impulsive, and disinclined to compromise, they were heading for a tragic collision.[5] Demonizing rhetoric came easily to both, with Dudayev playing on decades of Chechen mistreatment at the hands of Russians, and Yeltsin exploiting the peculiarly hard view that most Russians had of Chechens.

Tired and isolated, Yeltsin relied more and more on an inner circle of conservative power ministers and drinking companions, whose capacity for court politics exceeded their professional competence. Their argument to Yeltsin was that subduing Dudayev gave him a perfect opportunity to assert his control, outflank nationalist opponents, and show his wider international audience that Russia was beginning to reemerge after its moment of weakness. In the summer of 1994, with their encouragement, Yeltsin set in motion a series of escalating efforts to bring Dudayev to heel.

Serial humiliations were the result, first a failed coup d'état using Chechen oppositionists, and then a botched intervention in late November backed by Russian troops. The Chechens paid and recruited to undertake the operation fled at the last minute, and a number of Russian soldiers were captured and paraded before television cameras. There still may have been a chance to pressure Dudayev, whose position at home had been steadily weakening, and eventually negotiate an acceptable arrangement for Chechnya within the Russian Federation. Yeltsin, whose sense of embarrassment was now overflowing, instead doubled down and authorized a full-scale military invasion in early December. His defense minister, Pavel Grachev, assured him that the Russian army would easily overwhelm Chechen resistance. He could not have been more wrong.

Disregarding the advice of a number of senior army officers, Grachev sent three armored columns, poorly prepared and poorly led, into Grozny. Dudayev's forces, led by a former Soviet colonel, Aslan Maskhadov, slaughtered hundreds of Russian troops in fierce urban combat, and routed the rest. Beaten back, a furious Grachev began an intense aerial and artillery bombardment, determined to, as he said, "make the rubble bounce." Over the next few weeks, bombs and shells rained down on the city. Much of the bombing came from high altitude, and winter fog obscured targets. The result was devastating;

many of the civilian victims were elderly ethnic Russians living in the center of the city, who had been unable to flee.

On New Year's Eve, the Russians resumed their ground offensive, pushing most Chechen fighters out of the city by the end of February 1995. Grozny was left in ruins, with thousands of civilians dead. The violence and brutality of the conflict was heavily and openly covered by a still largely independent Russian media.

Back in the embassy, Ambassador Pickering asked me to take stock of the debacle for Washington. In a January 11, 1995, cable entitled "Sifting Through the Wreckage: Chechnya and Russia's Future," I laid out our preliminary thoughts.[6] "The Chechen crisis . . . has already laid bare the weakness of the Russian state and the tragic flaws of its first democratically-elected President." We worried about what all this meant for the future of reform in Russia, and whether this might trigger more separatism in other republics. The ineptitude of the Russian military left a powerful impression. "Probably even more than the loss of civilian lives which has so exercised Moscow's liberal intelligentsia," the blundering performance in the initial assault "has led Russians, and especially elites, to question Boris Yeltsin's competence to govern."

The cable argued that step-by-step over recent months, Yeltsin and his advisors had blundered further into a quagmire, with bad policy choices begetting worse ones. "The tragic irony is that the same mulish stubbornness that produced Yeltsin's greatest triumphs may now prove to be his undoing." While it was now too late for Yeltsin to recover the heroic democratic mantle he once wore, it was still not too late (assuming no catastrophic deterioration of his health) for him to maintain enough of his authority to limp along. He still appeared to retain support among political elites in Russia's regions, where the Chechen crisis so far did not have the resonance that it had in the capital. Blunders in Chechnya had severely tested military discipline, but it did not yet appear to be at the breaking point.

In Russian foreign policy terms, however, Chechnya had become a growing, self-inflicted disaster. The consequences for Russia were varied but uniformly bad—"isolating it internationally, exposing its weakness to other former Soviet states over which it seeks influence as well as to attentive regional powers like Iran, China, and Turkey, and playing into the hands of former Warsaw Pact states who will seek to accelerate the process of NATO expansion." In Moscow, it was hardening attitudes about the United States and its allies. "Russians across the political spectrum already feel an acute sense that the West is taking advantage of Russia's weakness, and that is likely to become more rather than less pronounced as a result of the deeply embarrassing experience in Chechnya."

The mood was hardening in Washington too. President Clinton had suffered a resounding defeat in the November 1994 midterm elections, with newly ascendant Republicans questioning many of his foreign policy assumptions, including about Russia. The administration itself was initially sympathetic to Yeltsin's predicament in Chechnya, with Vice President Gore comparing it at one point to the American Civil War, and Secretary of State Christopher calling it "an internal Russian affair."[7] Pickering was persistent in trying to explain how flawed that line of thinking was, but later noted with some frustration that "there was very little interest in the notion of whether the Russians actually provoked some of this or not."[8]

As fighting in Chechnya continued through the spring of 1995, the administration's attitude finally sharpened. Christopher warned Foreign Minister Andrey Kozyrev in Geneva in late March that the Chechen war was "foolhardy" and "tragically wrong." Meanwhile, pressure in Congress mounted to cut off or reduce aid to Russia, which then amounted to nearly a billion dollars annually. While the White House managed to forestall those efforts, we made clear from Moscow that we should not "overestimate the leverage that assistance gives us. Many Russian politicians, reformers included, would not mind an opportunity now to tell us to take our aid and shove it."[9]

Events in Chechnya continued to chip away at Yeltsin's waning authority. In June 1995, a daring Chechen commander, Shamil Basayev, led a group of rebels north, out of Chechnya and into the neighboring Russian region of Stavropol. Bribing their way through Russian military checkpoints until they ran out of cash, Basayev and his fighters seized some sixteen hundred Russian hostages in a hospital in Budennovsk. Yeltsin was en route to a G-7 summit in Halifax, Canada, as the attack unfolded. Rather than return immediately to Moscow, he left Prime Minister Chernomyrdin to handle the crisis. Negotiating directly with Basayev in a series of dramatic telephone calls, Chernomyrdin agreed to allow Basayev and his men to drive back to Chechnya with some one hundred hostages, freeing the remainder in Budennovsk. Once safely back in the mountains south of Grozny, Basayev released all those he had forced to accompany him. We reported from Moscow that "some in the Russian government thought at first that Budennovsk would be a plus at Halifax—an opportunity to show critics in the West that the Yeltsin regime had been right all along about what it was dealing with in Chechnya. The hostage crisis turned out instead to be a mortal embarrassment, painfully demonstrating Yeltsin's detached and erratic leadership and once again exposing Russia's weakness."[10]

The Chechen conflict continued in bloody fits and starts until the summer of 1996, when a more enduring cessation of hostilities was agreed upon. It reignited a few years later, providing Vladimir Putin with his chance to put a much different mark on Russian leadership, but the impact of that first brutal war would be felt in Russian politics and Russian attitudes toward the wider world for many years to come.

* * *

NOTHING BROUGHT THE brutality and chaos of the Chechen conflict into sharper relief for us in the embassy than the tragic case of Fred Cuny. I met Cuny only once, when he came to see Ambassador Pickering in Moscow in late February 1995. Six foot three, wearing cowboy boots and speaking in a quiet Texas drawl that oozed self-

confidence, Cuny was a magnetic presence. He had already built an
international reputation as a humanitarian relief expert, the "master
of disaster" who had worked his way through acute danger from Bi-
afra to Iraq. Most recently, he had braved the bombardment of Sarajevo to help restore the water supply for trapped civilians.

Cuny explained to Pickering that he had just returned from two
weeks in Chechnya, and had traveled widely in Grozny and to besieged towns and villages in its vicinity, on behalf of George Soros and
his foundation. He painted a sobering picture. He was particularly
concerned about the plight of thirty thousand mostly elderly, mostly
ethnic Russian civilians surrounded by fighting in southern Grozny.
Living in burned-out buildings and bomb shelters, many suffering
from pneumonia, most people there were not cooking for fear of
drawing Russian shelling, and most food was eaten raw. The fighting
was still intense, and humanitarian convoys couldn't reach Grozny's
southern neighborhoods. Cuny said those trapped there "could soon
be dropping like flies."[11] He described his contacts with local Chechen
commanders as well as Russian forces, and indicated that he planned
to return to Chechnya in about a month. Pickering thanked him for
his insights and Cuny agreed to stay in touch.

Cuny went back into Chechnya on March 31. His goal was to broker an agreement for humanitarian access, so that trapped civilians
could be extracted safely and supplies could be delivered. Cuny was
accompanied by two Russian Red Cross doctors, a translator, and a
Chechen driver. They headed first toward the Chechen-held town of
Bamut, southwest of Grozny, where Dudayev was believed to be
headquartered. When Cuny and his team reached Bamut, Dudayev
wasn't there. They tried to drive east, but on April 4 were apparently
detained at gunpoint by Chechen intelligence forces on the outskirts
of the village of Stary Achkoi. Later that day, Cuny's Chechen driver
reappeared in Ingushetia, with a brief message from Cuny noting that
he had been taken into custody but was "ok" and expected to be back

shortly. That was the last message from him, and neither he nor the Russian doctors or translator were ever heard from again.

Fred Cuny's disappearance set off a four-month search that occupied much of the embassy's energy and attention, and eventually drew the personal engagement of President Clinton. Our efforts on his behalf reflected an important dimension of what American diplomats do overseas. Few such efforts, however, were as dramatic or intense as the search for Cuny.

As the weeks and months passed, there were tantalizing rumors that Cuny and his colleagues were still alive, somewhere in the murky world of wartime Chechnya. Pickering tasked me with managing the day-to-day embassy effort to find him. We pressed senior Russian officials repeatedly for more information and help conducting a serious search. They promised a lot, and delivered very little. Our contacts on the Chechen side were limited, but we worked hard to use intermediaries in the government of Ingushetia to find out more. Cuny's son and brother, along with some of his staff and representatives of Soros's foundation, spent considerable time in Ingushetia that spring and summer and made a number of courageous trips inside Chechnya in pursuit of leads.

We set up our own informal outpost in Ingushetia, manned on a rotating basis by several of my colleagues. President Clinton raised the Cuny case with Yeltsin in May, as did Vice President Gore during his visit in June. I traveled to the region twice, and met at length with President Ruslan Aushev of Ingushetia both times. He insisted that he and his government were "working overtime" in the search.[12] "We have scoured the republic of Chechnya and even gone into Georgia to investigate a rumor that Cuny had been taken across the frontier," he told me. "Unfortunately, it did not check out."[13]

At one point, a report emerged of a corpse that resembled Cuny at a hospital in the rebel-held town of Shatoy, well south of Grozny in the foothills of the Caucasus Mountain range. Philip Remler, an

American diplomat serving in the Organization for Security and Co-operation in Europe (OSCE) peace mission in Grozny, volunteered to drive down to Shatoy and try to verify the report. A white flag flutter-ing on the front of his OSCE vehicle did not prevent a Russian tank from firing several rounds at him.

At the tiny hospital in Shatoy, Philip huddled with a local doctor as the badly decomposed body was brought out to be examined. Dusk was falling, and the lights in the makeshift examination room were flickering. Philip used his satellite phone to get me on the line in Moscow. Relying upon a medical record that his family had shared with us, I described Cuny's distinguishing physical characteristics, in-cluding a metal surgical pin in one of his thighs. Philip confirmed that the body was that of a tall man. In a calm voice, with the sound of Russian shelling audible in the background, he said decomposition had rendered most other features indistinct, but it was clear that there were no pins in either leg. It wasn't Cuny.

In August, after exhausting every possible lead, the Cuny team concluded that it was most likely that Fred had been killed early in April by Chechen forces in western Chechnya, soon after his initial detention in Stary Achkoi. The family gave a press conference in Moscow and ended their search. The embassy shared the family's judgment about Fred Cuny's fate. Based on what we had heard from a variety of Ingush and Chechen sources during the course of our four-month search, we noted in a cable to Washington that "we sus-pect (but cannot prove) that there were rumors spread prior to Fred Cuny's last entry into Chechnya that would have fed Chechen suspi-cions."[14]

We suggested that such stories "were originated or fanned" by the FSB, the Russian successor organization to the Soviet Union's KGB. We added that "the FSB was well aware of Cuny's earlier travels in Chechnya" and his previous meetings with Chechen military com-mander Maskhadov. There were also reports circulating in March in western Chechnya that the two Russian Red Cross doctors accompa-

nying Cuny were FSB agents. The FSB had ample incentive for a disinformation campaign, given the tensions swirling across Chechnya
in those months, and their interest in discrediting the Chechen fighters. Such a disinformation effort, we wrote, "would not necessarily
have been coordinated in Moscow (if the FSB had been well-
coordinated, it might not have gotten into such a colossal mess in
Chechnya in the first place)."

After months of painstaking effort, we came to a straightforward
conclusion: Cuny was likely caught in between two intelligence
services—the Chechens who pulled the trigger and the Russians responsible for setting the trap.

The whole tragic episode was wrapped in layer after layer of murk-
iness and deception. "It may well be that the double-dealing and dis-
ingenuousness of virtually all the parties with which we and the Cuny
family have been dealing reflect some measure of shared culpability,"
we wrote. The hard reality was that "none of this should come as a
surprise in the chaotic and often brutal world of the North Caucasus.
But Fred Cuny, while no stranger to risk-taking in dangerous situations, still deserved better." So did the poor Chechen civilians and un-
derfed, undertrained Russian conscripts who were both, in different
ways, victimized by a war that wasn't foreordained in that awful winter of 1994–95. It was another blow to a post-Soviet transition in
which problems were already overtaking possibilities. The Chechen
debacle was emblematic of a Russia still trapped in its complicated
past, struggling to find its way and regain its pride and purpose. And
it reinforced the limits of American agency in influencing a future
that only Russians could ultimately shape.

*   *   *

YELTSIN WAS BADLY wounded by the Chechen mess. After a heart
attack in the summer of 1995, he looked increasingly incapable, politically or physically, of avoiding a fatal blow in Duma elections in
December 1995, let alone running for reelection the following June.

The outlook for continued reform at home and the kind of partnership abroad to which both Yeltsin and Clinton still aspired was increasingly uncertain.

Despite the headwinds, Clinton continued to invest in their relationship, recognizing how central it was to any hope of keeping U.S.-Russian relations on a stable footing. In the face of domestic criticism and unease over Chechnya, Clinton went ahead with a long-planned visit to Moscow in May 1995 to join several other leaders from the victorious World War II alliance to celebrate the fifty-year anniversary of Hitler's defeat. Clinton knew how much this meant to Yeltsin, and to Russians more broadly. Even a half century later, the wartime sacrifices of the Soviet people, not least the loss of more than twenty million of their fellow citizens, and the pride that came with their indispensable role in crushing the Nazis, were powerful forces.

Any presidential visit is complicated, but this one was trickier than most, given the fragile policy backdrop. As the "control officer," I was responsible for coordinating negotiations with the Russians over the schedule and agenda for the visit and supporting Ambassador Pickering and the White House advance team. American presidents don't travel light. Clinton came with more than two hundred staff and security personnel, and a similar number of journalists. My team tried but failed to persuade the Russians not to have a unit fresh from combat in Chechnya join in the celebratory parade in Red Square. When an enterprising White House press official foolishly tried to forge a few extra credentials for American journalists, Kremlin security reacted with a predictable lack of amusement, but we avoided anything more than a mild scuffle and a few sharp words.

This was my first extended encounter with President Clinton, and I was impressed. He had a sure touch with Yeltsin, and an equally sure command of substance. Clinton understood Yeltsin's political constraints—both those imposed on him by Russia's turbulent weakness and those stemming from his own flawed decisions. "This guy is in a tough spot," Clinton said to us before heading to see Yeltsin. "We have to give him as much space as we can, because we're not going to find a better Russian partner."

President Clinton delivered a firm message on Chechnya, both privately in the Kremlin meetings and then publicly in a speech at Moscow State University. "Continued fighting in that region," he said in his televised remarks, "can only spill more blood and further erode support for Russia." Clinton was gracious with the overworked embassy staff and their families. The genuine appreciation that he conveyed in a brief conversation with Lisa and our two daughters, then six and three, helped make up for the long hours I had put in over the preceding weeks.

In broad foreign policy terms, Yeltsin had two principal concerns during Clinton's visit. Both would dominate much of the last year of my tour in Moscow—and much of the U.S.-Russian debate for many years to come. The first was maintaining a paramount Russian role among the states of the former Soviet Union. The second was preventing further erosion of Russia's position in post–Cold War Europe. As we reported in a cable a month after Clinton's visit, "nowhere are Russian sensitivities about being excluded or taken advantage of more acute than on the broad issue of European security. There is a solid consensus within the Russian elite that NATO expansion is a bad idea, period." The cable concluded that "it is very clear that the Russian elite sees NATO expansion . . . and Bosnia as parts of a whole—with concerns about NATO's role in Bosnia deepening Russian suspicions about NATO and its enlargement."[15]

Preoccupied with domestic issues early in his presidency, Clinton was reluctant to risk much American diplomatic capital in the Balkans, as the disintegration of Yugoslavia in the early 1990s spawned mounting ethnic bloodshed in Bosnia between the Muslim majority and a Bosnian Serb minority armed and supported by the new Serbian government in Belgrade. By 1994–95, the conflict consumed more attention and energy at the highest levels of the Clinton administration than any other foreign policy problem. NATO air forces

gradually stepped up their involvement to help protect Muslim civilians, especially after the massacre of some eight thousand Muslims in
Srebrenica in July 1995, and a brutal mortar attack on the central
marketplace in Sarajevo the following month that killed more than
three dozen innocent civilians. A renewed peacemaking effort was led
by Richard Holbrooke, then the assistant secretary of state for European affairs. Holbrooke was a brilliant diplomat, whose talents and
drive were matched only by his showmanship and sense of self—
memorably reflected in an otherwise routine State Department cable
noting his arrival in a Balkan capital, puckishly titled "The Ego Has
Landed."

For the Russians, the war in Bosnia served as another painful reminder of their weakness. While often frustrated by the brutality and
venality of the Serbian leadership, Yeltsin couldn't ignore the natural
affinity of Russians for Slavic kinsmen in Belgrade and among the
Bosnian Serbs. As NATO stepped up its air campaign, and as Holbrooke accelerated American diplomacy, the Russians resented their
secondary role. Holbrooke was not especially sympathetic, but took a
practical view of managing Russian sensibilities. "We felt that, despite
occasional mischief-making, Moscow would be easier to deal with,"
he later wrote, "if we gave it a place as a co-equal with the EU and the
United States" in the Contact Group.[16]

Holbrooke came to Moscow in October for a meeting of the Contact Group, the first hosted by the Russians. I met him at Vnukovo
Airport, and on the hourlong ride into Moscow was treated to a "full
Holbrooke," as he juggled calls to Secretary Christopher and Senator
Bill Bradley, unleashed a running commentary about Washington
politics, peppered me with questions about the already snowy landscape around us, made acerbic asides about the Russians, and complained bitterly about having to waste his time in Moscow when there
was more urgent work to be done in the Balkans. In the end, however,
Holbrooke's visit and Talbott's continuing, meticulous outreach to

counterparts in Moscow helped ease the Russian sense of grievance, and persuaded them to provide grudging support for the landmark 1995 Dayton Agreement and its implementation.

The issue of expanding NATO's membership to include Russia's former Warsaw Pact allies was a deeper challenge. Yeltsin and the Russian elite assumed, with considerable justification, that Jim Baker's assurances during the negotiation of German reunification in 1990—that NATO would not extend its reach "one inch" farther east—would continue to apply after the breakup of the Soviet Union. That commitment, however, had never been precisely defined or codified, and the Clinton administration saw its inheritance as fairly ambiguous. While Clinton himself was in no rush at the outset of his administration to force the question of enlarging NATO, his first national security advisor, Tony Lake, was an early proponent of expansion. Lake argued that the United States and its European allies had a rare historical opportunity to anchor former Communist countries like Poland, Hungary, and the Czech Republic in a successful democratic and market economic transition. A path to NATO membership would offer stability and reassurance, a compelling answer to historical fears of vulnerability to a revanchist Russia, as well as a newly reunified Germany. Amid the chaos of the former Yugoslavia, this argument struck a chord with Clinton.

Others in the new administration were less convinced. Talbott, and later Secretary of Defense Bill Perry, worried that starting down the road to formal enlargement of NATO would undermine hopes for a more enduring partnership with Russia, undercutting reformers who would see it as a vote of no confidence in their efforts, a hedge against the likely failure of reform. We shared similar concerns at Embassy Moscow. In a fall 1995 cable, we laid out the quandary: "The challenge for us is to look past the [government of Russia's] often irritating rhetoric and erratic and reactive diplomacy to our own long-term self-interest. That demands, in particular, that we continue to seek to build a security order in Europe sufficiently in Russia's interests so that a revived Russia will have no compelling reason to revise it—and so that in the meantime the 'stab in the back' theorists will have only limited room for maneuver in Russian politics."[17]

In an attempt to buy time and test Russian attitudes, the Pentagon developed the "Partnership for Peace," a kind of NATO halfway house that would build trust by offering all former Warsaw Pact states—including Russia—a formal relationship with NATO. Clinton indicated at the outset that PfP membership "can also lead to eventual membership in NATO," but there was no explicit signal of any decision to expand at that stage. Yeltsin and Foreign Minister Andrey Kozyrev indicated their interest in participating in PfP, dragging out talks in hopes of slowing down any movement toward NATO expansion. Nevertheless, momentum gathered over the course of 1994 toward enlargement, with Clinton declaring publicly in Warsaw in July that the question was not if but when. At an OSCE summit in Budapest in December, Yeltsin lashed back. He declared publicly that the end of the Cold War was in danger of becoming a "cold peace," and accused Clinton and the NATO allies of "giving up on democracy in Russia." In a later private conversation with Clinton, Yeltsin was equally direct about his concerns. "For me to agree to the borders of NATO expanding toward those of Russia," he said, "would constitute a betrayal on my part of the Russian people."[18]

"Hostility to early NATO expansion," we reported just after the Budapest outburst, "is almost universally felt across the domestic political spectrum here."[19] We tried to counter the characteristically American tendency to think that the right process could solve almost any substantive problem. "The Russian elite is much more focused on outcomes now," we wrote in a subsequent cable. "When consultations on Bosnia or NATO expansion or other neuralgic issues don't—in Russian eyes—affect Western behavior, resentment and disillusionment are bound to follow. In those circumstances, the process serves mainly to remind Russians of their own weakness."[20]

Clinton mollified Yeltsin by privately assuring him that no decisions on expansion would be made until after the Russian presidential elections in June 1996. Apart from the NATO issue, Yeltsin's health and political fortunes were both in poor shape as he maneuvered to win reelection. His heart ailments slowed him down, and heavy drinking didn't help. On one occasion in late 1995, when I was serving as chargé, Lisa and I joined a small party of senior Russian officials at Vnukovo Airport to welcome Yeltsin back from an overseas trip. He had clearly done a lot of unwinding on the flight home, and lumbered past us to his waiting limousine—a bodyguard steering the well-lubricated president by the elbow, while another aide mumbled the Russian equivalent of "nothing to see here folks, just move along."

With most of Russia's oligarchs banding together behind him, Yeltsin stumbled ahead to victory, defeating a gray, uncharismatic Communist candidate. His candidacy was also bolstered not so subtly by American advice and support, prompting a 1996 cover of *Time* that read "Yanks to the Rescue: The Secret Story of How American Advisers Helped Yeltsin Win." Vladimir Putin would later hold up that episode as evidence of American hypocrisy and political meddling, part of a bill of particulars that he would use to justify his own efforts to manipulate American politics.

After his reelection in November 1996, Clinton followed through on NATO expansion, with formal invitations extended to Poland, Hungary, and the Czech Republic in the summer of 1997. An elaborate NATO-Russia agreement was later reached, which helped address some of Yeltsin's concerns. Nevertheless, as Russians stewed in their grievance and sense of disadvantage, a gathering storm of "stab in the back" theories slowly swirled, leaving a mark on Russia's relations with the West that would linger for decades. No less a statesman than George Kennan, the architect of containment, called the expansion decision "the most fateful error of American policy in the entire post–Cold War era."

* * *

I FINISHED MY assignment in Moscow in early 1996, called back to Washington to become the executive secretary of the State Department, a senior career position that oversaw all the immediate staff support for the secretary of state. While it was a significant promotion, I missed Russia and the excitement of serving in a place in the midst of such consequential change.

In the years that followed, as debates about "who lost Russia" picked up steam, I thought often of what we had gotten right and what we had gotten wrong. The truth was that Russia was never ours to lose. Domestically, Russians had lost trust and confidence in themselves, and they would eventually have to remake their state and their economy. As the twentieth century wound to a close, Russians had been through generations of privation and tragedy. None of that could be fixed in a single generation, let alone a few years. None of it could be fixed by outsiders, even a United States at the peak of its post–Cold War dominance.

As Talbott later put it, "more therapy and less shock" would have been a better formula for easing Russia's transition to a market economy. But that was more a question of our sometimes flawed assumptions and advice than some grand missing economic initiative, a "Marshall Plan" that would have neatly transformed a broken post-Soviet economy. Russians would not have tolerated massive foreign intrusion reordering their economic life; they could only navigate that difficult landscape themselves.

When it came to international security arrangements, we were less Churchillian in our magnanimity. Sitting at the embassy in Moscow in the mid-1990s, it seemed to me that NATO expansion was premature at best, and needlessly provocative at worst. I understood and sympathized with the arguments for reassuring newly liberated Central European states, whose history created powerful reasons for anxiety about a revanchist Russia. I could plainly see the case for anchoring them quickly in Western institutions but thought a longer investment in the Partnership for Peace, prior to any move to formal NATO membership, made sense. It was wishful thinking, however, to believe that we could open the door to NATO membership without incurring some lasting cost with a Russia coping with its own historic insecurities.

Applied to this first wave of NATO expansion in Central Europe, Kennan's comments struck me as a little hyperbolic. It damaged prospects for future relations with Russia, but not fatally. Where we made a serious strategic mistake—and where Kennan was prescient—was in later letting inertia drive us to push for NATO membership for Ukraine and Georgia, despite Russia's deep historical attachments to both states and even stronger protestations. That did indelible damage, and fed the appetite of a future Russian leadership for getting even.

In the end, there proved to be no avoiding the sense of loss and humiliation that came with defeat in the Cold War and the collapse of the Soviet Union, no matter how many times we and the Russians told each other that the outcome had no losers, only winners. The forces of history would continue to reverberate, and Russia—as it had done throughout its tumultuous history—would eventually bounce back from catastrophe. There was bound to come a moment when Russia would have the capacity to toss off the junior-partner role that made it so uncomfortable, even as its long-term great power decline continued. That moment just came sooner than any of us anticipated.

4

Jordan's Moment of Transition: The Power of Partnership

KING HUSSEIN LOOKED awful. His face was drawn and pale, his eyes as cloudy as the sky on that piercingly cold January day in Amman. The king was near the end of a long battle with cancer, desperately ill and about to return to the Mayo Clinic in Minnesota for one last bone marrow transplant. Lisa and I joined the royal family and a handful of senior Jordanian officials at the airport to bid him farewell. The mood was heavy with anxiety and anticipation. After nearly a half century under Hussein's leadership, Jordanians were coming to grips with the prospect of losing the only ruler they had ever known.

A small receiving line formed on the way to the king's plane. He walked slowly, propping himself up with a cane in acute discomfort. His voice was uncharacteristically weak, but he was still as gracious as ever. I told him that our thoughts and prayers were with him, and that he—and Jordan—could count on our support. He squeezed my hand, smiled, and leaned in to whisper a few words of appreciation.

Queen Noor was in tears beside him, looking tired and sad, but trying hard to smile. Crown Prince Abdullah and Princess Rania, standing alongside Hussein and Noor, looked a little stunned, having learned within the last few days that they would become crown prince and princess—and before long, king and queen of Jordan.

After the king's plane had taken off, several of the royal guards—stalwart East Bank tribesmen—began to sob quietly. One elderly royal court official stopped me as I left, took me by the arm, and asked, "Do you ever think we'll see him again?"[1]

* * *

MY RETURN TO Jordan as ambassador, a little more than a decade after the end of my first diplomatic posting, was fortunate on several levels: It was unusual to have an opportunity to serve as ambassador so early in my career; it turned out to be an unusually interesting time to be in Amman, with the transition from Hussein to Abdullah emblematic of wider dramatic change in Jordan and the region; and it was as enjoyable a tour as our family ever had overseas. Lisa's work as the State Department's regional refugee coordinator often took her outside Jordan, driving her armored Suburban to visit Palestinian refugee camps from the outskirts of Damascus to the crowded center of Gaza. And my own job was a significant professional test, trying to steady and reassure a small but crucial partner at an historic inflection point.

I came to the assignment with the benefit of another demanding tour on the seventh floor behind me. Sitting between the offices of the secretary and the deputy secretary, I had spent more than two years leading the Executive Secretariat, a 160-person bureau that handled the relentless flow of information to the department's senior leadership; tasked material to prepare the secretary for meetings in Washington and abroad; organized the secretarial travel schedule; monitored implementation of secretarial decisions; and ran the Operations Center, the twenty-four-hour nerve center of the department, responsible for managing crises and connecting the secretary and senior officials to our embassies and their foreign counterparts.

It was a prestigious if mostly thankless job, with a punishing pace and recognition that usually came only when problems emerged or mistakes were made. The Operations Center typically juggled calls to foreign ministers and other senior foreign officials with remarkable dexterity, even in the most acute crises. On one memorable occasion early in my tenure, however, I got a late-night call from an irate senior department official, who had been accidentally connected to the wrong foreign minister. It hadn't helped that the minister on the line was a rival of the neighboring minister he had sought to speak to— and it really hadn't helped that my senior colleague had plowed through about five minutes of his talking points before realizing that he was speaking to the wrong person. Fortunately, the minister on the other end of the line had more of a sense of humor than my colleague, and calamity was averted.

Leading the Executive Secretariat was in a way the managerial and logistical complement on the seventh floor to the substantive work of the Policy Planning Staff. If Policy Planning was, especially in Baker's time, like a ship's navigation team, the Executive Secretariat was more like the engine room, where all the gears connected. The experience of leading both bureaus helped me understand how to marry policy ideas with policy action.

Warren Christopher was entering his last year as secretary when I began my new role as executive secretary in early 1996. Gentlemanly and deeply experienced, Christopher had served as deputy secretary under Secretary Cyrus Vance in the Carter years, and as deputy attorney general in the Johnson administration. Always well prepared, Christopher was as precise in his conversations with foreign counterparts or public statements as he was in his attire. In his bespoke suits, he could make even the most fastidious around him feel disheveled. I admired his quiet dignity and professionalism in a town that often prized self-promotion and chicanery. He was shy in public, but employed a dry wit, and took great pleasure in puncturing inflated egos. After one assistant secretary droned on at a morning staff meeting,

Christopher leaned toward me and deadpanned, "Remind me to bring my ejection button next time."

His successor, Madeleine Albright, thrived in her public role, and had a particular flair for putting foreign policy in practical terms. She could do diplomatic convolutions when she had to, but was much more in her element questioning the "cojones" of the Cuban regime after it shot down a defenseless civilian aircraft, or bluntly challenging Balkan despots. Proud to be the first woman to serve as secretary of state, Albright was a formidable presence on the international stage, extremely hardworking, and adept at managing hard issues and complicated personalities.

Along with Pat Kennedy, the acting undersecretary for management legendary for his bureaucratic wizardry, I led the department's transition effort from Christopher to Albright. This traditionally involved the preparation of dozens of voluminous briefing books on every conceivable issue that a new secretary might encounter, either in her confirmation hearing or in her early months in office. Given that Secretary Albright had already served as the U.S. ambassador to the United Nations for four years and was intimately familiar with most major policy questions, we tried to curb the department's enthusiasm for deforestation. Instead, we insisted that senior officials and chiefs of mission overseas craft their own personal notes to her. We knew that nothing would be more helpful to the incoming secretary than unvarnished first-person assessments of what had gone right and what had gone wrong during their tenures, what issues loomed on the horizon, and what strategies they would recommend going forward.

The results were mixed. Some of the first-person cables were exceptional—honest, insightful, and grounded in thoughtful policy prescriptions. Others were long-winded, whiny, self-absorbed, and deep in the weeds on issues that no secretary should have to address. For a new secretary, it was a useful introduction to the department she would now lead, with all its strengths, weaknesses, and idiosyncrasies.

"Friendly takeovers" in administrations of the same party, like the
transition from Christopher to Albright, are supposed to be easy.
Transitions from one party to another are assumed to be much more
difficult. The reality is more complicated. New secretaries, no matter
their party, want to put their own mark on personnel and policy.
Much as Baker respected Shultz, he wanted to mold the department
in his own way, and both he and President George H. W. Bush made
clear that they were shaping the first Bush administration, not the
third Reagan administration. Madeleine Albright was equally intent
on putting her own stamp on the department, but I survived the reshuffle.

The administration was under heavy pressure to cut costs and
streamline the foreign policy machinery from Senator Jesse Helms,
the chairman of the Senate Foreign Relations Committee, a caricature of a neo-isolationist and a longtime critic of the Department of
State and foreign assistance. With Helms leading the charge, Congress made clear its intention to cash in on the post–Cold War peace
dividend, eventually shrinking the size of the foreign affairs budget by
nearly half over the 1990s. Reading the tea leaves, the Clinton administration tried to get ahead of the cuts by laying out an affirmative
vision for the most substantial restructuring of Washington national
security institutions in a half century.

The secretary asked Pat and me to take the lead in managing one
significant aspect of this effort—the complicated task of absorbing
the Arms Control and Disarmament Agency (ACDA) and the U.S.
Information Agency (USIA) into the State Department. ACDA,
which my father led in the late 1980s, was much smaller than State,
with about two hundred staff and a mission that remained essential
but had shifted from its Cold War origins. Its consolidation into State
was relatively straightforward. We created a new undersecretary position to absorb its key elements and transferred its professional cadre
directly into the department.

USIA was a more difficult proposition. Its public diplomacy

mission—to expose other societies to American culture, ideas, and perspectives and make the case for American policy—was in many ways even more valuable in the post–Cold War world. It took years to fully merge the two personnel systems and bureaucratic cultures, and we lost much of USIA's public diplomacy expertise and program management skills along the way. That became painfully apparent in the aftermath of 9/11, especially in a roiling Islamic world. It became even more apparent when Putin's Russia mounted substantial disinformation campaigns a decade later.

The costs of the Helms-generated cuts and consolidation were long-lasting. At State, intake of new foreign service officers was virtually suspended for four years. This created substantial gaps at mid-level ranks a decade down the road, significantly hindering post–9/11 diplomacy as we struggled to find enough seasoned officers to fill key positions. History didn't end in the 1990s; we couldn't afford to rest on our laurels and await the inexorable march of globalization and American influence, and we paid a price for our shortsightedness.[2]

I learned more than I ever wanted to know about budgets, personnel, regulations, and congressional affairs during my two years as executive secretary. I knew, at least conceptually, that it was an investment that would pay off. But I missed doing diplomacy and was eager to return overseas.

Secretary Albright and Strobe Talbott, by now deputy secretary of state, could sense my impatience, and offered to support my candidacy to become ambassador to Jordan—if I agreed to extend for another year through the summer of 1998. It was a hard offer to refuse, not only because it would fulfill every young diplomat's dream to become an ambassador, but also because it would allow me to return to Jordan—and this time to experience it with Lisa and our daughters. I had a blessedly uneventful confirmation hearing before the Senate Foreign Relations Committee, and was sworn in by Madeleine Albright in late July. Sixteen years into the Foreign Service, I had come full circle.

* * *

IN A CABLE to President Clinton on the eve of King Hussein's funeral in Amman in February 1999, I reminded him of a comment attributed to John Foster Dulles in the early 1950s. "King Hussein is an impressive young fellow," Dulles said. "It's a shame that neither he nor his country will last very long."[3] Nearly five decades later, Jordan was still intact, and the king himself had become the region's longest-serving head of state. He had survived a coup attempt in 1957, the disaster of the Six-Day War in 1967, the events of Black September a few years later, and a series of assassination attempts along the way. He had not only kept Jordan afloat amid the unending turbulence of the Middle East, but created a sense of national identity and an operable, if still fragile, economy.

The practical dilemmas facing Jordan in the summer of 1998 were nevertheless daunting. Water scarcity was an urgent problem; per capita consumption was one-fortieth that of Americans. Unemployment ran at more than 20 percent, with underemployment an equally flammable problem. The population of roughly five million was growing rapidly, GDP growth was flat, and external debt was rising. Jordan had few natural resources. It ran a growing trade deficit, importing most of its food and heavily dependent on outside assistance. Hussein periodically had to employ austerity measures and tighten budgets, but cuts in subsidies brought popular unrest, and the king was generally unable to sustain serious economic reform programs.

As he neared his forty-seventh year on the throne, Hussein was the embodiment of Jordan, the singular guarantor of national unity. Down below, society was still riven by fault lines, some old and some new. Over half the population was of Palestinian origin. East Bankers, the townspeople and descendants of the Bedouin tribes who had populated the hard hills and deserts east of the Jordan River before the waves of Palestinian arrivals after the 1948 and 1967 wars, were fiercely protective of their political control and prerogatives. Several hundred thousand Iraqis had fled to Jordan after Desert Storm. Meanwhile, another newer fault line was widening, between the struggling poor of east Amman and other Jordanian cities and the conspicuously consuming residents of Abdoun and other neighborhoods in west Amman.

Political opposition was closely monitored by the General Intelligence Department (GID). Hussein sometimes let off steam through carefully managed political liberalization; in 1989, for example, he had allowed fairly open elections and the formation of a government that included Islamists. His rule was absolute, but wrapped in a tolerance and relative generosity of spirit that set Jordan apart from other regimes in the region.

If Hussein had a tough hand to play at home, his neighborhood was even rougher. While the king's longevity, shrewdness, and friends outside the region (in particular the United States) brought him some respect, it came mostly grudgingly. To the north, Hafez al-Assad's Syria looked down its nose at Jordan—which was a part of Greater Syria during Ottoman times, and was now a country most Syrians thought of as an historical anomaly. To the east lay Saddam Hussein's Iraq, isolated after Desert Storm but still menacing, a source of concessional oil and a market for Jordan's goods. To the south, Saudi Arabia often took a dim view of Hashemite Jordan, always mindful that the House of Saud had expelled Hussein's great-grandfather from the Hejaz in the 1920s. Across the Red Sea and Gulf of Aqaba was Egypt, self-consciously the center of the Arab world and usually disinclined to pay much attention to an inconsequential smaller Arab power like Jordan. And to the west was Israel, which had a strategic interest in a stable, moderate Jordan. Since the 1950s, Hussein had kept up secret contacts with the Israelis. After the Oslo Accords between the Israelis and the Palestinians, Hussein seized the opportunity to negotiate a peace treaty with Israel, solidifying his regional position and repairing the damage with the United States that lingered after the Gulf War.

By 1998, U.S.-Jordanian relations were quite healthy. President Clinton and Secretary Albright reintroduced me to King Hussein as their nominee for ambassador when the king visited Washington in June. I had been a background fixture in Hussein's meetings with senior Americans over the years, and his courtly mannerisms and deep, easy laugh were familiar. Clinton and the king had an excellent relationship. The president had obvious respect for Hussein's judgment and experience, and the king had an equally obvious, almost avuncular affection for Clinton's intellect and commitment to Arab-Israeli peace.

In that initial June conversation, Hussein was upbeat and looking ahead. "We'll do a lot together," he said. "You already know Jordan and our challenges. There is so much we can accomplish during this administration." Sadly, the king would return to the Mayo Clinic in July, before I arrived in Amman, with a recurrence of an even more deadly form of cancer. He would spend only a couple more weeks of his life in Jordan.

The embassy that I took over at the beginning of August 1998 was a much different place from the one I left in 1984. It occupied a new and much larger complex west of the old center of Amman, built in the early 1990s to fit the new security specifications for American embassies around the world. It contained 130 American employees and 270 Jordanians, roughly twice the staff of the embassy I had left. The compound was about the size of six or seven football fields, and was surrounded by a nine-foot wall. Inside were a sizable circular chancery building, a service annex and motor pool, a social club and swimming pool, and the ambassador's residence. Lisa and the girls and I enjoyed our new home; what it lacked in privacy it made up for in convenience, with my office a two-minute walk away.

Security was a persistent concern throughout our three years in Amman. On our third night in our new home, Lisa and I were awakened by a 2 A.M. phone call from the Operations Center, and a contingent of Marines in full combat gear barreling upstairs to help secure the residence. An urgent threat report warned that there would be an RPG attack on the embassy compound that night. Fortunately, the plotters were caught in time. A few days later, al-Qaeda struck two American embassies in East Africa, with massive loss of life.

Threats reemerged throughout our tour, and were particularly worrisome at the end of 1999, when a major al-Qaeda attack on Jordanian hotel and tourist sites was thwarted. We had entered a new era in diplomatic insecurity, in which risks—for many years a painful feature of embassy life—were increasing, and Washington's appetite for risk-taking was diminishing.

* * *

SITTING IN HIS hospital room in Minnesota in July 1998, King Hussein gave a television interview that jarred his Jordanian audience. "The doctors' diagnosis is lymphoma," he said with a weary smile. "My cancer is a new fight which I hope to win." There was reason for the king to be optimistic. He was only sixty-two, he'd already won a bout with bladder cancer earlier that decade, and he had one of the world's best teams of doctors treating him at Mayo.[4]

Jordanians, however, were uneasy. They had become utterly dependent on one man, and were not used to having him out of the country for months at a time. Through force of personality and political dexterity, Hussein had camouflaged societal divisions in Jordan and created a role for his country on the regional stage out of all proportion to its strategic weight and resources. Most Jordanians had grown unaccustomed to taking political responsibility, let alone thinking about what might follow after Hussein. There was no escaping that now.

Hussein's younger brother, Hassan, had served as crown prince since 1965, when the king had decided amid a particularly intense spate of assassination threats that it would be irresponsible to keep his oldest son, Abdullah, then only three years old, as his successor. Hussein and Hassan were eleven years apart in age, but the difference in their personalities seemed even wider. Intuitive and full of restless energy, the king had an easy rapport with Jordanians, at home with Bedouin sheikhs in the desert or military units in the field. Hassan was at heart an intellectual. It was hard to imagine him clambering atop a tank to speak to his troops, as Hussein had done so many times over the years. Oxford-educated and widely read, Hassan could come across as a bit detached from the world of most Jordanians—a disconnect reinforced by his official 1998 birthday portrait, in which he posed in full polo regalia, complete with helmet, mallet, and jodhpurs, seated on his favorite pony.

And yet beyond traits that were easy to caricature, Hassan was as devoted to Jordan as Hussein. He worked hard, was deeply knowledgeable about his country, and loyal to his brother. He also had more of a common touch than he was given credit for. When Secretary of Commerce Bill Daley visited Jordan in the fall of 1998, Hassan insisted on driving us back to Daley's hotel after dinner at his lovely old stone house on a hill overlooking downtown Amman. He got behind the wheel of his Land Rover, with a bemused commerce secretary riding shotgun and me in the backseat, and another vehicle full of royal guards in the rear. Pulling out of the palace gate, Hassan asked if we wanted to stop for tea in the Wehdat refugee camp, which was more or less on the way. Daley was haggard after a long day of meetings, but he knew it would be impolite to say no. And so the three of us wound up sitting at a tiny shop on one of the camp's densely packed streets at midnight, drinking tea surrounded by curious Palestinian teenagers and an increasingly nervous group of royal guards. Hassan was breezy and nonchalant, asking the shopkeeper about his family, engaging in small talk with other patrons, and basking in the moment.

King Hussein's long hospitalization in the second half of 1998 became, in effect, Hassan's dress rehearsal for the throne, after thirty-three years as crown prince. It didn't end well. There were all the hallmarks of Shakespearean drama—a dying king coming to terms with his own mortality; a beleaguered crown prince trying to show he was ready for a job that was fast receding from him; a royal family struggling with loss and dysfunction; sons coming of age in the midst of so much scrutiny and uncertainty; and courtiers angling for advantage. There were no real villains, just a chain of difficult circumstances and complicated personalities. The king had been drifting for some time toward a change in the line of succession. His illness merely accelerated that decision. His unease about Hassan was not about loyalty or intellect or commitment, but about whether he was the best person to lead Jordan through what the king knew would be a tough transition. And his sense of confidence in his sons had grown as they matured. Prince Abdullah, now in his late thirties, had become an accomplished and well-respected military officer. Prince Hamzeh, now eighteen and Hussein's eldest son by the last of his wives, Queen Noor, was a cadet at Sandhurst, with a manner and bearing much like his father's.

As uncertainties about the king's health and succession unfolded that fall and winter, my main task as ambassador was to place America's hand on Jordan's shoulder and do whatever I could to help steady a country on which the United States depended heavily. A stable Jordanian partner was essential to Israel's security and hopes for Palestinian-Israeli peace, and Jordan's geopolitical value as a moderate, reliable friend in a tough neighborhood was out of all proportion to its demographic and economic weight. This was a classic opportunity for American diplomacy, as the organizer and mobilizer of support from other countries and international institutions—and for an ambassador as conductor, orchestrating the varied instruments of the American bureaucratic symphony.

Crown Prince Hassan was gracious and welcoming from the start. Barely ten days into my new role, I had to call him a little after midnight to seek an urgent meeting and preview the cruise missile strikes that the United States was about to launch against al-Qaeda targets in Afghanistan in retaliation for the embassy attacks in East Africa.

Without hesitation, he agreed to see me, and we spent an hour or two drinking his favorite single malt scotch and discussing a variety of challenges beyond those lighting up the sky over Afghanistan. Hassan seemed a bit lonely, with few confidants outside his immediate family. That was partly a function of personality, but also partly because the king moved people in and out of his brother's inner circle and never allowed him to develop an independent political base. Hassan was understandably thin-skinned about stories drawing unflattering contrasts with his brother. He was too proud to look for sympathy but anxious for signs that people respected him in his own right. I went out of my way to make clear that I did.

Prince Abdullah and I were only a few years apart in age. He spent a year at Oxford soon after I finished there, and we had shared an academic mentor in Albert Hourani. At the time, Hourani described Abdullah to me in a letter as "smart and personable" but someone who seemed "destined more for a life of action than of books."[5]

In late August 1998, Prince Abdullah and his wife, Princess Rania, invited Lisa and me to an informal dinner at their home. A fan of Japanese cuisine, Abdullah was an accomplished cook, and prepared Kobe beef on the grill. The setting was relaxed and unpretentious, just like our hosts. The only other guests were from the royal family— Abdullah's brothers and sisters; his mother, Princess Muna, a lovely, down-to-earth person and King Hussein's second, British wife; and her father, Colonel Gardiner, a veteran of the Italian campaign in World War II. It was the first of a number of evenings that we would spend with Abdullah and Rania over the next few years, including each of the Thanksgivings we celebrated in Amman, when we supplied the turkey and they brought the pies. They were funny and unaffected, with Princess Rania a particularly good judge of people, and Prince Abdullah proud of his family and his growing responsibilities in the military.

With uncertainty about King Hussein's health hanging over everything, I tried hard to build as broad a set of relationships as I could, inside the royal family and across Jordanian society. I worked easily with the prime minister, Fayez Tarawneh, an affable East Bank technocrat, instinctively cautious but increasingly concerned about Jordan's economic predicament. The foreign minister, Abdul-Ilah al-Khatib, was a capable professional and good friend. Rima Khalaf, the minister of planning and one of the most senior women officials in the Arab world, was impressive and reform-minded. Samieh Battikhi was then the head of the General Intelligence Department, a shrewd and ambitious operator with a lifestyle obviously not purely a function of his government salary. The GID was already a crucial intelligence partner for the United States; it was also slowly becoming the power behind the throne.

Meanwhile, Crown Prince Hassan was trying to demonstrate that he could manage affairs in Hussein's absence, without appearing to usurp the king's authority. It was an extremely difficult balancing act. In September, Hassan stepped on the sensibilities of the Jordanian military leadership, questioning their budget submission and raising the issue of whether it would make sense to accelerate senior military retirements and make way for the next generation. Neither was an unreasonable thought—but military affairs were exclusively the king's preserve, and Hussein was upset when word filtered back to him at Mayo, undoubtedly flavored by the wounded sensitivities of his generals.

I had easy access to senior Jordanians throughout my time in Amman, and there were times when it seemed a little too easy, especially in this early period. On one occasion, Hassan invited me to sit in on an internal briefing from his military leadership in preparation for a forthcoming meeting of the U.S.-Jordanian Joint Military Commission. I did my best to be unobtrusive, but it was an awkward experience. The crown prince was pointed in his commentary, peremptory and a little patronizing in manner, interrupting the briefers repeatedly to question their arguments. His intent was straightforward. He wanted to ensure a tight presentation, and also to demonstrate his understanding of military realities. But it didn't go down well with the officers in the room. You could see them gritting their teeth—and thinking to themselves that King Hussein would never have treated them that way.

The crown prince stayed in regular contact with the king during his treatment, but chose not to visit him at Mayo. He thought his role was to mind the store in Jordan, and Hussein seemed to agree. But that put Hassan at a considerable tactical disadvantage, as other senior family members and officials, many of whom were not admirers of the crown prince, flew back and forth to see the king in the United States. The army chief, Field Marshal Abdul Hafez Marei Kaabneh, complained directly to the king on one visit that fall about Hassan, alleging that he was telling senior military officers that Hussein's condition was "irreversible," and that they would need to prepare for the possibility of a transition. Hassan later denied to me that he had ever said that. But the damage was done, and the king's irritation grew. Rumors reached Mayo that Princess Sarvath, Hassan's intelligent but occasionally sharp-elbowed wife, was agitating privately for Hassan to move immediately if he became king to make their son, Rashid, the new crown prince. Queen Noor, not a big fan of either Hassan or Sarvath, was with the king throughout his treatment, and fed his mounting discontent.

At President Clinton's request, Hussein flew from Mayo to Washington in late October to help prod the Israelis and Palestinians toward compromise at talks taking place at the Wye Plantation, on the Eastern Shore of Maryland. The king had a magnetic effect, and played a valuable role in producing the Wye River Memorandum, in which the Palestinians and Israelis finally settled on implementation of the redeployments and other interim arrangements in the West Bank that had been agreed to several years before. On the day of the White House signing ceremony, Hussein received a number of senior Jordanian visitors in Washington, among them former prime minister Abdul Karim Kabariti. They reinforced the king's concerns about the crown prince. Hussein told Kabariti that he was considering "major changes" when he returned to Jordan.

I heard versions of all of this from each of the protagonists as they returned to Amman. It was clear that the king's illness was sharpening his focus on the future, and that changes of some sort were looming. Their pace and scope obviously depended to some extent on his health. While the king was upbeat to Jordanians about his prognosis, the reports we were hearing were much more guarded and uncertain.

Hassan was concerned about his brother's health, and increasingly anxious about the reports of royal displeasure with his performance. He invited me and my exceptional CIA station chief, Rob Richer, to a private dinner soon after the Wye agreement, and fished politely for information on the king's health and disposition.[6] I was careful; there was no percentage in getting in the middle of what was a thorny royal decision. There had already been erroneous stories in the British press in the fall that the U.S. administration lacked confidence in Hassan. We had quickly knocked them down, and Madeleine Albright had even called Hassan to reassure him. Moreover, I was still not yet entirely convinced that the king would push Hassan aside. It seemed to me that our role in this delicate moment was to make clear our strong and enduring commitment to king and country, steer clear of political infighting, and keep our lines open.[7]

I had ample support from Washington. In November and December alone, we had visits to Amman from Secretary Albright, Secretary Daley, Secretary of Defense Bill Cohen, and CIA director George Tenet. I pressed the administration to do all we could to invest in our relationship with Jordan now; if Hussein's health worsened, more tangible backing at this point for Jordan's economy and security would put us in a stronger position to support the transition than if we had to scramble later to catch up with events.[8] The White House began to consider a supplemental assistance package and other contingency steps we might take to shore up the dinar and avoid financial panic.

By early January 1999, the king had completed his treatment at Mayo. It would take a couple weeks to determine whether his bone marrow transplant had cured his cancer, but popular expectations for a full recovery were high. I flew over to see him before he left the United States, just after New Year's. We met at the house the king had owned for some years in suburban Maryland, on a high wooded bluff overlooking the Potomac. It was a gloomy winter afternoon, with a clear view of the river through the leafless trees. He was weak, shivering beneath his heavy sweater. "I am eager to get home," he said. "It has been so long, and there is so much to do."

I congratulated him again on Wye. He smiled wanly, underscoring his skepticism about both Netanyahu and Arafat, but emphasized how much faith he had in President Clinton. "It will be good to work with you once I'm home," he continued. "I've had a lot of time to think about the future. I don't know how much time I have left in this world, and there are some things I need to do." Hussein left it at that, and made it clear that he didn't want to be drawn out. I returned to Amman convinced that a change in succession was coming.

Hundreds of thousands of Jordanians lined the streets to welcome the king back home on January 19. The next day, Hussein gave an interview to CNN's Christiane Amanpour, in which he hinted—for the first time in public—of changes to come. The king kept putting off a meeting with Hassan, and the crown prince knew what that meant. I saw him on the afternoon of January 21, and he told me that Princess Basma, the only sister of Hussein and Hassan, had just come over to tell him that he was on his way out. Hassan was in deep distress. "I truly can't understand why the king is so upset with me," he said. Nevertheless, he would handle the decision with dignity.

Finally, on the night of January 22, the king told Hassan he had decided to change succession. Earlier that day, he had informed Prince Abdullah that he would become crown prince. The king made his choice public on January 25, publishing an uncharacteristically mean-spirited letter detailing his disappointment in Hassan. His treatment had failed, and he would have to return to Mayo the next day for a last-ditch effort to save his life and a second bone marrow transplant.

At thirty-seven, Abdullah was nearly two decades older than his father had been when he took the throne. Jordan was a far more stable place than it had been then, but there was no shortage of challenges on the horizon, or regional predators. Abdullah knew how much he had to learn, but did not seem intimidated. Secretary Albright made a brief but timely visit to Amman on January 28, reassuring the new crown prince and pledging American support for Jordan. I saw Hassan again a few days later. There were no visitors waiting to see him, and he commented wryly that he didn't expect many to seek him out. He was clearly hurt by a turn of events that he still didn't fully comprehend, but he had no interest in seeking sympathy. I told him I admired the grace with which he was handling all this, and I meant it. For all his years of service as crown prince, Hassan's biggest contribution to the future of Jordan may have been the way in which he managed his biggest disappointment.

The king's second bone marrow transplant failed, and he headed home again one last time. He had lost consciousness by the time his plane landed in Amman on February 4, and his vital organs were beginning to shut down. In one final display of the stubborn courage that had taken him and Jordan so far, Hussein outlived his doctors' predictions of death for three more days. As I put it in a cable to Washington, "It was almost as if, conscious or unconscious, the King was determined to show that only he—not CNN or anxious foreign audiences or medical experts, or anyone else—would decide when he would make his exit. He lived a life that ran against the odds. John Foster Dulles was just the first in a long line of people to underestimate him, and Jordan. It is worth remembering that as all of us contemplate a future without King Hussein."[9]

February 7, the day King Hussein died, was another in the series of cold rainy days that seemed to reflect the Jordanian mood that winter. I made a point of walking around the embassy to talk to all of our Jordanian employees, individually or in groups. This was as wrenching a national moment as they had ever faced. Many had tears streaming down their faces. I wanted them to know that they could count on American friendship. Later that day, I talked again to King Abdullah. He was sad but unflustered as he prepared for what some would later call "the funeral of the century," which by Islamic tradition had to take place within twenty-four hours of his father's death.

It was an unforgettable tableau. Seventy-five countries sent representatives. President Clinton flew overnight to attend, along with the First Lady and three former presidents—George H. W. Bush, Jimmy Carter, and Gerald Ford. I couldn't imagine a more powerful gesture of American respect. The other leaders who came sent a similarly impressive signal. They made an unusual scene at Raghadan Palace, as strange a collection of bedfellows as I had ever witnessed, their tangled and occasionally lethal rivalries on full display.

There in one corner was the Israeli delegation, led by Prime Minister Netanyahu, looking warily across the room at Hafez al-Assad, whose own health was fading but who wanted to come in a curious show of admiration for the Hashemite ruler he had tried so hard to undermine over the years. Standing not far from the Israelis was Khaled Meshal, the Hamas leader whose assassination the Mossad had bungled in downtown Amman a year before. Arafat chatted amiably with Mubarak. Iraqi vice president Taha Mohieddin Maruf scowled from a distance, representing Saddam Hussein, who had only a month before employed his usual tact in referring publicly to King Hussein as a "throne dwarf." One of Muammar al-Qaddafi's sons talked with Crown Prince Abdullah of Saudi Arabia, whom his father would shortly plot to murder. Prime Minister Tony Blair and Prince Charles came from London, and President Jacques Chirac from Paris.

Even Boris Yeltsin came, ill and disoriented, and propped up in a corner of the room by two aides—intent upon honoring King Hus-

sein, and upon not missing such a remarkable gathering of his con-
temporaries. Bill Clinton worked the room as only he could, gripping
the arms of his counterparts and consoling Jordanian royal family
members. By early evening, the simple burial ceremony completed,
Air Force One had departed, and the other delegations had left for
home. Jordanians were left to consider the complicated world before
them, without the only leader most of them had ever known.

* * *

PRESIDENT CLINTON TOOK me aside at one point on the dreary
day of King Hussein's funeral, as we were walking across the tarmac
to Air Force One and his return flight to Washington. "The next few
months are going to be all about reassurance," he said. "I'm counting
on you to help support these people. Just let us know what you need."
The president was as good as his word, and over the next two years
the United States paid careful attention to Jordan's well-being. I drew
on everything I had learned over the years and every connection I had
in the executive branch and Congress to drum up and sustain interest
in supporting the Jordanians at this crucial moment. I was careful
not to oversell the risks King Abdullah faced, but determined to ex-
haust every possibility to show American reliability.

I believed it was profoundly in our interest to do so. As I wrote in
a cable soon after King Abdullah's accession, "We have a strong and
continuing stake in a stable Jordanian partner at the geographic and
political center of the Middle East. If we didn't have such a partner,
we'd have to invent one."[10]

The day before the funeral, President Clinton issued a public
statement stressing his confidence in the Jordanian economy, and
confirming that he would ask Congress for $300 million in supple-
mental military and economic aid. He pledged to work with G-7 and
Gulf Arab partners to mobilize more support, including steps to ease
Jordan's $7 billion external debt burden. He said he would work with
the World Bank and the International Monetary Fund to marshal ad-

ditional help. The president's vote of confidence helped stave off the run on the Jordanian dinar that officials in Amman had feared, and give the new king a little economic breathing space.

In succeeding months, the administration increased concessional wheat shipments to Jordan. It also expanded the Qualifying Industrial Zones (QIZ) program, which allowed duty-free access into the American market for goods produced in Jordan, so long as they had 8 percent Israeli content (one example was a luggage line manufactured at a QIZ in northern Jordan, in which Israeli-produced plastic handles accounted for the required percentage). By 2000, some forty thousand new jobs were created in Jordanian QIZs. More ambitiously, we provided enthusiastic support for Jordan's bid to join the World Trade Organization, which was accomplished in the spring of 2000. That was the essential first step in negotiating a bilateral free trade agreement, the first with an Arab country and only the fourth such U.S. agreement anywhere in the world.

When President Clinton and King Abdullah finally signed the free trade agreement in October 2000, it sent a signal of confidence in Jordan that was as much political as it was economic. Other than the precedential effect of the terms of the agreement, and making sure that American businesses could compete on a fair playing field in Jordan, there was relatively little consequence for the infinitely larger American economy. By contrast, it was an enormous psychological and practical boost for Jordan. Thanks to both the FTA and the QIZs, Jordan's exports to the United States shot up from barely $9 million in 1998 to over $1 billion by 2004. Annual U.S. assistance levels rose dramatically as well, from $7 million in 1996 to $950 million in 2003, as Jordan became the third-largest recipient of American aid in the world.

Meanwhile, King Abdullah plunged into his new role with considerable energy and drive. He quickly overcame doubts about his inexperience, and showed a flair for leadership at home and selling Jordan's case abroad. He understood that the outpouring of international and regional goodwill that followed his father's death would not last long. Without the baggage of the Gulf War and his father's refusal to join the Desert Storm coalition, Abdullah rebuilt bridges to the Saudis and Kuwaitis, and connected easily with next-generation leaders in Bahrain and the United Arab Emirates. Without the competitive tensions that had shaped his father's relationships with leaders like Hafez al-Assad, he solidified ties with Syria and other Arab neighbors. In his first year on the throne, he visited all of the G-7 capitals, including two productive trips to Washington, where he demonstrated even greater finesse than Hussein in cultivating Congress, and even less hesitation in asking for assistance.

At home, Abdullah built an appealing persona, exhibiting common sense and natural strengths as a unifier. Personable and practical, he got off to a good start with most of the sometimes cranky leaders of the East Bank establishment, and impressed many of the rising figures in Jordan's tiny and often inert and risk-averse private sector with his modernizing instincts. Abdullah could count on the loyalty of the military in which he had served for more than two decades. He tried to project a populist air, dressing in disguise as an elderly local and observing the bureaucracy at its plodding pace in Zarqa and other poorer parts of the country.

Prince Hassan kept his disappointment largely to himself, and his dignity intact. Samieh Battikhi remained at GID, watching the king's back but more and more prone to self-aggrandizement. A sturdy East Bank warhorse, Abdul Raouf Rawabdeh, a former mayor of Amman, became prime minister. Not exactly a poster child for reform, but good at soothing establishment sensibilities, the conservative Rawabdeh was balanced by the more risk-taking Abdul Karim Kabariti, now chief of the royal court. Kabariti reinforced the king's reformist impulses, and together they drove a fair amount of change: privatization of the telecommunications sector and several significant companies; legislation to protect intellectual property rights; a new economic consultative council; and a major initiative to attract investment in the information technology sector. The king himself didn't hesitate in that early era to roll up his sleeves and hold his ministers to timetables and action plans—a novel experience for most of them.

The king was easy to talk to, and we usually saw each other several times a week, whether at his office at the palace, at home in Amman or Aqaba, or at events around Jordan. I was always careful not to waste his time or abuse my access. I was equally careful to balance my relationships with the royal family and senior government officials with a range of other Jordanians, and to keep a sharp-eyed perspective on what was going right in this complicated transition and what challenges loomed.

"Clientitis" is a common affliction among diplomats, the tendency to gradually conflate the interests of the country you represent with those of the country in which you serve. One symptom is a selective blindness to the country's flaws, exacerbated by the seductive power of access and apparent influence. I tried hard to avoid that during my time in Jordan, but didn't always succeed. I kept my lines open to critics of the Jordanian elite and my attention fixed on obvious problems of economic stagnation; corruption that was small-bore by regional standards, but nonetheless pervasive; political repression that was modest compared to the practice of most of Jordan's neighbors, but nonetheless persistent; and institutional dominance by a Jordanian intelligence establishment that was a valuable regional partner for the United States and less thuggish than in most of the region, but nonetheless troublesome. I'm sure I occasionally sanded the edges of my judgments. A lot was at stake for the United States in the transition from Hussein to Abdullah, and in a region where imperfections were relative and successes rare, I had no doubt of the value of our support.

In one cable at the beginning of 2000, I wrote, "If you had asked most Jordanians a year ago, as King Hussein lay dying, how their country would fare without him, few would have predicted the impressive achievements in economic reform and regional diplomacy of

King Abdullah, whom they barely knew." I added, without hyperbole, that Abdullah "has done more to reform the structure of the Jordanian economy in the last six months than Jordan did in the entire previous decade." I was also quick to point out that the hard part was coming. I stressed that "if he is going to turn the promise and the glitter of his first year into enduring success in Jordan, the King will have to begin to show tangible results for structural economic reforms, start a process of opening up a sclerotic political system, and lay the basis for long-term protection of Jordanian interests in a region on the verge of some profound changes."[11]

The wider region remained a snakepit, despite the king's skill in navigating it. More than a decade before the Arab Spring, the social and economic forces building beneath the surface of the region were intensifying. In an April 2000 cable, I argued that "globalization, technological change and the expanding reach of independent media will only increase the pressures on the anachronistic, authoritarian regimes who dominate the Arab world—even ones as relatively tolerant and civil as the Hashemites."[12] On the immediate horizon were adversaries in the neighborhood, and troubles waiting to erupt. Two of the most obvious were Saddam Hussein's Iraq, badly wounded in the Gulf War but still a deeply complicated problem for Jordan, and the fragile relationship between Israelis and Palestinians on the other side of the Jordan River.

* * *

EVER SINCE THE end of the Gulf War in the spring of 1991, the United States had been engaged in a frustrating effort to contain Saddam Hussein, protect the Kurds, and prevent Iraq from menacing its neighbors. The UN Security Council had authorized no-fly zones in northern and southern Iraq, which the United States policed at considerable expense. A UN inspection regime (UNSCOM) had been established to work with the International Atomic Energy Agency to ensure that Saddam met his UNSC-mandated obligations to destroy

any remaining infrastructure and stocks of weapons of mass destruction, as well as ballistic missiles with a range of more than ninety
miles. Stringent economic sanctions remained in place to keep pressure on Saddam to comply.

Inevitably, this whole structure became increasingly difficult to
manage. Early in President Clinton's tenure, Saddam mounted an
unsuccessful plot to assassinate former president Bush in Kuwait.
Clinton retaliated with missile strikes against Iraq. As the years went
by, Saddam episodically challenged U.S. aircraft enforcing the no-fly
zones, and the United States responded. The Iraqis angered the
Americans with their practice of "cheat and retreat" in dealing with
UNSCOM—refusing access to sites for long periods, eventually offering limited concessions under pressure, and then repeating the whole
maddening process. Saddam declared eight large compounds, containing more than a thousand buildings, to be presidential palaces,
exempt from inspection. In December 1998, the United States
launched Operation Desert Fox, a series of air and missile strikes
against Iraqi targets, to punish Saddam for his intransigence.

Jordan was exposed on several fronts, leaving Abdullah with a
nettlesome set of competing demands. It was heavily dependent on a
concessional oil arrangement with Iraq, tacitly permitted by the
United States and the UN Security Council, and increasingly squeezed
as oil prices rose in the late 1990s. Iraq remained an important and
irreplaceable market for cheap Jordanian goods, especially pharma-
ceuticals. Jordanian popular sympathies also remained strongly with
the Iraqis, amplified by the human impact of sanctions and aggravated by broader antipathy toward American policy in the region.

King Abdullah had no illusions about Saddam. He continued the
quiet practice of exchanging information about Iraq with the United
States and supported our forces involved in the no-fly zones. But he
couldn't afford the economic or domestic political consequences of
outright opposition to Saddam. The Gulf Arabs might have eased his
calculus by substituting concessional oil for the Iraqi arrangement,

but whether for reasons of lingering animus toward Jordan's position in the Gulf War or inertia never followed through. Abdullah was in a bind.

His own encounters over the years with the Iraqi leadership had been dispiriting, and often bizarre. King Abdullah once told me about an especially strange encounter. Some years before, in the late 1980s, King Hussein sent Abdullah and his younger brother, Prince Faisal, to Baghdad to get acquainted with Saddam's sons, Uday and Qusay Hussein. Uday, then still in his twenties, had not yet achieved the notoriety of his later years, when he regularly showed off the pet lions in his Baghdad palace, beat the members of the Iraqi national soccer team when they lost matches, and kidnapped and raped female Iraqi university students who caught his eye. Qusay was less visibly thuggish, but already developing a reputation as his father's son when it came to cunning brutality.

On the second day of the visit, their hosts took Abdullah and Faisal for a boat ride on a large man-made lake outside Baghdad. Expecting a quiet afternoon, both were more than a little shocked when Uday—always the thrill seeker—pulled out an RPG and fired it just ahead of his own security patrol a few dozen yards away. No one was hurt, but Uday didn't seem at all bothered by the prospect, acting as if this were just another way to spend an afternoon. Abdullah and Faisal were horrified. As Abdullah put it, "There are many people in my generation of leaders in the region with whom I already have a good rapport—but Uday is not one of them."[13]

After Abdullah became king, he grew increasingly anxious about the direction of American policy toward Iraq. He was skeptical that the Iraq Liberation Act (ILA), passed by Congress and signed into law by President Clinton late in the autumn of 1998, represented anything more than wishful thinking. The ILA stated explicitly that it was the goal of the United States to change the regime in Baghdad, but Abdullah saw no compelling strategy behind the rhetoric—and a lot of risk for Jordan along the way. He thought many of those most prominent in the exiled Iraqi opposition movement were frauds, or at best naïve. He was particularly caustic about Ahmed Chalabi, who had been run out of Jordan a decade before as head of a prominent local bank, following allegations of embezzlement.

As he emphasized to me with mounting concern in 1999 and 2000, the king saw Western sanctions policy as self-defeating. Saddam had successfully manipulated the UN's Oil for Food Program, aimed at easing the plight of ordinary Iraqis, to tighten his own grip on power. By late 2000, Abdullah told me that "it's more likely that Saddam will be killed by a meteor than that sanctions will undermine him."[14]

By the end of the Clinton administration, the king was arguing consistently that the United States was helping, not hurting, Saddam, allowing him to play the victim and exploit an increasingly tense regional situation. He maintained that Washington should abandon economic or civilian sanctions, and instead intensify measures prohibiting the import of military or dual-use items. These so-called smart sanctions had obvious drawbacks, since Saddam could exploit the revenue from unrestricted oil sales to solidify his regime, but Abdullah's argument was that he was more or less doing this anyway, and the United States needed to regain the initiative. It was certainly a self-serving position for Jordan, but that didn't make it wrong.

* * *

AS JORDAN'S CHALLENGE to the east became more worrisome, its dilemma to the west grew larger too. In that same conversation in Aqaba in late 2000 about Iraqi sanctions, the king expressed mounting concern about the Second Intifada, the Palestinian uprising that had been triggered by Ariel Sharon's provocative visit to the Temple Mount several weeks earlier. As he pointed out, Saddam was using the ugly spectacle in the West Bank to divert attention and pressure, and to fan regional animus toward American policy. Jordan was stuck in the middle, politically and physically. I cabled Washington later that day, restating the glaringly obvious: "It is important to take a step back and look soberly at the collateral damage that the unfolding tragedy across the river could do to relatively moderate countries like Jordan, which are not exactly a growth industry in this region these days."[15]

When King Abdullah took the throne, things had looked more positive across the river. The Wye agreement, which his father had so heroically inspired, was the latest incremental step toward the two-state solution envisioned by the Oslo Accords of 1993. Progress had been painful and halting, but by the beginning of 1999 the Palestinian Authority, led by Yasser Arafat, exerted some degree of control over 40 percent of the West Bank, and most of Gaza. In May of that year, Labor's Ehud Barak won the Israeli elections and ousted Likud's Bibi Netanyahu, a leader in whom neither Abdullah nor his father had had much faith.

Early in Barak's tenure, a new target of September 2000 was set for completion of negotiations about the permanent status of the West Bank and Gaza, the latest in a series of moving goalposts since Oslo. Barak decided, however, to concentrate first on negotiations with Syria. He disliked the incrementalism of the Oslo process, which he thought maximized domestic political cost in Israel for minimal strategic gains. The Syria track offered a chance to produce a big strategic reward, removing the more serious security threat posed by the Assad regime, as well as building leverage on Arafat in subsequent negotiations. With Hafez al-Assad's health a growing question mark, Barak felt a sense of urgency to test the possibility of an agreement with Syria.

Not surprisingly, the Palestinians were upset by Barak's sense of priorities. They had been negotiating for years, and had made clear their commitment to reaching an agreement. Assad, who had not budged an inch, was being rewarded with Israeli attention. King Abdullah was nervous too. While he was supportive of an Israeli-Syrian deal, it was a two-state solution that mattered most to Jordan's future. Establishment of a sovereign Palestine in the West Bank and Gaza would cement a sense of Jordanian national identity on the other side of the Jordan River, solidifying the unity of both East Bank Jordanians and Jordanians of Palestinian origin that Abdullah's father had worked for nearly half a century to accomplish. It also promised economic opportunities for Jordan beyond the thus far meager results of the Israeli-Jordanian peace treaty of 1994. Nevertheless, Abdullah did what he could to support Syrian-Israeli negotiations, in hopes that a breakthrough there would accelerate Israeli-Palestinian progress.

Abdullah traveled to Damascus in April 1999, two months after Assad's unexpected appearance at King Hussein's funeral. Assad was relatively upbeat about improving relations with Jordan, including on the thorny issue of water resources, where Syria held the high cards through its control of the headwaters of the Jordan and Yarmouk rivers. Abdullah also spent substantial time on that trip with Assad's son and heir apparent, Bashar. On the surface, Abdullah and Bashar seemed to share a few traits. Both were in their thirties, part of a new generation of Arab leaders. Both had the experience of unexpected elevations, Bashar when his elder brother Basil died in a car crash, and Abdullah when his father changed the line of succession on his deathbed. And both thought of themselves as modernizers, although Bashar's self-image was thinly drawn, the product of a year in London studying ophthalmology and his role as head of the Syrian Computer Society, as close to a hotbed of innovation as the deeply repressive Assad regime permitted.

Bashar took the king to the Alawite stronghold of Latakia on the Mediterranean, and drove him around the city for several hours while they talked about the region and the world. The king was a little bemused by Bashar's apparent naïveté; he asked Abdullah at one point what jet lag felt like, explaining that the longest flights he had ever taken were to London and back. The king said, however, that he thought Bashar might be capable of breaking out of some of his father's knuckle-dragging habits, and following through on any prog-ress that might be made with the Israelis. Years later, the king ruefully acknowledged to me, "So much for first impressions."

In January 2000, the United States hosted Israeli and Syrian del-egations at Shepherdstown, West Virginia. Barak led the Israeli team. The Syrian delegation was headed by Foreign Minister Farouk al-Sharaa, whose demeanor hadn't grown much more flexible or concil-iatory in the decade since he had strained Jim Baker's patience at Madrid. The talks sputtered over nearly ten days with no break-through. In a final, high-stakes effort to reach a deal, Clinton met in Geneva in late March with a fast-failing Hafez al-Assad. Unconvinced that Barak would ever deliver the full return of Syrian territory occu-pied since the 1967 war, Assad refused to authorize the resumption of negotiations with the Israelis. The Syria track had run its course.

Barak and Clinton then turned to the Palestinian talks with re-newed focus. Prodded by Barak, and hoping to cap his presidency with a Palestinian-Israeli peace agreement, Clinton decided to invite Arafat and Barak to Camp David, the scene of Jimmy Carter's dra-matic success with Sadat and Begin more than twenty years earlier. It was a significant gamble. The Israelis and Palestinians were far apart on how much of the West Bank would be returned, and even further apart on the questions of Jerusalem and the right of Palestinian refu-gees to return. Arafat feared that he would be blamed for a break-down in talks, and knew how deep disillusionment already ran among Palestinians after all the unmet expectations of the Oslo years. Never a diplomatic risk-taker, Arafat came to Camp David with great reluc-tance, drawn largely by the investment he had made in Clinton and American leadership, and always confident that he could wriggle out of any tight political situation if he had to.

For King Abdullah, this was a difficult juncture. In barely two years on the throne, he knew that he couldn't replicate the influence or prestige of his father, but he understood instinctively the impor-tance of Jordan's unique position, enjoying healthy relations with all three key players—Palestinians, Israelis, and Americans. He found the Camp David experience frustrating. For reasons that were partly understandable but also partly mistaken, the U.S. team at Camp David kept a tight lid over the more than two weeks of intense negotiations at the secluded presidential retreat. Key Arab players who might have helped encourage Arafat became an afterthought, and when they were consulted it was often with only the skimpiest of background.

On one occasion late in the talks, for example, a senior American official at Camp David placed a call to the king to ask for his help in persuading the Palestinians to show more flexibility on Jerusalem, but never provided any context on what exactly we were hoping to achieve, or what had transpired so far. Much to my embarrassment, I wasn't any more successful in eliciting better information for the king. My concerns, however, were insignificant compared to the central dilemma: Despite herculean efforts by President Clinton, and unprecedented progress on the question of territory and the even more complex question of Jerusalem, the two sides were at an impasse. Camp David had come further than any previous effort but ultimately ended with no agreement and plenty of resentments.

Despite earlier promises to the Palestinians, the United States—attuned more to Barak's worsening domestic political predicament—appeared in the wake of Camp David to blame Arafat for the summit's failure. With popular Palestinian anger rising, Sharon's visit to the Temple Mount in late September set off a political firestorm, and in the ensuing violence a new Palestinian uprising was born. I accompanied King Abdullah to a meeting at Sharm el-Sheikh, where President Mubarak invited Barak, Arafat, and Clinton to try to find a way to ease the violence. It proved fruitless. The Israelis were intent upon driving home to the Palestinians that violence wouldn't produce any positive political results, and often responded with disproportionate force; Arafat, always sensitive to the popular mood and never shy about indulging in violence if it helped keep his position as political ringmaster intact, often played a double game.

Our ambassador to Egypt, Dan Kurtzer, and I were deeply concerned about where all of this was headed. Over the next few months, we took the unusual step of sending joint messages to Washington. We felt a responsibility to inject our perspective into the negotiating process from the outside, if we could not provide our views from the inside. In December, we sent the third and final message:

> As seen from Cairo and Amman, U.S. policy in the peace process and our overall posture in the region are still heading in exactly the wrong direction. With our interests under increasing scrutiny and attack, we are acting passively, reactively and defensively. There is no guarantee that a bolder, more activist American approach will stop the hemorrhaging—but it seems clear to us that things could get a lot worse unless we regain the initiative.
>
> Our stake in reversing the drift toward more violence, rebuilding American credibility, refocusing attention on the possibilities of a political process, and getting as far as we can over the next seven weeks toward a framework agreement is self-evident. What is less obvious is how to get from here to there. One option is to follow Barak's lead. That may serve what he sees to be his tactical interests at this point. But it's hard to see how it serves ours. A second option is to see if we can extract from the Palestinians a clearer sense of how far they're prepared to go right now, and then use that to craft an approach to Barak. But it's unlikely that Arafat will level with us at this point; and while recent Egyptian and Jordanian efforts with the Palestinians have been helpful, it's not at all clear that they will produce a workable starting point.
>
> That leaves it to us to lay out the hard truths—for all parties—that must underpin any enduring political solution. As we have tried to emphasize in our two previous telegrams, that will require the po-

litical will to stand up for what we have fought so hard for over the
past eight years, and a readiness to declare the independence of our
policy.[16]

The central recommendation we made was to "articulate a 'Clinton Vision' for the peace process." We argued that "we have a unique
but wasting opportunity to take advantage of a remarkable asset: the
personal reputation and demonstrated commitment of President
Clinton. He has built up substantial personal credit with the parties
over the years, and now is the time to use it. He can sketch a vision of
what he believes a comprehensive peace will require of all parties—
Palestinians, Israelis, and Arab states alike. He will have to be willing
to say things to each party that they will not want to hear, but that is
the definition of a balanced and credible approach."

Neither the White House nor the State Department probably
needed our cable to convince them to produce what became the
"Clinton Parameters"—a groundbreaking American proposal for a
comprehensive two-state solution that was presented to the parties in
late December and made public the following month, shortly before
President Clinton left office. It was too late, however, with Clinton's
term ending and the parties drifting further apart. Violence quickly
consumed nearly a decade of political progress.

* * *

KING ABDULLAH, LIKE the rest of us, was worried about the stalemate in diplomacy and the worsening of Palestinian-Israeli violence.
In a long conversation one afternoon in January 2001, he told me,
"I'm generally an optimistic person, but now I'm worried. This region is drifting in a scary direction. People are getting angrier, and
I don't have any good answers."[17] I didn't have much reassurance to
offer. In a cable a couple months later, I reported more troubling indicators: "The mood amongst Jordanians is increasingly angry and
disaffected—a mixture of intense frustration over rising violence

across the Jordan River, fury at American policies that are seen to be not just unbalanced but aggressively anti-Arab, and discontent with the meager practical results of economic reform."[18]

After nearly three years as ambassador, I was worried too—not about Abdullah's leadership, but about the pressures that Jordan faced, and the inevitable uncertainties about the new administration's policies. These uncertainties took on particular significance for me when President Bush's new secretary of state, Colin Powell, called me a week or so after he was named to ask if I would serve as assistant secretary for near eastern affairs.

I had never worked for anyone I respected more than Powell, and I was thrilled by what his leadership would bring to American foreign policy. I had similar respect for Rich Armitage, who had been nominated as deputy secretary of state. I was confident in my knowledge of the region, and familiar with the main policy issues; I was far less confident in my ability to rise to the leadership and management challenge of heading one of the department's largest bureaus. I was just as unsure about the new administration's Middle East policy and feared we were sailing into even more treacherous waters in that troubled part of the world.

It was hard to say no to Colin Powell, however, or to a request to serve in such a critical post at such a critical time. I quickly accepted, asking only that we stay in Jordan until as close to the end of the school year as possible (which, given the vagaries of the Senate confirmation process, was a probability anyway), and that I be able to choose my deputies in the NEA front office.

I had learned over the years that the key to success in any demanding job is to surround yourself with people who are smarter and more experienced than you are. That's exactly what I did in NEA, working the phones hard from Amman in early 2001 to enlist three of the most capable Arabists I knew, all of whom were serving, like me, as ambassadors in the field. Jim Larocco, ambassador in Kuwait, agreed to come back to Washington as principal deputy assistant secretary. David Satterfield, our ambassador in Beirut, with whom I had worked many years before as lowly staff assistants for Dick Murphy, also readily agreed. Ryan Crocker, leading our embassy in Damascus, was the toughest sell. One of the best officers I had ever known, Ryan far preferred the dangers and challenges of the Middle East to the petty intrigues and bureaucratic machinations of Washington. He eventually relented, calling me from Damascus one afternoon, after I had nearly given up. "I'll join you at the Alamo," he said in his usual laconic way.

I was confirmed by the Senate in April, and began my new job immediately. The king and queen invited Lisa and me to Aqaba for the weekend, just before we left. It had been a remarkable three years, and I told the king how glad I was to have had the chance to work with him, and how much Jordan would always mean to me and my family.

"Neither of us expected all the things that have been thrown at us," he said. "I'm proud of what we've done together. You should be too."

5

Age of Terror: The Inversion of Force and Diplomacy

IT WAS JUST after midnight on a cold February morning in 2005, at a tent encampment in the Libyan desert. My route had been as circuitous and eccentric as the man I was coming to see. I flew into Tripoli on a U.S. military aircraft, landing at Mitiga airfield, formerly Wheelus Air Base, the largest overseas U.S. Air Force installation in the 1960s. An officious protocol officer drove us across the tarmac where one of Muammar al-Qaddafi's jets was parked. We quickly boarded the Libyan aircraft. Its décor was a bedraggled version of 1970s chic, with worn lime-green shag carpeting and swivel chairs that had long since ceased swiveling. For security reasons, the Libyans refused to specify our destination. We flew east along the Mediterranean coast to another military airfield, near Qaddafi's hometown of Sirte. There, we were hustled into a convoy of Land Rovers and driven south at breakneck speed for two hours through desert scrub and successive rings of Libyan security.

We finally slowed at the entrance to a small wadi, where Qaddafi sat in spartan splendor. His cavernous camouflage tent was un-adorned save for a few white plastic lawn chairs, a sleeping mat, a small television, and a single light bulb hanging from the top of the tent. I was ushered in, and Qaddafi rose to greet me, wrapped against the nighttime chill in robes and a headscarf that covered most of his face. His attire was less flamboyant than in a previous encounter, when he wore a pajama-like outfit with a shirt featuring pictures of fellow African strongmen. Whenever he engaged in his disconcerting habit of pausing for two or three minutes in conversational midstream to stare at the ceiling, presumably to collect his thoughts, I would mentally try to name all the dictators so proudly displayed on his pajama top.

On this occasion, Qaddafi's mood and message meandered. We were nearing the end of a long and tortuous path to normalized relations, the product of many years of diplomacy—some covert, some overt—across administrations of both parties. Qaddafi complained mildly about the pace of change, but made clear that there would be no turning back from Libya's commitments to compensate victims of the Lockerbie bombing, renounce terrorism, and abandon its nuclear and chemical weapons programs. He bristled when I raised human rights concerns, and had not the slightest inclination to open up his profoundly weird and repressive system of "popular rule." He was unapologetic about his brutality, convinced that there could be no political order in his fractious society without it. In all the hours I spent with him and his lieutenants over four years, I never once forgot the blood on their hands. One of the 259 innocent victims on the Pan Am 103 flight bombed by Libyan operatives was my friend Matthew Gannon, a CIA officer with whom I had served in Amman in the early 1980s.[1] He had been on his way from Beirut to the States to spend Christmas with his wife and two young daughters. His loss had left me shaken.

Qaddafi rambled across the region in that early-morning discussion, offering views on people and problems that were, as I reported back to Washington, "a combination of the eerily insightful and the just plain eerie." Rarely making eye contact, speaking in a monotone, he limited his gestures to an occasional wave to a bodyguard stationed just outside the tent to refill our tea glasses. As in our previous conversations, Qaddafi went on at length about the Israel-Palestine issue, convinced that a two-state solution was receding, and a one-state "Isratine" inevitable. He predicted the fragmentation of Saudi Arabia into four separate states, reflecting his dim view of the House of Saud, and worried aloud that Iraq, already in the throes of sectarian conflict after the 2003 American invasion, was becoming "a breeding ground and magnet for extremists from around the Islamic world."[2] He got that out without a trace of irony—momentarily oblivious to Libya's long history as a terrorist haven.

I nevertheless came away hopeful. For thirty-five years, Qaddafi had tried to seize center stage with despicable acts and surreal performance art. Now he was starved to be taken seriously by the United States and others in the West. Neither the weirdness nor the ugliness and intractability of his own political system was going away, but maybe his attention seeking would evolve in less destabilizing ways.

At that moment in early 2005, the Libyan experience proved that diplomacy could accomplish significant changes in the behavior of difficult regimes. Of course it had to be backed up by other forms of leverage—many years of U.S. and multilateral sanctions; a solid international consensus, codified in UN Security Council resolutions; and the credible threat of force. It also mattered that we set consistent and achievable benchmarks for the negotiations on Lockerbie, terrorism, and weapons of mass destruction (WMD), delivered on our end of the deal, and over a period of years built up a fair amount of trust. Regime change was never the goal, and the Libyan leadership gradually developed a self-interest in changing behavior. It saw little benefit in winding up on the wrong side of the post–9/11 divide, and we provided a difficult but navigable pathway to a form of practical redemption.

Sitting there in that drafty desert tent, I was acutely aware that diplomacy with Libya was a model that paled in significance with the other model we had created during those same years—the shoot-first, dabble-in-diplomacy-later approach we took in Iraq. Shaped by post–9/11 apprehension and assertiveness, determination to preempt threats, and hubris and overreliance on force, we blundered our way into a war and its ugly aftermath. That inversion of force and diplomacy left scars that would long endure—for the region and for America's role in the world.

* * *

AS I PREPARED to leave Amman and return to Washington in the spring of 2001, a colleague warned that we'd be trying to grope our way through a wider Middle East that "really is the land of bad policy options." It was hard to argue with him.

I had watched with mounting concern as the violence of the Second Intifada worsened. Ariel Sharon's election victory over Ehud Barak in February 2001 signaled unmistakably that Israel's consuming focus would be on restoring order and security through force, not negotiations. Yasser Arafat remained risk-averse and duplicitous, maneuvering to stay atop an angry sea of Palestinians under occupation. Sharon and Arafat seemed locked in a stubborn war of attrition, each convinced that he could outlast the other, mutual enablers in a contest with no end in sight. In my Senate confirmation hearing in April, I tried to paint an honest picture: "Too many Israelis and Palestinians now feel less secure, less hopeful, and less certain that peace is possible. The result is an angry and disillusioned mood, much of it directed, fairly or unfairly, against the United States. Many Arabs think we don't care about their concerns; worse, many think we're actively hostile to them."[3]

Across the region, the deeper dysfunction of Arab societies and the autocrats who sat atop them was impossible to ignore. As the landmark Arab Human Development Reports would soon make clear, Arabs were falling further behind many other regions of the world. The combined GDP of all Arab countries, comprising a population of some three hundred million, was less than that of Spain, which had roughly one-tenth the number of people. Half of all Arabs were under the age of twenty, creating huge pressures that neither educational systems nor job markets could absorb, and only 2 percent had access to the Internet.

Amid this regional tumult, a new generation of leaders was emerging. Like King Abdullah of Jordan, new monarchs in Morocco and Bahrain were experimenting with economic and political openness. Even Bashar al-Assad briefly opened the window to a "Damascus Spring," with younger technocrats forming short-lived discussion groups to explore reform. The older generation was instinctively much more cautious. In the Gulf, there were abundant anxieties about risks from both Iraq and Iran, despite the reelection in June 2001 of Mohammad Khatami, the reformist president in Tehran. Hosni Mubarak, moored deeply in the status quo in Egypt, saw little reason for optimism in a region with so many unnerving changes afoot.

The view from Washington, as George W. Bush assembled his administration, was similarly cautious in the first half of 2001. President Bush's national security team was familiar, experienced, and tested. It seemed at the outset nearly as impressive as his father's, with Dick Cheney as vice president, Colin Powell as secretary of state, and Don Rumsfeld as secretary of defense. George Tenet stayed on as director of the CIA, and Condoleezza Rice became the national security advisor. Rice had captured succinctly the self-consciously realistic approach of the new administration in a *Foreign Affairs* article during the 2000 election campaign: In a Bush administration, there would be no more nation-building, no more overuse of the U.S. military as an instrument of humanitarian intervention, no more soft-headed multilateralism. The perceived fixation of the Clinton administration on the Middle East peace process would be a thing of the past. Rice was blunt about the use of force in general. The American military, she wrote, "is a special instrument. It is not a civilian police force. It is not a political referee. And it is most certainly not designed to build a civilian society." On Saddam, she was equally clear: "The first line of defense should be deterrence—if he does acquire WMD, his weapons will be unusable because any attempt to use them will bring national obliteration." Restraint and realism seemed to be the dominant guideposts, just as they were for Bush 41.

Colin Powell brought strong leadership to the State Department, and for all my misgivings about the Middle East at that moment and the challenges of my new role, I was genuinely excited to be working for him again. He and Rich Armitage were a formidable team, close friends and keenly attuned to the importance of building morale in the Department, modernizing its 1980s-era technology, and dragging American diplomacy into the twenty-first century. Powell enjoyed walking around the building, poking his head into offices, and offering passing employees a ride up in his private elevator. When President Bush visited the State Department for the first time to get a briefing for an early meeting with his Mexican counterpart, Powell had two junior desk officers sit across from the president and handle the presentation. That kind of empowerment set the tone throughout the department. Armitage worked hard to de-layer the institution and push responsibility downward wherever he could. He was always accessible, with a no-nonsense style leavened by an irreverent sense of humor. If you were summoned to his office after six in the evening, Motown tunes would be blaring down the august seventh floor corridor, and scotch would be served to ease the tensions of the day.

Powell and Armitage helped make it a good time to lead a regional bureau. They expected initiative, creativity, and loyalty, and didn't mind thoughtful disagreement. They emphasized the importance of leaders taking care of their people, and had little patience for martinets or senior officers who admired the problem rather than trying to solve it. I tried as best I could to help create that same atmosphere in NEA.

NEA was arguably the most challenging, if not the biggest, of the regional bureaus. With about forty-five hundred staff spread over

Washington and some two dozen embassies and consulates in the region, I was constantly preoccupied with security threats, policy dilemmas, or management problems of one stripe or another.

Sworn in to my new post at the beginning of May 2001, I set out to visit each of the sixteen countries in which we then had embassies. Over the next four years, I spent about half my time on the road. In a region as idiosyncratic and autocratic as the Middle East, modern communications technology was still no substitute for building personal relationships and face-to-face interactions.

My first trip was to Israel and the West Bank. Our aim was to orchestrate a cease-fire and stop the violence that had erupted nearly a year earlier. I joined George Tenet on a couple of those efforts, as he worked to persuade Palestinian and Israeli security officials to cooperate. "The situation we confront is bleak," I wrote at the time. "Arafat and Sharon are locked into a death dance in which each is looking to best or get rid of the other."[4] Prime Minister Sharon was courteous but unyielding in his determination to hit back hard against Palestinian violence, and to isolate and undermine Arafat, whom he was convinced was not only turning a blind eye to terrorist attacks but tacitly encouraging them. Arafat was just as dug in, manipulating violence for his own purposes and determined not to yield in the face of disproportionate Israeli force. On one visit, I arrived in Tel Aviv a few hours after a vicious suicide attack on a beachfront nightclub, in which twenty-one Israelis had been killed, most of them teenagers. I stopped by the site to lay flowers that morning, as Israeli emergency personnel were still searching for body parts and identifying the victims.

The savagery of Israeli-Palestinian violence was high on the agendas of most of the other Arab leaders I visited that summer. Hosni Mubarak was worried about the mood on the Egyptian street, and the impact on Egypt's treaty relationship with Israel. He had a grudging respect for Sharon's toughness, but worried that he was relying so much on force and so little on offering any kind of political future for

Palestinians that he would ultimately just dig the hole deeper. Mubarak was well acquainted with Arafat's slippery disposition, and knew that the weakness of his hand made him even less likely to concede much under Israeli pressure. Waving his arms in the air dismissively near the end of one conversation, he said, "Those two deserve each other, but we can't let them drag us all down." King Abdullah was even more exposed in Jordan, and shared Mubarak's frustration.

Distance insulated leaders in the Maghreb to some extent from the passions of the Levant. Morocco's King Mohammed VI was more concerned with establishing himself on the throne and the apparently inexhaustible conflict with the Algerians over the Western Sahara than the ugliness farther east. In Algiers, President Abdelaziz Bouteflika's comb-over remained one of the country's true architectural marvels. He dominated our three-hour conversation with his impressions of other leaders and their conflicts, without any hint of introspection. President Zine El Abidine Ben Ali in Tunisia professed to want to fight corruption and open up his political system, with an enthusiasm that seemed heavily contrived.

In Beirut, the political cast of characters eyed one another nervously, as they had for decades. Prime Minister Rafik Hariri took a wary view of Sharon, who had helped drive the Israeli invasion of Lebanon in 1982, and of Arafat, the proximate target of that invasion. Hariri was then still somewhat optimistic about Bashar al-Assad in Syria, who seemed to lack his father's guile and experience, but might give Lebanon more room to maneuver.

My first meeting with Bashar in Damascus offered a glimpse at the banality of an evil that would emerge in its full and horrific form ten years later. He asked me to see him at home, which was still the relatively modest house in which he had lived before becoming president. He greeted me at the door with his wife, Asma, alongside, a few of his children's toys visible in a corner of the living room. Asma had been raised in London and spoke fluent English. Bashar's was more halting, and we switched back and forth to Arabic.

Bashar was pleasant but cocksure, betraying none of the tentative-ness that you might expect from someone who had been in power for little more than a year. He pronounced himself with conviction on regional events and American policy (about which he had nothing good to say). He dismissed Arafat as vain and indecisive, and said air-ily that the only thing Sharon and Israel understood was force. He was patronizing about King Abdullah in Jordan, and displayed little deference toward Mubarak or the senior Gulf leaders. Bashar's fasci-nation with modernity seemed more about gadgets and technology than political or economic progress. As I later told Powell, the most generous conclusion you could draw was that Bashar was a work in progress, but we should have no illusions about any dramatic shift in Syrian behavior. His regime's capacity for mendacity and brutality would remain the cold heart of its survival strategy.

On the Arabian Peninsula, leaders were preoccupied with leader-ship transitions and domestic challenges, along with the emotions aroused in their own societies by nightly television images of violence in Palestine. I saw Ali Abdullah Saleh, Yemen's mercurial president, in Sanaa. He punctuated his comments with expansive waves of the camel riding crop he kept in his hand, which his aides ducked with a practiced air. Sultan Qaboos of Oman, with whom I would deal fre-quently years later when he hosted secret talks with the Iranians, was full of wise insights and quiet dignity. Amir Hamad in Doha engaged in the favorite Qatari sport, poking fun at the Saudis and asserting his own independence. Bahrain and Kuwait were eager to sustain strong relations with the United States, and not to get caught in any of the various regional crossfires.

I met Crown Prince Abdullah of Saudi Arabia, de facto ruler of his country given King Fahd's infirmity, at his horse farm outside Riyadh. In that conversation and a number of others over the succeeding years, I found him to be refreshingly direct and candid. He found American officials to be energetic but slow-witted students, naïve about the Middle East and often oblivious to the consequences of their actions (or inaction). In the summer of 2001, Abdullah's anxieties were mostly about the unfolding mess in Palestine. He urged greater White House interest and activism. Despite his frustrations, he was hospitable and warm. That evening, he challenged me to join him in a Bedouin form of bocce. With a twinkle in his eye, he asked if I knew how to play. When I said no, he smiled broadly and said, "Good." Although he had eased himself out of his chair with some apparent difficulty, he managed to bend his knees when he tossed, and had some well-honed flair in his wrist motion. His agility and experience more than compensated for our thirty-year age difference—and I knew when I was being played. The crown prince beat me handily.

I also stopped in Abu Dhabi to meet Sheikh Zayed, the aging but thoroughly engaging leader of the United Arab Emirates. Zayed made clear how pained he was by American policy on the Arab-Israeli issue. "Ten years ago," he said, "I had such hopes for the region and America. Now I don't have much hope left. I know that George Bush and Colin Powell are good men. Please help open their eyes to the consequences of what's happening." American political stock in the Middle East faced a bear market, and in the summer of 2001 the most pressing priority was to stop the hemorrhaging of capital caused by Israeli-Palestinian violence.[5]

Iraq and Saddam featured in all of these conversations, but didn't overwhelm them. Nor did they overwhelm debate in Washington. While the vice president and the Pentagon quietly agitated for a tougher line on Saddam and more active support for the exiled Iraqi opposition, there was not much sense of urgency. The immediate task was to try to put the sanctions regime on a more sustainable path and strengthen containment of Saddam. Powell took the lead in fashioning a new "smart sanctions" approach—lifting most of the ineffectual or even counterproductive sanctions on Iraqi civilians and substituting a more narrowly focused arms control regime to deny military and dual-use technology. The administration, like its predecessor, remained committed to the long-term goal of regime change in Baghdad, but also remained concerned about overreaching. In a closed briefing for some key senators after I returned from my travels in July 2001, I repeated that we had no doubt that Iraq and the region would be better off without Saddam, but added that that outcome obviously couldn't be imposed from the outside. I had no idea how quickly the mood in the administration could change.

* * *

I WAS AT my desk in the State Department on the morning of Tuesday, September 11, 2001, reading my daily intelligence briefs, when the first images of the attack on the World Trade Center in New York flashed across my television screen. I watched in horror as the second tower was struck, and as the full magnitude of the assault began to sink in. The department was evacuated amid reports of possible further attacks; thousands of employees, many with tears in their eyes, filed quietly out of the building. I walked hurriedly among the crowds, found Lisa, and hugged her tightly. I went back to my office an hour or so later, along with a small number of colleagues, uncertain of what to expect—beyond a vastly transformed world.

By that point, another hijacked aircraft had crashed into the Pentagon. Looking out my window on the sixth floor of the department, I could see the plumes of smoke across the Potomac. My thoughts turned quickly to ensuring that NEA personnel overseas were safe. Jim Larocco took the lead in calling each of our posts, and the bureau responded with its usual discipline and professionalism. On the seventh floor, Rich Armitage stayed in touch with the White House and with Secretary Powell, who was in Peru for a meeting of the Organization of American States. Powell began the eight-hour flight home as soon as he learned of the attacks, but wouldn't arrive until early evening.

That afternoon, sitting in a virtually deserted building, I tried to collect my thoughts and think ahead. It was already clear that al-Qaeda was responsible for the attacks. The first step would obviously

be a sharp strike against them and their Taliban protectors in Afghanistan. Three thousand innocent people had just been slaughtered in the worst assault on American soil since Pearl Harbor. We
had to respond decisively. But we also had to look for opportunities
amid crisis. In the first few hours after the attacks, there was a huge
outpouring of international sympathy and support. Vladimir Putin
was one of the first leaders to call the president and offer Russia's
solidarity, and the Iranian leadership was quick to denounce the attack. Was there a chance to mobilize regional and international action
around a shared sense of revulsion? At this grim and painful moment, could the United States take advantage of almost unprecedented global support and retake the initiative in the Middle East?
Could we shape a strategy that would not only hit back hard against
terrorists and any states who continued to harbor them, but also lay
out an affirmative agenda that might eventually help reduce the
hopelessness and anger on which extremists preyed?

Our computer systems were down most of that day, so I sat at my
desk and wrote a note to the secretary in longhand, as legibly as I
could. It was a hurried effort, covering four pages of yellow legal paper.

My thinking was straightforward. The use of force and American
military and intelligence leverage would be crucial in Afghanistan,
but there were also considerable opportunities for imaginative and
hard-nosed diplomacy. Adversaries like Iran had a stake in the removal of the Taliban, and a solid grasp of Afghan politics. Exploring
cooperation with them might prove useful and create long-term
openings.

The demonstration effect of success against the Taliban and al-
Qaeda could also help focus the minds of other states dabbling (or
immersed) in terrorism, like Libya and Syria. Tough diplomacy and
the weight of post–9/11 international opinion could have a decisive
effect on Qaddafi and Assad, and we should exploit the moment. I
doubted that Saddam was capable of any such epiphanies, but argued
that this was the best opportunity we had had in years to strengthen

containment of Iraq and build international support for "smart sanctions." We could use the terrible events of 9/11 as the antidote to containment fatigue, and shore up constraints that were bent but not yet broken.

I added that we might also have opportunities to create the cooperative security arrangements among the Gulf Arab states that we had discussed after Desert Storm a decade before but never made systematic. Amid all the awful violence of the Second Intifada, we might have an opening to reassert American leadership, press hard against violence, and re-create a sense of political horizon for Israelis and Palestinians. Finally, I encouraged a renewed focus from the new administration on the longer-term drivers of instability across the Middle East, on the value of carefully promoting greater economic and political openness. A regional economic development bank was one possibility; a new regional assistance initiative was another, with incentives linked to measurable progress on reforms and cooperation against terrorism.

The trauma of 9/11 confronted us with the reality that the Islamist movement spawned in 1979—the year in which the Iranian Revolution, the Grand Mosque attack in Mecca, and the Soviet invasion of Afghanistan unleashed lethal regional and ideological rivalries—had become more extreme, more violent, and more global. There could be no wishing it away. What was unfolding was less a clash of civilizations than a clash within a civilization, a deeply battered Islamic world in the midst of a desperate ideological struggle. There were limits to what we could do directly to shape that debate. What we could do, however, was to help create a sense of geopolitical order that would deprive extremists of the oxygen they needed to fan the flames of chaos, and give moderate forces the sustained support they needed to demonstrate that they could deliver for their people.

I handed the note to the secretary after he returned. He was tired and understandably preoccupied, but appreciative. One of the things I had admired most about Powell was the way he exuded confidence, even in the worst of circumstances. I could feel that now, unspoken but unmistakable. As I walked out, I said he could count on NEA. He smiled wearily and said, "I know I can."

We followed up over the next few days with more specific memos on Iran, Libya, and the Israeli-Palestinian issue, along the same lines as my hastily handwritten note. At a senior staff meeting on September 13, the first after 9/11, Powell echoed some of these themes, stressing alongside a message of American firmness and resolve that we had to be attentive to opportunities for diplomacy in even the worst national tragedies.

As the U.S. military and the CIA moved swiftly in the fall of 2001 to support the Afghan opposition and overthrow the Taliban government in Kabul, we pedaled ahead slowly on a number of the Middle East initiatives we had suggested. In late September, Ryan Crocker began a direct dialogue with the Iranians about Afghanistan that helped produce a new Afghan government. In early October, I met quietly in London with a Libyan delegation led by Musa Kusa, Qaddafi's intelligence chief, resuscitating talks about Lockerbie and terrorism that had begun in the Clinton administration. I returned to Damascus that same month and met Bashar, who soon thereafter began a modestly useful information exchange, which in one instance provided advance warning of a terrorist plot against U.S. facilities in Bahrain.

In November, using the diplomatic momentum of the immediate post–9/11 period, Powell won Russian acceptance and UN Security Council passage of a "smart sanctions" framework for Iraq, which tightened controls on military and dual-use items, and loosened restrictions on civilian goods. That same month, he gave a speech in Louisville, Kentucky, emphasizing the importance of renewing a peace process between Israelis and Palestinians. He talked movingly about ending the daily humiliations of Palestinians under Israeli occupation, and with equal passion about Israel's right to security. He appointed retired General Tony Zinni, the former commander of U.S.

Central Command (CENTCOM), as a senior advisor to help negotiate a cease-fire and reopen the way to negotiations. All this was at least a start on the agenda I had tried to sketch, alone in my office, on that grim afternoon of September 11.

That agenda was soon eclipsed by an alternative view. The new administration had been shaken badly and felt a call to action—the more decisive the better. "Containment" didn't have much of a ring to it in the months after the al-Qaeda attacks on the homeland. It was not the season for nuance, caution, and compromise. It was the season for the risk-tolerant and the ideologically ambitious, bent on inserting ourselves aggressively into the regional contest of ideas, militarizing our policy, and unbuckling our rhetoric.

After the pain and surprise of 9/11, it was time for the muscular reassertion of American might, time to remind adversaries of the consequences of challenging the United States. For many in the White House and the Pentagon, that was a message best served unilaterally, unencumbered and undiluted by elaborate coalition-building. Lost in the moment was the reality that the approach we advocated at State was no less hard-nosed, just more sustainable and more mindful of risks.

Regime change in Iraq became the acid test of the administration's post–9/11 approach. The overthrow of the Taliban had come almost too quickly and too easily. For "paleoconservatives" like Dick Cheney and Don Rumsfeld, the message sent in Afghanistan was necessary but insufficient. Another, bigger blow had to be struck to deter enemies in a region in which force was the only language people understood. For "neoconservatives," like Deputy Secretary Paul Wolfowitz and Undersecretary Doug Feith at the Pentagon, Saddam's forcible ouster was not just a message, it was an opportunity to create a democratic model in Iraq, begin the transformation of the whole region, and reassert American hegemony after a post–Cold War decade of naïve attachment to the promise of a peace dividend.

For President George W. Bush, the world had changed after September 11, and the humble realist lens that he had used in the months before no longer seemed to illuminate. Impatient and proud of his decisiveness, the president found containment of Saddam to be too passive, inadequate to the challenges of this moment in history. After 9/11, the policy terrain tilted rapidly away from the wider agenda for which we argued, and toward a single-minded focus on toppling Saddam. So did the bureaucratic playing field, with Powell increasingly isolated and considered by antagonists at the White House and the Pentagon to be too independent, too popular, and too moderate—and NEA considered a den of defeatists and Cassandras. In a Washington that rarely lacked for infighting and policy combat, the road to war in Iraq was distinctive for its intensity and indiscipline.

* * *

FOLLOWING 9/11, MY colleagues and I continued to believe we could contain Iraq and avoid war. We worried that an ill-considered, unilateral war to topple Saddam would prove to be a massive foreign policy blunder. We did not, however, argue frontally against the bipartisan policy of eventual regime change, nor did we argue against the possible use of force much further down the road to achieve it. Instead, sensing the ideological zeal with which war drums were beating, we tried to slow the tempo and direct debate in a less self-injurious manner. None of us had any illusions about Saddam or the long-term risk that his regime posed for the region. His brutality deserved every bit of international condemnation and ostracism it had received. We did not, however, see a serious, imminent threat that would justify a war. While most of us suspected that Saddam was concealing some residual WMD capacity, the evidence was hard to establish, and he always deliberately obscured his intentions in order to deceive and intimidate regional and domestic enemies. His conventional military capabilities had been shattered in Desert Storm, and his economy was in tatters after a decade of sanctions, and decades more of mismanagement.

As a result, there was little sense of urgency in the region about Saddam, and even less interest in supporting a military effort against him. "At age 74, Mubarak remains proud, cautious, and deeply preoccupied with stability at home and in the region," I wrote in one cable after a conversation with the Egyptian leader. Mubarak repeatedly warned me about the complexities of Iraqi society, the unpredictability of a post-Saddam world, and the negative regional consequences of any eventual use of force.[6] "Burns," the Egyptian president would say, "you must not underestimate how much trouble those Iraqis can be. They spend their whole lives plotting against each other." Most other Arab leaders were far more worried about the images of Palestinians being killed in the West Bank and stories of Iraqi civilian hardships under sanctions than they were about a near-term threat from Saddam. Broader international opinion was similarly unfocused on any immediate Iraqi threat. Even in London, where Prime Minister Tony Blair was determined to stay close to President Bush after 9/11, there was a strong sense that it would take time and considerable effort to build a legitimate case for Saddam's removal.

At the State Department, we were at first lulled into thinking that our arguments were getting traction. Before 9/11, the new administration's episodic interagency discussions about Iraq were long and painful, the kind of bureaucratic purgatory that exists when issues are being sharply debated but everyone knows there is neither the political will nor urgency to resolve them. Civilian officials from the Pentagon, often allied with the vice president's growing and increasingly independent national security staff, would press for more radical steps against Saddam. A particular favorite was to create a safe zone in southern Iraq, similar to the zone protecting the Kurds in the north, that could provide a launching pad for Iraqi oppositionists to undermine Saddam. Most of these ideas foundered on the obvious concerns—lack of internationally legitimate grounds for acting; lack of enthusiasm in the region; the potential military consequences; and the opportunity costs for other priorities on the early Bush 43 agenda.

The wiliest, most active, and least trustworthy of the Iraqi oppositionists agitating for American intervention to overthrow Saddam
was Ahmed Chalabi. I had first met him in Amman in the early
1980s. An Iraqi national from a well-connected Baghdad family, he
had fled the country after Saddam took power. In Amman, he ran the
Petra Bank and was a large fish in the relatively small pond of Jordanian high society. Smooth and smart, Chalabi established himself as
a leading figure among exiled Iraqi oppositionists during the 1990s,
based mostly in London, but spending increasing amounts of time
working the halls of Congress. He became head of the main umbrella
opposition group, the Iraqi National Congress, in 1992, and was one
of the principal architects of the Iraq Liberation Act.

Always a fertile source of ideas and information, much of it contrived but all of it delivered with conspiratorial enthusiasm, Chalabi
cultivated particularly close contacts at senior levels of the Pentagon
and the White House. He kept a disdainful distance from the Powell
State Department, an attitude we reciprocated. "That guy is a weasel,"
Rich Armitage said, in the least earthy description he could manage.
"And he will only lead us into trouble."

9/11 provided the opening for regime change proponents. Powell
mentioned to me on September 12 that Rumsfeld had raised the
threat posed by Saddam at the previous evening's NSC meeting, and
Wolfowitz pressed the issue again at a principals meeting at Camp
David a few days later. President Bush was intrigued enough to ask
the NSC staff for a quick investigation of whether Saddam had a role
in the 9/11 attacks. The answer was an unambiguous no. The president made clear that the immediate priority would be action against
the Taliban and al-Qaeda in Afghanistan. Nevertheless, the idea of a
preemptive strike to topple Saddam was slowly gathering steam. In
November, with the president's blessing, Rumsfeld instructed CENT-
COM to update contingency planning for Iraq, with the aim of "de-
capitating" the Iraqi leadership and installing a new provisional
government.

Before a White House meeting that same month, I sent a note to Armitage emphasizing that it was the "wrong time to shift our focus from Afghanistan." I explained that we needed "to show that we will finish the job [and] restore order, not just move on to the next Moslem state."[7] I added that the case for war was extremely weak. There was "no evidence of an Iraqi role" in 9/11, "no [regional or international] support for military action," and "no triggering event." There was a "relatively weak internal opposition [in Iraq]," and little clarity on what might happen on the day after. Other than that, it made perfect sense.

But the drumbeat only grew louder after the president's State of the Union speech at the end of January, when he took aim at the "axis of evil"—Iraq, North Korea, and Iran. That killed the diplomatic channel that Ryan Crocker had so skillfully developed with the Iranians. The headline role for Iraq was hardly a surprise, and a preview of the case for preemption that was building. Frustrated by the inconclusive evidence offered up by the intelligence community of Iraqi complicity in 9/11 and continuing WMD activities, senior civilians in the Pentagon and the vice president's staff probed even harder for any shred of information or analysis that would fit their predispositions. An "independent" intelligence unit was set up at the Pentagon under Doug Feith, charged with ferreting out the real story. As Armitage later put it, the war party within the administration was "trying to connect dots which were unconnectable."[8]

Despite efforts of Pentagon civilians and the vice president's office to lead the witnesses, many in the intelligence community continued to offer honest analysis, however unsatisfying it was to administration hawks. At State, the Bureau of Intelligence and Research reported repeatedly to Powell that it saw no firm evidence of reconstitution of Iraqi WMD. In the spring of 2002, the Defense Intelligence Agency forcefully and convincingly labeled one of the main sources for information on continuing Iraqi WMD activities to be a fabricator. In early 2002, a former State Department colleague, Joe Wilson, went to Niger on the CIA's behalf to track down a story that Saddam was trying to obtain yellowcake for an alleged covert uranium enrichment program, but found no corroboration.

After yet another trip to the Middle East in February, I told Powell that there was still no regional enthusiasm for any near-term military effort against Saddam. I was particularly struck by my conversations with Crown Prince Mohammed bin Zayed (MbZ) and other Emirati leaders. They warned that if the images on Al Jazeera showed American tanks occupying Iraq alongside Israeli tanks sitting atop the Palestinians, "it won't take long for anger to boil." MbZ concluded our meeting by putting the stakes in sharp relief: "You have an opportunity to do a very good thing for the region by overthrowing Saddam—or a very bad thing if the outcome is messy, Iraq breaks apart, or other regional problems are left untouched afterwards. You and we will either benefit or suffer from the consequences for many years to come."[9] He made no secret of which outcome he thought was the most likely.

And he wasn't alone. Mubarak, King Abdullah, and other Arab leaders worried "that [the United States] will come in, create a mess, and then leave them to deal with the consequences." Their anxiety reflected "a cold calculation that the risks posed by the uncertainties of regime change outweigh the current threat from Saddam." I noted that "the current Iraqi opposition is fractured, feeble, and incapable of organizing itself, much less bringing security, stability and civil society to a post-Saddam Iraq." I emphasized again my conviction, which I knew Powell shared, that "getting into Iraq would be a lot easier than getting out"—that the post-conflict situation would be a far bigger problem than the initial military operation.[10] In the face of such risks, I told a meeting of NEA ambassadors that February, "That's exactly why we would never go at this alone."

Unpersuaded by what we were reporting about attitudes in the region, and keen to underscore the gravity of the administration's concerns about Saddam, Vice President Cheney decided to travel to

the Middle East himself in March. I joined his delegation as the senior State Department representative. The vice president, who combined a quiet, even-tempered exterior with a sharp intellect and rigid
views, was gracious toward me throughout the ten-day trip. He included me in most meetings and welcomed my participation, if not
always my perspective. I had a faint hope before the trip that firsthand exposure to the reluctance of regional leaders, and their preoccupation with quieting Israeli-Palestinian violence, would help
convince the vice president that thoughts of war should wait until we
had a better case and a better regional environment. Armitage was
skeptical, and proved to be right. If anything, the trip seemed to solidify Cheney's view that early, forcible regime change would be the
key to transforming the regional environment, not the other way
around.

It didn't help that several of the Arab leaders appeared more re-
strained in their comments about Iraq than they had been with me.
Arab political culture is full of winks and nods, and the message conveyed to Cheney in a number of capitals was essentially "Do this if you
must, but do it right, and wake us when it's over." In London, Cheney
said bluntly that the president was determined to overthrow Saddam,
leaving the British unsettled about his willingness to go it alone if
necessary. "A coalition would be nice," the vice president said, "but not
essential."

For the rest of the spring and early summer, interagency debate
continued. The NSC staff ran a process that tended to paper over
sharp differences, mainly between Powell on one side and Cheney
and Rumsfeld on the other, and at least from our point of view indulge the vice president's staff and the Pentagon civilians. Rumsfeld
made no real attempt to conceal his contempt for the process, often
claiming that he hadn't had time to read papers for major meetings
and obfuscating or retreating into Socratic questions when he didn't
want to show his hand.

We still thought we could "slow the train down," as Powell used to put it, but the truth was that it was gathering speed. I used a different, and equally mistaken, metaphor in a note to the secretary before an April 2002 meeting with the president. I urged him to "play 'judo' with the crazier assertions from OSD [Office of the Secretary of Defense]" and hope that by exposing the risks of war and its aftermath we could gain leverage.[11] That tactic had only marginal effect, especially in that post–9/11 moment when there was a bias for action, and prudence looked like weakness. In early June, the president gave a speech at West Point that underscored his growing impatience and sense of purpose. In the post–9/11 world, offense was the key to security, not defense. On Iraq, that meant that preventive action would be the default position. It was a deeply misguided prescription, but one that was far easier to sell within the administration and to the American public.

We took one last run later that summer at the argument for avoiding war—summarizing, all in one place, the profound risks of an ill-prepared and ill-considered conflict. David Pearce, a Foreign Service classmate then serving as head of the Iraq/Iran office in NEA, produced an initial draft outlining everything that could go wrong if we went to war. Ryan and I joined him in what quickly became the most depressing brainstorming session of our careers. The resultant memo, revised by David, was more a hurried list of horribles than a coherent analysis, a hastily assembled antidote to the recklessly rosy assumptions of our bureaucratic antagonists.

Many of the arguments in the memo, which we entitled "The Perfect Storm," look obvious in hindsight.[12] We highlighted the deep sectarian fault lines in Iraq, on which Saddam had kept such a brutal lid. We emphasized the dangers of civil unrest and looting if the Iraqi military and security institutions collapsed or were eliminated in the wake of Saddam's overthrow, and the risk that already badly degraded civilian infrastructure would crumble. We noted the likelihood that regional players would be tempted to meddle and take advantage of

Iraqi weakness. Iran could wind up as a major beneficiary. With no tradition of democratic governance and market economics, Iraq would be a hard place to test the upbeat assertions offered by Paul Wolfowitz and other advocates of regime change. If the United States embarked on this conflict, and especially if we embarked on it more or less on our own, and without a compelling justification, we'd bear the primary responsibility for post-conflict security, order, and recovery. That would suck the oxygen out of every other priority on the administration's national security agenda.

Looking back, we understated some risks, like the speed with which Sunni-Shia bloodletting in post-Saddam Iraq would fuel wider sectarian conflict in the region. We exaggerated others, like the risk that Saddam would use chemical weapons. Yet it was an honest effort to lay out our concerns, and it reflected our collective experiences and those of our generation of State Department Arabists, seared by the memory of stumbling into the middle of bloody sectarian conflict in Lebanon in the 1980s.

What we did not do in "The Perfect Storm," however, was take a hard stand against war altogether, or make a passionate case for containment as a long-term alternative to conflict. In the end, we pulled some punches, persuading ourselves that we'd never get a hearing for our concerns beyond the secretary if we simply threw ourselves on the track. Years later, that remains my biggest professional regret.

I gave the memo to the secretary late one day in mid-July. I don't think he ever forwarded the paper to the White House, but he later told me he used it in the dinner conversation that he had with the president and Condi Rice on August 5, when he laid out his reservations bluntly. As he later recounted to journalist Bob Woodward, Powell warned the president that if he decided to go to war, he'd wind up as "the proud owner of twenty-five million people. . . . This will become your first term." He stressed the risks of regional destabilization, the difficulty of encouraging democracy in Iraq, the unpredictability of postwar politics in such a deeply repressed society, and the potential for damage to the global energy market. In light of all those dangers, he repeated his case for building pressure on Saddam deliberately through the United Nations, first attempting to get weapons inspectors back in, and then obtaining an authorization to use force if necessary.

At least for a while, the president took Powell's concerns to heart and approved an effort to obtain a new UN Security Council resolution to test Saddam. The reality, however, was that we had shifted from trying to avoid war to trying to shape it. In a note to Powell later in August, I acknowledged that we were past the point of arguing with others in the administration about "whether the goal of regime change makes sense; now it's about choosing between a smart way and a dumb way of bringing it about."[13]

We had only marginally greater success in this next phase than we had in the first. Having lost the argument to avoid war, we had two main goals in shaping it and managing the inevitable risks. First, we sought to internationalize as much as possible the road to war. That was less about the military necessity of a coalition and more about the need for international support and involvement in postwar Iraq. If this meant delay and difficult diplomacy, it was worth it. In a read-ahead memo prior to a Principals Committee meeting in January 2003, I highlighted to Powell the gulf between State and the Pentagon: "DOD's plan calls for a military government with a civilian face, run out of OSD, lasting months or years, then turning control from U.S. to Iraqis. Our plan calls for U.S. handover ASAP to an interim international authority which monitors development of Iraqi institutions."[14]

To complement a push for international legitimacy and buy-in, the second concern was about domestic legitimacy in post-Saddam Iraq. Skeptical of Chalabi and some of the other external oppositionists, we argued vociferously with staffers in the Pentagon and the vice president's office against their preference, which was essentially to "have the U.S. government install a member of the external opposition as a Karzai-like figure in post-Saddam Iraq." I argued that "some oppositionists favored by Washington are largely despised by the Iraqi public." I emphasized that Iraqis "would resent not having a significant voice in choosing new leadership" and that "ensuring the cooperation and support of Iraqis inside the country will be critical." Armitage noted in the margin, "Exactly right."[15]

We began as early as March 2002 to try to organize a number of Iraqi exiles and technocrats around an effort to consider all the challenges of post-Saddam Iraq, and how best to cope with them. It was born in large part of Ryan Crocker's experience in post-Taliban Afghanistan, when he saw the urgent need to mobilize exiled oppositionists and technocrats to help build effective governance in Kabul. Dubbed the "Future of Iraq" project, this effort resulted over the following months in a seventeen-volume set of planning documents. They ranged from the future of Iraq's agricultural sector, to dealing with immediate security challenges, to a framework for a national consultative process for putting together a provisional government.

Chalabi saw the Future of Iraq project as a threat to his interest in monopolizing post-Saddam planning, and worked with his advocates in Washington to sideline it. The Pentagon mounted its own planning operation and ignored the work we had done. When Saddam was toppled, those seventeen volumes continued to gather dust.

As the domestic legitimacy debate wound on inconclusively, there were some tactical successes on the international legitimacy front. But they didn't come without considerable grumbling from hardliners in the administration, who saw the whole UN effort at best as a waste of time and at worst as a sign of weakness. Vice President Cheney squabbled with Powell in several principals meetings in August and September, and gave two speeches late in the summer pressing the case for regime change and downplaying any need for wider international backing. One Saturday that September, I was sent to represent State at a last-minute principals meeting on Iraq. Sitting across from the vice president, with Condi Rice chairing the meeting, I dutifully made the case for working through the UN to build international legitimacy and to enhance the leverage of coercive diplomacy. After listening politely but impatiently, the vice president replied, "The only legitimacy we really need comes on the back of an M1A1 tank."

Pressed also by the British, the president stuck with his commitment to Powell and joined in a high-level push for a new Security Council resolution. In October, a new U.S. National Intelligence Estimate made the sweeping assertion that Iraq "is reconstituting its nuclear program" and "has now established large-scale, redundant and concealed biological weapons agent production capabilities." That same month, by substantial majorities in both the Senate and House, Congress gave the president authorization to use force against Iraq. The margins for the congressional vote authorizing the use of force more than a decade before were far narrower, despite the more compelling reality of Saddam's invasion of Kuwait. It was yet another reminder of how much 9/11 had changed the political atmosphere. In early November, the UN Security Council passed Resolution 1441. It declared Saddam in "material breach" of his obligations, gave Iraq a "final opportunity" to comply, and warned of "serious consequences" if it did not.

At the end of November, with his attention focused by the new resolution and the congressional vote, Saddam suddenly took steps to comply, providing a first tranche of documents and allowing UN inspectors to return to Iraq for the first time in nearly four years. In December and again in January 2003, suspicious UN inspectors reported that Saddam remained in violation of his obligations and had not yet provided complete information or access. A number of us in the department made the case to Powell that we should give the inspectors more time and let 1441 play out a little longer, in the slim hope that Saddam would come clean. By that point, however, the secretary had run out the string with the White House.

On February 5, Powell made his famous presentation to the UN

Security Council about Saddam's noncompliance and continuing WMD activities. He said that the evidence of Iraq's breach of its obligations was "irrefutable and undeniable," and that Saddam was "determined to keep his WMD and determined to make more." The secretary had worked hard to peel away unsubstantiated material pressed on him by the vice president's staff and others, but most of what remained was eventually discredited. In the moment, it felt like the most persuasive—and honest—case that the administration could muster, from its most credible spokesperson. Over time, the damage done became more obvious, to both Powell's reputation and our country's. Powell would later call his speech "painful" and a permanent "blot" on his record. It was a hard lesson for all of us in the complexities of duty.

Late on the evening of March 19, the president announced in a nationally televised speech that we were at war again with Saddam. A dozen years before, I had sat with Lisa and watched the president's father make a similar, equally sobering speech. I had much deeper trepidation this time. This was not a war that we needed to fight.

* * *

THE MILITARY OPERATION proceeded with predictable efficiency. Iraqi forces crumbled, Baghdad fell in early April, and Saddam fled into hiding. The mood in much of the administration was triumphant, and the president declared "mission accomplished" in early May. It didn't take long, however, for many of the troubles we had foreseen to surface. After a visit to Baghdad at the beginning of July, I reported bluntly to Powell that "we're in a pretty deep hole in Iraq."

Looting and lawlessness had already taken a huge toll. Rumsfeld's determination to display the new lean, mobile, technologically innovative American way of war had made short work of conventional Iraqi military resistance, but was inadequate to the task of ensuring postwar order. Less than one-third the size of the Desert Storm coalition force, the U.S. military was badly overstretched on the ground in Iraq, especially as the Iraqi army and police melted away and insecurity mushroomed. The problem was compounded by two tragically misguided American decisions in May, first to ban Baath Party members from public-sector roles, and second to disband the Iraqi army. In that same July message to Powell, I relayed an anecdote from a friend in the CIA who had recently returned from Baghdad. Interrogated after an RPG attack on U.S. troops, an ex–Iraqi army captain admitted that he had taken fifty dollars from insurgent leaders to conduct the operation. "They took away my job and my honor," he explained. "I can't feed my family. There are many more like me."[16]

In the aftermath of the toppling of Saddam, the decision-making process in Washington was even worse than the prewar experience. In NEA, we continued to push for internationalizing the civilian administration of Iraq, with an immediate emphasis on security and order, preserving the Iraqi army and police, and engaging both Sunni and Shia leaders. We also continued to make the argument for careful cultivation of a new Iraqi governance structure, whose legitimacy would come largely from people inside the country, with exiled oppositionists playing a significant but supporting role.

Our colleagues in the Pentagon had a different view, far more suspicious of ceding oversight to international partners or the United Nations, and still far more attached to central roles for Chalabi and returning exiles. Setting them atop a provisional government would be a much quicker and less complicated way to establish new Iraqi leadership. Just three days after the launch of the war, on March 22, I stressed to Powell that it was already clear we were "being pushed in a dangerous direction on some critical postwar planning issues. . . . OSD and OVP have been working steadily to . . . [hand over] postwar Iraq to 'our' Iraqis (Chalabi and company), while keeping at bay other Iraqis, the rest of the U.S. Administration, and the UN and other potential international partners."[17]

Events in Iraq and incoherence in Washington soon overwhelmed the fledgling steps we managed to take toward a more inclusive political process. Jay Garner, the retired Army general leading the early transition effort, was well-intentioned but badly miscast. The atmosphere within his group was tangled, to put it mildly. One British colleague described Garner's team as "a bag of ferrets."[18]

Garner was quickly replaced by a retired diplomat, Jerry Bremer. Smart, disciplined, and supremely self-confident, Bremer seemed like a solid choice. He reported to the Pentagon, but had enormous room to maneuver. Rumsfeld was already experiencing periodic bouts of amnesia about his hard prewar press to manage the aftermath, and the White House was all too willing at the outset to defer to a strong-willed proconsul on the ground. Described to Secretary Powell by Henry Kissinger as a "control freak," Bremer was intent upon swiftly establishing his leadership and convincing Iraqis that there would be no return to the old political order.

Just before Bremer left for Baghdad, I joined Powell and Armitage for a quiet conversation with him at Powell's home in Virginia. The secretary made clear that he wanted to do all he could to help, and that Bremer could count on State to provide whatever support we could. Powell was candid about his frustrations with the interagency process and emphasized the importance of building an international structure in Baghdad to shepherd the transition and to keep focused on a legitimate, inclusive Iraqi political process. Bremer seemed appreciative.

He didn't mention anything in that discussion about his intention to issue sweeping orders shortly after his arrival in Iraq on de-Baathification and formal dissolution of the Iraqi army. Ahmed Chalabi was put in charge of implementing the broad injunction against Baath Party members, which he applied to its illogical extreme, tossing aside not only senior officials with blood on their hands, but schoolteachers and lower-level technocrats for whom party membership was an essential basis for employment. In different hands, implementation of the de-Baathification decision might have been far

less catastrophic, but Chalabi ensured that it would have ruinous effect.

The disbanding of the regular military was similarly shortsighted,
casting thousands of Sunnis with lethal training and an equally lethal
sense of grievance into the hands of the insurgency. It was true that
most of the Iraqi armed forces had not been physically defeated in
battle; when the Turks blocked the movement of U.S. ground forces
into northern Iraq, and the Americans quickly took Baghdad, most of
the Iraqi military beyond the capital simply melted away. It would
have been hard to reassemble them, and any such effort would likely
have alienated the Shia majority. The cardinal sin, however, was to cut
them off entirely, and not immediately ensure some form of payment
or support to disbanded soldiers. In August, UN special envoy Sérgio
Vieira de Mello was killed in an insurgent truck bombing of UN
headquarters in Baghdad, and prospects for international administration of the Iraqi transition as well as for a provisional government
that could bridge sectarian differences rapidly receded.

The Bremer-led Coalition Provisional Authority was a curious
amalgam of American hubris, ingenuity, courage, and wishful thinking. It didn't take long for the CPA to mirror the wider dysfunction of
the society Bremer was seeking to mold. Its reporting to Washington
was constrained by Bremer's disinclination to be second-guessed and
the fact that what little reporting there was had to come through the
Pentagon. I told Powell at one point that "we learn more from *The
Washington Post* than we do from CPA."

Partly for that reason, but mostly because of the sheer significance
of our unfolding predicament, I visited Iraq a half dozen times during
the CPA's yearlong existence. Each trip had an element of the surreal.
After one of my visits to the Green Zone, I described CPA headquarters in Saddam's old Republican Palace to Secretary Powell as "remi-
niscent of the bar scene in *Star Wars*." In the faded and still creepy
grandeur of Saddam's corridors, American and other coalition personnel swarmed busily at all hours of the day and night—military and

civilian, armed and unarmed, veterans of post-conflict situations and young Republican neophytes, the hardworking and committed and the certifiably clueless. Ambitious young ideologues talked earnestly about remaking ministries and educational systems, or building a securities and exchange system whether the Iraqis knew they needed one or not. On one trip, I stopped in to see Bernie Kerik, the former New York Police Department commissioner who had come to advise the Ministry of Interior. He seemed perplexed by Iraq, and perked up only when an aide informed him of another urban explosion. He rushed out, eager to get to the scene and give a television interview, reassuring Iraqi viewers in Arabic translation that order was being restored and the perpetrators would be caught, much as he might have done in the more familiar boroughs of New York City.

I traveled widely outside Baghdad that year, from Erbil and the Kurdish north to Basra and the Shia-dominated south. The two principal Kurdish leaders, Jalal Talabani and Masoud Barzani, circled each other warily but made a united front in defending the autonomy that they had spent much of the previous decade building. In my visits to Mosul, Tikrit, and Baquba in late 2003, evidence of a mounting Sunni Arab insurgency was all too obvious. By the end of the year, Shia militia groups had begun to spring up too, with Muqtada al-Sadr emerging as a particularly difficult and incendiary voice. Iran and its Revolutionary Guards deepened their meddling, feeding off the sectarian strife. Turkey kept a careful eye on the north, and opened up channels of communication to the Iraqi Kurds. Across much of the country, security was fragile and infrastructure painfully inadequate. By the spring of 2004, the early self-assurance that had fueled the CPA was fading fast.

Violence in Anbar Province, where Sunnis were an aggrieved and well-armed majority, boiled over. The towns I had driven through on my misbegotten trip from Amman to Baghdad twenty years earlier filled American television screens with awful images. First were the scenes of the burned corpses of four Blackwater security contractors being dragged through the streets and hung from a bridge in Fallujah, then it was images of detained insurgents being brutalized and humiliated by their American captors at Abu Ghraib. That was only more tinder for Abu Musab al-Zarqawi, the Jordanian extremist who was already fanning the flames in Iraq and organizing the particularly vicious group that would later be known as al-Qaeda in Iraq. It was an ugly spring, with reverberations that would stretch across the next few bloody years.

Meanwhile, the White House finally agreed to replace the proconsular CPA with a more normal embassy structure, as the Iraqis moved toward national elections and establishment of a new government. Jerry Bremer left Baghdad in late spring, and John Negroponte took over as ambassador. We set up a sizable mini-bureau inside NEA in Washington to provide support for Embassy Baghdad, which remained a huge and exceptionally complicated diplomatic mission. Much as Powell had predicted to President Bush in August 2002, war in Iraq sucked the oxygen out of the administration's foreign policy agenda, and left lasting scars on America's influence and an already complicated region.

* * *

AS IRAQ BECAME the main event, the Israeli-Palestinian conflict became a painful and distracting sideshow. It was hardly the most promising diplomatic possibility that the administration had inherited. The White House thought the Clinton administration had wasted political capital on a problem neither central to American interests nor ripe for solution. Like so much else in foreign policy, that attitude hardened after the September 11 attacks, with Palestinian violence looking increasingly like a part of the wider terrorist problem, Yasser Arafat its enabler, and Ariel Sharon a partner whose hard, uncompromising reputation fit the mood in Washington. Nevertheless, the grinding violence of the Second Intifada was impossible to ignore, and America's Arab friends were agitated about the impact on their own populations, if not so much about the plight or aspirations of Palestinians themselves.

The net result was a policy of relative detachment, with the administration trying to do just enough to placate the Arabs without leaning too hard on Sharon or diverting from the emerging post–9/11 goals of regime change in Iraq and regional transformation. Middle East policy in the first term of the administration was a world of two parallel bureaucratic and conceptual universes. In one corner stood the vice president and his activist staff, the civilian leadership of the Defense Department, and most NSC staffers. Their view, shared increasingly by the president after 9/11, was not only that the road to a better future for the region lay through toppling Saddam, but also that the road to Israeli-Palestinian peace lay through toppling Arafat and thorough democratic reform of the Palestinian Authority. Too much talk about what such a future might hold for Palestinians, or about the corrosive impact of Israeli settlement activity in the meantime, was seen as a reward for bad Palestinian behavior and a distraction from the main challenge. They sought to park the peace process—and decades of bipartisan diplomatic convention—until the broader regional goal was accomplished.

In the other corner stood Powell and his team at the State Department, often supported analytically by CIA. Deeply skeptical about the rush to take on Iraq and its likely consequences in the region, we argued for more focus on the immediate fires that were burning, to create better long-term conditions for considering what to do about Saddam. We largely shared the view that Arafat had become an obstacle to progress. We also realized that the Clinton administration had underplayed the importance of Palestinian reform in its zeal for a political settlement, and that we had to put a higher priority on better Palestinian governance.

The inconvenient reality, however, was that the more Arafat posed as the victim, the more popular he became among Palestinians. There was considerable frustration with the Palestinian Authority's corruption in the West Bank and Gaza, but far more anger about Israeli use of force, the ritual humiliations of life under occupation, and the absence of hope for a two-state solution. In a note to Secretary Powell, I argued that the more we focused on those issues, the more pressure we could bring to bear on Arafat. "If we are prepared to lay out for all our partners some plain truths about what a two state solution will look like, and a clear roadmap for getting there . . . a great deal is possible. If we're not prepared, however, to speak those plain truths, we will get nowhere on Palestinian reform, achieve no real security for Israel, and our Arab friends will head in other directions." I continued, "This will require us to piss everybody off to some extent, and address our message to the peoples involved, not just to the stubborn old men who lead them."[19]

Against the backdrop of continuing Israeli-Palestinian violence, American policy moved fitfully and ineffectually down its two parallel tracks. Powell's Louisville speech in November 2001 launched an effort by Tony Zinni, the former CENTCOM commander, to achieve a cease-fire and the resumption of security cooperation between Israel and the Palestinian Authority. There couldn't have been a better person to lead such an effort, or a worse set of circumstances in which to try. Zinni was supported by Aaron Miller, my longtime friend and colleague at State, with his encyclopedic knowledge of the peace process and passion for promoting it. They were an unlikely but capable duo—the brawny and cerebral former Marine general, an Italian Catholic from Philadelphia, and the lanky Jewish peace process lifer from the suburbs of Cleveland—but their mission was nearly impossible. Then came the Israeli seizure of an Iranian-origin ship loaded with arms for Palestinian fighters. The failed voyage of the *Karine-A* was a damning indictment of Arafat, and effectively buried the chances that Zinni and Miller would get anywhere.

Trips to the region by Cheney and Powell followed in March and April, respectively. They offered a graphic illustration of the administration's parallel policy universes. Cheney's purpose was largely to test the waters on Iraq. He came away convinced that there was enough regional support for decisive action against Saddam, and that there was no point in investing much in the Palestinian issue in the meantime. Powell's purpose, by contrast, was to create some sense of possibility on the Israeli-Palestinian front, calm the situation on the ground as well as regional anger, and harness the energies of other international players before they set off on their own high-profile peace initiatives.

Powell's conversations in Arab capitals, and with Sharon and Arafat in particular, were a slog. As he put it to me late one evening over the rum and Cokes that he occasionally enjoyed, "This is the closest thing to a diplomatic root canal I've ever experienced." Saudi crown prince Abdullah had helped produce a promising initiative at the Arab League summit in Beirut at the end of March, which offered a vision of peace and normalization with the wider Arab world if Israel and the Palestinians reached a two-state solution. A terrorist attack in Netanya the week before the Beirut summit, in which thirty Israeli civilians were murdered at a Passover dinner, cast a huge cloud over Powell's efforts. Nevertheless, he managed to get the key players to agree to the possibility of a regional conference to discuss ways of ending the violence and getting back to a political process. We had kept the White House carefully informed about this effort during the trip, which only amplified Powell's ire when he was overruled, and informed in a series of calls with Washington late one night in Jerusalem at the end of his trip that he could not announce this publicly the next day, as we had planned. In the minds of many in the administration, the time to launch such an effort would be after the presumed transformative impact of Saddam's fall, not before.

I had rarely seen Powell so angry. I was sitting with him in his hotel suite, long past midnight, as he finished a White House call. He slammed the phone down, his jaw clenched and eyes flashing, and said, "Goddamn it. They never stop undercutting me. Don't they understand that we're just trying to prevent a bad situation from getting worse?" At his last stop in Cairo the next day, he asked me to stay in the region and keep trying to dampen tensions. "I've burned up my heat shield," he said. "Do the best you can."

I kept at it for most of the rest of April, with each depressing meeting or event flowing seamlessly into the next. After a string of bloody terrorist attacks, the mood in Israel was edgy. Israel had begun Operation Defensive Shield in late March, after the Netanya massacre, and was reasserting direct Israeli security control in areas ceded to the Palestinians under the Oslo Accords. Arafat himself was under a form of house arrest, bottled up in the presidential compound in Ramallah.

Prime Minister Sharon was invariably courteous in our discussions, but immovable. He had little appetite for what he often saw to be American naïveté, and operated on the conviction that the best diplomacy came when your adversary was pinned firmly to the floor. (He would always greet me by saying, "You're mostly welcome"—which my U.S. embassy colleagues would ascribe to his imperfect English, but that I always suspected reflected his ambivalence about my arrival.) Much as he used an intricate network of chutes to corral and direct the cattle at his beloved ranch in the Negev, Sharon was a master at keeping people focused on security and away from longer-term political issues. Arafat made it easy for him.

The Palestinian leader seemed strangely at home under siege in Ramallah—secure in his victimhood and eerily self-assured about his ability to wriggle out of yet another predicament. The scene around his sandbagged office building in the small presidential compound, the Muqatta, was stark, with vehicles in the surrounding area turned into rusting metal pancakes by Israeli tanks, and Israel Defense Forces snipers visible in the windows of nearby structures. Inside, corridors were lit by candles, black-clad security guards grasped their weapons, and twenty-something volunteer "human shields" from Europe and America crowded the hallway, a few surreptitiously handing me notes asking for help to return home. "Please call my mother and tell her I'm ok," one read, with a name and number neatly printed below. Arafat would sit beaming when you entered his makeshift meeting room, his machine pistol prominently displayed on the table in front of him for all—especially the cameras—to see. His aides and bodyguards would smile nervously, not quite as relaxed as Arafat about where all this was headed.

Salam Fayyad, the immensely decent Palestinian minister of finance, was trapped in the Muqatta for days at a time. He later told me a story that captured perfectly Arafat's hyperpersonalized approach to governing the Palestinian Authority. There was only one functioning air conditioner in the presidential office building in those months, in a room in which Arafat and several other senior PA officials worked and slept. Ever the micromanager, the Palestinian president would turn the air conditioner off at night, despite the heat and increasingly gamey smell of too many men with too little opportunity to wash. He slept while clutching the AC's remote control, one of the few remaining totems of his authority. One night, egged on by his colleagues, Fayyad pried the remote out of the sleeping grip of Arafat and turned the air-conditioning back on. With tongue in cheek, he concluded the story by drawing a larger lesson: "You really can devolve power if you assert yourself."

As Arafat and Sharon continued their zero-sum contest, the costs for people on both sides continued to rise. From the Dolphinarium Club in Tel Aviv to the Park Hotel in Netanya to the terrible bus bombing in Hadera, Palestinian suicide attacks took an awful human toll. The human tragedy on the other side was equally painful to watch. During that late April trip, I went with United Nations Relief and Works Agency for Palestine Refugees (UNRWA) officials to visit the Palestinian refugee camp in Jenin. It was one of the grimmest scenes I ever witnessed.

Ambushed by Palestinian extremists in the narrow alleyways of the camp, IDF units had laid waste to most of it, leaving 40 percent of the camp, an area roughly the size of five football fields, flattened into rubble. The IDF had withdrawn the day before, and the stench of decomposing bodies was overpowering. Survivors were digging with shovels, picks, and their bare hands, looking for bodies of relatives. The vacant expressions on the faces of the camp's children went straight through me. There was unexploded ordnance all around, and during our visit a local Palestinian physician trying to tend to the wounded was badly injured by an accidental detonation. The UNRWA medical clinic, the only such facility in the camp, was vandalized. The refrigerator containing vaccines was shot up, spoiling the medicine inside. Miraculously, a fifteen-year-old Palestinian boy was pulled alive from the rubble that afternoon, after being trapped for nearly two days.

It was the images of Palestinian suffering that animated Saudi crown prince Abdullah when he visited President Bush at his ranch in Crawford, Texas, on April 25. The crown prince showed Bush a binder of photos of Palestinian victims, and at one point threatened to leave Crawford early if the United States wasn't prepared to act more vigorously. Taken aback by Abdullah's vehemence, the president made clear that we'd weigh in with the Israelis to prevent them from expelling or killing Arafat, and would look for ways to make our broader concerns clear. Even the staunchest proponents of giving priority to taking down Saddam and "parking" the Palestinian issue began to realize that winning the acquiescence of key Arab partners for action against Iraq would require some semblance of diplomatic commitment on the Israeli-Palestinian front. Two months later, the result was the president's June 24 speech in the Rose Garden.

In American foreign policy, there are two kinds of major speeches: frameworks for action, and substitutes for action. The June 24 address was mostly the latter, an effort to deflect Arab and European pressures for active American diplomacy and buy time for the near-term priority of action against Saddam. Reflecting the untreated schizophrenia in the policy process, it was really two speeches, with only a thin connection between them. In the first part, the president laid out the transformative notion that the path to Palestinian state-hood could only come through the removal of Arafat, serious democratic reform of the Palestinian Authority, and a cessation of violence. The second part laid out, in much more general terms, what might be possible for Palestinians at the end of the rainbow: a Palestinian state living side by side in peace and security with Israel. The clear implication was sequential, putting the onus squarely on the Palestinians to carry out unilateral regime change before there could be any progress toward a two-state solution.

The bureaucratic infighting over the drafting of the speech was ugly. While Condi Rice was a prime proponent of a presidential address, Vice President Cheney and Secretary Rumsfeld opposed the idea, which they saw as both an unnecessary diversion from the Iraq campaign and an undeserved reward for Palestinians. Powell and I made the argument that the second half of the speech had to be strengthened, spelling out in more detail what a state might look like and what responsibilities the Israelis would have along the way, especially regarding the cessation of settlement construction. That, we maintained, would be essential to get a serious hearing from Palestinians who understood the need for reform. The early White House drafts, however, were heavily weighted toward the front end of the speech. I didn't mince words with Powell. "Mr. Secretary," I wrote in a note in early June, "I have to be honest with you: this draft is junk. It contains no real sense of endgame. It vastly overestimates the attractiveness of a 'provisional state' for Palestinians. . . . Its tone is patronizing and preachy. No one—not even you—could sell this in the region."[20]

The Sharon government played an active role in the editing process, emphasizing Palestinian obligations as the precondition for eventual final status negotiations, and resisting anything more than an extremely light touch in sketching the possible contours of the outcome. Dov Weisglass, a senior advisor to Sharon, led a delegation to the White House in mid-June and suggested in one meeting that "the Palestinians are fed up with Arafat and just waiting for the Americans to give a signal that he's finished." I countered that "the one thing Palestinians are more fed up with than Arafat is the occupation. . . . If you want to marginalize and manipulate Arafat, give the Palestinians a real political horizon. The Prime Minister has not given Palestinians a whiff of hope for ending occupation, nor any kind of compelling political plan. If he had done so, we might be having a different conversation."[21] The reaction not only from Weisglass but also from most of the Americans in the room was polite but utterly dismissive.

By about the twentieth draft, we began to make a little headway, but it was a hard and unsatisfying debate. In one memorable conference call to review yet another draft, two of my senior colleagues from the Pentagon and the vice president's office tried to argue that there had to be parity in any reference to cessation of settlement activity in the West Bank, and that we should call on both Israelis and Palestinians to stop construction activity during negotiations. I didn't know whether to laugh or cry. In the end, the two halves of the speech hung uneasily together, with just enough in the latter part to give some slight credibility to the first. The reaction from the Sharon government was effusive. As one noted Israeli columnist wrote the next day, "The Likud Central Committee could not have written a speech like that." Arab reaction was swift and negative. Rice called me to ask what I was hearing from regional leaders, and I tested my capacity for understatement by replying that "it's pretty rough."

While the White House had hoped that the speech would tamp down international clamor for American diplomatic action, it predictably invited the question of how the administration intended to operationalize the president's vision. On June 25, I told Powell that "our most immediate challenge is the absence of a practical roadmap in the speech to end violence, transform Palestinian leadership, and restore hope."[22] In July, the Jordanian, Egyptian, and Saudi foreign ministers came to Washington to make a similar argument. Powell engineered a meeting for them with the president in hopes that they could help reinforce the case we were trying to make. Bush acknowledged the need for follow-up, but remained wary of investing much American capital. His view was that the speech had put the ball squarely in the court of the Palestinians and Arabs, and now they needed to act. Marwan Muasher, the gifted and energetic Jordanian foreign minister, pressed the president gently in this meeting and then during an August visit by King Abdullah to put together a plan to implement the June 24 vision. He pushed for a "roadmap" that would include benchmarks, timelines, mutual obligations, and a monitoring group to measure performance. The president eventually accepted the argument. In the Oval Office with King Abdullah in August, Bush motioned to me and told the king that "Bill can work with Marwan on this." That was the beginning of the Roadmap initiative, which became a classic illustration of how motion can imitate movement in diplomacy.

The Roadmap never suffered for lack of effort at State or among our Quartet partners: the UN, EU, and Russia. Its fatal flaw was lack of commitment and political will—in Jerusalem and Ramallah, as well as in Washington. The White House's priorities were elsewhere, and outside State there was no interest in the exercise. Doug Feith later called it "just a halftime show," occupying the space between the June 24 speech and the invasion of Iraq and "whatever serious diplomacy was going to be after the Iraq action."[23] To those of us in the halftime marching band crisscrossing the region in late 2002 and early 2003, that was not a very edifying image, but Feith certainly captured our irrelevance.

The Roadmap laid out three phases, with parallel Palestinian and Israeli actions in each, aimed ultimately at a two-state solution. We floated early drafts with the Israelis and Palestinians in the fall of 2002. Weisglass objected vehemently to the lack of strict sequencing in the Roadmap, insistent on postponing Israeli steps until the Palestinians had acted decisively on reform and ending violence. The Palestinians pushed for both sides to take steps in parallel. Meanwhile, reform began to gain some momentum, with the Palestinians producing a provisional constitution and Salam Fayyad accomplishing near miracles on budget transparency.

In the spring of 2003, Mahmoud Abbas was appointed prime minister, a first step toward devolving power away from Arafat. Long an advocate of negotiations but generally risk-averse and without any independent political base, Abbas at least offered the possibility of easing Arafat off center stage and opening up diplomatic opportunities with the Israelis. Taking advantage of this step, and the early if short-lived success of the invasion of Iraq, the White House finally assented to public release of the Roadmap at the end of April. The Palestinians grudgingly went along. The Israelis offered highly conditioned acceptance, with fourteen reservations aimed at ensuring strict sequencing within each phase of the Roadmap and the deferral of significant Israeli concessions or responsibilities. It was not an auspicious start, but there was nevertheless finally a small opening, which would require real American diplomatic muscle and willpower to explore, and a readiness to press both sides persistently on some uncomfortable issues. The White House's limited appetite for peacemaking soon became clear, especially as the debacle in Iraq unfolded.

I accompanied Powell on a trip to the region in early May, and returned later in the month with Elliott Abrams, the senior Middle East advisor on the NSC staff. Our main goal was to prepare the way for two summits. The first was hosted by President Mubarak in Sharm el-Sheikh at the beginning of June, and brought together a number of international and regional leaders to highlight a common front against terrorism. The second was hosted by King Abdullah in Aqaba immediately afterward, and included Sharon and Abbas. Its focus was launching the Roadmap process. Both events were long on ceremony and short on practical follow-through, although the president did have an admirably direct conversation with Sharon in Aqaba

about curbing settlement activity and stepping up to Israel's responsibilities under the Roadmap. Bush was equally blunt with Abbas. A
U.S. monitoring mission was set up, but by late summer a tenuous
cease-fire in the West Bank and Gaza collapsed. Abbas resigned
shortly thereafter, disillusioned both by American detachment and
Arafat's refusal to empower him.

Late in the fall, Sharon told Abrams privately that he was considering a unilateral withdrawal from Gaza. It was a step that appealed
to Sharon. Demographically, it removed from Israeli control and responsibility a large Palestinian population. Strategically, it offered a
way for Israel to regain the initiative, keep the Roadmap in the glove
compartment, divest itself of the troublesome Gazans, tighten its
hold on the West Bank, and deflect any pressure for wider territorial
concessions. As Weisglass put it in an interview in 2004, "The disengagement is actually formaldehyde. . . . It is the bottle of formaldehyde within which you place the President's formula so that it will be
preserved for a very lengthy period."[24] Bush announced formal U.S.
support for Gaza disengagement during an April 2004 visit by Sharon, adding public statements essentially endorsing Israel's positions
on Palestinian refugees and on the permanent retention by Israel of
the large settlement blocs along the 1948 Green Line. Both positions
were generally consistent with the parameters that Bill Clinton had
offered the Israelis and Palestinians in 2000, but Bush's reaffirmation
directly to the Israelis, in the absence of any active negotiation, was
notable, unnecessary, and poorly received by the Arabs.

With the already severely stricken Roadmap overdosed on Weisglass's formaldehyde, and the White House content to follow Sharon's
lead on Gaza disengagement, there was little inclination to seize the
last opportunity that arose in the administration's first term—the
sudden death of Yasser Arafat in November, just a few days after President Bush's reelection. I was dispatched as the senior American representative to Arafat's official funeral in Cairo, a gesture of respect

from the White House for Palestinians, if not for the Palestinian leader himself. It was a chaotic scene. At one point, I found myself in a receiving line just behind the leader of Hamas, Khaled Meshal, who looked only marginally more worried about being seen near me than I was about being seen near him.

In hindsight, it's hard to see how we could have gotten much traction on the Israeli-Palestinian issue once the White House had set Saddam's overthrow as its overriding regional objective. Arafat's default position had become inertia, riding the wave of Intifada violence rather than trying to tame it, content to drift in hopes that outside events might once again change his luck. Sharon had no interest in serious territorial compromise, and happily took advantage of Arafat's evasiveness. When a few modest openings emerged, such as Abbas's selection as prime minister in 2003 and then Arafat's death in 2004, the United States was too preoccupied with Iraq and too uninterested in the kind of hands-on role that Bush thought Clinton had fallen into. Purely as a diplomatic device, the Roadmap helped create the appearance of seriousness, preserved some sense of political possibility, and avoided stray international peace initiatives. In the end, however, it reflected a general post–9/11 habit of viewing diplomacy as an afterthought—as the halftime show, not the main event.

* * *

THERE WERE EXCEPTIONS, however, to the general pattern of dismissiveness toward diplomacy. Libya was one of them. Dealing with Qaddafi in this period was complicated, but certainly more heartening than the bitter failure of Iraq and the endless frustrations of dealing with Palestinians and Israelis. Diplomacy worked in Libya with painstaking effort over several administrations, producing a resolution of the Lockerbie terrorist attack, and Libya's abandonment of terrorism and weapons of mass destruction. It worked because we applied American and international leverage methodically to change Qaddafi's calculus and sharpen his self-interest in changing his behavior so he could preserve his regime. And it worked because we had far more running room for diplomacy in the Bush administration on this issue than we did on Iraq or the peace process.

The stage had been set over the previous decade, by the Bush 41 and Clinton administrations. In 1991, the United States and the United Kingdom formally indicted two Libyan intelligence agents in connection with the Lockerbie bombing, and made a set of five demands, which remained consistent over the next dozen years: The Libyans had to surrender the suspects for trial; accept responsibility for the actions of Libyan officials involved in the bombing; disclose all it knew of the bombing and allow full access to witnesses and evidence; pay appropriate compensation; and commit itself to cease all forms of terrorist action and assistance to terrorist groups. Fulfillment of all five demands would result in the lifting of the multilateral sanctions that had been imposed by the UN Security Council after Lockerbie.

When Qaddafi met the first demand and turned over the two suspects for trial in 1999, the Clinton administration opened direct, secret talks with the Libyans, led by Assistant Secretary of State Martin Indyk, in cooperation with the British. Indyk made clear that the lifting of U.S. national sanctions, built up since the Reagan-era conflicts with Qaddafi, would depend upon Libya giving up its nuclear and chemical weapons programs, which U.S. intelligence had been following closely since the 1970s.

When I resumed the secret channel in London in October 2001, I was careful to reiterate the main lines of the positions conveyed earlier by Indyk, including on WMD. Over the course of the next two years, in roughly a dozen meetings in London, Rome, and other locations, we made considerable progress. There were several reasons for this. First, Qaddafi was feeling the pressure of concerted U.S. and international sanctions. The energy sector was starved for investment, and the country's infrastructure was in shambles. Unemployment ran at 30 percent, and inflation at nearly 50 percent. Qaddafi worried about his restive population, and in 1998 had sent troops to Benghazi to put down an Islamist rebellion.

Second, we established a reliable diplomatic channel with serious Libyan counterparts, well connected to Qaddafi. As had been the case in the talks with Indyk, Musa Kusa, one of Qaddafi's closest aides, led the Libyan delegation. Tall, thin, and poker-faced, Kusa had studied sociology at Michigan State in the late 1970s, before returning to Libya and a series of senior intelligence jobs—a line of work far removed from his academic stint in America. Kusa was accompanied by two senior Libyan diplomats, Abdelati Obeidi and Abdel Rahman Shalgham. From that first meeting in the fall of 2001, I found Kusa and his colleagues to be cautious but capable, committed to making progress, if always nervous about hidden agendas from us and the whims of their mercurial boss. We offered him a "script" in that initial discussion, which laid out exactly what we expected from the Libyans, and what we were prepared to do in return. We spent hours and hours in tangled debate over subsequent months, in bilateral sessions as well as trilateral discussions with the British. Slowly we began to reach understandings on language and how to verify commitments—and we also began to build up trust and personal rapport.

Third, we could rely on excellent intelligence coordination with our CIA and MI6 colleagues. We tracked systematically Libya's gradual disengagement from the business of terrorism, from the high-profile expulsion of the notorious Palestinian terrorist Abu Nidal to the lower-key severing of financial and training links to other groups. We also tracked the much less promising evidence of persistent Libyan efforts to expand their chemical and nuclear weapons programs, which featured contacts with former Soviet scientists as well as the A. Q. Khan network in Pakistan. U.S. intelligence helped interdict a shipment of uranium enrichment technology from A. Q. Khan to Tripoli in the fall of 2003. That played a crucial role in persuading Qaddafi to finally give up his WMD programs and realize he could no longer deceive us. Finally, we could rely on the credible threat of force in the event that diplomacy failed, reinforced by the examples of Afghanistan in 2001 and Iraq in 2003.

By the early spring of 2003, Kusa was ready to confirm Libyan acceptance of the terms we had laid out on Lockerbie a decade earlier. Meanwhile, lawyers for the families of the victims were negotiating with the Libyans about compensation. In several wrenching meetings with the families that spring, I briefed them on the progress we had made, and stressed that we would not conclude any settlement until the compensation question was resolved. Those were among the most painful conversations I ever had in government. The dull, antiseptic State Department conference room in which we met only put in sharper relief the anguish of the family members around the table. No form of words, and no amount of compensation, could erase their loss or atone for the murders of so many innocent people, dozens of whom were American college students on their way home for the holidays after a semester abroad. The grief and anger in that room could not be bridged by empathy or rational diplomatic explanation, and I understood that. One furious mother told me to "go to hell with your Libyan friends" in a session that spring, but most of the families were appreciative of what we were trying to do and the limits of what we could produce. I wish we could have done more. In August, the lawyers reached a compensation agreement providing $2.7 billion to the families, $10 million for each of the victims.

Meanwhile, we began to move ahead on the WMD issue. In each of our private conversations over the previous year and a half, I had reminded Kusa that this question would have to be solved before any normalization of relations. He made no effort to deny that Libya had active nuclear and chemical weapons programs, and I made clear that we had solid evidence that it did. Libya would have to take fast, dramatic, concrete steps up front to rid itself of WMD and advanced missile programs, which we would verify before normalization. I always emphasized that there was no ulterior motive in this—we had no interest in regime change, but a powerful interest in Libya making the strategic choice to abandon WMD. We were demonstrating in the Lockerbie negotiations that we would follow through on our end of commitments if the Libyans acted on theirs. This was a moment when Qaddafi, ever the contrarian, could gain in stature by renouncing weapons that would only buy him trouble, especially in the new and more perilous post–9/11 world. Kusa indicated to me that he thought Qaddafi was increasingly drawn to that logic, especially as he learned to trust America's word in the Lockerbie talks. On the margins of our March 11, 2003, meeting in London, after he had finally confirmed acceptance of the Lockerbie terms, he told me quietly that Qaddafi "is ready to move decisively" on the issue of WMD.[25]

That same month, Saif al-Islam, Qaddafi's son and an erstwhile postgraduate student in London, conveyed much the same message to MI6. His father, he said, wanted to "clear the air." Strongly encouraged by Prime Minister Blair, President Bush agreed to send Steve Kappes, a senior CIA officer, to join British intelligence counterparts for follow-on conversations with Saif and Kusa. The WMD interdiction in the Mediterranean in the fall finally convinced Qaddafi that it was time to move. After a last round of talks in December, Qaddafi agreed, and announced on December 19 that he was giving up WMD. It was a significant achievement for Bush and Blair, at a time when the Iraq fiasco was becoming more and more difficult to manage.

I made three trips to Libya in the following year to ensure strict implementation. The Libyans stressed repeatedly their commitment to follow through. Their sensitivities were predictable, and focused mainly on the need to be careful to characterize our WMD efforts in Libya as "assistance" rather than "inspection," and the importance of showing the Libyan public concrete benefits of Qaddafi's decision to get out of the terrorism and WMD business.[26]

For all of our progress, we continued to have plenty of difficulties with the Libyan leader—we caught him plotting against Crown Prince Abdullah of Saudi Arabia in the fall of 2003; he detained a group of Bulgarian medical personnel on trumped-up charges in

2004; and his human rights practices continued to attract, rightly and regularly, our criticism. But his abandonment of terrorism and WMD was a substantial accomplishment, and a reminder of the value of diplomacy.

There was a lively debate within the Bush administration about why Qaddafi had acted, with Vice President Cheney and other hawks drawing a direct connection to Iraq and the demonstration effect of Saddam's removal. I always thought that was part of the answer, but only part, and not necessarily the decisive part. Afghanistan was evidence enough of our determination and capabilities after 9/11. Moreover, the track record we built up with the Libyans, on the foundation of what the previous administration had pursued, underscored that we were focused on changing behavior, not the Qaddafi regime, and that however difficult the choices and the pathway for the Libyans, our word could be trusted. Sanctions had taken a long-term toll. Qaddafi's political isolation in the international community was tightly sealed. He needed a way out, and we gave him a tough but defensible one. That's ultimately what diplomacy is all about—not perfect solutions, but outcomes that cost far less than war and leave everyone better off than they would otherwise have been.

* * *

BY THE END of the first term of Bush 43, and four years in NEA, I was exhausted. I had been proud to serve under Powell and Armitage and proud of the dedication, skill, and courage of my colleagues in the Near Eastern Affairs bureau. I was also deeply worried about the mess we had made in the Middle East, and disappointed in my own failure to do more to avoid it.

In January 2005, Condi Rice succeeded Powell as secretary. In the note I sent to her before our two-hour transition conversation, I wrote, "The Near East is a region dangerously adrift. . . . Across the Arab world a sense of humiliation and weakness is becoming more and more corrosive. Most regimes are perceived by their people to be corrupt and self-absorbed." Blunt about the depths to which America's standing in the region had fallen, with more than four out of every five Arabs expressing strong disapproval of the United States, I warned of further strategic setbacks in the second Bush term unless we shifted our approach. There could be "terminal chaos and warlordism in Iraq, the death of the two state solution for Israelis and Palestinians, the birth of a nuclear-armed, hegemonic Iran, and mounting popular pressures against Arab governments . . . unless we make common cause with regional partners in a coherent strategy for constructive change. . . . We have to be seen as part of the solution, not as part of the problem. That is not the case today."[27]

Arafat's death in November and the election of Mahmoud Abbas as the new Palestinian president in January 2005 offered an opening to reorient our approach. So did the tragic assassination of Lebanese prime minister Rafik Hariri in February, orchestrated by the overreaching Syrians, who now faced a huge popular backlash in Lebanon. We managed to take advantage of the moment to build international pressure and push Syrian forces out of Lebanon, for the first time since the Lebanese civil war began in the mid-1970s. The wreckage of the administration's first-term efforts, however, overwhelmed. The policy sins of commission were glaringly apparent, the sins of omission harder to measure but no less significant.

The Iraq invasion was the original sin. It was born of hubris, as well as failures of imagination and process. For neoconservative proponents, it was the key tool in the disruption of the Middle East—the heady, irresponsible, and historically unmoored notion that shaking things up violently would produce better outcomes. In a region where unintended consequences were rarely uplifting, the toppling of Saddam set off a chain reaction of troubles. It laid bare the fragilities and dysfunctions of Iraq as well as the wider Arab state system—proving that Americans could be just as arrogant and haphazard in their impact on Middle East maps as the original British and French mapmakers.

The chaos that spread across Iraq after 2003 created opportunities for Iranian mischief and influence, and helped reawaken broader competition between Sunni and Shia for supremacy in the Middle East. By 2004, King Abdullah in Jordan was already talking about fears of a "Shia crescent," arcing from Iran across Iraq and sympathetic Alawite allies in Syria to Lebanon. Afflicted by sectarian violence and Sunni Arab alienation, Iraq became a magnet for jihadists and regional terrorism. While we made halting attempts to promote greater political and economic openness throughout the Middle East, the debacle in Iraq, including the miserable images from Abu Ghraib, poisoned America's image and credibility. If this was how Americans promoted democracy, few Arabs wanted any part of it.

Poverty of imagination was another problem. Although we had tried in NEA to emphasize—repeatedly—all the things that could go wrong, all the reasons to avoid an ill-conceived war, and all the plausible alternative policy paths, none of us asked enough basic questions. None of us thought seriously enough about the possibility that Saddam had no WMD anymore and was obfuscating not to conceal his stockpiles but rather to hide their absence in the face of domestic and regional predators.

There was also a failure of process. Military interventions, especially in the dysfunctional circumstances of the modern Middle East, are always fraught with peril. Our capacity for underestimating that has become habitual. The polarization of views in the administration in the run-up to war in 2003 was stark and crippling, and never really resolved. Sometimes that was simply a function of wishful thinking, such as the neocon fantasy that Iraqis would quickly rise above a history devoid of consensual national governance and replete with sectarian rivalries, or the Rumsfeld notion that we could do regime change on the cheap. Prewar planning was erratic and stovepiped, with too little attention to the most fundamental questions about consequences and how best to anticipate and manage them. Immediate postwar policy suffered badly from seat-of-the-pants judgments, such as the momentous CPA decisions to disband the Iraqi army and cut its members loose financially, and to put Ahmed Chalabi in charge of a recklessly sweeping implementation of the ban on Baath Party members.

There was a continuous fixation on policy capillaries—hours and hours of discussion in the White House Situation Room about the ins and outs of restoring electricity across Iraq, or reconstruction of local health or education systems—without enough focus on the arterial issues of security and national governance, of how to keep the Kurds in, the Sunni Arabs engaged, and the Shia tempered in their new-found political advantage. There was all too often a massive discon-nect between bold pronouncements in the cloistered Situation Room and the messy challenge of connecting them to the realities of the Middle East.

And then there were the more elusive sins of omission. Some were deeply personal. Having tried to highlight all the things that could go wrong, all the unanswered strategic and practical questions, and all the flaws in going it alone, why didn't I go to the mat in my opposi-tion or quit? These are hard decisions, filled with professional, moral, and family considerations. I still find my own answer garbled and unsatisfying, even with the benefit of a decade and a half of hindsight. Part of it was about loyalty to my friends and colleagues, and to Sec-retary Powell; part of it was the discipline of the Foreign Service, and the conceit that we could still help avoid even worse policy blunders from within the system than from outside it; part of it was selfish and career-centric, the unease about forgoing a profession I genuinely loved and in which I had invested twenty years; and part of it, I sup-pose, was the nagging sense that Saddam was a tyrant who deserved to go, and maybe we could navigate his demise more adeptly than I feared.

In the end, I stayed, and my efforts to limit the damage had little effect. I wasn't alone in my uncertainty in those years. "There's honor in continuing to serve," said one longtime colleague, "so long as you're honest about your dissent. But you never entirely escape the feeling that you're also an enabler."

The wider sins of omission are really about opportunity costs, about the road not taken. How might things have been different for America's role in the world and for the Middle East if we had not invaded Iraq in the spring of 2003? What if we had tried to harness the massive outpouring of international goodwill and shared concern after the terrible attacks of September 11 in a different—more constructive—direction?

The eighteen months between 9/11 and the invasion of Iraq were one of those hinge points in history, whose contours are easier to see today than they were at that uncertain and emotional time. If we had avoided the debacle in Iraq, and instead projected American power and purpose more wisely, it seems obvious today that American interests and values would have been better served. That would have required a real attempt at coercive diplomacy in Iraq—not the one we employed, which was long on coercion and short on diplomacy. That would also have required patience in our diplomacy and a readiness to share in its design and execution. Instead, we opted for the more immediate satisfactions of unilateral impulses and blunt force, and kept the sharing part to a minimum. It was beyond our power and imagination to remake the Middle East, with or without the overthrow of Saddam, but we could certainly make an already disordered region worse and further erode our leadership and influence. And we did.

6

Putin's Disruptions: Managing Great Power Trainwrecks

VLADIMIR PUTIN HAS never been at a loss for tactical surprises, and he didn't disappoint this time. Sitting in a hotel near Red Square, we waited for the Kremlin to summon us. Well acquainted with Putin's penchant for one-upmanship, Secretary of State Condi Rice was relaxed and a little bemused as the first hour of delay stretched into a second. Her staff circled nervously, staring at their watches. The secretary was a pro, watching a Russian sports channel on television as she waited for Putin's inevitable trick play. It finally came as we approached the third hour. We got the call, but Putin was no longer at the Kremlin. We'd have to travel forty minutes to his compound at Barvikha, on the outskirts of the city. Diplomatic Security didn't like these kinds of surprises, but they had no choice. Rice shrugged. "Shall we?"

When we arrived, a presidential assistant escorted us to a lavishly appointed dining room. Arrayed around the long rectangular table, with Putin at its center, was nearly the entirety of Russia's Security Council. With a sardonic half-smile, Putin said he thought Rice, as a student of Russian history, would appreciate the setting. This was the modern Politburo, the court of the new Russian tsar. The point was as subtle as Putin himself: Russia was back.

Putin greeted the secretary and explained that the occasion for the celebration was the birthdays of Igor Ivanov, the sixty-one-year-old Security Council secretary and former foreign minister, and Dmitry Medvedev, the forty-one-year-old first deputy prime minister. It was a jovial meal, punctuated by frequent vodka toasts and liberal resort to Ivanov's supply of special reserve Georgian wine. Russia had recently embargoed a variety of Georgian products, but Ivanov, whose mother still lived in Tbilisi, evidently had a dispensation from the tsar.

Sitting across from Putin, Rice held her own. Putin played the instigator, poking and prodding about the war in Iraq, the prisoners in Guantanamo, and other unpleasant topics. Sergey Ivanov, the urbane defense minister, piled on at one point with a few acerbic comments about Ukraine, where the afterglow of the Orange Revolution in 2004 was quickly fading. "How's your beacon of democracy looking now?" he asked.

After dinner, Putin invited Secretary Rice to a separate sitting room. Foreign Minister Sergey Lavrov and I joined them in front of a roaring fire. Putin and Rice got straight to business. Rice raised a couple of concerns about the ongoing negotiations over Russia's entry into the World Trade Organization. Putin showed off his mastery of the dreary details of poultry imports and food safety standards, but seemed bored by it all. His mood changed abruptly when the secretary raised Georgia, cautioning the Russians to avoid escalation of frictions with President Mikheil Saakashvili over the breakaway republics of Abkhazia and South Ossetia. Standing up in front of the fireplace, Putin wagged his index finger and grew testy. "If Saakashvili uses force in South Ossetia, which we are convinced he is preparing to do, that would be a grave mistake, and the Georgian people would suffer the most. If he wants war, he will get it."

Rice stood at this point too, giving no ground to Putin and looming several inches taller than him in her heels. She repeated the risks for U.S.-Russian relations if there was conflict in Georgia. Having to look up at Rice hardly improved Putin's attitude. "Saakashvili is nothing more than a puppet of the United States," he said. "You need to pull back the strings before there's trouble." Gesturing toward the dining room next door, he added, "I'm going to tell you something that no one in there knows yet. If Georgia causes bloodshed in Ossetia, I will have no alternative to recognizing South Ossetia and Abkhazia, and responding with force." The conversation gradually deescalated, and Putin and Rice sat back down. Putin was exasperated, but concluded calmly, "We could talk for ages about this, but that's the point I want you to understand. If Saakashvili starts something, we will finish it."[1]

Having made his point, Putin excused himself to say good night to the birthday celebrants. He passed the baton to Sergey Ivanov, who reinforced Putin's message on Georgia. It hardly needed reinforcing. Putin's pugnacity left an impression. This was not the Russia I had left a decade earlier, flat on its back and in strategic retreat. Surfing on historically high oil prices and nursing fifteen years of grievances, convinced that the United States had taken advantage of Russia's moment of historical weakness and was bent on keeping it down, Putin was determined to show that he was making Russia great again and we better get used to it.

* * *

SERVING AS U.S. ambassador in Moscow was my dream job. Russia can be a hard place, especially for American diplomats, but the relationship between Russia and the United States mattered as few others did. Still struggling with its post-Soviet identity crisis, and a considerably less potent player on the international stage than the Soviet Union had been, Russia remained a force to be reckoned with. Its nuclear capacity was formidable. Its hydrocarbons were a significant factor in the global economy. Its geographic sprawl and history gave it influence across a range of international issues. Its diplomatic skill and permanent membership on the UN Security Council meant that it would have a say.

Having lived through Russia's complicated post-Soviet transition, I was fascinated by the great historical canvas on which Russians were now trying to paint their future. Often as preoccupied with their sense of exceptionalism as Americans were, they sought a distinctive political and economic system, which would safeguard the individual freedoms and economic possibilities denied them under Communism, and ensure them a place among the handful of world powers. I liked Russians, respected their culture, enjoyed their language, and was endlessly fascinated by the tangled history of U.S.-Russian diplomacy.

Following in the footsteps of Kennan and Bohlen, and the remarkable ambassadors who succeeded them, was a daunting challenge. It almost didn't happen. Late in my tenure as assistant secretary for near eastern affairs, Colin Powell had asked what I hoped to do next. I told him that I'd love to go back to Moscow, and he said he'd do everything he could to make that happen. He and Rich Armitage recommended me to the White House as the career Foreign Service candidate. There was precedent for noncareer appointees to Moscow, but they were the exception, and there didn't appear to be any such contenders as the transition to President Bush's second term unfolded in the winter of 2004–5. Nevertheless, several months passed without any decision, and I began to wonder about my chances, especially given all the reservations that my colleagues and I had expressed in the lead-up to the Iraq War.

In January, shortly after succeeding Powell as secretary of state, Rice approached me about serving as ambassador to Israel instead, making a strong case that she intended to make a priority of the Arab-Israeli peace process during her tenure. I was intrigued, but burned out on Middle East issues after four long years in NEA, and not enthusiastic about relitigating many of the same policy disagreements with many of the same personalities. I decided to push hard for Moscow, and Rice agreed to back Powell's recommendation. Eventually, the White House approved my nomination in the spring of 2005. I was confirmed by the Senate in July, and Lisa and the girls and I arrived in Moscow in early August.

Spaso House, named after the quiet little square on which it sits in central Moscow, was the immense neoclassical residence of the American ambassador and our new home. We often reminded our daughters not to get too used to its proportions or grandeur. The house we owned in Washington could easily fit into Spaso's Great Hall. The massive chandelier hanging from the two-story-high ceiling, with its dozens of crystals weighing twenty-five pounds apiece, left us in chronic fear that a guest would be impaled and U.S.-Russian relations imperiled. Beyond the Great Hall was the State Dining Room, with a table that seemed as long as a bowling lane, and, past that, a huge ballroom. A long gallery ran around the second floor of the house overlooking the Great Hall, with a series of bedrooms with twenty-foot ceilings, and a small family kitchen and dining room. In the basement, there was a much bigger kitchen and a labyrinth of storerooms, staff quarters, and mysterious passageways.

I never tired of legendary Spaso stories. One party in 1935, on the eve of the great purge trials, attracted most of the Soviet leadership save for Stalin. Few of the senior officials on the guest list that evening survived. Featuring a variety of acts from the Moscow circus, the party became the model for the famous ball scene in Mikhail Bulgakov's *The Master and Margarita*. The best act was accidental—when a trainer put a rubber nipple on a champagne bottle and fed a baby bear liberally, with predictably chaotic consequences. In the early 1950s, Kennan amused himself during his brief and lonely tenure as ambassador by reading Russian poetry aloud late at night in the darkened Great Hall. He assumed that his habit would only confuse his Soviet minders, who were of course recording virtually everything that was said in Spaso. Little had changed on the surveillance front by the time we arrived, and Lisa and I always assumed that the only way to have a private conversation in Spaso was to either go for a walk in the garden or turn on the radio to mask our voices.

We had a busy residence during those three years, welcoming tens of thousands of guests. Foreign Minister Sergey Lavrov and other cabinet officers came to private lunches. We hosted three thousand Russians for the Fourth of July. During the two hundredth anniversary of U.S.-Russian diplomatic relations in 2007, we held a series of events, including jazz concerts, films, lectures, and even a fashion show with Ralph Lauren. We celebrated space cooperation with astronauts and cosmonauts. I especially enjoyed sports diplomacy—bringing the NBA's Los Angeles Clippers, the Davis Cup tennis team, and the U.S. men's junior hockey team to Spaso and Russia. We even hosted Lizzy's senior prom, which conveniently allowed me—and my security detail—to keep her date within our sights for the duration of the evening. Lisa and I worked hard to include people from across generations and Russian society, from prominent Kremlin officials to political oppositionists and human rights activists. Barely a day went by without some event or reception. Spaso House was a huge asset, and we put it to full use.

The embassy itself was now operating out of the new chancery building, which had stood empty and forlorn during our previous tour, and whose top floors were now secure enough for classified work. The staff was still one of the largest in the world, with nearly 1,800 employees, including about 450 Americans, divided across Moscow and our consulates in St. Petersburg, Yekaterinburg, and Vladivostok.

With an exceptional team behind me and a fair amount of leeway from Washington, I threw myself into my new role. Real progress would be hard to come by. The Russia policy knot mostly just seemed to get tighter, with Washington increasingly preoccupied with troubles in the Middle East, and Moscow consumed by its grievances and captivated by its newfound ability to do something about them.

* * *

WHEN I LEFT Moscow after my first tour in 1996, I was worried
about the resurgence of a Russia at once cocky, cranky, aggrieved, and
insecure. I had no idea it would happen so quickly, or that Vladimir
Putin would emerge over the next decade as the extreme embodiment
of that peculiarly Russian combination of qualities.

Neither process moved in a straight line. Boris Yeltsin had stumbled repeatedly in his second term, lurching from a desperate financial crisis in 1998 to another war in Chechnya and diplomatic
embarrassment in Kosovo. Late in his term, with his health failing,
and anxious to protect his family and legacy, he anointed his successor, a man who had in the span of a few years vaulted from gray ano-
nymity in the St. Petersburg mayor's office to a senior position in the
Kremlin, leadership of the FSB, and finally the prime ministry. Putin
had an unremarkable career in the KGB, but a string of St. Petersburg
patrons helped him up the ladder, and he eventually earned Yeltsin's
trust. He seemed in many ways the anti-Yeltsin—half a generation
younger, sober, ruthlessly competent, hardworking, and hard-faced,
he offered promise for Russians tired of Yeltsin-era chaos and disorder.

Putin's most striking characteristic was his passion for control—
founded on an abiding distrust of most of those around him, whether
in the Russian elite or among foreign leaders. Some of that had to do
with his professional training; some had to do with his tough upbringing in postwar Leningrad. The only surviving child of parents
scarred by the brutalities of World War II—his father badly wounded
in the defense of Leningrad, his mother nearly dying of starvation
during the siege—Putin shaped his worldview in urban schoolyards,
where, as he put it, "the weak get beat." He learned to fend for himself,
mastering judo and its techniques for gaining leverage against stronger opponents. However indifferent his record had been in university
and the KGB, he didn't lack self-confidence. Nor did he doubt his

capacity for reading his opponents and exploiting their vulnerabilities. He could charm as well as bully, and he was always coldly calculating.

The Russia that he inherited was full of troubles. In addition to the apparent political challenges that came with a crumbling state, the economy had descended into turmoil. After the August 1998 economic crisis, in which the stock market crashed, the government defaulted, and the ruble collapsed, unemployment and inflation soared, GDP contracted by nearly 5 percent, and oil production dropped to half its Soviet-era high. A rapid rise in hydrocarbon prices and aggressive economic reforms helped turn the Russian economy around during Putin's first term as president. By the summer of 2005, early in his second term, Russia's annual growth rate was averaging 7 percent, and unemployment had dropped by nearly half. Economic progress fueled Putin's popularity and gave him space to impose his brand of political order. He tamed the oligarchs by brokering an implicit deal—if they stayed out of his business, he'd stay out of theirs. If they waded into politics, he'd wade into their pockets. He made a brutal object lesson of the billionaire Mikhail Khodorkovsky in 2003, seizing his oil and gas company, Yukos, and sending him to prison. Others, like Boris Berezovsky, his former patron, were hounded into exile.

Putin's obsession with order and control, and restoring the power of the Russian state, was abundantly clear and widely popular. His formula was straightforward: Revive the state and its authority over politics, media, and civil society; regain control over Russia's natural resources to fuel economic growth; and reverse nearly two decades of strategic retreat, rebuild Russian prerogatives as a great power, and reassert Russia's entitlement to a sphere of influence in its own neighborhood. As I put it in a cable to Secretary Rice early in my tenure, "Uncomfortable personally with political competition and openness, [Putin] has never been a democratizer."[2]

Putin's view of relations with the United States was infused with suspicion, but early on he tested with President Bush a form of partnership suited to his view of Russia's interests. He was the first foreign leader to call Bush after 9/11, and saw an opening through which Russia could become a partner in the Global War on Terrorism. He thought the war on terror would give Russia a better frame in which to operate than the "new world order" that had dominated U.S. policy since the end of the Cold War. The implicit terms of the deal Putin sought included a common front against terrorism, with Russia backing the United States against al-Qaeda and the Taliban in Afghanistan, and Washington backing Moscow's tough tactics against Chechen rebels. Moreover, the United States would grant Russia special influence in the former Soviet Union, with no encroachment by NATO beyond the Baltics, and no interference in Russia's domestic politics. Putin quickly set out to show that he could deliver on his end of the presumed bargain. In the face of considerable misgivings from his own military and security services, he facilitated U.S. military access and transit to Afghanistan through the Central Asian states.

As Putin quickly learned, however, this kind of transaction was never in the cards. He fundamentally misread American interests and politics. From Washington's view, there was no desire—and no reason—to trade anything for Russian partnership against al-Qaeda. We didn't have to purchase Russian acquiescence in something that was so much in its own interest, and we certainly didn't need to discard long-standing bipartisan priorities and partnerships in Europe to buy Putin's favor. He also misread American behavior, tending to see contrary American actions as part of some careful, duplicitous conspiracy to undermine him, not as the product of an administration that was desperately consumed with its response to 9/11, indifferent to Putin's calculus, and generally disinclined to concede or pay much attention to a power in strategic decline.

Putin gave us more credit than we deserved for careful plotting against Russian interests. For Putin, the September 2004 Beslan school siege was a turning point. The whole world saw live the massacre of more than three hundred teachers, staff, and students. Putin saw Bush's response, which included warnings against overreaction and a dalliance with "moderate" Chechen elements to try to defuse tensions, as nothing short of a betrayal. The Orange Revolution in Ukraine that same year, and the Rose Revolution in Georgia before that, led Putin to conclude that the Americans were not only undercutting Russia's interest in its sphere of influence, but might eventually aim the same kind of color revolution at his regime. These disappointments were piled on top of his anger over the Iraq War, a symbol of America's predilection for unilateral action in a unipolar world, and President Bush's second inaugural address and its "freedom agenda"—which Putin believed included Russia near the top of the administration's "to-do" list. Democracy promotion, in his eyes, was a Trojan horse designed to further American geopolitical interests at Russia's expense, and ultimately to erode his grip on power in Russia itself.

By the summer of 2005, mutual disillusionment weighed heavily on attitudes in Moscow and Washington. The Bush administration saw a Russia uninterested in democratic values, unlikely to evolve anytime soon into a deferential member of an American-led international club or become a reliable junior partner in fighting terrorism. Putin had already begun to tilt in a more adversarial direction, increasingly persuaded that an American-led international order was constraining Russia's legitimate interests, and that chipping away at that order was the key to preserving and enlarging space for Russian influence. He also believed that he had a reasonably strong hand to play, with unprecedented domestic approval and support. "Outside Russia's borders," I argued in a cable, "Putin sees considerable room for maneuver in a world of multiple power centers, with the U.S. bogged down with difficulties, China and India on the rise in ways which pose no immediate threat to Russia, and the EU consumed with internal concerns. After years of being the potted plant of Great Power diplomacy, Putin, and many in the Russian elite, find it very satisfying to play a distinctive and assertive role."[3]

The diplomatic challenge was foreboding, and the stakes enormous. From the outset of my tenure as ambassador, I urged realism about the unlikely prospects for broad partnership with Putin's Russia, and pragmatism in our strategy. Realism demanded that we come to terms with the fact that relations were going to be uneasy, at best, for some time to come. We should shed the illusions that had lingered since the end of the Cold War, recognize that we were bound to have significant differences with a resurgent Russia, and seek a durable mix of competition and cooperation in our relationship. Pragmatism required that we draw clear lines around our vital interests, pick our fights on other issues carefully, manage inevitable problems with a cool head, and not lose sight of those issues on which we could still find common ground.

Putin understood as well as anyone that Russia had more than its share of vulnerabilities and blind spots, from demographic decline, to worsening corruption, to seething troubles in the North Caucasus. He was not inclined, however, to use Russia's moment of oil-driven prosperity to diversify and innovate, and unleash Russia's human capital. The risk to political order and control was too great. I was pessimistic that his outlook would change. As I wrote in an early cable to Washington:

> Over the next few years, at least, it's hard to see any fundamental rethinking of priorities on the part of Putin or his likely successors. . . . Some might argue that this suggests a "paradigm lost," a sense that a partnership that once was firmly rooted is now gone. The truth is that the roots for a genuine strategic partnership have always been pretty shallow—whether in the era of euphoric expectations after the end of the Cold War, or in the immediate aftermath of September 11. Russia is too big, too proud, and too self-conscious of its own history to fit neatly into "a Europe whole and free." Neither we nor the Europeans have ever really viewed Russia as "one of us"—and when Rus-

sians talk about "nashi" ("ours") these days, they're not talking about a grand Euro-Atlantic community.

So where does that leave us? Basically, we're facing a Russia that's too big a player on too many important issues to ignore. It's a Russia whose backsliding on political modernization is likely to get worse before it gets better, and whose leadership is neither overly concerned about its image nor much inclined to explain itself to the outside world. It's a Russia whose assertiveness in its neighborhood and interest in playing a distinctive Great Power role beyond it will sometimes cause significant problems.[4]

Pessimistic analysis, of course, did not constitute a strategy. My argument was that if the strategic partnership that had fitfully and loosely framed aspirations in Washington and Moscow for much of the 1990s was out of reach, it was worth testing whether a partnership on a few key strategic issues was possible. That might put the relationship on a steadier track, with limited cooperation balancing inevitable differences.

* * *

I REALIZED THAT stabilizing the relationship, after all the ups and downs of the previous decade and a half, would be a long shot. In our last conversation before I left for Moscow, Secretary Rice made clear that she shared my skepticism, although she encouraged the effort. A student of Russia, Rice was hard-nosed about Putin's repressive behavior at home and his determination to expand Russian influence in its neighborhood, but sympathetic to the notion that we ought to be able to work more effectively together on certain issues. She highlighted in particular nuclear cooperation, where Russia and the United States shared unique capabilities and unique responsibilities. We had a common interest in promoting the security of nuclear materials in our two countries and around the world. We had a similar interest in nonproliferation, especially the challenges posed by Iran and North Korea. And we had a stake in the stable management and further reduction of our existing arsenals.

We also discussed our shared interest in creating more economic ballast in our relationship. U.S. investment in Russia was minuscule, and bilateral trade insignificant, but possibilities were growing in sectors like energy and aerospace. Moreover, Putin had revived Russia's campaign to join the World Trade Organization. That would require a bilateral agreement with the United States, and the lifting of the Jackson-Vanik Amendment of 1974, which had denied the Soviet Union a normal trading relationship because of its restriction of Soviet Jewish emigration. That purpose had long since been achieved, but congressional reservations about other aspects of Russian behavior remained, and there were also continuing concerns about Russian barriers against agricultural products and piracy of intellectual property. Rice agreed that it made sense to make another push, as part of a long-term investment in a more open and competitive Russian economy. WTO accession would help reinforce the rule of law, and create a model of progress in the economic system that might someday spill over into the political system. The expansion of trade and investment would give both countries something positive to safeguard in the relationship, and more to lose if differences got out of hand.

I highlighted a third priority, encouraging the gradual increase of exchange programs, mainly aimed at bringing young Russian students and entrepreneurs to the United States and developing the network of some sixty thousand exchange alumni around Russia. With a mostly bleak outlook for any rapid improvement of relations, it made sense to continue to invest in the next generation of Russians and in their deepening stake in individual freedoms and interaction with the rest of the world.

I knew that each of these initiatives could easily be swallowed up by mounting friction over Ukraine and Georgia, as well as the Kremlin's tightening political squeeze at home. The next couple of years would be critical. Putin was term-limited, and at least according to the Russian constitution would step down as president in 2008. The Russian elite's obsession with succession would mount as that date grew closer, and it would be important to do all we could to anchor our relationship well before then.

In my first few months in Moscow, I was persistent in engaging senior Russians. One of the most important challenges for any ambassador is to develop wide-ranging contacts, to gain as solid a grasp as possible of the views of different players and their interactions. Russia in those years was particularly difficult terrain, with many senior officials suspicious of American diplomats, and oppositionists under intense scrutiny and pressure.

After I presented my credentials in an elaborate ceremony at the Kremlin, Putin took me aside and stressed his personal respect for President Bush, along with his disappointment in American policy. "You Americans need to listen more," he said. "You can't have everything your way anymore. We can have effective relations, but not just on your terms."

Sergey Ivanov, the minister of defense, was a longtime friend and former KGB colleague of Putin. A fluent English speaker, able to charm or bludgeon as circumstances required, Ivanov had aspirations to succeed Putin. Not shy about projecting strength, he had limited popular appeal, and not much of a political base beyond his personal bond with Putin. His steely personality and ambition unsettled others in Putin's orbit, and the fact that he had been a far more accomplished KGB officer than his friend may have unsettled Putin a little too. Alone in his office at the Defense Ministry, Ivanov was matter-of-fact about relations with the United States in our first meeting, sharply critical of American naïveté and hubris in underestimating the complexities of Iraq, as well as of Russia's neighbors. He said forthrightly that it was important to have stable relations between Russia and the United States, but a few "course corrections" were necessary.

Dmitry Medvedev, then the chief of presidential administration at the Kremlin, was another friend of Putin's with ambitions to succeed him. Medvedev was younger than Ivanov and softer around the edges. Unlike Putin and Ivanov, Medvedev was never a Communist Party member; his whole professional life had unfolded after the collapse of the Soviet Union. Like Putin, he came from St. Petersburg, but from the better side of the tracks. He grew up in a stable, well-educated suburban family that had escaped the purges and rejected atheism when it became politically possible. Diminutive, polite, lawyerly in manner, and utterly loyal to Putin, Medvedev nevertheless had a spine, and no shortage of drive. As I put it in a cable to Washington after our first meeting, "He would not have survived as long as he has in the dark and unforgiving corridors of the Kremlin if he did not."[5]

After an initial meeting in his office, Foreign Minister Sergey Lavrov came to a one-on-one lunch at Spaso House. Lavrov was a world-class diplomat and adept negotiator, with a keen eye for detail and an endlessly creative mind. He could also be prickly and obnoxious, especially if he had a dim regard for his counterpart or had to defend positions he knew were indefensible. A veteran of the peculiar form of multilateral torture that comes with long service at the United Nations, where he was Russia's permanent representative for nearly a decade, Lavrov had survived deadening hours of UN debate by becoming a gifted sketch artist and cartoonist. (I still have one of his doodles, a wolf's head whose detail betrays a particularly boring session with a visiting American delegation.) At lunch, after a large glass of his favorite Johnnie Walker Black, Lavrov dissected the mistakes he perceived in American foreign policy in the Bush administration. He took some pleasure in underscoring the ways in which he thought they opened up scope for Russian diplomacy, and warned of trouble ahead over Ukraine and Georgia. He was too smart and too skilled to ignore the potential for cooperation, especially on the economic and nuclear fronts.

One of my most interesting early encounters was with Vladislav

Surkov. Surkov was a young Kremlin political advisor—undoubtedly the only Kremlin official with a photo of the rapper Tupac Shakur on his wall. He was also the architect of Putin's then-fashionable concept of "sovereign democracy," which put a lot more emphasis on the first part of the term than the second.

Surkov and I later appeared together on a program at MGIMO, Russia's elite international affairs university for aspiring diplomats and entrepreneurs, focused unusually on the 125th anniversary of Franklin Delano Roosevelt's birth. With speculation running high about Putin's intentions in 2008, Surkov cleverly spun FDR's legacy to highlight his four terms in office, and their significance for the United States at a moment of crisis and transformation. I replied that the main lesson was not FDR's four terms, which were permitted at the time under our constitution, but rather his historic accomplishments in establishing the political and economic institutions that propelled America out of the Great Depression, through to victory with the Soviet Union in World War II, and into postwar prosperity. Personalities mattered, but democratic institutions endured. Surkov wasn't convinced.

Nor was he convinced by my pitch to think hard about the consequences of continued democratic rollback for the success of the upcoming G-8 summit in St. Petersburg. Like it or not, I stressed, the summit would bring eight thousand of his closest friends in the international media to Russia. They would have only a passing interest in the main summit theme—energy security. The stories on the domestic front would be far more captivating, and not very uplifting. Surkov just shrugged, reflecting his patron's utter disregard for international opinion.

I worked just as hard to cast a wide net for contacts and conversations beyond current government officials. Since traffic had become horrendous, I'd sometimes take advantage of the Moscow Metro, to the consternation of my security detail. The Metro retained its Soviet efficiency, with all its jostling and familiar wet wool smells in winter.

I met regularly with Putin's most outspoken opponents, including Garry Kasparov, the legendary former chess champion. Boris Nemtsov, a onetime presidential hopeful turned Putin critic, was always accessible and full of energy and opinions. (He would be murdered a few hundred meters from the walls of the Kremlin in February 2015.) I met frequently with a stalwart group of human rights activists, from the indomitable Lyudmila Alexeyeva, unbowed in her eighties, to younger advocates passionate about concerns that ran the gamut from brutality in Chechnya to environmental degradation and the rights of the disabled.

Moscow had no shortage of larger-than-life personalities. Reviled by many as the breaker of the Soviet empire, Mikhail Gorbachev kept a low profile, sitting in a spacious office in central Moscow, lonely after the death of his wife and concerned about Putin's increasingly authoritarian instincts. He seemed wistful about what might have been, and a bit lost in the new, gleaming, frantically acquisitive Moscow. Aleksandr Solzhenitsyn continued to write relentlessly at a small dacha complex outside Moscow, secure behind a tall green fence. When I went out to see him one late autumn afternoon, he spent a couple hours, as the light was dimming outside, talking about his life, the privations of the war and Communist rule, and the hope he had for Putin and for Russia. He distrusted the materialism of a Russia intoxicated by oil and excess, and emphasized his belief in the spiritual underpinnings of Russian exceptionalism. He saw nothing out of the ordinary about a Russia with predominant influence in the former Soviet space, "including our brothers in Ukraine." Although he had spent almost two decades in Vermont after his exile from the Soviet Union, he was not a convert to liberal internationalism, and especially not its hawkish neoconservative variant on full display in Iraq.

I made the best use I could of Russian television and newspaper interviews to convey American policy concerns and my commitment to healthier U.S.-Russian relations. I also took the somewhat unusual initiative of offering to appear before the Duma foreign affairs committee to answer questions about American policy. However imperfect my Russian-language skills, the nearly three hours I spent with Duma members that day were a good investment in our relationship. Several apologized afterward for being too harsh in their comments and questions. I assured them that congressional hearings in Washington could be at least as contentious.

I was convinced by my previous experience that no one could hope to understand Russia without exposure to the country beyond Moscow and St. Petersburg, nor could Russians understand America if all they had to draw upon was the caricature fed them by the Russian media, most of which was by now a wholly owned subsidiary of the Kremlin. I made some fifty extended trips outside Moscow during my three years as ambassador, from Kaliningrad in the west to Vladivostok in the east, and from the frigid Arctic north to Sochi on the Black Sea. Lisa and I traveled a good chunk of the Trans-Siberian Railway, still the best way to grasp Russia's sheer size. I spent a fascinating couple of days in Chukotka, just across the Bering Strait from Alaska, where Roman Abramovich, one of Russia's wealthiest men, served as governor by long distance, investing heavily in local infrastructure as part of what had become in Putin's Russia a kind of community service for oligarchs. I had poignant conversations with aging Soviet war veterans in Volgograd, the former Stalingrad.

There were plenty of vodka-filled evenings in Siberia and the Urals, where local governors and their aides tried to drink the visiting American ambassador under the table. Like my predecessors, I practiced all the tricks of the trade—surreptitiously draining my shot glass in the houseplants, slipping water into my glass, sipping instead of chugging—but I was badly outmatched. I continued to indulge my fascination with the North Caucasus, but never managed to return to Chechnya, now ruled harshly by Putin's rent-a-thug, Ramzan Kadyrov.

* * *

WE WORKED HARD to add more economic weight to the relationship and finally overcome trade disputes. Our aim initially was to
reach a bilateral trade agreement by the time of the G-8 summit in St.
Petersburg in July 2006, which seemed to fit Putin's agenda and give
us some negotiating leverage. The pace of negotiations was painfully
slow. Rapid progress in parallel U.S. negotiations with Ukraine, which
resulted in a bilateral accord and a normalization of trade relations in
the spring of 2006, only rubbed more salt in the wound for Putin. In
a classified email to Rice in April, I painted a gloomy picture. "We
have hit the point of diminishing returns in the negotiations. Absent
a bold move by the President to close the deal, the Russians are going
to slide backwards very quickly, as only they can do, into a swamp of
real and imagined grievances. Unfortunately, Putin is taking an increasingly sour attitude toward us on WTO. . . . He's now at the stage
where he's quite capable of shooting himself (and Russia) in the foot
by declaring that Russia doesn't need the WTO, and the U.S. can
shove it."[6]

U.S.-Russian negotiations lurched along, and a bilateral deal was
finally signed in November 2006—more than a dozen years after negotiations had begun. WTO accession and repeal of Jackson-Vanik
would drag on for another several years, and Russia grew to resent the
regulatory colonoscopy to which it was subjected—including revisions of hundreds of domestic laws and more than a thousand international agreements. This was nevertheless the single biggest step in
our economic relationship in more than a decade.

Meanwhile, we continued to work hard to enlarge two-way trade
and investment. I spent considerable time with American business
representatives, from the biggest energy companies to medium-sized
enterprises trying to get a foothold in the elusive Russian market.
Doing business in Russia was not for the fainthearted; one senior
American energy executive wound up in his company's version of the
witness protection program, shielded from rapacious Russian part-

ners taking apart a major joint venture. Despite the risk, there were profits to be made and markets to be opened, and I lobbied everyone from the most senior Kremlin officials to regional governors and local administrators on behalf of a level playing field for American companies. American direct investment in Russia increased by 50 percent in 2005–6, and business picked up in both directions.

The most ambitious commercial deal was a nearly $4 billion purchase of Boeing aircraft, including the new 787 Dreamliners. Boeing had a savvy local head of sales and operations, and had made Russian titanium an important component of the new, lighter-weight 787. It had also set up a research and design operation in Moscow that employed some fourteen hundred Russian engineers. It was a smart investment in Russian interest in acquisitions, and a powerful advertisement for what Russia had to offer at the high end of the technology industry. Formally signed in mid-2007, it was the largest nonenergy U.S. venture in post–Cold War Russia, and it encouraged other businesses in other sectors to give the Russian economy a try.

Our progress on nuclear cooperation was equally positive, and equally incremental. Bush and Putin had made broadly similar proposals for global civilian energy cooperation, aimed at boosting nuclear energy as a cleaner alternative to hydrocarbons, and reducing the risks of nuclear weapons proliferation. Among their common ideas was creation of multilateral enrichment facilities to eliminate the need for countries to enrich nuclear material or store and reprocess spent fuel—all of which posed serious proliferation risks. There was also shared interest in a variety of initiatives to ensure the safety and security of nuclear materials. Chafing at remaining the object of U.S. and international concerns about nuclear safety, Putin was eager to widen the lens and show cooperation in dealing with third-party challenges. We saw value in that too. When Qaddafi turned over enriched materials after we negotiated the end of his nuclear program, we arranged for the Russians to take custody. It was striking, and strangely satisfying, to see containers of enriched uranium that had been the object of so many of our efforts in Libya a couple years before sitting in a facility outside Moscow.

To codify our work in this field, we negotiated a bilateral civilian nuclear cooperation agreement in early 2007. Progress on civilian nuclear cooperation helped improve the atmosphere for collaboration on critical nonproliferation issues, especially Iran and North Korea. Although never an easy negotiating partner on UN Security Council resolutions, Russia joined in two significant sanctions measures against both countries in late 2006.

In addition to our efforts on the economic and nuclear fronts, I made a high priority of sustaining and expanding our exchange programs. Secretary of Education Margaret Spellings visited to discuss new bilateral education initiatives with her Russian counterpart, including university partnerships and exchanges of secondary school teachers in math and science. We looked for ways to expand English-language training programs in Russia, and Russian-language programs in the United States.

As we pushed forward on these initiatives, we relied on a high tempo of senior-level visits and meetings throughout 2005–6. President Bush met with Putin four times, and Secretary Rice led a steady stream of other cabinet visitors in 2006. Steve Hadley, Rice's successor as national security advisor, visited too, and was a sensible voice in the sometimes fractious Russia policy debates in Washington. High-level attention helped significantly, but didn't insulate the relationship from the troubling currents that were gathering momentum.

* * *

DESPITE ALL THESE efforts, the steadier track we were looking for in relations with Moscow seemed no closer at the end of 2006 than when I arrived eighteen months before—and in some ways even more remote. For understandable reasons, the patience of pragmatists like Rice and Bob Gates, who succeeded Don Rumsfeld at Defense late in

2006, and President Bush himself, wore thin, and neoconservatives saw an opening to push for a tougher approach. As he became more assertive about Russia's sense of entitlement in the former Soviet space, the dark side of Putin's rule at home clouded any remaining glimmers of political openness.

As Putin's fireplace exchange with Rice in the fall of 2006 made clear, he was growing impatient with Georgia and its president. Mikheil Saakashvili made no secret of his interest in NATO membership and closer ties to the West, and flaunted his relationships in Washington, where he had been lionized by many for his political dexterity during the Rose Revolution and his impressive economic success since then. Although he professed to seek a good relationship with Putin, his glee in poking the Russian bear was unbearable in the Kremlin. Russian policy was based on the presumption that it was entitled to expect—and if not forthcoming voluntarily, to enforce—a substantial degree of deference to its interests on the part of a small and poor neighboring country like Georgia. To Putin's growing annoyance, Saakashvili was defiantly nondeferential. Not unreasonably, he made clear his determination to recover Abkhazia and South Ossetia, parts of Georgia that had been under de facto Russian occupation for years. He was eager to make tangible progress toward NATO membership, and relished the leverage that any steps forward might give him with Moscow.

There was a growing danger that Saakashvili would overreach and the Kremlin would overreact. Reporting to Washington after a meeting between Putin and Saakashvili in June 2006, I noted, "No one evokes greater neuralgia in Moscow these days than Saakashvili." Putin's not-so-subtle message to the Georgian leader was: "You can have your territorial integrity, or you can have NATO membership, but you can't have both."[7]

Earlier that year, I had stressed in another cable that "nowhere is Putin's determination to stop the erosion of Russia's influence greater than in his own neighborhood."[8] Georgia was the proximate concern, but Ukraine remained the reddest of red lines for Putin. The Orange Revolution in 2004 was a massive blow for the Kremlin, a warning shot that Ukrainians might drift away from historic dependence on Moscow and toward formal association with the West. The next couple years brought some relief in the Russian leadership, as the victors in Kyiv indulged in the traditional Ukrainian habit of squabbling among themselves and bogging down the economy in corruption and bureaucratism. Putin was acutely sensitive to any signs that the Ukrainian government might encourage Washington to lay out a clearer path to NATO membership, and he was paranoid about American conspiracies.

Russia's domestic landscape was hardening too. As Putin looked ahead at the likely 2008 succession, he sought to eliminate any potential wild cards and to cow his opponents. Late in 2005, with his encouragement, the Duma introduced a draft law to severely restrict nongovernmental organizations, especially those receiving foreign funding. At the embassy we made strenuous efforts to push back, consulting with Russian NGOs as well as U.S.-based organizations still operating in Russia, and meeting with a variety of Duma leaders and Kremlin officials. I also enlisted my European counterparts in the effort, conscious that the Russian government was more likely to pay attention if we were part of a chorus of concerns, not a solo act. We made a little headway, and the legislation approved by the Duma in the spring of 2006 was slightly less onerous. Nevertheless, the trend line was clear. In case I had missed the message, Surkov drove the point home in a conversation that spring. "NGOs won't be able to act in Russia as they did in the color revolutions in Ukraine and Georgia. Period. In the '90s we were too weak and distracted to act. Now Russia will defend its sovereignty."

Ahead of the uncertain 2008 transition, many in the Russian elite were scrambling for wealth and power. Meanwhile, structural problems—corruption, the absence of institutionalized checks and balances, pressure on the media and civil society—were getting worse.

"The real danger," I cabled Washington at one point, "is that the excesses of Putin's Russia are eating up its successes."[9] Murders of dissidents and prominent journalists were, sadly, not uncommon in Russia in this era. Paul Klebnikov, a courageous American journalist working for *Forbes*, had been killed in Moscow the year before I arrived. In the fall of 2006, the pace accelerated. Aleksandr Litvinenko, a former Russian security officer turned outspoken critic of the Kremlin, was poisoned in London and died a horrible, protracted death. Responsibility for his killing was traced directly to the Kremlin. Anna Politkovskaya, a fearless journalist for the liberal newspaper *Novaya Gazeta*, who had covered the wars in Chechnya and a variety of abuses in Russian society, was gunned down outside her Moscow apartment. Some suspected that it was no coincidence the murder fell on Putin's birthday.

As a mark of respect, I went to Politkovskaya's funeral. I had only met her once, but her reputation and life deserved to be honored, and it was also important for me to make a point about where the United States stood. I recall the day vividly—a cold late-autumn afternoon, dusk settling, a few snowflakes beginning to fall, long lines of mourners, about three thousand altogether, shuffling slowly toward the hall where Politkovskaya's casket lay. I was asked to speak, along with one of my European colleagues and a couple of editors at *Novaya Gazeta*. Speaking for a few minutes in Russian, I said that Politkovskaya embodied the best of Russia, and that the best way for all of us to honor her memory was to continue to support the ideals she cherished and the kind of Russia she sought. Not one representative of the Russian government showed up.[10]

* * *

AGAINST THAT DARKENING backdrop, 2007 began with another jolt. In early February, Putin became the first Russian leader to attend the Munich Security Conference, an annual gathering of transatlantic security experts and officials. He didn't waste the opportunity to unburden himself. He bitterly criticized American unilateralism, which had "overstepped its national borders in every way."[11] Warning his audience sardonically that his comments might be "unduly polemical," Putin plowed ahead, assembling in one edgy speech the criticisms he had been making for years. The audience was taken aback, but the senior American official there, Secretary of Defense Gates, responded with aplomb. He noted drily that he shared Putin's background in intelligence, but thought that "one Cold War was quite enough."

In an email to Rice shortly afterward, I tried again to explain the mindset in the Kremlin. "The Munich speech," I wrote, "was the self-absorbed product of fifteen years of accumulated Russian frustrations and grievances, amplified by Putin's own sense that Russia's concerns are still often taken for granted or ignored." Understanding the Kremlin was as much about psychology as about geopolitics. "It's immensely satisfying psychologically," I continued, "to be able to take a whack at people after so many years of being down on their luck, and for Russians nothing is more satisfying than poking at Americans, with whom they have tried to compare themselves for so long." This was a moment that had particular appeal for Russia's president. "A large element was pure Putin—the attraction of swaggering into a den of transatlantic security wonks, sticking out his chin, and letting them have it with both barrels."[12]

There was an element of political convenience for Putin too. Certainly trumpeting about enemies at the gate and overbearing American behavior was a way to divert attention from domestic insecurities. It was also a matter of deep conviction—his sense that Russia had been taken advantage of in the 1990s by oligarchs at home and hypocritical Western friends abroad, and that Putinism was at its core all about fixing the playing field for the Russian state. Putin was giving voice to the pent-up frustrations of many Russians, not just striking an expedient pose. His view of his legacy at that point, and the source of his popularity, was that he had restored order, prosperity, and pride to a Russia sorely lacking in all three when Yeltsin left office.

I had attempted a more detailed stocktaking a couple of weeks earlier in another personal note for the secretary. I reported that Putin's Russia remained a paradox. On the one hand, Putin and those around him had contracted a case of *golovokruzhenie ot uspekhov,* "dizziness from success," an old, Stalin-era slogan appropriate for a new post-Soviet elite awash in petrodollars. The international landscape looked more promising than it had in years, which fed their hubris:

> For most of the Russian elite, still intoxicated by an unexpectedly rapid revival of Great Power status, the world around them is full of tactical opportunities. America is distracted and bogged down in Iraq; China and India are unthreatening and thirsty for energy; Europe is consumed with leadership transitions and ultimately pliable; and the Middle East is a mess in which vestigial connections to troublemakers like Syria offer openings for diplomatic station identification. From the Kremlin's perspective, Russia's own neighborhood looks a lot better than it did a year ago, with NATO expansion less imminent, Ukraine's color revolution fading, Georgia at least temporarily sobered, and Central Asia more attentive to Russian interests.[13]

The picture at home, at least on the surface, looked similarly promising. Putin was now running at 80 percent approval in the polls. The annual economic growth rate was 7 percent, and Russia had put away $300 billion in hard currency reserves. A middle class was emerging, focused on rising standards of living and individual choices that their parents could only have dreamed of, and mostly oblivious to politics. The oligarchs were quiescent, and Putin and his circle, never content to live off their government salaries, were steadily monopolizing major sources of wealth.

"Behind the curtain, however," I continued, "stands an emperor who is not fully clothed." As elites became more convinced that Putin was leaving the presidency in 2008, he was finding it harder than he thought to manage a neat succession. The only real checks and balances in Russia revolved not around institutions, but around a single personality. It therefore fell to Putin to convince the motley crew in and around the Kremlin—from the hard men of the security services to the remaining economic modernizers—that his successor would not threaten the current order.[14]

Beneath all the impressive macroeconomic indicators and apparent stability, troubles lurked. Demographic decline was not an abstract problem if you were one of the lonely thirty million Russians east of the Urals—distributed sparsely over a vast swath of the earth, sitting on vast natural resources, and staring across a long border at nearly a billion and a half Chinese. Corruption was worsening rapidly, as was Russia's overdependence on unsustainably high-priced hydrocarbons and an equally unsustainable energy infrastructure showing its age and decay from serial underinvestment. The North Caucasus was deceptively quiet, with a security lid on its dysfunctions but no real solutions in sight. And even though it was hard to see a rational prospect for color revolutions bubbling up in Russia, the Kremlin was paranoid about external meddling and insecure about its own grip.

So where did that leave American strategy? I warned that the Russians would likely become even more difficult to deal with, noting that it was a safe prediction they would often "exhibit all the subtlety and grace of the 'New Russian' businessmen of the 1990's—with lots of bling, and a kind of 'I'm going to drive my Hummer down the sidewalk just because it feels good' bluster."[15] The Russians' thirst for respect was insatiable, their sensitivity to being taken for granted always turned on high.

For all its irritations, we couldn't afford not to engage Putin's Russia, tempting as that might sometimes be. We'd have to build on common ground where we could, and limit the damage where we couldn't. I urged that we keep the Europeans close, and be careful about pushing too hard on issues where our key allies might start to back away from us. I stressed in particular that we ought to be "careful about our tactical priorities; if we want to have every issue our way, simultaneously, we'll make it harder to get what we want on the most important questions."[16] That became a broken-record theme in my messages and conversations over the remainder of my tenure. I knew how hard it was to break the post–Cold War habit of assuming that we could eventually maneuver over or around Moscow when it suited us, and I knew that was especially difficult as an administration looked to cement its legacy on issues like European security and missile defense. I also knew that we were running out of room for maneuver with Putin, and risked bigger collisions on critical issues like Iran if we weren't careful.

As 2007 unfolded, the question of who would succeed Putin when his second term ended in 2008 weighed increasingly on the Russian elite and clogged up much of the bilateral bandwidth. It was always a mistake to assume anything about Putin, except that he would always do all he could to keep people guessing. There was certainly the possibility that he would engineer a constitutional change to permit a third consecutive term; Duma votes were not exactly a prohibitive challenge for him. But most indications I had from him, as well as from Sergey Ivanov, Surkov, and others, were that Putin at least cared enough about appearances that he would step down. Surkov hinted broadly on several occasions that Putin might well return for a third, nonconsecutive term in 2012, which the constitution permitted. It was also likely that no matter who became president in 2008, Putin would remain the power behind the throne, in whatever role he chose. Nevertheless, it would not be a small thing for a relatively young, healthy, politically unchallenged leader to leave office voluntarily for the first time in a thousand years of Russian history.

Putin was not, however, in any rush to show his hand, and hardly ready to start crating his papers for the presidential library. Medvedev and Sergey Ivanov were clearly the early front-runners. Medvedev, then forty-two, seemed the more modern candidate, but he was also seen as a little soft, an uneasy fit in the rough-and-tumble world of

Russian elite politics and international affairs. Ivanov, then fifty-four, was the more traditional model, like Putin a veteran of the KGB, with years of experience as minister of defense; but he was also seen as a little hard, his ambition and self-confidence an uneasy fit for the other hard men in Putin's circle, and perhaps for Putin himself.

Medvedev had been given a boost at the end of 2005, when Putin moved him from the Kremlin to become first deputy prime minister. He had a chance to mold a more independent political image, and was given charge of the "national priority projects," which targeted significant chunks of the federal budget toward improvement of housing, healthcare, and education. In January 2007, he led Russia's delegation to Davos and gave a well-received speech. But Putin was not content to become a lame duck so early. In February 2007, he moved Sergey Ivanov from Defense to become another deputy prime minister. His portfolio focused on reorganizing the aviation, shipping, and high-tech industries, and also included the increasingly profitable arms trade. It also freed him from the endless controversies of the Ministry of Defense, where hazing deaths of recruits and other scandals were political deadweights. Both Ivanov and Medvedev seemed well positioned.

Putin's concern that outside influence might undermine his orchestration of events bordered on the paranoid. The sharpest exchange I ever had with him came in a private conversation at the St. Petersburg Economic Forum in early June 2007. He accused the embassy and American NGOs of funneling money and support to critics of the Kremlin. "Outside interference in our elections," he said, "will not be tolerated. We know you have diplomats and people who pretend to be diplomats traveling all over Russia encouraging oppositionists." With the most even tone I could manage, I replied that the outcome of Russia's elections was obviously for Russians alone to decide. The United States had no business supporting particular candidates or parties, and simply would not do so. We would, however, continue to express support for a fair process, just as we did any place in the world. Putin listened, offered a tight-lipped smile, and said, "Don't think we won't react to outside interference."[17]

He was convinced we were bent on tilting the political playing field in Russia, and drew a straight line from the color revolutions in Georgia and Ukraine in 2003–4, which he genuinely believed were the product of American conspiracies, to his own 2008 succession drama. The rich irony of Putin's threat is not lost on me more than a decade later, after Russia's brazen interference in the 2016 American presidential election.

As 2007 drew to a close, Putin finally tipped his hand and declared that he would support Medvedev as his successor in the March 2008 presidential election. The logic of that choice became clearer in the next couple months, as rumors swirled that Putin would remain in government as prime minister—perfectly acceptable under the Russian constitution. It made sense to have the more malleable and less experienced Medvedev as his partner in this new "tandem" arrangement; it was hard to see Sergey Ivanov being comfortable in that role, or Putin comfortable with him. Russia's political landscape appeared to be stabilizing. U.S.-Russian relations, on the other hand, were heading in the opposite direction.

* * *

THE LIST OF irritants between us continued to grow, but several stood out. One was Kosovo, where the United States had championed a UN-led process to organize Kosovar independence from Serbia. The effort made practical and moral sense. The Kosovars overwhelmingly wanted independence, the status quo was unsustainable, and long delay invited another eruption of violence in the Balkans. For Putin, Kosovo's independence brought back bad memories of Russian impotence, and loomed as a test of how different his Russia was from Yeltsin's.

He also had worries, not entirely unfounded, that Kosovo's independence would set off a chain reaction of pressures, with some in the

Russian elite urging him to recognize the independence of Abkhazia, South Ossetia, and other disputed territories in the former Soviet Union. Putin was not at all shy about using those conflicts as levers, especially with Saakashvili, but his preference was to keep them frozen. He also knew that separatist tendencies in the North Caucasus, inside the Russian Federation itself, had not been fully extinguished, and he did not want to see them rekindled. "The notion that Russia can't be pushed around again as it was in 1999, and that the issue of North Caucasus separatism has been settled," I wrote in the summer of 2007, "are two of the cardinal elements of Putin's own sense of legacy, and he will fiercely resist revisiting either of them."[18] Nevertheless, the UN plan authored by former Finnish president Martti Ahtisaari was moving down the track, with Kosovo's independence within sight by the end of 2007.

A second problem was the question of NATO expansion, this time to Ukraine and Georgia. There had been two waves of NATO expansion since the end of the Cold War: Poland, the Czech Republic, and Hungary were offered membership in the second half of the 1990s, and then the Baltic states and four more Central European states a few years later. Yeltsin had gnashed his teeth over the first wave, but couldn't do much about it. Putin offered little resistance to Baltic membership, amid all the other preoccupations of his first term. Georgia, and especially Ukraine, were different animals altogether. There could be no doubt that Putin would fight back hard against any steps in the direction of NATO membership for either state. In Washington, however, there was a kind of geopolitical and ideological inertia at work, with strong interest from Vice President Cheney and large parts of the interagency bureaucracy in a "Membership Action Plan" (MAP) for Ukraine and Georgia. Key European allies, in particular Germany and France, were dead set against offering it. They were disinclined to add to mounting friction between Moscow and the West—and unprepared to commit themselves formally and militarily to the defense of Tbilisi or Kyiv against the Russians. The Bush administration understood the objections, but still felt it could finesse the issue.

Completing the trifecta of troubles was the vexing issue of missile defense. Anxious about American superiority in missile defense technology since the Soviet era, the Russians were always nervous that U.S. advances in the field, whatever their stated purposes, would put Moscow at a serious strategic disadvantage. Putin had swallowed the U.S. abrogation of the Anti-Ballistic Missile (ABM) Treaty early in the Bush administration, but resented it deeply as another example, in his eyes, of the United States throwing its weight around at Russia's expense. By 2007, the United States had begun fielding missile defense capabilities in Alaska and California, aimed at the emerging North Korean threat. More worrying for Putin were American plans to build new radar and interceptor sites in the Czech Republic and Poland to counter a potential Iranian missile threat. Putin didn't buy the argument that an Iranian threat was imminent; and even if it was, his specialists told him (not unreasonably) that it would be technically smarter to deploy new missile defense systems in the southeast Mediterranean, or Italy, and that Aegis shipborne systems could be an effective ingredient. No amount of argument about the technological limitations of systems based in the Czech Republic and Poland against theoretical Russian targets, however soundly based, swayed Putin and his innately suspicious military. Their longer-term concern was not so much about the particular technologies that might be deployed in new NATO states in Central Europe as it was about what those technologies might mean as part of a future, globalized American missile defense system. At the core of their opposition was also the weight of history. For many in Russia, especially in Putin's orbit of security and intelligence hardliners, you could build a Disney theme park in Poland and they would find it faintly threatening.

I had done my best over the previous two and a half years to signal the brewing problems in the relationship and what might be done to head them off. I knew I was straining the patience of some in Washington, who chafed at my warnings of troubles to come when they were consumed with the challenges that had already arrived. I decided, however, that I owed Secretary Rice and the White House one more attempt to collect my concerns and recommendations in one place.

On a typically dreary Friday afternoon in early February 2008, with snow falling steadily against the gray Moscow sky outside my office window, I sat down and composed a long personal email to Secretary Rice, which she later shared with Steve Hadley and Bob Gates. While more formal diplomatic cables still had their uses, classified emails were faster, more direct, and more discreet—in this case a better way to convey the urgency and scope of my concerns.

"The next couple months will be among the most consequential in recent U.S.-Russian relations," I wrote. "We face three potential trainwrecks: Kosovo, MAP for Ukraine/Georgia, and missile defense. We've got a high-priority problem with Iran that will be extremely hard ... to address without the Russians. We've got a chance to do something enduring with the Russians on nuclear cooperation ... and we've got an opportunity to get off on a better foot with a reconfigured Russian leadership after Medvedev's likely election, and to help the Russians get across the finish line into WTO this year, which is among the most practical things we can do to promote the long-term prospects for political and economic modernization in this proud, prickly and complicated society." I tried to be clear about what should be done:

> My view is that we can only manage one of those three train-wrecks without doing real damage to a relationship we don't have the luxury of ignoring. From my admittedly parochial perspective here, it's hard to see how we could get the key Europeans to support us on all three at the same time. I'd opt for plowing ahead resolutely on Kosovo; deferring MAP for Ukraine or Georgia until a stronger foundation is laid; and going to Putin directly while he's still in the Presi-

dency to try and cut a deal on missile defense, as part of a broader security framework.

I fully understand how difficult a decision to hold off on MAP will be. But it's equally hard to overstate the strategic consequences of a premature MAP offer, especially to Ukraine. Ukrainian entry into NATO is the brightest of all redlines for the Russian elite (not just Putin). In more than two and a half years of conversations with key Russian players, from knuckle-draggers in the dark recesses of the Kremlin to Putin's sharpest liberal critics, I have yet to find anyone who views Ukraine in NATO as anything other than a direct challenge to Russian interests. At this stage, a MAP offer would be seen not as a technical step along a long road toward membership, but as throwing down the strategic gauntlet. Today's Russia will respond. Russian-Ukrainian relations will go into a deep freeze. . . . It will create fertile soil for Russian meddling in Crimea and eastern Ukraine. On Georgia, the combination of Kosovo independence and a MAP offer would likely lead to recognition of Abkhazia, however counterproductive that might be to Russia's own long-term interests in the Caucasus. The prospects of subsequent Russian-Georgian armed conflict would be high.

I pushed my luck a little in the next passage. If, in the end, we decided to push MAP offers for Ukraine and Georgia, I wrote, "you can probably stop reading here. I can conceive of no grand package that would allow the Russians to swallow this pill quietly." On missile defense, I urged that we not be in a rush on the Polish and Czech deployment plans, continue to seek ways in which we might find a basis for cooperation with Russia, and work harder to link this issue to Russian collaboration in countering the Iranian missile and nuclear threats—which were, after all, the proximate reasons for our initiative. If we could get the Russians to work more closely with us and slow or block Iranian advances, that would serve the main strategic purpose that animated our plans in Central Europe.

I repeated my arguments for pressing ahead on economic and nuclear cooperation as Putin prepared to launch the "tandem" arrangement with Medvedev. We ought to engage the Russians on the possibility of a new strategic arms reduction accord, beyond the START agreement that would soon expire. We should continue to work hard on nonproliferation challenges. Iran was one important example. North Korea was another. The Russians had far less direct influence in Pyongyang than did the Chinese, but wanted to play a role.

My case for economic cooperation was still built around WTO accession and supporting American trade and investment. I always thought that over the longer term, that was one of the best of the limited bets available to us to advance the president's freedom agenda in Russia, helping slowly to deepen the self-interest of Russians in the rule of law. "That wouldn't change the reality," I noted, "that Russia is a deeply authoritarian and overcentralized state today, whose dismal record on human rights and political freedoms deserves our criticism." But over time it might reinforce the instincts for protecting private property and market-driven opportunity that were slowly building a middle class, and open up a massively undertapped market for American companies.[19]

Rice was appreciative and encouraged me to keep pressing my views. Both she and Gates shared at least some of my concerns on MAP, but I sensed that the debate in Washington was still tilting toward a strong, legacy-building effort to engineer a MAP offer for Ukraine and Georgia at the April 2008 NATO summit in Bucharest. There was similar fin-de-administration momentum behind the missile defense project in Poland and the Czech Republic, now that Kosovo's independence was a done deal.

Both Rice and Gates, and President Bush himself, had spent a lot of time in 2007 trying to engage the Russians on all these issues. Gates visited in April, not long after his encounter with Putin at Munich, and displayed a sure feel for the Russians, the product of decades of experience during the Cold War and his own savvy, pragmatic judgment and good humor. The latter was especially useful in his formal conversations with the new defense minister, Anatoliy Serdyukov, a former furniture trader from St. Petersburg who had endeared himself to Putin as chief of the federal tax collection service, and implementer of the brutal demolition of Mikhail Khodorkovsky several years before. Serdyukov was entirely unschooled in defense matters or diplomacy, and mostly read his talking points from a stack of index cards. Gates parried his points respectfully, occasionally passing me notes with his unvarnished thoughts about our host, who he concluded should have stuck to furniture sales.

Rice, determined to do what she could to ease tensions, came to Moscow in May. President Bush saw Putin on the margins of the G-8 summit in Germany in June, where Putin suggested the use of a Russian-operated radar facility in Azerbaijan, which he intended as an alternative, not a complement, to a Central European site. When Putin came to Kennebunkport, Maine, in July, the Russian leader added the possibility of using an existing early-warning facility at Armavir, in southern Russia. The two leaders agreed that their experts should study the ideas, in hopes of developing a joint approach. Extensive working-level discussions ensued. The limited technical capacity of the two Russian-proposed sites was one concern; the bigger issue was that the Russians saw their offers as a substitute for U.S. plans in Central Europe, while Washington was willing to consider them (at most) as add-ons.

The Kennebunkport meeting showed both the cordiality of the Bush-Putin relationship and its limitations. Relaxed and gracious at their summer home, the Bush family wrapped Putin and his delegation in warmth and hospitality. I told President Bush afterward that I thought Putin had been genuinely touched by the invitation, and he was not someone easily touched by gestures of any kind. But I left feeling that Russians and Americans were still talking past one another and hurtling down the track toward a wreck of one kind or another.

In March 2008, just before Medvedev was elected as president, I had an unusual conversation with Putin, which only reinforced my worries. President Bush had asked me to deliver a message to Putin. Its contents were straightforward: outlining again our position on Kosovo; emphasizing our hope that we could still work out some acceptable formula on missile defense; indicating that any move forward at the Bucharest summit toward NATO membership for Ukraine and Georgia should not be seen as threatening; and underscoring our continued commitment to Russia's accession to the WTO. President Bush also confirmed that he'd accept Putin's invitation to visit Sochi and hope they'd take advantage of their last meeting as presidents to discuss a "strategic framework" to guide the U.S.-Russian relationship.

Putin didn't often agree to separate meetings with me, and almost never saw other ambassadors. Most of our encounters during my tenure were on the margins of other events, or with visiting senior U.S. officials. This time I was invited to come to the presidential dacha at Novo Ogaryovo, just outside Moscow. I was asked to come alone. Arriving at the appointed time, I was ushered into a reception room, with the usual assortment of bottled Russian mineral water and snacks. Putin was just finishing a meeting with the Security Council, a protocol assistant told me. I half expected a replay of the experience Rice and I had had, and wondered if I was going to have to navigate that not especially receptive audience before my session with Putin. I was also thinking through how best to convey my fairly lengthy message, well aware that Putin had little patience for long-winded presentations.

Almost as if to spare me from my mounting anxiety, I was ushered into Putin's conference room. It was bright and airy, with light pine walls and furniture. Adding to the brightness, I quickly realized, were a dozen press cameras. Having been in Russia long enough to cultivate a bit of paranoia, I immediately thought this was a trap, an opportunity for Putin to lace into U.S. policy and its quavering representative.

I was wrong. With the cameras running, Putin made some general comments about the potential of the Russian-American relationship, despite our differences. Noting that my tour as ambassador was nearing its end, he thanked me for being an honest and professional envoy for my country. I stumbled around a little in Russian in my reply, emphasizing how much I enjoyed serving in Russia. We would inevitably have disagreements, sometimes sharp ones, but stable relations were in the interests of both our countries, and of the wider world. Putin nodded, the camera lights went off, and the press left.

With Sergey Lavrov sitting beside him and the rest of the room cleared, Putin looked at me with his customary expressionless demeanor and invited me to deliver the message I was bearing. I condensed my points as best I could, without losing any of their meaning or precision. It took me about ten minutes. Somewhat to my surprise, Putin didn't interrupt at all, and didn't roll his eyes or make side comments to Lavrov. When I finished, he thanked me politely and said he would look forward to seeing President Bush, and would offer a few preliminary comments—none of which, he added, would surprise me.

Putin's intimidating aura is often belied by his controlled mannerisms, modulated tone, and steady gaze. He'll slouch a bit and look bored by it all if not engaged by the subject or the person across from him, and be snarky and bullying if he's feeling pressed. But he can get quite animated if he wants to drive home a point, his eyes flashing and his voice rising in pitch. In this exchange, Putin displayed his full range.

As I took careful notes, he said, "Your government has made a big mistake on Kosovo. Don't you see how that encourages conflict and monoethnic states all over the world?" Shaking his head ruefully, he observed, "I'm glad you didn't try to tell me that Kosovo is not a precedent. That's a ridiculous argument." I smiled a little to myself, grateful that that was one point I had persuaded my colleagues in Washington to delete in the drafting process. Then Putin moved on to MAP. "No Russian leader could stand idly by in the face of steps toward NATO membership for Ukraine. That would be a hostile act toward Russia. Even President Chubais or President Kasyanov [two of Russia's better-known liberals] would have to fight back on this issue. We would do all in our power to prevent it." Growing angry, Putin continued, "If people want to limit and weaken Russia, why do they have to do it through NATO enlargement? Doesn't your government know that Ukraine is unstable and immature politically, and NATO is a very divisive issue there? Don't you know that Ukraine is not even a real country? Part of it is really East European, and part is really Russian. This would be another mistake in American diplomacy, and I know Germany and France are not ready anyway."

On other issues, Putin was mostly dismissive. Looking perturbed and waving his arm, he said the United States wasn't listening on missile defense. "Unfortunately, the U.S. just wants to go off on its own again." He was scathing on Jackson-Vanik. "You've been teasing us on this for years." It was "indecent" to keep prolonging the process, or leveraging Jackson-Vanik to settle agricultural trade issues. Even Soviet-era refuseniks, he said, were insulted by the continuation of the policy. They complained to him, "We didn't go to jail for the sake of poultry."

We went back and forth over some of these issues for over an hour. Putin's patience was wearing thin, and Lavrov was doodling intently, which I took as a signal to wrap things up. I thanked Putin for his time and said I would convey all his comments to Washington. I congratulated him on winning the Winter Olympics for Sochi in 2014, an effort in which he had invested significant personal energy, working hard on his English for the presentation to the International Olympic Committee, and even harder to grease the palms of its commissioners. Putin finally brightened, smiled, and said the Winter Olympics would be a great moment for Russia. He shook my hand, and I went back out to my car for the ride back to Moscow.

* * *

THE BUCHAREST NATO summit had moments of high drama, with President Bush and Secretary Rice still hoping to find a way to produce MAP offers. Chancellor Angela Merkel and President Nicolas Sarkozy were dug in firmly in opposition. In the end, the curious outcome was a public statement, issued on behalf of the alliance by Merkel and Rice, that "we agreed today that Ukraine and Georgia will become members of NATO."[20] There was no mention of MAP, which disappointed Kyiv and Tbilisi, but what the statement lacked in practical import it seemed to more than make up for in clarity of direction. Putin came the next day for a charged NATO–Russia Council meeting, and vented his concerns forcefully. In many ways, Bucharest left us with the worst of both worlds—indulging the Ukrainians and Georgians in hopes of NATO membership on which we were unlikely to deliver, while reinforcing Putin's sense that we were determined to pursue a course he saw as an existential threat.

President Bush arrived in Sochi two days later. Sochi was Putin's pride and joy, an old Soviet spa town on the Black Sea, with a temperate climate, pebbly beaches, and a few forlorn-looking palm trees set against snowcapped mountains an hour's drive away. Putin had built an expansive retreat just outside town, where he spent increasing amounts of time and received foreign visitors. The basic infrastructure, like so much of the rest of Russia outside the emerald cities of Moscow and St. Petersburg, was extremely run-down. The few hotels had all the beat-up charm that I remembered from the late Soviet era, and the Olympic skating, ice hockey, and skiing venues were still on the drawing board. A new airport was planned but construction had not yet begun; Air Force One looked out of place on the bedraggled runway, with weeds popping up through the concrete and the terminal building a ramshackle affair.

In a cable to the president and Secretary Rice before the visit, I had predicted that "while cocky and combative as ever, still without a mellow bone in his body, Putin will likely soften his roughest edges in Sochi."[21] To my relief, that had proven mostly true. Putin was certainly mad about NATO opening the door to Ukrainian and Georgian membership, and was already thinking of ways to tighten the screws on both to make his displeasure even clearer. Yet he also liked Bush and didn't want to embarrass him on his valedictory visit. Moreover, he was anxious to get the "tandem" experiment off to a good start and show both his international and domestic audiences that he could make it work. The Russian elite was still a little uncertain about the whole idea. In my message to the president, I had recounted an experience at an event in Moscow the previous week, during which I listened to longtime mayor Yuri Luzhkov pontificate at some length to a group about the merits of the tandem arrangement. When I asked him afterward if he really believed that, he laughed uproariously and said, "Of course not. It's the craziest thing I've ever heard."[22]

Relaxed by the setting, Putin and Bush covered the familiar range of issues thoroughly and civilly. Putin was pointed on Ukraine and Georgia in a smaller session with the president, repeating his view that we didn't understand what an unwieldy place Ukraine was, and how close Saakashvili was to provoking him. He didn't belabor his concern, however, and the overall atmosphere was remarkably cordial. At a concluding dinner, Putin and Medvedev sat with the president, talking and joking, and generally conveying a sense that our relationship was solid enough to endure whatever troubles lay ahead. The after-dinner entertainment featured Russian folk music and a group of local dancers who invited members of the delegations to join them on the small stage. Several Russian officials, their alcohol consumption outpacing their abstemious president, climbed up and danced energetically. I wasn't brave enough, clinging to what remained of my ambassadorial dignity. A few of my less inhibited colleagues made up in enthusiasm what they lacked in rhythm. Chuckling, President Bush said as we were walking out, "I didn't see you up there, but maybe that was smart. Our folks looked like mice on a hot plate."

* * *

I WOULD LEAVE Moscow a month later. Earlier that spring, Secretary Rice had asked me to return to the State Department as undersecretary for political affairs, the third-ranking position in the department and traditionally the highest post to which a career officer could aspire. I departed with a sense of foreboding. For all our efforts to steady the relationship, some kind of crash seemed more and more likely.

Putin was determined to take Saakashvili down a peg, and perhaps also to show, in the wake of the Bucharest statement, that the Germans and French were right to see Georgia's not-so-frozen conflicts as a long-term obstacle to NATO membership. He was clearly baiting the impulsive Georgian president, who may have wanted for his own reasons after Bucharest to act in South Ossetia and force a resolution of the disputes there and in Abkhazia. Rice visited Tbilisi in July and pushed Saakashvili hard not to take the bait. He heard other, more encouraging voices in Washington, including in the vice president's office, and couldn't resist the temptation to move, as the Russians continued to prod and provoke, their trap carefully laid. On the night of August 7, the Georgians launched an artillery barrage on Tskhinvali, the tiny South Ossetian capital, killing a number of Ossetes and Russian peacekeepers. Already poised, the Russians sent a large force through the Roki Tunnel between North and South Ossetia, routed the Georgians, and within a few days were on the verge of seizing Tbilisi and overthrowing Saakashvili. European diplomatic intervention led by French president Sarkozy, in close coordination with the United States, produced a cease-fire. The damage was done, however, leaving U.S.-Russian relations in their worst shape since the end of the Cold War.

The slow-motion trainwreck in U.S.-Russian relations that had its flaming culmination in Georgia in August 2008 had more than one cause. Certainly, the complexes of Putin's Russia were on vivid display—pent-up grievance, wounded pride, suspicion of American motives and color revolutions, a sense of entitlement about Russia's great power prerogatives and sphere of influence, and Putin's particular autocratic zeal for translating all those passions into calculated aggression. Saakashvili's impulsiveness didn't help. Neither did our own post–Cold War complexes, born of the self-confidence of the unipolar moment after the collapse of the Soviet Union and the searing experience of 9/11. Restraint and compromise seemed unappealing and unnecessary, given our strength and sense of mission. They seemed especially unappealing with Putin's Russia, a declining power with a nasty repressive streak.

Whether a crash could have been avoided, and a difficult but more stable relationship constructed, is a hard question. The next administration would take its own run at answering it, with a sustained effort to "reset" relations with Russia that produced early dividends. It ended, however, with an even bigger trainwreck, and not much to show for my quarter century of episodic involvement in relations between Russia and America. It was another lesson in the complexities of diplomacy, and the risks of wishful thinking—both about the disruptive Mr. Putin and our own capacity to maneuver over or around him.

Over the next decade, Putin's confidence and risk tolerance would deepen further. Increasingly convinced of his ability to "play strongly with weak cards," increasingly disdainful of "poor players" of stronger hands like the irresolute and divided Americans and Europeans, Putin gradually shifted from testing the West in places where Russia had a greater stake and more appetite for risk, like Ukraine and Georgia, to places where the West had a far greater stake, like the integrity of its democracies.

7

Obama's Long Game: Bets, Pivots, and Resets in a Post-Primacy World

IN THE SUMMER of 2005, Barack Obama, a newly elected Democratic senator from Illinois, was one of my first guests in Moscow. I had arrived with my family earlier that week, and Spaso House was still littered with unpacked boxes. I had yet to meet with all the members of my team, let alone complete my first round of courtesy calls with Russian officials. Obama, sensing my professional and domestic disorder, could not have been more gracious. With two young daughters of his own, he instantly connected with Lizzy and Sarah. He could sense that they were just getting their bearings in yet another new home and new school. He knew precisely what that felt like and went out of his way to relate, reassure, and comfort them.

Obama's travel partner was Republican senator Dick Lugar from Indiana—one of the most respected voices in the Senate, with enormous foreign policy expertise and credibility across the aisle and around the world. For more than a decade, he had been a regular visitor to Russia with Senator Sam Nunn of Georgia—his Democratic friend and co-sponsor of legislation that secured loose nuclear material and weapons left behind in the dissolution of the Soviet Union.

With Nunn now retired, Lugar hoped Obama would step into his shoes. Obama had a long interest in nuclear policy, and Lugar a keen eye for talent.

Obama and Lugar joined Lisa and me for an informal dinner at Spaso House one evening, together with Senator Chuck Hagel of Nebraska, a decorated Vietnam veteran and a leading Republican voice on foreign policy, who was on a separate visit to Russia. We talked until nearly midnight. Obama wanted to know about my experiences in Russia in the 1990s, and what I thought about Putin. He was curious about the run-up to the Iraq War in 2003 and where things were headed as the Sunni insurgency picked up steam. He seemed particularly interested in what it was like to work for Secretary Baker and how the Bush 41 administration coped with such an avalanche of transformative international events. "That was an impressive bunch," he said.

Lugar and Obama spent a couple days in Moscow. We had lots more time to talk, bouncing around in embassy minivans to and from meetings. At a former biological weapons lab outside Moscow, Obama watched warily as Lugar handled dusty old jars of toxins perched precariously on the shelves. As we sat down for lunch, Obama was equally wary of the green Jell-O mold on our plates. He looked to me, pointed at my untouched plate, and said, "You first, Mr. Ambassador. This is what diplomats get paid the big bucks to do."

The following day, Lisa and I were busily unpacking our boxes when my cellphone rang. The embassy duty officer had some inconvenient news: Officials at Perm airport were demanding payment of an exorbitant landing fee (from which official delegations were supposed to be exempt) before clearing the congressional delegation and its U.S. military plane to take off. Over the next three hours, I hunted frantically for a senior Russian official to spring Obama and Lugar. Sunday afternoons in August are not the most accessible moment for senior Russians, but I managed to track down the groggy first deputy foreign minister at his dacha near Moscow. He pulled the necessary strings, and Lugar and Obama made it to Ukraine later that day. I was lucky that my first (and only) senatorial detainees in Russia were two of the least affected members of Congress. Nevertheless, Obama would occasionally tease me about the incident in later years. "You're not going to pull another Perm on me, are you?" he'd ask, semi-kidding.

Perm-gate was a reminder that no matter how thoughtful the effort, no matter how carefully laid the plan, other forces and players had a vote too. It was a lesson I learned time and time again during the course of my diplomatic career, and it would rear its head regularly during President Obama's tenure in the White House. He inherited a world in which America's post–Cold War dominance—thanks to the forces of history and our unforced errors—was coming to an end. Although America's relative power and influence were diminishing, its myriad strengths seemed to ensure its preeminence for decades to come. The question for Obama was how to make best use of that preeminence to secure American interests and values in a more competitive world.

That required playing a long game—molding an emerging international order, realigning relationships with major powers like China, India, and Russia, and revitalizing diplomacy to achieve goals like preventing Iran from acquiring nuclear weapons. It also required a relentlessly adaptable short game, navigating through a landscape in which terrorism was still a threat, the weight of the military-intelligence complex was still far greater than diplomatic tools, and the pull of old dysfunctions in the Middle East would threaten to swallow the foreign policy agenda. It was a world of unsynchronized passions, full of collisions between the ambitions of the long game and the vexations of the short game.

* * *

IN QUESTIONS OF temperament, instinct, and worldview, President Obama and his secretaries of state, Hillary Clinton and John

Kerry, diverged in a number of ways, but they all saw the importance of getting America off of its war footing and reclaiming its diplomatic leadership. During the campaign, Obama's diagnosis of U.S. foreign policy was harsh: The United States had failed to prioritize interests and investments; had inverted the roles of force and diplomacy; had been stubbornly reluctant to engage adversaries directly; and had been too attuned to the siren song of unilateralism and often deaf to the hard task of coalition-building in a world in which both power and problems were more diffuse.

Obama's suspicions about the foreign policy establishment in Washington ran deeper than his predecessor's mistakes. He was skeptical, and eventually publicly dismissive, of its tendency to homogenize analyses and reduce complicated problems to simple tests of American credibility. For Obama, the "blob" was not a term of endearment, but a self-absorbed bipartisan elite whose insular judgments had led the United States into troubles, from Vietnam to Iraq.

Obama took office determined to break the chains of U.S. foreign policy pathologies and shift the terms of America's engagement in the Middle East. He sought to position the United States for long-term success by pivoting more attention and resources to Asia, where China's rise was rapidly unfolding; making bets on emerging geostrategic players like India; and resetting relations with critical if declining rivals like Russia.

Obama saw the Bush 41 model—the instinctive modesty of George H. W. Bush and the dexterity and restraint of Baker and Scowcroft—as one to emulate. The world he inherited, however, was far less propitious than theirs. Nor did he enter office with their experience and a Rolodex full of world leaders. For all the impossibly inflated expectations that greeted his inauguration, Obama would discover that the world was full of events that would make pushing the reset button on America's role infinitely difficult. After the recklessness of his predecessor, Obama's mantra of "not doing stupid shit" was a sensible guideline. But there were other scatological realities in foreign policy:

Shit happened too, and reacting to events outside neat policy boxes would be a persistent challenge.

If Obama was innately suspicious of the Washington establishment, Clinton and Kerry had come to embody it. Both had been on the national stage for decades. Both had voted for the 2003 Iraq War in the Senate. Both reveled in the personal relationships with world leaders that were the daily stuff of diplomacy, and prized their long connections with friends in high places. Their convictions about American leadership were traditional and assertive.

Clinton was most self-confidently an American exceptionalist, and least self-flagellating in her assessment of U.S. foreign policy and its blind spots. She was comfortable with the muscularity of America's role, and attuned to the benefit of being the hawk in the room. She was unfailingly sober and well prepared in her approach, unflappable when hard decisions had to be made but generally risk-conscious, and sometimes risk-averse, about big diplomatic bets.

I first met Hillary Clinton when she accompanied President Clinton to King Hussein's funeral in February 1999. In November of that year, she returned to Jordan to visit King Abdullah and Queen Rania. The backdrop was complicated. The day before in Ramallah, she had had to sit through a particularly nasty rant by Yasser Arafat's wife, Suha. In the midst of a public ceremony, and with the First Lady by her side, Suha accused the Israeli government of using poison gas against Palestinians. The simultaneous interpretation had apparently broken down or was garbled and Clinton—already bone-tired—missed much of what Mrs. Arafat was saying. When she embraced Suha at the end of the event, a mini-scandal erupted. Criticism in Israel and the United States quickly mounted, an unhelpful storm on the eve of her campaign for a Senate seat in New York.

Arriving in Petra in southern Jordan to tour the fabled Nabatean city before heading to Amman, Clinton seemed unfazed. There was very little angst or finger-pointing. Clinton decided to make a short statement to the press before leaving Petra, explaining what had happened and rejecting Mrs. Arafat's vile rhetoric. When that was done, we flew on to Amman, and Clinton was focused and even-keeled over the rest of a busy schedule. The following night, she invited Lisa and me to join her and her immediate staff for an after-dinner drink in her hotel suite. The First Lady was funny and relaxed, full of good questions about how the king and queen were coping with their first year on the throne, and how Jordan was faring. As we talked on the way home, Lisa and I were both struck not only by how smart and genuinely devoted to her staff Clinton was, but also by how quickly she picked herself up after setbacks and moved on.

John Kerry shared Clinton's tireless energy and perseverance. Kerry never met a diplomatic problem that he didn't want to take on, or that he thought would prove immune to his powers of persuasion. He was far more prone to improvising, always willing to be caught trying, and unintimidated by long odds or historical patterns. His was in some respects a more classical approach to diplomacy, focused on ending big conflicts and negotiating big international agreements, with a readiness to take big risks and even bigger falls.

I had met Senator Kerry off and on over the years, in Senate hearings and briefings. It was not until May 2012, when we wound up as roommates at a small retreat of Arab and international political leaders hosted by King Abdullah in Aqaba, that I got the chance to get to know him better. Abdullah kept these weekend gatherings informal and exclusive, with no staff or media allowed.

The king ensured that there was plenty of time for Hashemite hospitality and bonding. He organized a cookout in Wadi Rum, the spectacular desert setting not far from Aqaba where T. E. Lawrence had orchestrated the Arab Revolt against the Turks a century before. There was a shooting range, and dune buggies to race. Kerry and Senator John McCain, political opposites but longtime friends, roared off into the desert sunset, huge grins on their faces. That was John Kerry. He loved a challenge, loved competition, and loved being in constant motion.

With Lisa during A-100 training in early 1982 *(Courtesy of the author)*

With President Reagan, Secretary of State George Shultz, National Security Advisor Colin
Powell, and other senior advisors in the Oval Office in December 1988
(Courtesy Ronald Reagan Presidential Library)

Listening (back row, second from left) as President George H. W. Bush addresses the Madrid Peace Conference on October 30, 1991 (*Courtesy of the author*)

Secretary of State Madeleine Albright greeting Lisa, Sarah, and Lizzy during a 1998 ceremony marking the end of my term as executive secretary (*Courtesy of the author*)

Visiting the Palestinian refugee camp in Jenin on April 20, 2002 (*Courtesy of the author*)

With President George W. Bush and other senior foreign policy advisors in the
Oval Office in February 2003 *(Official White House Photo)*

With King Abdullah II in
Amman in November 2003
*(Yusef Allan/Jordanian Royal
Palace/Getty Images)*

With Egyptian president
Hosni Mubarak in Cairo in
September 2004
*(Amro Maraghi/AFP/
Getty Images)*

Celebrating a birthday on the road with
Secretary of State Colin Powell
(Courtesy of the author)

With Muammar al-Qaddafi in
2004 *(Courtesy of the author)*

During a December 2006 visit
to a school in Beslan, Russia,
where more than three
hundred died in a 2004
Chechen terrorist attack
*(Kazbek Basayev/AFP/
Getty Images)*

Meeting with Russian president Vladimir Putin at Novo Ogaryovo, the presidential dacha outside Moscow, in the spring of 2008 *(Alexander Zemlianichenko/ AFP/Getty Images)*

At a meeting between President Obama and Prime Minister Vladimir Putin held at Putin's dacha on July 7, 2009 *(Official White House Photo by Pete Souza)*

Meeting with President Obama and Secretary of State Hillary Clinton in the White House Situation Room on September 29, 2009, in advance of P5+1 negotiations with Iran *(Official White House Photo by Pete Souza)*

Leading the U.S. delegation (third from left, far side of table) in P5+1 talks with Iran in Geneva, Switzerland, on October 1, 2009 (*Dominic Favre/AFP/Getty Images*)

With Syrian president Bashar al-Assad prior to a meeting in Damascus in February 2010 (*Louai Beshara/AFP/ Getty Images*)

In the Oval Office (fourth from left) during a call between President Obama and Egyptian president Hosni Mubarak on February 1, 2011 (*Official White House Photo by Pete Souza*)

With President Obama on Marine One during
a trip to the Korean DMZ in March 2012
(*Official White House Photo by Pete Souza*)

Speaking with President Obama
in the Oval Office in June 2013
(*Official White House Photo by Pete Souza*)

With Secretary of State John Kerry
during negotiations with Iran in
Geneva in November 2013
(*Courtesy of the author*)

With Chinese vice president Li Yuanchao in Beijing in January 2014 *(Photo by Jason Lee—Pool/Getty Images)*

At the makeshift memorial honoring slain Maidan protesters in Kyiv, Ukraine, on February 25, 2014 *(State Department Photo)*

Greeting Indian prime minister Narendra Modi at Andrews Air Force Base during his first visit to the United States on September 29, 2014 *(Courtesy Government of India Press Information Bureau)*

Kerry and I shared a bungalow on the Aqaba compound, modest by most royal standards. Late at night, we had a couple beers and talked at length about American foreign policy. I found him incisive and well informed, with a conviction that it was far riskier to miss diplomatic opportunities than to throw yourself into them. He bore little resemblance to the stiff and self-important portrayal favored by critics. He was, as he so often liked to say about others, "the real deal."

For all their differences, however, Obama and his secretaries of state shared a broad view of the world they faced and the challenge for American diplomacy. While neither could be as close in personal and policy terms as Baker was with Bush 41, Clinton and Kerry were just as loyal to Obama and both became effective partners. Like the Bush 41 administration, they would confront a world undergoing seismic change with all its turbulence, uncertainty, and impossible balancing acts.

* * *

WHEN OBAMA WAS elected in 2008, and soon thereafter chose Hillary Clinton to be his secretary of state, I doubted that I would be asked to continue as undersecretary for political affairs. New administrations and new secretaries almost invariably made new appointments to the most senior jobs at State. So I was delighted when Clinton asked me to stay on soon after her nomination was announced, and even more enthused after we met on her first day in the transition office on the department's first floor. I realized that we had already inundated Clinton with massive briefing books, in the best State Department tradition that anything worth doing is worth overdoing. Figuring that a canned presentation was the last thing the incoming secretary needed or wanted, I put down a few notes on a single index card, focused on the main trend lines, the most significant troubles and opportunities ahead. I'd be the first senior career officer she'd be meeting as she got ready for her new role, and I didn't want to screw it up.

Our scheduled forty-five-minute session ran nearly two hours. We covered the waterfront of policy issues. Clinton had lots of questions—about substance, foreign personalities, and how best to work with the Pentagon and the NSC staff. I was impressed both by the depth of her knowledge and her easygoing style.

I introduced Secretary Clinton on her first day in office to an uncharacteristically raucous crowd of employees at the main C Street entrance. The next day, President Obama made a visit, a visible early sign of his support for her, the department, and, as he said, "the importance of diplomacy and renewing American leadership." He backed those words with actions. He and Clinton moved quickly to win an increase in the international affairs budget, and issued a presidential directive emphasizing development as a core element of American foreign policy.

There was no question about the importance of strengthening diplomacy and development alongside defense. But there were significant questions about what kind of investments we should make now and to what ends. The military was struggling with how to adapt itself to an uncertain era defined by both potential great power collisions and small wars in far-off places. The State Department similarly struggled to settle on a theory of the case for what loomed over the horizon and the most realistic way to adapt given growing risks and scarce resources. There were plenty of slogans bandied about but less hard-nosed priority setting, and even less success in translating Obama's electoral mandate into a domestic political coalition to support serious reforms and his long-term foreign policy ambitions.

Organizing the national security bureaucracy for this new era was an ongoing challenge. Having lived through the bureaucratic blood feuds of the Reagan and Bush 43 eras, I found the interagency atmosphere of the Obama administration to be congenial and disciplined. The president set the tone. He brooked no backbiting or gameplaying, and expected that issues would be considered thoroughly and deliberately. He had limited patience for verbosity, and even less for melodrama. Obama's focus was on a "tight" process—rigorous review of the facts and problem at hand; patient examination of the various options; careful attention to second- and third-order consequences; and "buttoned down" execution of decisions. He understood right from the outset that a disciplined decision-making process would help ensure disciplined implementation. His national security advisors were sticklers for "regular order" and avoiding analytical or procedural shortcuts.

Obama's national security advisors, Jim Jones, Tom Donilon, and Susan Rice, chaired the Principals Committee (PC). This was the group of cabinet agency heads—with State, Defense, the Joint Chiefs, CIA, the director of national intelligence, and Treasury at its core, and other agency counterparts sometimes joining, depending on the subject. Vice President Biden always came to NSC meetings chaired by the president, and frequently to PC meetings. His experience in national security went back to the Vietnam era, and his was a significant and thoughtful voice at the table. Clinton and Bob Gates were almost always of like mind on key issues, a formidable pairing that carried on the informal alliance that Condi Rice and Gates had built late in the previous administration. That was a huge asset for State, and for the quality of decision-making, and a sharp contrast to the pitched battles we endured during Powell's tenure. It also filtered down to the next level, the Deputies Committee.

As undersecretary, and then later as deputy secretary, I probably spent more time with my colleagues in the claustrophobic, windowless confines of the White House Situation Room than I did with anyone else, including my own family. The meetings of the Deputies Committee, which comprised sub-cabinet officials led by the deputy national security advisor, were serious affairs. Our job was to propose, test, argue, and, when possible, settle policy debates and options, or tee them up for the decision of cabinet officials and the president. None of the president's deputy national security advisors, however, lost sight of the human element of the process. Denis

McDonough, who later became the president's chief of staff for the entire second term, was adept at poking holes in policy arguments and keeping people honest. His good humor and humanity also helped keep us sane and focused—his scribbled thank-you notes or expressions of sympathy for family emergencies were legendary.

We were, after all, a collection of human beings, not an abstraction—always coping with intense time pressures, in the era of instantaneous news cycles; always operating with incomplete information, despite the unceasing waves of open-source and classified intelligence washing over us; often trying to choose between bad and worse options. After a quarter century of sitting in the back benches in that room, it finally dawned on me that I had crept up distressingly close to the top of the policy food chain. In a lull between meetings one day during Obama's first term, I leaned over and said to Denis, "You know, I've finally realized that we're the adults now. We're it."

"Yup," he replied with a smile. "Scares the crap out of me sometimes. But we better make the most of it."

For all the quality and camaraderie of the interagency process in the Obama administration, it had its imperfections. The increasing complexity of issues, the increasing number of agencies engaged, and the need for White House oversight of the use of force in an age of frequent drone strikes and limited military operations bred overcentralization. Too many problems got pushed up too high in the interagency process, with the most senior officials sometimes consumed by tactical questions and the details of implementation.

That was compounded by the steady mushrooming of the NSC staff with each administration. At its Obama-era peak, it grew to a policy staff of three hundred, compared to just sixty in the Colin Powell NSC staff I had served on more than twenty years before. The deliberative, patient style of decision-making that was usually one of the strengths of the Obama administration could also sometimes become a weakness—a substitute for action, or a dodge. On challenges where there were no good choices, like Syria, tasking the ninety-seventh paper from the intelligence community on what Assad might do next was sometimes a convenient way to kick the can to the next meeting.

Despite the emphasis on diplomacy, the arm of American military might was extending, not diminishing. During the course of the Obama administration, reliance on drones and special operations grew exponentially. No one in the administration had to be lectured about the blowback risks, but no one managed to slow the addiction, either. It was too inconvenient to challenge the conventional wisdom about the seemingly low-risk, high-reward nature of drone strikes. Yet the conventional wisdom had some painful limits, not just for the impact of occasional botched strikes and the extrajudicial nature of our operations on our standing with Muslim societies around the world, but the ways it would warp our diplomatic relations and skew—and sometimes upend—our diplomatic agenda.

* * *

ONE OF THE best examples of both the quality of Obama's decision-making process and his capacity to navigate the often treacherous short-game choices posed by terrorist threats was the raid that killed Osama bin Laden. In early March 2011, CIA director Leon Panetta briefed Secretary Clinton privately about intelligence that had recently emerged on bin Laden, the best lead on his whereabouts since soon after 9/11. It indicated that he might be holed up in a walled compound near Abbottabad, Pakistan, north of Islamabad and not far from the Pakistani military academy. For obvious reasons, the information was being tightly held. Secretary Clinton was authorized to bring one other person at State into the circle, and she asked me to help her think through the options and the consequences of action. I joined her in a series of close-hold discussions in the Situation Room throughout the rest of the spring.

The intelligence on the compound continued to suggest that bin Laden might well be there, along with a number of family members. But it was never a sure thing. Obama and his cabinet principals carefully weighed the options. The first was a joint raid with the Pakistanis, which was quickly dismissed. There was simply too high a chance that the Pakistanis were already complicit or would tip off bin Laden. Other alternatives included aerial bombing of the compound or a targeted drone strike. The former carried a substantial risk of collateral civilian casualties; neither would allow for confirmation that bin Laden had been killed, or for collection of other intelligence at the site.

The final option was the riskiest—a special operations raid. This would mean a nighttime helicopter movement from a U.S. base in Afghanistan, a dangerous operation on the ground by a team of Navy SEALs, and then their extraction by helicopter back across Pakistan to Afghanistan. A lot could go wrong, as it had in the Desert One debacle in 1980 when the United States lost eight servicemen in an aborted attempt to rescue the embassy hostages in Tehran. But by 2011, American special forces had carried out hundreds of similar raids in Iraq and Afghanistan; when Admiral Bill McRaven, head of Joint Special Operations Command, laid out this option for the president in the Situation Room, it was impossible not to feel his confidence.

The president convened his senior advisors for a final discussion on Thursday afternoon, April 28. I rode over with Secretary Clinton, and we agreed on the way that this was too important an opportunity to miss, even if the odds were no better than fifty-fifty that bin Laden was there, and that the special operations raid was the best of the options. It was hard to know how the Pakistanis would react, and a failed raid could be a disaster for the president. But not attempting it carried substantial risks too.

The intelligence update presented to the president that afternoon was still inconclusive. When the president went around the room asking for views, Vice President Biden recommended waiting for more definitive intelligence. Bob Gates, who had lived through the Desert One ordeal as an aide to the CIA director, agreed. Clinton, in a rare break with Gates, laid out a calm, well-reasoned case for action, which Panetta reinforced. Most of the rest of the participants also favored action, and I joined them when the president polled the deputies in the room too. Obama concluded the meeting by saying that he would think about things overnight. The next morning, he told Donilon that he'd decided to launch, and McRaven began to set the operation in motion for Sunday.

On Sunday morning, I drove into the State Department on my own, parked my car, and walked the five blocks to the White House. I joined Clinton and the rest of Obama's team in the Situation Room for the long wait. At 2:30 P.M., we watched on a small video map as two Black Hawk helicopters took off for Abbottabad from Jalalabad in eastern Afghanistan. The next couple hours seemed like an eternity, and the raid itself began with gut-wrenching drama, when one of the two helicopters made a hard landing in the courtyard of the compound. The SEALs were unhurt, but they had to destroy the helicopter and adapt quickly. McRaven narrated the whole operation with incredible calm from a command post in Afghanistan. As the president and his senior aides sat in rapt attention, there wasn't a hint of second-guessing or backseat commentary. Then McRaven's voice came on the line to confirm "E-KIA"—the enemy had been killed in action. Bin Laden was dead. Never had I been prouder of the U.S. military, or of a president who had so coolly taken such a big risk. For a diplomat accustomed to long slogs and victories at the margins, this was an incredible moment.

The president announced the successful operation to the nation and the world at around 11 P.M. that night. Secretary Clinton and I divided a series of phone calls to notify key allies and leaders around the world. Late that night, my calls completed, I walked out the White House gate, heading back to my car. In front of the White House, all across Lafayette Square, was a large and boisterous crowd, waving flags and shouting "USA, USA, USA." I couldn't help but think, as I walked back to the State Department, of a much different moment nearly a decade before, standing in front of State with Lisa as the full import of the 9/11 attacks began to sink in. It had taken a long time, but a measure of justice had been done.

Amid the deliberations about the bin Laden raid that spring, Clinton called late one afternoon and asked me to come down to her office. The issue on her mind was not bin Laden, but finding a successor to Jim Steinberg, who had just decided to step down as deputy secretary. Smiling broadly, she got right to the point. "I'd like you to take Jim's place," the secretary said. "I trust you, the president trusts you, and everyone in this building trusts you. It would mean a lot to me personally if you'd agree." I smiled back, surprised but flattered, and mentioned that it was a little unusual to have a career person in that role.[1] "I know," she replied. "But you're the right choice, and I like the message it sends." I quickly accepted. This was a vote of confidence in the professional diplomatic service, not just me.

My work as undersecretary and deputy secretary stretched me across the whole range of issues in American foreign policy. On many days, it was a little like taking ten exams on ten different subjects, some of which I knew well, and some of which I didn't. I filled in for the secretary at meetings of foreign ministers, going to a G-8 ministerial in Italy on short notice, after Clinton fell and broke her elbow in the State Department parking garage, and later accompanying the president to the G-8 summit and Moscow. I spent considerable time testifying and consulting on Capitol Hill, and my travels took me to every part of the globe, from Africa and Latin America to the Balkans and Southeast Asia. Inevitably, I spent more time on some issues than others. And the issue that was at the core of the long game, and the heart of our revitalized diplomacy, was the effort to manage changing relations with the major powers, especially India, China, and Russia.

* * *

OBAMA INHERITED FROM Bush an emerging partnership with India. The world's biggest democracy, and soon to be the world's most populous country, India had begun an economic transformation in the early 1990s and was growing at a rapid clip. It remained, however, a nation of vast contradictions. Hundreds of millions of people had been lifted out of poverty and into a new middle class, but hundreds of millions more still lived on less than two dollars a day, without toilets or regular access to electricity. The tech sector was beginning to boom, but infrastructure was crumbling and pollution and urban overcrowding were worsening. Expansive national ambitions were slowed by a constipated, corrupt, and overbureaucratized political system. India was sometimes schizophrenic in its international ambitions, caught between a future that argued for a more assertive and agile role and a past that bogged down Indian diplomacy in the pedantic quarrels of a nonaligned world left behind by the end of the Cold War. As a matter of policy, India had been "looking east" to its future in a wider Asia for two decades. When Obama took office, it was still doing more looking than acting.

What had accelerated dramatically in the George W. Bush administration was the improvement in U.S.-Indian ties that had begun at the end of the Clinton administration. Sensing the historic opportunity that a rising India provided, Bush made a big strategic bet at the beginning of his second term. He decided to cut through the most difficult knot in our relationship with India—its nuclear program. India's decision to remain outside the Treaty on the Non-Proliferation of Nuclear Weapons (NPT), alongside Pakistan, Israel, and North Korea (which withdrew in 2003), and its refusal to put its nuclear facilities under international safeguards, proved for decades an immovable practical and symbolic roadblock to closer relations.

The president believed that bringing India in out of the nuclear cold would be a net plus for American strategy. The result, in the summer of 2005, was a crucial understanding announced by President Bush and Indian prime minister Manmohan Singh. India would seek to separate its military and civilian nuclear facilities and put the latter under the most advanced international safeguards, called the

Additional Protocol; it would put in place effective export control systems consistent with the Nuclear Suppliers Group (NSG), and would not transfer enrichment and reprocessing technologies to states that did not already have them; and it would continue its "unilateral moratorium" on nuclear testing. In return, the United States would bend domestic and international rules to accommodate the reality of India's nuclear program and its commitment to act responsibly.

It was not an easy call. Questions remained on just how aligned India would be with us, how significant the costs of the India exception would be to nuclear diplomacy and the broader nuclear nonproliferation regime, and whether the economic benefits for the American nuclear industry would ever live up to the hype. Proponents of the deal tended to overstate the promise and understate the risk; critics did the opposite, lambasted by Indian officials as "nuclear ayatollahs" whose nonproliferation zeal blinded them to wider possibilities. As a long-term strategic investment, however, Bush's decision was bold and smart. It was the essential prerequisite to unlocking the possibility of a strategic partnership that would be a huge asset in shaping the unfolding Pacific Century. The downsides were real but manageable, the returns promising, if delayed. There are no guarantees in diplomacy, but this was a bet worth making.

Producing that initial accord proved difficult, but Secretary Rice, National Security Advisor Hadley, and my predecessor as undersecretary for political affairs, Nick Burns, led a formidable diplomatic campaign. Congress passed the Hyde Act, laying out its expectations for implementation and amending U.S. law to permit civilian nuclear cooperation with India, but there continued to be resistance from members primarily concerned with nuclear proliferation. It was tough going in the Indian Parliament too, with opposition members complaining about infringements on Indian sovereignty. By the time I returned to Washington in the late spring of 2008, the process had stalled, and it looked as if this would be yet another challenge for the next administration to pick up.

Then Prime Minister Singh, in a burst of unforeseen political risk-taking, decided to press ahead in Parliament. With India's next national elections looming in the spring of 2009, time running out for his allies in the Bush administration, and uncertainty about the attitudes of their successors, Singh pushed for and won a confidence vote, clearing a major hurdle on the Indian side. The president and Secretary Rice made clear that they wanted to make a hard push to complete the agreement before the end of their term. Rice called me into her office in mid-June and said, "I know the odds on this are long. But Singh has taken a real risk, and we need to pull out all the stops." I dove in—the beginning of a three-month sprint to finish the civil nuclear agreement, and of another six years of active personal involvement in deepening and normalizing the U.S.-Indian partnership.

We had three more forbidding obstacles to clear: approval of India's nuclear safeguards program by the International Atomic Energy Agency (IAEA); agreement by the NSG to allow a so-called clean exemption for India, permitting it to engage in civil nuclear cooperation with other countries; and finally, passage by both houses of Congress of the civilian nuclear agreement. Of these, the NSG hurdle looked the highest, with six or seven member states in vocal opposition, and consensus a requirement. Passage by Congress would be tough on such a short timetable, but we had to move in sequence and hope that there'd be a small window left for hearings and a vote in September.

We had a skillful team, and Indian counterparts who had received similarly urgent marching orders from Manmohan Singh. President Bush, Secretary Rice, and Steve Hadley were indefatigable in making phone calls and leaning on other leaders, and our ambassador in New Delhi, David Mulford, was not shy about pushing the Indians to show maximum flexibility. John Rood and Dick Stratford, senior arms control officials at State, were excellent partners.

On August 1, the Indians won IAEA approval, clearing the first and lowest hurdle. The NSG was another matter. At an initial meeting of the NSG board in late August, consensus proved elusive. A number of the four dozen member states balked, with Austria, Ireland, and New Zealand among the most outspoken about the concern that India's nonproliferation commitments weren't strong enough. I was candid with Rice. "We really are at a crunch point," I wrote to her in a memo on August 27, "and the Indians are extremely nervous about their domestic politics, and not giving us much to work with at the NSG. . . . The obstacles on both sides are pretty steep."[2]

Both the secretary and the president urged Singh to sharpen the Indian text, and worked the phones with reluctant NSG members. Armed with a somewhat tighter draft, we set off with the Indians for the follow-on NSG board meeting in early September in Vienna. Rice asked me to lead the American delegation, a higher level than we would normally have used, to signal our determination.

This was an exercise in diplomatic blunt force as much as persuasion. I had to wake up senior Swiss and Irish officials in their capitals at four in the morning to push for a final yes. I argued our case but didn't belabor it. The point was simply that we needed this vote and were calling in a chit. There was no point in going back and forth on the merits; we were not looking to do any convincing. This was not elegant diplomacy. This was about power, and we were exercising it.

The votes eventually began to fall into place, and on September 6 the NSG finally approved India's exemption, following a formal pledge by New Delhi that it would not share sensitive nuclear technology or materials with others, and would uphold its moratorium on testing. There was still a lot of uneasiness within the NSG over the purely declaratory nature of the Indian commitments, but in the end it was enough. It was a few years before I was welcome again in Bern or Dublin, but we had cleared the second hurdle.

Although legislative days were limited with the November elections approaching, the congressional leadership agreed to give us a shot at passage in the fall of 2008. Rood and I testified before the

Senate Foreign Relations Committee on September 18 and made our pitch—looking to take seriously the nonproliferation concerns but overwhelm them with the strategic argument. By the end of the month, both the Senate and the House voted to approve the deal. Prime Minister Singh made a last visit to have dinner with President Bush at the White House, a moment of genuine mutual satisfaction, and a moment in which the promise of U.S.-Indian partnership seemed tangible. The ever-polite Singh looked more bemused than offended when his plate was whipped away with his fork still poised in midair. It was his introduction to President Bush's penchant for culinary speed dating, where business was the first and only course. However abbreviated their dinner, their sense of pride was enduring, and so was their achievement.

* * *

THE ADVENT OF the Obama administration initially unnerved the Indian leadership. Fresh from their successful partnership with Bush, Singh and his chief advisors were worried that Obama was less enthusiastic. In the near term, they feared the new president's campaign focus on the "right war" in Afghanistan would "re-hyphenate" the relationship, seeing it through a wider lens that balanced American priorities with Pakistan and Afghanistan against strategic investment with India. In the longer term, they were anxious that he would subordinate partnership with India to a "G-2" worldview, in which the U.S.-China relationship was paramount. Obama's ambitious agenda on nuclear issues was another source of concern—for all the unburdening of the nuclear deal, India was still a square peg in the round hole of the nonproliferation regime. As the most senior U.S. representative of continuity in relations with India, I worked hard to overcome misimpressions and sustain momentum.

It didn't take long to reassure the Singh government, and making the case for India's significance was pushing on an open door with Clinton and Obama. In an early memo, I reminded Clinton of the heavy lift required to finalize the civil nuclear agreement the summer before, and added that "despite the difficulties—the reversals, recriminations, and negotiating brinksmanship—I was taken by the potential of our relationship. India is as remarkable as it is complicated, a democracy of many and competing voices, and without doubt an emerging Great Power with a growing role in Asia and beyond. I don't believe it will be an easy or quick task, but building a true American alliance with India is a mission worthy of our patience and investment."[3]

Obama and Clinton fully appreciated the importance of partnership with India, both on its own merits and as a key element in the "rebalance" toward Asia that they were beginning to shape. Step-by-step, we expanded the bilateral agenda, strengthening counterterrorism cooperation; looking for opportunities to work together in education and science; deepening two-way trade and investment; starting a systematic discussion on climate change; and significantly increasing defense cooperation. By the end of Obama's first term, India was conducting more military exercises with the United States than with any other country, and its acquisitions of American defense equipment had risen from a little over $200 million to $2 billion.

The president and Prime Minister Singh had a cordial first encounter in London on the margins of the G-20 summit in April, and Obama invited him to make a state visit—the first of his administration—in November 2009. The symbolism of that went a long way to assuage Indian anxieties, and Obama and Singh hit it off. The next year, Obama made a reciprocal state visit to India. He and Singh pressed ahead in a number of areas, as both the economic and defense dimensions of the relationship continued to grow. There were headaches, of course; nothing came easily in U.S.-Indian relations, and the Singh government lost political altitude and clout steadily after its reelection in the spring of 2009.

Pakistan remained a neuralgic topic; despite the president's best efforts with Singh, and my own quiet conversations with Shivshankar

Menon, the prime minister's national security advisor, the Indians had no interest in opening up much with us about their relations with the Pakistanis. Active back-channel talks between them had nearly brought about a breakthrough over Kashmir and other disputes in the spring of 2007, but the collapsing political position of Pakistani president Pervez Musharraf had brought them to an abrupt halt, and they had made no more than fitful progress since then. We were increasingly worried about the risks of nuclear confrontation, but the Indians were not much interested in talking about their perceptions or how to avoid escalation, let alone any American mediation role.[4]

The president took advantage of his 2010 visit to take another dramatic step to highlight his commitment to U.S.-Indian partnership. Speaking to India's Parliament, Obama repeated that the U.S.-India relationship was "one of the defining partnerships of the twenty-first century," and indicated for the first time his support for Indian permanent membership in a reformed UN Security Council. The announcement fit the moment and the setting, but it was not an easy decision. The United States had made only one other similar statement, some years before, in support of Japan's candidacy. The whole issue of expanding permanent membership was fraught with difficulty—in terms of procedures; preserving the efficacy of the institution; navigating the reservations of other permanent members; and managing the sensitivities of a number of players, including close allies and Security Council aspirants like Germany.

Susan Rice, our ambassador to the UN, was understandably concerned about taking this step, not least because the Indians hadn't exactly been reliable partners in New York over the years. On the morning of his speech to Parliament, I sat with the president and Tom Donilon, newly elevated as national security advisor, for one last secure conference call with Susan, who repeated her reservations and argued for more conditional language. I fully acknowledged the risks, but said I thought it would be a mistake to miss this opportunity.

Tom agreed. The president ultimately decided to go ahead—but made a point of stressing to Singh privately the difficulties involved in expanding permanent membership, and the importance of India doing its part to earn the seat in New York.

Over the next few years, U.S.-Indian relations continued to deepen. John Kerry followed in Clinton's footsteps and worked with Secretary of Commerce Penny Pritzker in the second Obama term to deepen the promise of economic ties. Implementation of the civil nuclear agreement was a slog. Menon and I finished a required nuclear reprocessing agreement in 2010, but that same year the Indian Parliament passed nuclear liability legislation that discouraged domestic, American, and other foreign firms from taking advantage of the commercial opportunities that were one of the attractions of the civilian nuclear deal. It took several years to develop a workable compromise. It was a deeply frustrating exercise, one that tested the patience and goodwill of Congress and much of the U.S. bureaucracy—and served as a gnawing reminder that whatever the long-term gains might be from the agreement, the near-term pains would not be inconsequential.

Narendra Modi succeeded Singh as prime minister after a landslide victory for his Bharatiya Janata Party (BJP) in the spring of 2014. Modi embraced a more confident role for India on the world stage, committed to making it a great power and its partnership with the United States far more strategic. He had bold ideas to propel India's economy and bureaucracy into the twenty-first century. The BJP, however, had harbored for years some worrying sectarian, Hindu nationalist tendencies. During Modi's tenure as chief minister of Gujarat, anti-Muslim violence had claimed more than a thousand lives, denting his image and complicating his relationship with the United States, which denied him a visa for more than a decade. The Indian electorate, however, was thirsty for a strong man to deal with domestic drift, and Modi's energy and vision offered a sense of possibility, both for India and for our partnership.

I was the first senior U.S. official to visit Modi in New Delhi, a week after his inauguration. I found him full of ambition, with a dry sense of humor and no evident hard feelings about the visa issue. He made clear his determination to invest in U.S.-Indian relations, and emphasized that he saw our partnership as one of the keys to his own domestic and regional ambitions. Modi was curious about American politics and how the next presidential contest was shaping up, and what could be done in the meantime to cement cooperation between Washington and New Delhi. He immediately accepted the invitation I conveyed from President Obama to visit Washington in September.

Obama and Modi developed a close rapport, and the September visit went well. Obama was the honored foreign guest on India's Republic Day in January 2015, a further sign of the strength of the relationship. While it was always going to be impossible to duplicate the drama of the civilian nuclear breakthrough, and while we would continue to have our differences on important questions of geopolitics and trade, the Obama administration deepened the roots of a partnership whose consequence for international order was growing, and whose utility in the administration's rebalance toward Asia was increasingly apparent.

* * *

A LITTLE BEFORE 10 P.M. on a Wednesday evening in April 2012, I got a call at home from the State Department Operations Center asking me to join a secure call with Secretary Clinton. I climbed up the stairs to my tiny attic office, ducking to avoid hitting my head on the beams. I had had my secure phone installed up there to avoid bothering Lisa and our daughters with the late-night calls that they had so often endured over the years. Chief of Staff Cheryl Mills, Policy Planning Director Jake Sullivan, and Assistant Secretary for East Asian and Pacific Affairs Kurt Campbell were already on the line.

When the secretary joined, with her usual even-keeled "now what?" tone, Campbell explained the dilemma before us: A blind, self-taught, forty-year-old Chinese human rights activist named

Chen Guangcheng had escaped house arrest in Shandong Province. Despite having broken his ankle, he had made his way to the Beijing suburbs, with the assistance of friends along the way. On the run from the state security services, he had telephoned a U.S. embassy contact, who drove out along with another embassy officer to meet with him a few hours later. Chen asked for refuge inside the U.S. embassy. The officers relayed this to the chargé, Bob Wang, who immediately sought guidance from Kurt. Wang said he thought the chances were slim that Chen could get into the embassy on his own, given his condition and the layers of Chinese security, but judged that the odds were high that American diplomats could drive him in if they went out and brought him back in their embassy vehicle. Wang added one more thing: His guess was that Chen had less than an hour before state security caught up with him.

It was not your average late-night phone call, but it was all too typical of the imperfect choices that secretaries of state often faced. The moral argument for bringing Chen in was powerful; this was yet another test of how much the United States was prepared to risk in defense of its values. On the other side was the obvious political problem: The Chinese government would be outraged. There was no clear pathway to negotiating an acceptable way out for Chen once he came in. To make matters even more complicated, Secretary Clinton was scheduled to fly to Beijing five days later for the next round of the Strategic and Economic Dialogue (S&ED)—the Obama administration's flagship cabinet-level meeting with the Chinese. The timing could not have been worse.

Clinton was matter of fact: no hand-wringing, no lamentation about lousy choices, no second-guessing of the embassy. She asked a few more questions about Chen and his background, and asked each of us what we thought. We all acknowledged the downsides, but recommended bringing Chen in. Clinton didn't hesitate. She knew there'd be a political storm with the Chinese, but suspected it was navigable, and she couldn't in any case justify saying no. She didn't try to pass the buck to the White House, recognizing the time pressures. She simply asked Jake to inform the NSC staff, in case they wanted to object, and authorized Kurt to give the green light to Bob Wang. I joined Jake for a secure call to Tom Donilon, who was not thrilled by the news and channeled Baker in reminding us that the dead cat would be on our doorstep if we messed this up.

At about 3 A.M. Washington time, Wang confirmed that Chen had made it into the embassy. Then we strapped ourselves in for the roller coaster. Kurt flew out to Beijing to begin discussions with an extremely unhappy Cui Tiankai, the vice foreign minister responsible for relations with the United States. Cui emphasized that the only solution was to turn Chen over to the Chinese authorities immediately, and left hanging the risk of blowing up the S&ED. I arrived a day later, on the evening of April 30, to lead another round of the Strategic Security Dialogue, a semiannual meeting aimed at some of the trickiest problems on the bilateral agenda—including cybersecurity, maritime security, and the future of nuclear arms and missile defense. Kurt and I had a long, hard two-hour conversation with Cui that night. I made the case as calmly as I could that the least messy of the options before us was to let Chen go to a Beijing hospital for treatment, let his family come from Shandong to join him there, and then let him do what he wanted—which was study law at a Chinese university. Cui initially balked. But as the night wore on, the political temperature lowered and he began to seem more amenable. It was obvious that neither he nor his superiors were eager to see the upcoming ministerial meeting sunk by the Chen affair. By the next morning, the Chinese had agreed to the approach we outlined.

But that didn't stop the roller coaster. In the hospital, Chen suddenly changed his mind. He now wanted to go to the United States immediately with his wife, and signaled the same thing in cellphone interviews with Western journalists. Cui was livid. "You can't do this," he said. "You have no idea how badly this will affect our relations." Eventually, with Clinton's direct intervention with her Chinese counterpart, Chen was allowed to go directly to New York as he had hoped. We breathed a huge sigh of relief—and so did the White House.[5]

This affair was far from the most significant crisis with the Chinese during the Obama administration, but it left a few lasting impressions. One was about Clinton's equanimity and leadership style in the face of the inevitable trade-offs and smothering time pressures of many policy choices. Another was about China's increasingly assertive direction. And still another was about the growing maturity of U.S.-China relations, whose resilience in the face of unavoidable difficulties required constant attention and investment. As I neared the end of a long diplomatic career, it was clearer than ever that nothing mattered more in American foreign policy than management of that relationship.

By now, China was no longer a great power on the rise, but one whose moment had come. The Iraq War and the financial crisis five years later had exposed American vulnerabilities. An increasingly feisty Chinese leadership saw an opening and began to question the wisdom of Deng Xiaoping's "hide your strengths and bide your time" philosophy, and it accelerated its ambitions not only to establish itself as a global economic peer of the United States, but to supplant it as the leading power in Asia. That did not mean that conflict was foreordained; the mutually beneficial entangling of the American and Chinese economies was a powerful incentive to avoid it. It did mean that the most critical test of American statecraft for President Obama and Secretary Clinton was managing competition with China, and cushioning it with bilateral cooperation and regional alliances and institutions. This was surely not a novel challenge—ever since Nixon and Kissinger, U.S. strategy had paid careful attention to China's emergence, and the Bush 43 administration had put considerable effort into encouraging China to be a "responsible stakeholder" in a changing international system. 9/11 and the Middle East sucked up high-level attention and resources, however, and Obama and Clinton were determined to rebalance American strategy back to Asia.

Clinton became the first secretary since Dean Rusk a half century earlier to take her first overseas trip to Asia, and returned often during her tenure. Obama surpassed every American president by making more than a dozen visits during his two terms. Beyond just showing up, they invested heavily in relationships across the region, with India as a western bookend, expanding ties to the fast-growing economies of Southeast Asia, and reaffirming crucial alliances with Australia, South Korea, and Japan. They began to expand the U.S. military and diplomatic presence in the region, explore a new trading arrangement that eventually emerged as the Trans-Pacific Partnership, and cultivate new, region-wide institutions like the East Asia Summit. Assistant Secretary Kurt Campbell was the leading sub-cabinet architect of the rebalance and its tireless champion. Once Tom Donilon became national security advisor partway through Obama's first term, he immersed himself in relations with China, traveling regularly to Beijing and building strong personal ties. So did Susan Rice after she succeeded Donilon.

Roaming across other issues and places, however, I was struck by the quality and increasing self-confidence of Chinese diplomacy. Leading the American delegation to the African Union summit in Addis Ababa one year, I found the Chinese presence nearly overwhelming, with President Hu Jintao at the head of a delegation many times the size of ours, and a gleaming new Chinese-constructed and -financed African Union headquarters building as the backdrop. I traveled to Beijing often to consult on Iran, Afghanistan, and Russia, among many other issues. I enjoyed long discussions with Dai Bingguo, Hu's principal foreign affairs advisor. Trained as a Soviet specialist, Dai had a clever, orderly mind, and a sure feel for how other leaderships operated. When I described to him at one point the progress that Obama and Medvedev were making in repairing relations, Dai smiled blandly and interjected, "You realize, of course, that nothing happens in Moscow without Putin's assent." His tone was polite, his expression amused, and his implication unmistakable—he really wasn't sure that we knew how things worked.

I spent a fair amount of time during the Obama years traveling in both Southeast and Northeast Asia. China had begun to throw its weight around in the South China Sea, intent upon—quite literally—shoring up its territorial claims through the creation of artificial islands, and staking out its commercial and resource interests. Irritated by Secretary Clinton's forthright statement at a meeting of the Association of Southeast Asian Nations (ASEAN) in Hanoi in the summer of 2010 that the United States had national interests in the South China Sea too, Foreign Minister Yang Jiechi basically warned the assembled ministers that China was the biggest player in the neighborhood, and they had better get used to it. Clinton astutely took advantage of Chinese overreach to strengthen our own ties in Southeast Asia. I tried to help with several visits to Vietnam and Indonesia, and stops in Australia and each of the other ASEAN capitals over the course of the next few years.

My father had fought in Vietnam in 1966–67, but there were few traces of war or resentment decades later in the boomtown cacophony of Ho Chi Minh City. In Cambodia, a survivor of Pol Pot's genocide guided me through the moving Tuol Seng Genocide Museum in central Phnom Penh, formerly the prison where he had once suffered. "Cambodia," I wrote Secretary Clinton afterward, "offers hope in the fundamental resilience of human beings, even after a whole society self-destructs amidst unspeakable horrors." Meeting Cambodia's current leader helped keep my expectations in check. "Having spent most of his adult life waking up every morning wondering who was going to try to kill him that day, Hun Sen remains a cunning, tough survivor, for whom political openness is not necessarily a natural condition." I went to Burma too, supporting the opening that Obama and Clinton had worked hard to create. After a lengthy conversation with the formidable Aung San Suu Kyi in 2012, I reported back to the secretary that it was already clear that "the mix within her of global human rights icon and steely Burmese politician is bound to be uneasy."[6]

After becoming deputy secretary in the summer of 2011, I became a more regular visitor to Tokyo and Seoul, and joined in trilateral meetings with both crucial allies, whose historical differences sometimes got in the way of common concerns about North Korea's nuclear ambitions and China's rise. I wasn't directly engaged in our fitful diplomacy on North Korea, but I shared my colleagues' frustration over the fruitlessness of the Six Party Talks, our inability to get a serious back channel with the North Koreans going, and our similar lack of success in beginning a quiet strategic conversation with the Chinese about the future of the Korean Peninsula. "Strategic patience" had a deceptively reassuring ring to it, but only seemed to narrow our strategic choices and fuel long-term impatience on all sides—especially after Kim Jong-un succeeded his father in 2012.

My involvement in U.S.-China relations became much more active and direct after 2011. Succeeding Steinberg, I led the American side in the semiannual Strategic Security Dialogue with the Chinese. These meetings brought together diplomats and senior military and intelligence officials. That sometimes made for an uneasy combination on the Chinese side, where my Foreign Ministry counterpart, Zhang Yesui, took the lead, with a number of People's Liberation Army (PLA) generals and senior security services representatives sitting alongside, most looking as if they'd like nothing better than to beam themselves out of the room.

The exchanges were rarely fun. We spent seven hours in one stretch laying out and debating specific information that we had about cyber-enabled commercial espionage by Chinese state organs, including the PLA. The Chinese summarily rejected our evidence. But there was a broader kind of cognitive dissonance at work too—for the Chinese, at least at that stage, the distinction we were drawing between espionage for national security purposes and cyber-spying for commercial advantage seemed artificial. In their view, governments used whatever means they could to build advantage, whether political or economic. We emphasized that we were determined to uphold that distinction, and we showed some teeth too. When our long presentation of concrete evidence got nowhere, and when the president's concerns were rebuffed or ignored, we announced indictments against several Chinese security officials. While the chances that they'd ever be offered up to the American judicial system were nil, our point was made, and the Chinese eventually reached a general understanding with us, significantly reducing cyber-enabled commercial thefts.

John Kerry's tireless efforts on climate change, and the Chinese leadership's belated realization that poisoning their population was a recipe for inconvenient domestic disturbances, led to the diplomatic breakthrough of the 2015 Paris climate agreement. Unfortunately, there were few other breakthroughs to celebrate. The gulf between us was growing, as were the risks of collision. Diplomacy played a critical role in keeping the temperature down and finding ways to get business done where there was obvious benefit to both of us. Obama believed that the Pacific Century could accommodate a risen China and a resilient and adaptable United States, and he worked hard to demonstrate American commitment to that idea. But as Chinese self-confidence grew and their sense of American drift deepened, it was inevitable that we'd test one another on whose version of regional order was ascendant. Nothing would matter more in American foreign policy than how that new great game played out.

* * *

AS PRESIDENT OBAMA attempted to rebalance American foreign policy for the long term, with new emphasis on Asia, he knew we needed to continue to invest in our closest allies in Europe. Obama and Clinton sought to strengthen transatlantic ties, especially with Germany, France, and the United Kingdom. The president built a particularly effective relationship over time with German chancellor Angela Merkel, whose cool intellect and no-nonsense style he greatly valued. While our core European allies would occasionally suffer from "pivot envy" as the Obama administration focused more and more visible attention on Asia, nothing remained more critical to our global interests than the transatlantic alliance. Strong ties to our European partners were essential to another long-game priority, a renewed effort at managing relations with Russia.

Obama's approach to Russia began cautiously. He told a television interviewer during the transition that he thought it made sense to explore a "reset" in relations. Differences over Russian aggression in Georgia remained serious, and there were plenty of other problems, but there was also common ground that could be plowed more effectively. Obama had talked during the 2008 campaign about his determination to reduce the dangers of nuclear war, his willingness to directly engage the Iranian regime, and his interest in a more successful approach to the war in Afghanistan. All of those priorities would benefit from a healthier U.S.-Russian relationship.

The Georgia conflict had further sobered my expectations, and my view continued to be that we'd be operating within a fairly narrow band of possibilities in relations with a Russia that was still far more Putin's than Medvedev's. We still could, however, seek a better balance between areas of cooperation and inevitable differences. I found a kindred spirit in Mike McFaul, the new senior Russia expert on the NSC staff. Mike and I had first met on the basketball court at the embassy in Moscow in the 1990s, during my first tour and his stint at the Carnegie Endowment's Moscow Center. He was as energetic in government as he had been on the court, driving the reset with similar determination and creativity.

McFaul was not, however, wildly enthusiastic about my first suggestion. I thought it would help reinforce the seriousness of the administration's approach to lay out our thinking comprehensively in a presidential letter, and then have the two of us deliver it in Moscow.

To Mike, this seemed very nineteenth-century; all that was missing was the quill pen. But I argued that the Russians tended to be traditionalists in their estimation of diplomatic seriousness, and that this would help. I eventually wore him down. We produced a long, systematic draft for the president, which Obama approved, and flew to Moscow in early February 2009. I also took along a handwritten note from Secretary Clinton to Foreign Minister Lavrov. Clinton was skeptical about how much could be accomplished in the reset, but believed it was worth a shot.

McFaul and I spent two days in intensive discussions with Lavrov and other senior officials. It went better than we expected. I told the secretary on February 13, "I left Moscow convinced that we have a significant opportunity before us, but realistic about how hard it is going to be to shift gears with a Russian leadership deeply distracted by a worsening economic predicament, and still conflicted about whether their interests are better served by a thaw in relations." I was struck by high-level anxiety in Moscow about the global financial crisis, which had quickly undercut Russia's boom. "The construction cranes that dominated the city skyline during my years as ambassador now sit idle," I wrote. "The bankers and senior officials gathered in the Finance Minister's anteroom while we were waiting to meet him . . . had none of the swagger I remember before, and their gloom was palpable." The authoritarian modernization model of Putin and Medvedev was under considerable strain, and that strengthened the case in the Kremlin for testing a relaxation of tensions with us.[7]

On specific issues that the president raised in his letter to Medvedev, the Russians seemed cautiously receptive. Obama had made clear our areas of difference, particularly our disagreement over the status of Abkhazia and South Ossetia. He was equally straight about our human rights concerns. The Russians didn't belabor the Georgia conflict or beat their chests over U.S. policy in the former Soviet Union. Lavrov signaled immediate interest in talks about a new arms reduction agreement, with START due to expire at the end of 2009.

"No passage in the President's letter caught the Russians' attention more," I told Clinton, "than the paragraph on Iran and missile defense." Choosing his words carefully, the president had emphasized that he was in the process of reviewing U.S. missile defense strategy, including the plans for sites in Poland and the Czech Republic that had so exercised the Russians, and that—logically—progress in reducing the risks posed by Iran's missile and nuclear programs would have a direct impact on our review, since those were the threats against which our European plans were primarily targeted. The Russians couldn't miss the implication.[8]

In early March, Clinton had an introductory meeting with Lavrov in Geneva. It was marred only by a minor embarrassment, when Clinton sought to break the ice during a press availability at the outset by handing Lavrov a red button that was supposed to say "reset" in Russian, but instead was mistranslated as "overload." Gimmicks and Lavrov rarely mixed well. Lavrov didn't rub it in (at least not too much), and the secretary took it in stride. The media, however, had a field day.

The president had his first meeting with Medvedev in London at the beginning of April, on the margins of a G-20 meeting focused mostly on the continuing economic tidal wave caused by the 2008 financial crisis. They met at Winfield House, the elegant residence of the U.S. ambassador, in a tranquil corner of Regent's Park. As we waited in the dining room for Medvedev and his delegation to arrive, I must admit that I was thinking less of the nuts and bolts of the reset agenda and more of the first time I walked into that room, a shy twenty-two-year-old in a bad suit trying to fade into the elegant woodwork at a welcome reception for Marshall Scholars. The woodwork still beckoned, and my sartorial standards were only marginally improved, but I was feeling a little more at ease this time.

It was clear from the start that Medvedev was eager to build rapport with Obama and try to make some version of the reset an advertisement for his effectiveness as a president and world leader. That didn't mean that he was going to be a pushover; he was a tough defender of Russian interests, without his mentor's snark but operating within the bounds of Putin's hard-nosed views. He underscored his commitment to finalizing a successor to the START treaty by the end of the year, at substantially reduced levels of strategic nuclear weapons. He offered to allow the United States to fly troops and material through Russian airspace to Afghanistan—a big advantage for a U.S. administration eager to lessen dependence on supply lines through Pakistan. Most surprisingly, he admitted to Obama that Russia had underestimated the pace and threat of the Iranian nuclear and ballistic missile programs—probing to see how far a tougher line on Iran might get him on the missile defense issue. Despite Medvedev's sharp criticisms on missile defense and Georgia, the overall tenor of the conversation was surprisingly positive, with Medvedev at pains to show how comfortably he was settling into his presidential role.

It was not at all clear, however, that there was space in a one-man political system for a second player—and also not at all clear that that one man shared Medvedev's apparent enthusiasm for the reset. President Obama agreed to an early visit to Moscow to test both propositions. Caution might have dictated a slower pace, especially since Obama wouldn't visit Beijing for the first time until November, and had a massive domestic agenda to contend with and a steep recession still consuming much of his time and attention. Yet the president was in a hurry, on a number of fronts, and he wanted to see if the reset with Russia could get traction. He flew to Moscow during the first week in July, and I went along as the senior State Department representative.

The Medvedev meeting went smoothly. Most of it—three hours out of a little less than four altogether—took place in a small group. Both presidents were on top of their briefs, and had an easy rapport as they went back and forth over the issues. Obama put particular emphasis on the need to accelerate the New START negotiations, and on his concerns about Iran. Medvedev continued to hammer away at

Russian reservations about missile defense, stressing their general interest in some form of constraints on missile defense alongside strategic arms reductions, and specifically their opposition to the two Central European sites, which he argued would do little to address the modest medium-term Iranian threat. The practical accomplishments of their first six months working together, however, were already substantial, and hinted at even greater potential.

The following morning, Obama drove out to meet Putin at his Novo Ogaryovo dacha just outside Moscow. Jim Jones, McFaul, and I rode along with him in the "Beast," the heavily armored limousine that is flown out in advance to transport and protect the president on his overseas trips. Mike and I sat facing the president, and we talked generally about the meeting and how best to approach Putin. I described a few of my own interactions with him over the years, and suggested that he usually didn't react well to a long presentation, especially since he would see himself as the more senior and experienced leader. Why not ask him at the start for his candid assessment of what he thought had gone right and what he thought had gone wrong in Russian-American relations over the past decade? Putin liked being asked his opinion, and he certainly wasn't shy. Maybe it would set a good tone to let him get some things off his chest up front. The president nodded.

After President Obama's initial question produced an unbroken fifty-minute Putin monologue filled with grievances, raw asides, and acerbic commentary, I began to wonder about the wisdom of my advice, and my future in the Obama administration. The meeting was supposed to last one hour, and Putin had already eaten up most of the clock. He had arranged an impressive setting, sitting under a canopy on an elaborate patio, with waiters in eighteenth-century costumes bringing out an endless variety of dishes. I just drank coffee and listened to Putin's familiar litany—how he liked George W. Bush, but saw his efforts to build solid relations after 9/11 go unrequited; how the Bush administration had bungled Iraq and orchestrated color revolutions in Ukraine and Georgia. He was less concerned than Medvedev about the Iranian threat, and more caustic about missile defense and what he perceived to be the unwillingness of the Bush administration to listen to him. His manner was blunt, his language sometimes crude, and his overall demeanor self-servingly dismissive of the value of working with Americans. He had tried with Bush. It hadn't panned out. Why get burned again?

Obama listened patiently, and then delivered his own firm message on the reset. He was matter-of-fact about our differences, and made no effort to gloss over the profound problems that Russia's actions in Georgia had caused. He said it was in neither of our interests to let our disagreements obscure those areas where we could each benefit by working together, and where U.S.-Russian leadership could contribute to international order. We should test that, he explained, without inflating expectations. After all, we already had a lot of experience testing the alternative approaches—either getting our hopes up too high or retreating into more familiar adversarial stances—and they hadn't worked out so well. Putin didn't look persuaded, but he conceded that it made sense to try. "These issues are Dmitry's responsibility now," he said airily. "He has my support."

The discussion between Putin and Obama went two hours longer than planned, but it was well worth the anxiety it caused schedulers on both sides. As we rode back to Moscow, the president said Putin's capacity for venting didn't surprise him. The challenge, Obama recognized, was to "stay connected to this guy, without undercutting Medvedev." That was to prove much harder than we thought at the outset. When we suggested that Putin co-chair the new Bilateral Presidential Commission with Vice President Biden, he didn't bite; Putin didn't view vice presidents as his peers. We came up with other ideas—like Putin leading a Russian business delegation to the United States, which would give him occasion to visit Washington—but none stuck. Rank and structure, and Putin's own wariness, combined to make him elusive throughout the reset effort, leaving a vulnerability that we were never able to patch. By the time Putin and Obama met again, three years later, the reset had collapsed.

Despite my doubts about whether we could stay connected to Putin, there was no question that we were making progress on the reset. The transit arrangements that we had negotiated for moving materiel and troops to Afghanistan through Russian and Central Asian airspace proved invaluable. To help solidify our ties, McFaul and I set off on a trip to all five Central Asian states just after Obama's Moscow summit in the summer of 2009. Woody Allen famously observed that 90 percent of life is showing up; that certainly applies to American diplomacy in places like Central Asia, whose leaders were habitually autocratic, sensitive to American inattention, and squeezed between their big, ambitious Russian and Chinese neighbors.

In Kazakhstan, President Nursultan Nazarbayev appreciated the timely briefing on the Moscow talks, supported our pragmatic approach, and emphasized shrewdly that one of the keys to sustaining it would be finding a way to work with Putin as well as Medvedev, about whom he was politely dismissive. In Uzbekistan, President Islam Karimov wondered why Americans always stopped in Astana first and failed to grasp that Tashkent was the center of gravity in the small Central Asian solar system. His two-hour opening monologue was impressive for its sheer stamina, as well as for his dismal opinions of other regional leaders, whom he clearly regarded as venal lightweights (presumably in contrast to his weightier venality). Karimov was frosty about our human rights concerns, and pessimistic on Afghanistan, but willing to help. So was Kyrgyzstan's leadership. In Turkmenistan, President Garbanguly Berdimuhamedov was a distinct improvement on his clinically unbalanced predecessor. I survived our stop in Tajikistan, where my major accomplishment was to consume the deer's ear I was served as the guest of honor at a presidential banquet, a digestive exercise for which no amount of vodka seemed sufficient.

Back in Washington, the administration was focused on an intensive interagency review of the missile defense strategy that it had inherited. Obama made clear that he wasn't interested in catering to the Russians. He wanted to make sure that we were moving in the most effective way possible for dealing with the emerging Iranian missile threat.

The result of the review was a strong recommendation, supported by both Bob Gates and Hillary Clinton, to pursue an alternative, relying at least initially on systems based on Aegis cruisers in the Mediterranean and in southern Europe. The review concluded that this "phased adaptive approach" would be a technically superior defense against a potential Iranian threat over the near and medium term, and more sustainable politically in Europe. It left open the possibility of revisiting the original Polish and Czech plans further down the road. I pointed out in a note to Clinton in early September an obvious corollary benefit: "A fresh start on missile defense, entirely defensible on the technical merits, gives you and the President a stronger hand to play" with the Russians. "Far from letting the Russians off the hook, this approach is our best bet to corner them on Iran, and to press ahead on post-START and wider European security issues."[9]

We moved quickly to take advantage of the improving atmosphere with Russia to advance one of the president's central priorities—preventing Iran from developing a nuclear weapon. Cooperation with Moscow was at the heart of that effort; if we could prevent the Iranians from driving a wedge between us and the Russians, the chances for mobilizing the Europeans, Chinese, and other players in a united front improved substantially. Medvedev was persuaded by our willingness to work with Russia in good faith, negotiate directly with the Iranians, and offer reasonable compromises before pivoting to an effort to build more economic pressure against Iran. The result was UN Security Council Resolution 1929 in June 2010, the platform on which we were able to build unprecedented pressure against the Iranians, and ultimately bring them back to the negotiating table.

We made similar headway on the New START agreement. A determined U.S. negotiating team, after lots of ups and downs along the way, worked out a solid accord in late 2009, just before the expiration of the original START treaty. It further reduced strategic nuclear arms, bringing them to their lowest levels since the dawn of the nuclear age. The president himself played a critical role in this, hammering out key compromises with Medvedev by phone and in meetings on the margins of international conferences. Hillary Clinton was instrumental in selling the deal on the Hill. The Senate voted in favor before the Christmas recess, with Republican opposition mollified by an agreement to invest billions in nuclear weapons modernization, some of which had questionable utility. It was another reminder of the costs of getting diplomatic business done in an increasingly polarized political system.

I accompanied Clinton to Moscow in March 2010, a moment when it felt like the reset might be taking hold. She had useful discussions with Medvedev and Lavrov, and we then went out to see Putin at his dacha. He was mildly combative at the outset of their meeting, while the press was still in the room, poking at continuing difficulties in the American economy and his skepticism about Washington's seriousness about deepening economic ties to Russia. Slouching a little in his chair, his legs spread wide in front of him, Putin looked every bit the kid in the back of the classroom with an attitude problem (an image that Obama once, undiplomatically, cited in public). Clinton took it all in stride, laughed off his barbs, and engaged in a crisp back-and-forth with Putin once the media were gone and the meeting unfolded. Accustomed to pushing people around and finding their weak spots, Putin seemed a bit frustrated by Clinton's measured reaction.

The secretary and I had talked earlier that day about Putin's love of the outdoors and fascination with both big animals and his own bare-chested persona. Shifting gears in the conversation, she asked him to talk a little about his well-publicized efforts to preserve Siberian tigers. A light seemed to go off, and Putin described with uncharacteristic excitement some of his recent trips to the Russian Far East. With what for him was borderline exuberance, he stood up and asked

Clinton to come with him to his private office. I trailed them down several hallways, past startled guards and assistants, as Putin led the way. Arriving at his office, he proceeded to show the secretary on a large map of Russia covering most of one wall the areas he had visited on his Siberian tiger trips, and those in the north where he planned to go that summer to tranquilize and tag polar bears. With genuine enthusiasm, he asked if former president Clinton might like to come along, or maybe even the secretary herself?

I had never seen Putin so animated. The secretary applauded his commitment to wildlife conservation, and said this might be another area where Russia and America could work more together. She politely deflected the invitation to the Russian Far North, although she promised to mention it to her husband. Riding back to her hotel in Moscow afterward, Clinton smiled and said that neither she nor the former president would be spending their summer vacation with Putin near the Arctic Circle.

The high point of the reset, in many ways, was Medvedev's visit to the United States in June 2010. New START had been ratified and signed. A strong new Security Council resolution signaled U.S.-Russian cooperation on Iran. Russian logistical support had enabled the president's Afghan surge. Medvedev's political stock was still dwarfed by Putin's in Russia, but he clearly saw an opportunity to show that he could promote Russian interests on the world stage—with his cordial relationship with Obama as exhibit A. That might be his ticket to a second term as president, amid rumors already beginning to swirl that Putin would return to the Kremlin instead.

Medvedev began his trip to the United States in Silicon Valley. He was intent upon developing Russia's technology sector, and had already launched a kind of tech hothouse just outside Moscow, aimed at incubating innovative new companies and technologies. Supported by the Russian state and a handful of oligarchs, it was a top-down model far removed from the West Coast garages in which Bill Gates and Steve Jobs had started their ascent, with little of the freewheeling entrepreneurial spirit that energized Silicon Valley. McFaul arranged for Medvedev to speak at Stanford, which he did with distinctly un-Kremlin-like flair, wearing blue jeans and reading his remarks from an iPad. He interacted with tech pioneers from Apple, Google, and Cisco, as well as with young Russian émigrés working in the Valley. For someone like me, who had long argued that Russia needed urgently to diversify its economy beyond what came out of the ground, it seemed like a hopeful moment.

Obama's conversations in Washington with Medvedev were similarly encouraging, focused on creating economic ballast that might support the relationship beyond the reset. They agreed to work together to complete Russia's entry into the World Trade Organization.

Even a spy scandal, which became public soon after Medvedev returned home, did not derail the reset. U.S. investigators had been piecing together for some months information about a network of Russian "sleeper" agents—Russian nationals who had taken on false American identities and burrowed into American society, preparing to eventually take on active espionage tasks. It was a story that later became the basis for a popular television series, *The Americans*—whose protagonists were a good deal more accomplished than the actual Russian sleepers. Nevertheless, the long-term risk they posed was real. After long sessions in the Situation Room in which we debated the options, the president decided to pursue a swap shortly after the Medvedev visit. The eleven sleeper agents were arrested, and then traded for four individuals imprisoned by the Russians on espionage charges. It was in some respects a classic Cold War tale—and a reminder that, for all the apparent promise of the reset, ours was still a fraught relationship.

* * *

IN 2011, THINGS began to get a lot more fraught and the reset began to lose altitude. Ever since the color revolutions in Georgia and Ukraine, Moscow had grown increasingly apprehensive about popular uprisings that might soon wash up on the walls of the Kremlin. The Arab Spring—the revolutions that erupted in Tunisia, Egypt, and across the region in early 2011—sent much of the Russian leadership into a cold sweat, as did Washington's evident sympathy for popular movements in the Arab world.

The case of Qaddafi's Libya was particularly challenging. As a revolt spread across Libya, Qaddafi threatened to slaughter rebels in Benghazi and other cities where the uprising was strongest. Key European states called for outside intervention to prevent massive bloodletting. In a break from past practice, the Arab League also was outspoken in its call for the United Nations to act and authorize intervention to protect civilians. The Russians supported a first Security Council resolution in February. And then in mid-March, after a direct request delivered persuasively by Vice President Biden to Medvedev in Moscow, Russia abstained and allowed passage of a second resolution authorizing "all necessary means" to safeguard Libyan civilians.

I accompanied the vice president on that trip, and the contrast between his conversations with Medvedev and those with Putin was striking. Medvedev acknowledged the humanitarian risks, and hinted that he was inclined to acquiesce in a limited military mission. He was also invested in Obama by this point, and that seemed to be a factor in his thinking. Putin was neither invested in Obama nor overly concerned about humanitarian risks. His main concern was the chaos that might result from outside intervention, and the precedent that would be set if another autocrat was toppled. Putin was dyspeptic about American policy in the Middle East, and sharply critical of our "abandonment" of Mubarak a month earlier.

While Putin clearly had serious doubts about the wisdom of catering to American preferences amid the Arab Spring, he deferred to Medvedev on the decision to abstain. If it didn't end well, he made clear he would add yet another black mark in his estimation of Medvedev's judgment and capacity to protect Russian interests in a rough and cold-blooded world—and another in his long list of grievances about American duplicity. In the fall of 2011, after Western military strikes that soon drifted beyond the original intent of the Security Council resolutions, Qaddafi was overthrown. In gruesome footage that Putin reportedly viewed repeatedly, rebels caught the Libyan dictator hiding in a drainage pipe and beat him to death.

Putin worried that Russia's vulnerabilities had grown, not diminished, since he had left the presidency, and concluded it was time to take back full control of the reins. The 2008 global financial crisis had hit Russia hard, sending hydrocarbon prices plummeting and curbing the high growth rates that Putin had enjoyed during his first two terms in the Kremlin. Although from Putin's perspective the war in Georgia and the sympathetic government of Viktor Yanukovich in Ukraine had put the brakes on the erosion of Russian influence in the former Soviet Union, the wider world looked more uncertain, with authoritarian leaderships falling across the Middle East and the United States throwing its weight behind regime changes. His self-assurance reinforced by years of sycophancy from the Russian elite and enviable public approval ratings, Putin concluded with the hubris that autocracy breeds that his was the only strong hand that could right Russia's course and steer it ahead. He announced in September his decision to run for president again in the March 2012 elections, and that Medvedev would replace him as prime minister.

Putin misjudged the reaction among the rising urban middle class in Moscow, St. Petersburg, and other major Russian cities. Resentful of his fait accompli, and restive for economic modernization and a more serious effort to combat corruption, they helped deliver a blow to his ruling party in the December 2011 Duma elections, which won only 49 percent of the vote, far less than its 64 percent total in 2007. When allegations of vote rigging and manipulation to produce even that unimpressive result began to build immediately after the elections, tens of thousands of demonstrators marched in the streets of Moscow and St. Petersburg in protest. Putin was surprised, angry,

and more than a little unnerved.[10] By instinct and professional training a control freak, he was discovering that the growing middle class
that he had helped create over the last decade wanted more than just
consumerism. It also wanted a political voice.

I warned Clinton that there was more combustibility ahead. Putin
and the tough guys around him were likely to invent or exaggerate
American involvement in Russian affairs, partly to deflect attention
from the unexpected domestic storm he had barreled into. It didn't
take long for that to materialize. When Clinton made public comments critical of the conduct of the Duma elections—consistent in
tone and substance with what we would have said in similar circumstances anyplace in the world—Putin lashed out, accusing her of
sending the "signal" that drew demonstrators into the streets, and the
State Department of quietly supporting opposition parties. Putin had
a remarkable capacity for storing up grievances and slights and assembling them to fit his narrative of the West trying to keep Russia
down. Clinton's criticism would rank high in his litany—and generate
a personal animus that led directly to his meddling against her candidacy in the 2016 U.S. presidential election. Putin was an apostle of
payback.

In early January 2012, Mike McFaul walked into this nasty set of
circumstances as our new ambassador to Russia. He was well prepared for the job—an excellent Russian speaker with long years of
experience in Russian affairs, and the White House architect of the
reset. By the time of his arrival in Moscow, however, the Kremlin was
in an increasingly edgy and vindictive mood, and Mike's hopes to
start slowly and tread carefully proved elusive. I wanted him to get off
on a good footing, and I intended to use a long-planned visit to help.
The inadvertent result, however, was to help make his life even more
complicated.

I arrived in Moscow during McFaul's first week as ambassador. We
made the rounds of senior officials in the Kremlin and the Foreign
Ministry, and encountered nothing unusual in our conversations. On

my second morning, just before my departure, we met first with a group of political opposition leaders and then with a number of civil society activists. These kinds of sessions were a regular part of any such visit, and I had taken part in them throughout many years of service at the embassy and as a visitor from Washington. I don't recall much that was unusual about those conversations either, nor did we go out of our way to call attention to them. We mostly listened.

The Kremlin was poised to seize on any such contacts, however routine, as evidence of American plotting. State television ran a long, vituperative piece that same night, alleging that Russian opposition-ists had come to see Mike and me to "get their instructions" for the further disruption of Russian politics. This began a carefully choreo-graphed campaign against McFaul, whose proud history prior to gov-ernment service of study and support for democracy movements made him a convenient target for the Kremlin. As Medvedev and Surkov later acknowledged, McFaul's arrival was a perfect opportu-nity to manufacture a narrative about American meddling and rouse Putin's nationalistic political base in the run-up to the March presi-dential elections.[11] The nastiness never stopped, continuing long after Putin's election. It was a campaign clearly planned before McFaul's arrival or my visit, and would have been triggered at some early point. I just wish I hadn't provided such an immediate and visible trigger.

Relations relapsed quickly in 2012. Putin returned as president after winning 63 percent of the vote in March, but pointedly declined to come to the G-8 summit in Washington in May, sending Medve-dev instead. We were increasingly at loggerheads over how to manage the reverberations of the Arab Spring as the Kremlin clung to its cli-ent in Damascus and resisted outside pressure for a political transi-tion. With American support, Russia finally joined the World Trade Organization in August. That forced the issue of repeal of the Jackson-Vanik Amendment, without which the United States couldn't benefit from Russia's WTO accession. Repeal also reinforced a push in Con-gress to hit back at the Russian leadership in other ways—especially through the passage of the Magnitsky Act in December, which sanctioned Russian officials implicated in the terrible prison death of a young lawyer who had uncovered evidence of high-level corruption.

Just before stepping down as secretary of state in February 2013, Clinton sent a memo to President Obama cautioning that relations with Russia would get worse before they got better, and that Putin's return to the Kremlin had brought the curtain down on the reset. We would still manage to work with the Russians on the Iran nuclear negotiations, and Clinton's successor, John Kerry, would labor mightily to reach an understanding with Moscow on Syria. But the overall downward drift was hard to brake. In August 2013, the Russians granted temporary asylum to Edward Snowden, the former U.S. intelligence contractor who had leaked massive amounts of highly classified material, infuriating Washington. In response, Obama canceled a planned bilateral summit with Putin on the margins of a G-20 meeting in St. Petersburg in September. It seemed like we had hit bottom in the relationship.

Then Putin's pugnacity in Ukraine took us much deeper. Throughout 2013, the plodding, corrupt Yanukovich government in Kyiv was the object of a tug-of-war between the European Union and Russia. The EU sought to engage Ukraine in an association agreement, the first step on a long and uncertain road to membership. Putin's main geopolitical aspiration was the formation of the Eurasian Economic Union, a collection of former Soviet states that Russia could control— and that would be hollow without Ukraine. For Putin, Ukraine would never be just another country and tethering it to the West was an existential issue for him. He was determined to play hardball, convinced that Russia's future as a great power depended upon predominant influence in Ukraine. Yanukovich, whom Putin viewed as weak-willed, predictably vacillated, torn between his Russian patrons and a population solidly in favor of association with the EU and the long-term economic benefits that would flow from it. Finally, he backed away from a scheduled signing event with the EU in late November and accepted a $15 billion subsidy from Putin to opt for the Eurasian Economic Union.

Disgruntled Ukrainians poured into the Maidan, the historic main square in Kyiv, setting up camp and venting their frustration with Yanukovich. A full-fledged political crisis ensued. Violence broke out in February 2014, with government snipers killing several protestors and hard-right oppositionists responsible for the deaths of a number of police officers. An EU mediation effort produced a last-minute agreement to deescalate, but Yanukovich—by now fearful for his own life—fled to eastern Ukraine and then across the border to Russia. The protestors celebrated, the Rada impeached Yanukovich and elected an interim president, and this all seemed to be yet another historic chance for Ukrainians to shape a more promising future.

At that moment, I was in Sochi, leading the U.S. delegation to the closing ceremony of the 2014 Winter Olympics. Mike McFaul was there with me, only a couple days from the end of his tour in Moscow. We quickly agreed that Putin wasn't going to accept quietly the demise of Yanukovich and all his hopes for a deferential Ukraine. We tried to arrange a meeting with Putin in Sochi, but he was in no mood to talk. The White House asked me to stop in Kyiv, which I did two days later. The mood was exuberant but apprehensive, with senior officials worried about what Putin might do next. I went down to the Maidan one cold evening and visited the makeshift medical clinic that had been set up by protesters at St. Michael's Monastery near the square. You could feel the pride among the volunteer doctors and nurses, and the wounded demonstrators who were still there. I told Secretary Kerry that I thought this might be the moment when Ukraine got it right. It seemed that hope might finally triumph over experience in a country whose landscape was littered with two decades of political failure, squabbling leaders, endemic corruption, Russian meddling, and unfulfilled expectations.

Soon after I left Kyiv, Russia's "little green men" began to appear in Crimea, the first of a wave of Russian military and security personnel in unmarked uniforms who would occupy Ukraine's Crimean Peninsula. Putin formally announced the annexation of Crimea in mid-March, and stepped up Russian military and separatist activity in the Donbass, the heavily industrialized swath of southeastern Ukraine long home to many ethnic Russians. Putin's message was typically unsubtle: If Russia couldn't have a deferential government in Kyiv, plan B was a dysfunctional Ukraine, in which the Kremlin used an annexed Crimea and a violent and unstable Donbass to exert leverage over Kyiv. The Western response was a series of sanctions against Russia, demonstrating a solidarity between the United States and key European allies that Putin didn't expect. It helped blunt his push into the Donbass and relieve the pressure on Kyiv, even if it could do little in the short term to reverse the annexation of Crimea.

In the early summer of 2014, after a difficult phone call between Obama and Putin, I was sent along with Jake Sullivan, then the national security advisor to Vice President Biden, to meet quietly with two senior Russian representatives—one from the Foreign Ministry and the other from the Kremlin—and see if back-channel conversations might lead anywhere useful, particularly on the Ukraine crisis. Over a long day in Geneva, at a hotel overlooking the lake, we went round and round. The senior Russian diplomat was an old friend, but had little to offer. The Kremlin official specialized in Borscht Belt humor and meandering, politically incorrect stories about Russia and its neighbors. Echoing Vladimir Putin to George W. Bush in 2008, he insisted that "you Americans don't understand that Ukraine is not a real country. Some parts are really Central Europe, and some are really Russian, and very little is actually Ukrainian. Don't kid yourselves." His smarmy, patronizing air wasn't very endearing. "And you shouldn't kid yourselves," I replied. "You've managed to create an even stronger sense of Ukrainian nationalism than existed before. You've swallowed up two million Crimeans, but made the other forty-two million people a lot more Ukrainian, and a lot more determined to keep out from under your influence."

Jake and I took turns losing our patience as the day wore on and the conversation went nowhere. We left discouraged about the near-term prospects for implementation of the Minsk agreement that the Germans and French had been hammering out with the Russians and Ukrainians. Our bigger concern was that the Russians might up the ante and increase military pressure in the Donbass rather than deescalate. We sent a note back to the president that night outlining the Russian failure to take seriously this back channel and our own failure to convince them of the wisdom of taking the diplomatic off-ramp we tried to telegraph.

The reset was long dead.

* * *

THE ARC OF relations with Russia in the Obama era was achingly familiar. Inheriting the mutual acrimony of the war in Georgia, Obama made some tangible early progress in the relationship. We took significant strides together on Iran, Afghanistan, and strategic arms reductions. We helped the Russians finally overcome the last barriers to formal WTO accession, but never succeeded in putting much economic weight in the relationship, certainly not compared to China, nor even to the halting promise of economic ties with India. Early cooperation between us in response to the Arab Spring collapsed in recrimination, especially over Libya. For all the potential of the president's rapport with Dmitry Medvedev, we were never able to sustain an effective connection to Putin. There was also a certain hubris in the notion that we could somehow enhance Medvedev's political position by investing in the relationship between Obama and someone so utterly dependent on Putin for his role and influence.

While he was intrigued by Obama initially, it remained for Putin a matter of both conviction and convenience to paint the United States as a hostile force, maneuvering to undermine Russia's influence in its neighborhood and his own grip at home. Putin had created a trap for himself and for Russia; willful failure to diversify the economy and adopt the rule of law led to slow stagnation, from which foreign adventure offered only a temporary diversion. Like the experience of George W. Bush, early potential in U.S.-Russian relations was eclipsed by a relapse, and a new post–Cold War low. It was a pattern that hinted sometimes at historical immutability. It was also, however, the product of the personalities, preconceptions, disconnects, and choices of leaders on both sides. Like the rest of post–Cold War relations between Russia and the United States, it was a fascinating—and often depressing—story.

Obama's effort to keep pace with a changing international landscape and invest energy and political capital in shaping relations with that landscape's most significant players was admirable. Unlike George H. W. Bush, he was not moving from a world of bipolarity to rising unipolarity, but from a world of diminishing unipolarity to something far messier. It was a time for big bets, like the rebalance to Asia and the strategic partnership with India, both wise and well executed, if less ambitious and complete than initially hoped. It was a time for steadiness in dealing with China, and patient effort to avoid unnecessary collisions. It was also a time to test the proposition of more stable relations with Russia and hard-nosed cooperation on issues of shared interest.

For all the agility and imagination of the time, we didn't have the freedom to play our diplomatic cards like Bush 41. Diplomacy could open doors, or prevent them from slamming shut, but ultimately others had to decide whether to walk through them. Obama hoped that this new era of U.S. leadership would unleash faster and more dramatic adjustments. History had other ideas.

8

The Arab Spring: When the Short Game Intercedes

ON THE AFTERNOON of February 1, 2011, President Obama joined his senior advisors in the Situation Room to review the unfolding drama of Egypt's revolution. He was pensive and steady, seized by the sense of possibility for Egypt and the region but sober about all the ways in which things could go wrong—for them and for us. "I'm worried that Mubarak is falling farther and farther behind events," he said. "I don't want us to."

A week into the revolution, the crowd in Tahrir Square had swelled to nearly one hundred thousand defiant and determined people. Now in his early eighties, President Mubarak was weary after three decades in power but stubbornly convinced that he knew what was best for Egypt. A lot was at stake. Since the 1979 peace treaty with Israel, Egypt had been a centerpiece of American strategy in the Middle East. It was a reliable security partner in the region, despite continuing political and economic corrosion at home. The compact between rulers and ruled had become more brittle, with the benefits of economic growth limited to a privileged few, a leadership growing more remote, and a young population increasingly consumed by a sense of indignity—fueled by their mounting awareness in a digital world of what others had that they did not.

Over the previous few days, Obama and Hillary Clinton had pressed Mubarak to address the legitimate demands of the protestors, indicate that he would step down soon, disavow any inclination to install his son as successor, and begin a shift to a new, democratically elected government. His fate was sealed. The scale and persistence of the protests made that clear. The hope was that Mubarak would come to grips with reality and set in motion an orderly transition. But he was not ready to go nearly that far. Hoping to stunt the momentum of the protests, he took the modest step of filling the long-vacant vice presidency with his intelligence chief, Omar Suleiman. Mubarak was reluctant to concede more, even as the ground continued to shift rapidly beneath him.

The Situation Room meeting began with an update from our embassy in Cairo, an intelligence assessment, and a review of the diplomatic state of play. An hour in, word was passed to the president that Mubarak was about to make a hastily arranged televised address. Hopeful that the Egyptian leader was finally ready to move, Obama interrupted the meeting to turn on CNN's live coverage, and we all sat there, watching expectantly. Secretary Clinton stood next to the president, clutching a cup of coffee from the White House Mess. Those around the table contorted their heads every which way to catch a glimpse of the television. Tom Donilon, seated to the left of the president, didn't even bother. He knew what was coming.

Predictably, Mubarak offered half a loaf. He promised not to run again in the fall elections, but had nothing to say about not grooming his son as successor or beginning to transfer some of his powers in the meantime. "That won't cut it," Obama concluded. The television screen faded to black, and the room fell quiet. Obama, as he often did, went around the table and asked us to offer our views on whether to ask the Egyptian leader to leave office now. There was no disagreement —our entreaties were falling on deaf ears in Cairo, and our hopes for an orderly transition were fading. The president decided to call Mubarak and press him to step down immediately, while he could still shape a transition and avoid greater chaos and violence.

I joined the president and several of his White House aides in the Oval Office for the call. I always admired how any president managed to focus on a phone conversation with a foreign leader with so many aides buzzing around. Donilon, Denis McDonough, and Deputy National Security Advisor Ben Rhodes were huddled in one corner looking over the president's talking points. The president's two senior Middle East advisors, Dennis Ross and Dan Shapiro, took notes furiously against the back of the Oval Office couch, where Chief of Staff Bill Daley was sitting and listening intently. Robert Gibbs, the president's spokesperson, shed his suit jacket and began to pace. Obama was leaning back in his chair, legs crossed, working through his argument.

As I stood off to the side listening, I could piece together Mubarak's patronizing and inflexible response. The Egyptian leader thought Obama was hopelessly naïve—unaware of just how indispensable Mubarak was to order in Egypt. As the call continued, I could see Obama's frustration rising, and I couldn't help thinking of scenes I had witnessed there going back to the Reagan administration. Each of Obama's recent predecessors had been sucked, some more willingly than others, into the morass of a region that remorselessly drained their political capital and consumed their attention.

Obama had entered office determined to change the terms of American involvement in the Middle East. He had no illusions about massive disengagement from a region he knew he couldn't ignore; what he sought was a different kind of engagement, a reversal of the unilateral and overly militarized habits of his predecessor. He would wind down America's troop presence in Iraq, rely on a smaller counterterrorism footprint made up of drones and special operations forces, and place a bigger emphasis on diplomacy to deal with Iran's nuclear program and the Israeli-Palestinian peace process. He would shift more of America's strategic bets to Asia, and a whole range of other pressing global questions, like nuclear nonproliferation and climate change, that had sometimes been neglected or undermined in the decade since 9/11. But now the Arab Spring, the revolutionary drama of which Egypt was only one act, was inexorably tugging him back to the crisis-driven Middle East focus that he had hoped so much to escape.

* * *

THE BRITISH PRIME minister Harold Macmillan may or may not have actually said, in response to a question about what most affects the course of government strategies, "Events, dear boy, events." But it's an apt observation. Statesmen rarely succeed if they don't have a sense of strategy—a set of assumptions about the world they seek to navigate, clear purposes and priorities, means matched to ends, and the discipline required to hold all those pieces together and stay focused. They also, however, have to be endlessly adaptable—quick to adjust to the unexpected, massage the anxieties of allies and partners, maneuver past adversaries, and manage change rather than be paralyzed by it. "Events" can create openings and opportunities; they can just as easily reveal the limits of even the most thoughtful and nuanced strategies. Playing the long game is essential, but it's the short game— coping with stuff that happens unexpectedly—that preoccupies policymakers and often shapes their legacies.

The Middle East is particularly challenging terrain for American strategy. By the time the revolts of the Arab Spring began to erupt, the region had twice as many people as it did when I arrived at my first post in Amman in the early 1980s. Sixty percent of the population was under the age of twenty-five, and it was urbanizing nearly as fast as Asia. Job markets couldn't cope, and youth unemployment ran higher than in any other part of the world. Corruption was endemic. The emerging middle class was frustrated, with economic growth siphoned to elites. Arab political systems were almost uniformly authoritarian, generally repressive and unresponsive to demands for political dignity and better governance. A generational change in leaderships had been under way for more than a decade, but hopes of new directions wilted quickly. Educational systems had little to offer young people eager to compete in a relentless twenty-first-century world, and the deficit in women's rights was robbing societies of half their potential.

The Arab order in early 2011 was still one that had the United States as its principal frame of reference. The Arab street despised most aspects of American policy, whether in Iraq or Palestine or elsewhere, and its leaders resented the Bush 43 administration's crusades and blunders. They were, however, accustomed to America's centrality in their world, schizophrenic in their simultaneous resentments and expectations of American influence. They continually exaggerated our ability to affect events, and we did the same.

We also both underestimated how unsettling a changing American role might be. When Obama laid out his broad strategy for the region in an eloquent speech in Cairo in June 2009, the immediate reaction across the Arab world was enthusiastic. He was the anti-Bush—in tone and substance. He promised a "new beginning," and conveyed an understanding of the many ills of the Arab world, and a realization that jobs, security, opportunity, and dignity were the keys to a better order, not democratization through the barrel of a gun. Many Arab leaders, not surprisingly, cherry-picked from the speech—embracing Obama's willingness to reexamine America's role while ignoring his call for them to undergo their own reexamination. His message also inflated expectations in Washington and the region far beyond his ability to deliver. That was certainly true when his early efforts to bridge Israeli-Palestinian differences ran aground on Bibi Netanyahu's artful intransigence, the habitual inclinations of an aging Palestinian leadership, and the lack of interest of most of the Arab states in investing in the issue. It was true when it became clear that there was little appetite and even fewer resources to support political and economic reform more robustly and creatively. And it became even more evident when another element of Obama's Middle East policy came into sharper focus—his intention to reduce our military role and shift America's strategic investments to other parts of the world.

Extricating ourselves from the central security role to which regimes had become accustomed proved far harder than Obama anticipated. Nervous Arab autocrats feared American abandonment nearly as much as the reckless exercise of our power. The new U.S. administration discovered that it was tied to the old regional order in more ways than it had first thought. When the early rumblings of the Arab revolts began, the difficulty of the trade-offs between significant security relationships and aspirations for change—and the sheer unpredictability and erratic course of events—became painfully apparent.

Few people in the Obama or George W. Bush administrations needed to be persuaded of the fragilities of the Arab political and economic order. Obama's Cairo speech made clear his concerns. Clinton was even more pointed in an address she gave in Doha in January 2011, just a dozen days before Tahrir Square erupted, warning that "the region's foundations are sinking into the sand." After 9/11 and the Bush administration's shift from a traditional Republican foreign policy of restraint and containment to unilateralism and preemption, Secretary Rice had spoken bluntly about the weaknesses of autocratic rule, and the risks of confusing authoritarian order with stability. It was the right message; after the Iraq War, however, the Bush administration was the wrong messenger.

Career diplomats in the Middle East had been arguing for decades that stability was not a static phenomenon, and that the United States shouldn't be blind to changes that were inevitable. I had tried to make the same arguments going back to my time as a junior officer in Jordan in the early 1980s. Like many of my colleagues, I continued to make them from the Policy Planning Staff, as an ambassador in the region, and from the Near Eastern Affairs bureau. None of this was particularly new.

What was new, and profoundly challenging, was the speed with which change moved once it began—propelled by advances in technology and social media. On December 17, 2010, Mohamed Bouazizi, a twenty-six-year-old proprietor of a street stall, self-immolated outside a local municipal building in Tunisia, in a desperate final protest against the harassment of local police. Demonstrations and violent clashes followed, spreading rapidly across the country. Within a month, President Zine El Abidine Ben Ali fled, and secular and Islamist oppositionists began to negotiate transitional arrangements. When I visited shortly thereafter, my report to Secretary Clinton was cautiously upbeat: "Tunisia's revolution is still incomplete, and its transition only just begun, but so far Tunisians are handling the challenges before them with more steadiness than most would have imagined before Ben Ali's sudden ouster, and considerable national pride in being the first of the Arabs to set out to reclaim their sense of dignity."[1]

The revolution in Tunisia quickly spread to the biggest and most consequential Arab state of all, Egypt. On January 25, the first crowds began to form in Tahrir Square, calling for extensive reforms and the end of Mubarak's rule. Most of the protestors were young, peaceful, passionate, tech-savvy, and energized by what had happened in Tunisia. The scenes were incredibly powerful, especially for someone like me, who had walked on that square and long admired Egyptians and the stoicism with which they coped with poverty and an overweening state. This all seemed hopeful, a genuine bottom-up movement to bend the arc of history. But events were soon to get a lot more complicated.

* * *

THE FIRST OFFICIAL American reactions to the Tahrir demonstrations were guarded. Egypt had weathered countless political storms over seven millennia, and after thirty years in power Mubarak's rule seemed tattered but durable. The military was the one truly national institution. It was vested in the status quo, and in the large slice of the Egyptian economic pie that it possessed. The United States was similarly vested in that status quo, with $1.3 billion in military aid and a substantial economic assistance program reinforcing Egypt's willingness to keep the peace with Israel, allow the American military access and overflight rights, share information about regional threats, and cooperate (more often than not) diplomatically.

In the initial aftermath of the January 25 protests, Clinton said in a press conference, with more hope than conviction, that "our assessment is that the Egyptian government is stable and is looking for ways to respond to the legitimate needs and interests of the Egyptian people." Vice President Biden said he "would not refer to Mubarak as a dictator."[2] Obama himself, mindful of what the United States had at stake, and of growing agitation among regional leaders desperately hoping that the Arab Spring fever would break in Egypt, shared the instinctive caution of his most senior advisors.

That all changed swiftly over the next week. While the armed forces kept a studied distance, Egyptian police and security forces clamped down hard, beating and arresting hundreds of protestors. After Obama's early calls failed to make a dent in Mubarak's thinking, and after Suleiman's appointment as vice president failed to impress the Tahrir crowds, concerns in the administration grew. On the Sunday talk shows on January 30, Clinton dodged questions about whether Mubarak should resign, but emphasized the need for an "orderly transition," warning of the dangers of chaos in the absence of a careful process.

Her comments masked an increasingly uneasy debate in unending meetings that week in the Situation Room, as some of the president's younger advisors pressed for a more forceful stance. At different times and in different ways, Susan Rice (then ambassador to the United Nations), Ben Rhodes, and Samantha Power (then a senior

NSC staff official) all argued that the United States risked being "on the wrong side of history," and should identify itself much more clearly with the demands of the protestors and insist publicly upon Mubarak's immediate resignation. Biden, Clinton, Gates, and Donilon were more wary, concerned about the consequences of too strong an American push on Mubarak, both in Egypt and in the wider region.[3]

I understood the power of what was unfolding in Tahrir Square, and the injustices and indignities that so energized the protestors. It was clear to me that Mubarak had to go; the question was how to get him to move before events overtook whatever agency he still had left. I was skeptical of the "right side of history" argument, simply because in my own experience in the Middle East, history rarely moved in a straight line. Revolutions were complicated, and most often ended messily, with the best-organized rather than the best-intentioned reaping the immediate gains.

Riding back with Clinton from yet another White House meeting that week, I suggested sending a private envoy to see Mubarak and deliver a firm message from the president. It would be a last effort to persuade him to agree to step down before we would have to call for his departure explicitly and publicly. The emissary needed to be someone Mubarak knew and trusted. I mentioned Frank Wisner, a retired diplomat who had grown close to Mubarak as ambassador in Cairo in the late 1980s. Clinton liked the concept, and recommended it to the president, who agreed. Wisner met with Mubarak in Cairo on Monday, January 31, and conveyed a set of points that mirrored what the president had conveyed in earlier calls. A savvy and vastly experienced diplomat, Wisner found the points prepared by the NSC staff to be painfully precise—like the helpful prompt to "pause for reaction" after the initial passage—but delivered the message faithfully and effectively. He reported that he thought Mubarak would be responsive.

He was not. Mubarak continued to offer too little too late, to take steps that even a week earlier might have had some chance of producing a dignified departure for him, and the more orderly transition for Egypt that we sought. The situation worsened on February 2, when thugs supporting Mubarak rode camels and horses into Tahrir Square, clubbing and beating demonstrators. Appalled, the White House stepped up its rhetoric, pressing the case for Mubarak to begin the transition "now," but stopped just short of calling for his immediate exit.

Wisner inadvertently complicated matters further when he said publicly in a video appearance at the Munich Security Conference on February 5 that he believed it was "critical" that Mubarak stay in office until the fall elections to steer the transition. He was speaking as a private citizen, but by this point his trip to Cairo had become public and it was easy for people to confuse his views with those of the administration. For exactly that reason, we had urged him not to do the Munich appearance, but evidently not strongly enough. The president and Donilon were furious, and Jake Sullivan and I tried to outdo one another's contrition in the immediate aftermath. I wrote to Jake that evening that he should shoot me if I ever suggested another emissary.

The Egyptian president gave another televised speech on February 10, a meandering and embarrassing performance that did nothing to ease the intensifying anger of the protestors. The armed forces, under Defense Minister Mohamed Hussein Tantawi, finally made clear to Mubarak that they would no longer defend him, and that it was time to step down. He resigned on February 11, handed power over to the military, and flew off to his residence in the Sinai resort town of Sharm el-Sheikh. The Mubarak era was over. The scenes of jubilation in Tahrir Square were as remarkable as they were heartening. It was hard not to feel hopeful, and the president had steered U.S. interests through extremely complicated terrain as skillfully as anyone could have. In many respects, however, the challenge for American policy was just beginning.

The Supreme Council of the Armed Forces (SCAF), led by Tantawi, became the interim arbiter of governance, and pledged early elections for a new civilian government. Inevitably, there was a certain amount of well-intentioned flailing around in Washington as we sought to stay in touch with Egyptian officers and officials. At one particularly prolonged Deputies Committee meeting, we set off on a wild exercise in Rolodex diplomacy, with agencies tasked with compiling lists of virtually every Egyptian who had ever been to a U.S. military staff college or on an exchange program. I pointed out that that was what we had an embassy for, but in the characteristically American rush to "do something," a pile of spreadsheets with phone numbers was dutifully compiled and then largely neglected. It was an early indication of the White House's understandable but ultimately self-injurious instinct to micromanage from Washington and under-utilize its embassies abroad.

In addition to the challenges of Egypt's transition, we faced an extremely nervous group of regional leaders. Mubarak's overthrow was stunning for them, and many would remain bitter for years about perceived American disloyalty. In a long conversation with me a few months later, King Abdullah of Saudi Arabia was blunt: "You abandoned your best friend. If you had stood firmly with Mubarak right at the beginning, he would still be with us."

My arguments made little difference to Saudi leaders who saw the fires of the Arab Spring burning all around them, with unrest already breaking out in Bahrain and Yemen. The truth was that it was beyond America's power to throw Mubarak under the bus; powered by decades of repression and corruption, the bus was already rolling over him by the time Obama called for transition. I flew quietly to Amman on February 12, the day after Mubarak's resignation, to encourage King Abdullah to stay ahead of the wave of change. It was our most direct conversation in nearly two decades, and he said he was already thinking about steps that he might take to open up Jordan's political and economic systems.

I visited Cairo on February 21–22, the first senior American official to arrive since the revolution. The mood in Tahrir Square was exuberant, with thousands of people still camped out, reveling in a national pride that many had never felt before. Walking along the Nile corniche to the Foreign Ministry, we passed piles of barbed wire and dozens of armored vehicles in front of the partially burned-out state television building. Banks had reopened without a disastrous run on the Egyptian pound, and the economy was sputtering back to life. "The political class," I wrote to Clinton, "is filled with genuine enthusiasts for change, as well as ex post facto revolutionaries, eager to declare their heretofore well-concealed antipathy for the Mubarak regime and claim that they were really with the revolutionaries in Tahrir Square all along."[4]

I cautioned, however, that "expectations are unrealistically high." The military leadership was struggling with transparency, a concept that didn't come naturally. A number of political leaders were worried by the military's rush to hand off to civilian rule. Cramming constitutional revisions and parliamentary and presidential elections into the next year, I predicted, would "benefit only the Muslim Brotherhood and the remnants of the NDP [the old official party]—the only organized parties on the playing field for early Parliamentary elections."[5]

The youth leaders I met, many of whom had orchestrated the sweeping Tahrir Square movement, were equally skeptical of the SCAF and the United States. Their energy and commitment were apparent and admirable, but they were already struggling to translate their success on the street into results at the ballot box. Organizing effective political parties was proving much harder than mobilizing crowds at Tahrir. They were determined to break down the web of privilege and protection that the elite had long enjoyed under Mubarak, but unsure how to get started. Still a little surprised at how quickly their movement had toppled a president, they were—like most revolutionaries in the first flush of victory—starting to squabble among themselves.

Secretary Clinton traveled to Egypt in March, and I returned in

June and then again in January 2012. Several other senior American officials came through as well, doing our best to amplify the hard work of an embassy constrained by security conditions, reduced staffing levels, and the ordered departure of family members. We tried to help bolster economic confidence, but offered more free advice than tangible assistance—limited partly by the reluctance of the SCAF to risk necessary reforms, and partly by budgetary stringency and partisan paralysis in a Washington still working its way out of the 2008 recession. Our message on the political side was also a bit conflicted. On the one hand, we emphasized to the SCAF the dangers of moving to elections too quickly, before giving a chance for new political parties to organize. On the other hand, we worried about the perpetuation of military rule, especially as intermittent violence continued, with the U.S.-supplied Egyptian security forces at center stage. A rapid move to civilian rule seemed attractive from that point of view. In the end, it probably didn't make much difference what we thought, since the SCAF was anxious to make a handoff and get out of the unaccustomed political limelight, and the Egyptian public even more sensitive than before the revolution about foreign encroachment.

President Obama made a speech at the State Department in May 2011, highlighting our support for post-revolutionary transitions in Egypt and Tunisia, as well as outlining longer-term strategy for the region and the Israeli-Palestinian peace process. The tone of his remarks was pitch perfect, making clear our intention to support forces for reform. There was little to offer, however, beyond words. The speech reflected Obama's fidelity to his long-game strategy and the priorities that underpinned it; his sober sense about the generational nature of the unfolding challenge and steep near-term odds facing voices of openness and pluralism; the risk of making the Arab Spring about us, as opposed to about the people in the region; and the harsh reality that the political and fiscal climates at home would in any case prevent the administration from providing anything close to the kind of support transitional regimes needed over the long term.

After my June 2011 trip, I told Clinton and the White House what they already suspected: Further progress toward a successful democratic transition was "certainly not a sure thing now."[6] When I came back to Cairo in early 2012, parliamentary elections had produced a strong showing by the Muslim Brotherhood (MB), which had won nearly half of the seats in the lower house. Combined with another quarter of the seats won by Salafists, the result was a dramatic victory for Islamist parties. The United States had largely avoided interaction with the Brotherhood up to this point, both because of their anti-American ideology and in deference to Mubarak. The Brotherhood reciprocated our reluctance and suspicion, but they had clearly emerged as a political force in Egypt, and I was authorized along with our new ambassador in Cairo, Anne Patterson, to meet with senior MB representatives and test the waters.

Our first encounter was in a nondescript office at the headquarters of the Brotherhood's Freedom and Justice Party, in downtown Cairo. Our host was Mohamed Morsi, the party's secretary-general and nominal head. Short and stocky, with a trim black beard, Morsi was circumspect, as unsure of how to approach a meeting with Americans as we were with him. While he had studied at the University of Southern California decades before, Morsi's English was halting, and he stuck to Arabic in our conversation. I stressed that the United States had no business backing particular parties in Egypt; what we supported was a broader evolution toward democratic institutions, shaped by Egyptians themselves. I emphasized that we hoped to sustain partnership with Egypt, in our mutual self-interest, built around economic progress for Egyptians, regional security, and continued adherence to existing agreements, especially the Egyptian-Israeli peace treaty. Morsi said that was all consistent with the Brotherhood's outlook, but I left our meeting not entirely convinced. It was a bit surreal sitting with Morsi and two of his colleagues, who had probably done a total among them of forty or fifty years in Mubarak-era jails. They had been on their best behavior, but it was hard to tell whether to take self-avowed moderation at face value, or whether it cloaked a more complicated agenda. They were a movement used to life in the shadows, distrustful of outsiders, and not inclined to share power once they obtained it.

My overall impression of Egypt a year after the revolution was decidedly mixed. It was, I told Clinton, "a pretty confused place."[7] The economy was sliding, with the SCAF tarnished and uncertain and the revolutionary youth who dominated Tahrir Square a frustrated and politically disconnected bunch. Meanwhile, some senior civilians in the interim government overseen by the SCAF had decided to burnish their own revolutionary and popular anti-American credentials instead of moving swiftly on reform. Chief among them was Minister of International Development Fayza Abul Naga, a longtime Mubarak supporter who had, I suspected, quickly turned his photo face first against her office wall when he was deposed. She instigated trumped-up cases against a number of American NGOs, eventually resulting in the arrests and detentions of several U.S. citizens, which we labored for months to undo.

Contrary to initial MB promises that they wouldn't run a candidate in the June 2012 presidential elections, the Freedom and Justice Party put forward Morsi as its nominee. Supported in no small part by Qatar, and to a lesser degree Turkey, he won by a narrow margin, revealing a deeply polarized electorate. I visited in early July, soon after his inauguration, and Clinton returned later that month. We urged him to govern inclusively, focus on the economy, and stick to the treaty with Israel. He was careful about the last point, not interfering with the operational channels that the Egyptian military and intelligence services maintained with the Israelis, and working constructively with Clinton to avert a major Israeli clash with Hamas in Gaza in November. Morsi, however, got nowhere on the economy, and was a disaster at inclusive governance. He and the MB had no experience running public-sector institutions, and little interest in sharing the burden with other politicians or technocrats. Late in the fall, he began an effort to further revise the constitution to entrench presidential prerogatives, and in turn the Brotherhood's centrality in Egyptian politics.

By the spring of 2013, tensions were rising rapidly. Street demonstrations intensified, drawing together a flammable mix of disgruntled revolutionary youth and Cairenes frustrated by economic decline and two years of uncertainty. The armed forces, now led by General Abdel Fattah el-Sisi, hung back at first, always anxious to protect their reputation. After massive street protests in late June, however, Sisi decided to act. Morsi was arrested on July 3, and the military again took power. Most of the Egyptian public seemed relieved, eager for order and predictability, the luster of their revolution long worn away.

Sisi moved quickly to crush the Brotherhood, encouraged by Saudi Arabia and the UAE, both of whom poured billions of dollars into stabilizing the Egyptian economy. The military's actions clearly fit the classic definition of a coup, notwithstanding the considerable popular support for Sisi's decision. Under U.S. law, formally designating Sisi's intervention as a coup would have required an automatic cutoff of U.S. security and economic assistance. The president was unhappy with the military's move, which set a complicated precedent in a region still in the throes of revolts of various stripes and guaranteed even greater polarization in Egyptian society and ever greater civilian strife. He was also mindful, however, of the mood of the Egyptian public, our continuing reliance on security partnership with Egypt, and the value of retaining some leverage over Sisi and a post-revolutionary transition that seemed unending.

We spent long hours in the Situation Room trying to thread the needle and avoid cessation of assistance. Lawyers and those of us pretending to be lawyers edited and reedited formulas we thought could finesse the problem. Finally, we split the difference. The White House asserted that no judgment on whether this was a coup or not was required by law, and therefore it was choosing not to choose. Looking back, we should have simply given a straight answer, called the coup a coup, and then worked with Congress to avoid the blunt tool of complete aid suspension. Instead, to make clear his displeasure with the coup that wasn't a coup, and the subsequent steps Sisi took against the Muslim Brotherhood, the president suspended shipment of certain weapons systems, including F-16s and M1A1 tanks, which were never essential to Egypt's main security priority—fighting a growing Islamist insurgency in the Sinai. In the end, we won favor with no one and managed to antagonize just about everyone—besieged Islamists, repressed revolutionaries, our regional friends and partners, and of course the Egyptian military and Congress.

* * *

SECRETARY KERRY ASKED me to return to Egypt and assess the situation, which I did in mid-July, ten days or so after Sisi overthrew Morsi. I found Sisi in a not-so-conciliatory mood. Some in his new interim government, like Vice President Mohamed ElBaradei, the former IAEA head, advocated a focus on economic recovery, renewing the political transition, and leaving the door open to the Brotherhood to reenter politics in the future. In our conversation, Sisi was unmoved by that view, and dismissive of differences within the Brotherhood over how to approach its predicament and whether to try to sustain itself as a political party. He was already enamored of his popular standing and taken by his image as the man on the white horse. Seemingly overnight, his photos appeared on walls all over Cairo. Dressed in uniform, his eyes hidden behind 1970s-era Arab strongman sunglasses, he exuded an air of mystery and command. More trouble was already brewing, with thousands of Brotherhood members and their families camped out at Raba'a Square in central Cairo, demanding Morsi's release and reinstatement. I told Kerry that this was not going to end well.

The secretary sent me back to Cairo again in August to try to dampen tensions. I spent the next eight days working with a European Union counterpart, Bernardino Leon, whose optimism and persistence in trying to find ways to deescalate had an infectious effect on me—but not on Sisi or the Brotherhood leadership. We shuttled back and forth between Sisi and two former MB government ministers who had not yet been arrested and were still in touch with their underground leaders, including the aging MB Supreme Guide. They were, however, unable to talk to either Morsi, who had been moved to a prison in Alexandria, or Khairat el-Shater, the Deputy Supreme Guide and number two in the organization, now in Cairo's notorious Tora Prison. The two former ministers agreed to consider an initial series of confidence-building measures at Raba'a—moving people out of the square, in return for a thinning out of security forces in the area and the opening of a dialogue with the new government. They also sought the release of a senior MB official at Tora, Saad al-Katatni, as a gesture of goodwill, and to create a more authoritative channel for further discussions with Sisi and his subordinates. Sisi was reluctant to agree to any of this, distrustful of the MB and inclined to press his advantage. He seemed slightly more open at the outset on the issue of Katatni, but within a few days had lost interest in that too.

We did manage to persuade the Egyptian authorities to let us visit el-Shater at Tora, along with two visiting Gulf Arab foreign ministers, Abdullah bin Zayed of the UAE and Khalid Attiyah of Qatar. The improbable idea was to try to get el-Shater's support for deescalation.

After a long wait in the lobby of our hotel, surrounded by muscular Egyptian security personnel in suits talking nervously into their headsets, we set off for Tora late one night. It took about forty minutes for our convoy of cars to reach the forbidding century-old prison complex on the southern edge of the city. We arrived well after midnight.

El-Shater was being held in the maximum security, or "Scorpion," block in Tora. Scorpion had about a thousand political prisoners, many of them hardcore MB members, held in about three hundred cold stone cells. Stories of torture and mistreatment were legendary here, and you could feel the grimness of the place as we walked down several dimly lit and foul-smelling corridors toward the warden's office.

The four of us arranged ourselves in front of a desk, behind which sat the unsmiling warden. He offered us tea, and a few minutes later el-Shater was escorted in by two prison guards. Clad in prison pajamas and wearing cheap plastic sandals, he was still an imposing figure—six foot four, solidly built and bearded. He was pale and had a hacking prison cough, but appeared unbowed by his confinement. He shook hands with each of us, sat down, and engaged us for the next two hours, unintimidated by the company, unapologetic about anything the Brotherhood had done, and definitely unhurried—since he clearly had no place else to go.

El-Shater's tone was polite, but there was no mistaking his bitterness as he denounced the UAE for complicity in the coup and the United States for its acquiescence. His gestures grew animated. At one point he accidentally bumped my shoulder. One of the prison guards sprang into action, but backed off quickly when el-Shater smiled broadly and said he was just punctuating his comments, not intending to threaten anyone. Bernardino and I outlined the deescalatory steps we had been discussing with the two MB ex-ministers, and the two Gulf Arab ministers asserted their interest in a nonviolent resolution.

El-Shater listened carefully. He said it was hard for him to comment on the particulars in confinement, cut off from his colleagues and the situation at Raba'a. But he asked practical questions about our proposal, and emphasized his commitment to nonviolence and a serious political dialogue. It just couldn't be a dialogue between "prisoners and jailers." He closed on a hard note, reminding us that neither he nor the Brotherhood were strangers to privation, and would be unyielding in the face of pressure. "I'm sixty-three years old," he said. "I've spent many years in Egyptian jails, and I am ready to spend many more."

As we drove back to the hotel, I told Bernardino that our effort had been worthwhile, but I doubted we'd get any more traction. We briefed our MB interlocutors the next day on the conversation with el-Shater, but they were immobilized by the mounting tensions and the difficulty of getting clear signals from their leadership. Sisi was hardening his stance too, sensing that this was the time to bludgeon the Brotherhood into submission and reassert order for Egyptians tired of more than two years of unrest.

In the end, we only postponed the moment of reckoning. Convinced we had reached a diplomatic dead end, I flew home on August 8. A few days later Egyptian security forces swept into Raba'a Square and the nearby al-Nahda Square, killing nearly one thousand Brotherhood supporters. It was a brutal move, as bloody as it was unnecessary. Sisi had cemented his authority at Egypt's expense, sowing the seeds of an even more violent Islamist movement in the future.

Undoubtedly, we had made our share of tactical mistakes in handling Egypt's transition. We should have pressed harder for a more deliberate transition timetable right after the revolution, giving secular parties more time to organize. We should have pushed more vigorously against Morsi's power grab in late 2012; instead, we misread the depths of the popular groundswell that Sisi seized so quickly and effectively, and were inhibited by fears that we would be accused once again of cutting legitimate Islamist politics off at the knees. A more direct declaration that July 3 was a coup might have sobered the Egyptian military and given us more leverage with other political players.

Even with the passage of time, however, I still suspect that American influence was incapable of fundamentally altering the course of events. Mubarak waited too long to act, and it was beyond our power to save him. Of course, we bore some of the responsibility for his autocratic rule, given the significance of our support over three decades. Of course, we could have done more to encourage him to undertake serious reforms. We never, however, had the capacity to transform him into a modernizer, no matter how hard we might have tried.

Egypt's Arab Spring—like some of the other uprisings in the region—was more of a decapitation than a revolution. It failed to redefine the military's grip on the country, and as a result, it was inevitable that the generals would reassert their authority as soon as their interests were threatened. There was little we could have done to alter the military's calculus or stage-manage the collision between Sisi and the Brotherhood. Nor could we have easily erased the deep sense of betrayal and grievance felt by some of our Gulf Arab partners, as well as the Israelis, all of whom saw our handling of Mubarak's demise and Egypt's transition as further evidence of our "withdrawal" from the region and lack of resolve. Those perceptions, however unfair, still linger and corrode.

* * *

ARAB AUTOCRACIES HAD seemed alike in their surface stability, but in 2011 each revolt was unstable in its own way. They erupted in parallel, each casting its own shadow onto the others. We struggled to draw meaning from one experience that might help decipher and manage the next. It was hard to find consistency amid the jumble of societies and idiosyncratic personalities and frantic—frequently violent—changes.

Most idiosyncratic of all was Qaddafi. He had stuck to his part of our deal on terrorism and the nuclear issue. But he continued to rule with weirdness and repression, convinced that a strong and sometimes brutal hand was essential to hold together a country that a colonizing Italy had invented from a mishmash of loosely connected regions and tribes. He had atomized the Libyan armed forces and security services to protect against coups, and for similar reasons deliberately prevented the emergence of real courts, legislative bodies, or political parties that could challenge his authority. Qaddafi's personal style remained decidedly unhinged. His bizarre ninety-minute speech to the UN General Assembly in the fall of 2009 was hardly an advertisement for his soundness of mind. He rambled and ranted, occasionally consulting scraps of paper that he had scattered on the podium, veering from one crazy comment to another. His interpreter was so frustrated that after seventy-five minutes he shouted, "I just can't take it anymore," slammed down his headphones, and stormed out.

We kept our end of the bargain, however—normalizing relations, removing sanctions, and setting up an embassy in Tripoli. Led by Gene Cretz, the embassy managed to decipher the Qaddafi regime and all its strangeness and interpret its behavior to Washington. For his sins, Gene became one of the early casualties of WikiLeaks when his cables became public. In one especially vivid telegram, he described Qaddafi's "voluptuous Ukrainian nurse," a passage that did not endear him to the Libyan leader.[8] After one of Qaddafi's henchmen told us with chilling candor that "people get killed here for writing things like that," Clinton withdrew Cretz from Tripoli at the end of 2010.

It was not a surprise when Libyans' fractiousness spun up after the breathtaking revolutions on either side of them, first in Tunisia and then in Egypt. It was also not a surprise when Qaddafi reacted with characteristic venom and violence. Soon after Mubarak's resignation next door, emboldened Libyans staged large-scale protests in Tripoli and Benghazi, traditionally a stronghold of anti-Qaddafi and Islamist movements. Intent on restoring fear in his domestic audience, and not particularly concerned about his wider audience, Qaddafi ordered the army to retake Benghazi, a city of seven hundred thousand, and "wipe out the rats and dogs" who resisted. "We will find you in your closets," he declared. "We will have no mercy and no pity."[9]

We tried and failed to dissuade Qaddafi. I telephoned my old negotiating partner, Musa Kusa, now Libya's foreign minister, three times in February. In the first call, he complained that we had stabbed Mubarak in the back and didn't understand the ugliness that was likely to unfold across the region. In our subsequent conversations, I told him that Qaddafi's violence against his own people had to stop. I warned him that it would undo not only what we had worked to achieve over the past decade, but the Qaddafi regime itself. Kusa repeated that we didn't understand the situation or the implacability of his leader. But when I told him again that this would not end well, he sighed heavily and said, "I know." Kusa defected to the United Kingdom one month later.

President Obama was wary of direct American military involvement, but the pressure to act mounted as Qaddafi's forces neared Benghazi. There were significant splits among Obama's advisors, although as is often the case in the retelling of policy debates, I don't remember them to have been quite as sharply defined as later reported. Biden and Gates made clear their reservations, arguing that there was no vital U.S. national interest at stake; that we already had our hands full trying to wind down wars in Iraq and Afghanistan; and that we had no idea where intervention might lead. Others maintained that the United States had a responsibility to protect innocent civilians. Acknowledging that the searing experience of Rwanda weighed on her, Susan Rice was especially outspoken. So was Samantha Power. And Hillary Clinton, in one of those rare moments in which she and Bob Gates diverged, eventually spoke out in favor of U.S. military action. No one dismissed or downplayed the risks.

In the end, Obama told Gates, it was a "51–49" call. A number of factors ultimately tipped the balance in favor of military action. First was the likelihood of a bloodbath, and the risks for the United States, moral as well as political, of not acting to prevent it. Some observers later argued that it might have been possible to negotiate a deal with Qaddafi to avert further violence and begin a political transition. I saw little evidence of that. When I later met Kusa, by then living in exile in Qatar, he said he knew Qaddafi as well as anyone, and believed in the spring of 2011 that the mercurial Libyan leader was living in his own world, determined to fight to the end. This was existential for Qaddafi, not the kind of strategic choice he had made with us a decade before. A meeting between an American delegation led by NEA assistant secretary Jeff Feltman and Libyan regime representatives in July 2011 went nowhere, and revealed no signs of Qaddafi's willingness to step down or concede anything. I always thought the alleged readiness to negotiate of Saif al-Islam, Qaddafi's son and sometime mouthpiece in the West, was vastly overstated. His rhetoric as the revolution grew was as nasty as his father's, and his capacity for self-delusion nearly as large.

Second, Obama had to weigh action or inaction in Libya against the wider backdrop of the Arab Spring. In mid-March 2011, the revolutions in Tunisia and Egypt looked complicated but promising, with relatively little bloodshed. Unrest was bubbling across the region, from Syria to Yemen and Bahrain. To watch while Qaddafi put a violent end to the Libyan uprising would send an awful signal, both about the possibilities for peaceful change and America's seriousness in encouraging it. Moreover, Qaddafi was the one Arab leader who united his peers in common antagonism. Nothing brought the region's leaders together like antipathy for the Libyan dictator and his regime. Over four decades, Qaddafi had tried at one time or another to sabotage—or assassinate—just about everyone around the Arab Summit table. They didn't doubt his vengefulness, and the Arab League called in March for the UN to intervene.

For Obama, Libya was one case where he didn't have to worry about regional reaction. Several Arab states, including the UAE and Jordan, had even made clear that they'd join in an air operation in Libya. With Gulf Arab sensitivity about our "abandonment" of Mubarak still stinging, this was also an opportunity for us to recover some of their confidence.

Third, while post-Qaddafi Libya would be uncharted territory, it appeared to contain the ingredients for a relatively stable transition. Libya's oil wealth provided a financial cushion, and an incentive for cooperation. The country's population was small and significant expertise existed in the Libyan diaspora. The leadership of the political opposition, most of whom had been in exile for some time, seemed responsible.

Fourth, our principal European allies were champing at the bit to act militarily. President Sarkozy was full of bravado about the need to protect Libyan civilians in Benghazi, ideally with the United States and with NATO organizing the mission, but independently if necessary. With Libya just across the Mediterranean, the Europeans had a profound self-interest in getting the post-Qaddafi transition right.

Finally, a UN Security Council resolution authorizing intervention seemed achievable, and would give the operation the international stamp of legality and legitimacy that America's second Iraq war lacked. The Russians and Chinese had already supported one resolution, in late February, condemning Qaddafi's brutality. President Medvedev had indicated to the vice president on March 10 that Russia would likely abstain on a new resolution, and Putin had been unenthused but disinclined to countermand his protégé. The U.S. Congress was also strongly in support of limited military action, with the Senate unanimously backing a March resolution endorsing American participation in a no-fly zone.

The potential downsides were not insignificant. A decade before, we had employed careful diplomacy to pry Qaddafi away from international terrorism and the pursuit of weapons of mass destruction, on the proposition that he could keep his regime if he changed his behavior. Abetting his overthrow now could undo that message for other proliferators. The still-raw wounds of post-Saddam Iraq were also a reminder of everything that could go wrong once authoritarian lids were removed from pots seething with sectarian and tribal troubles. Nevertheless, I thought the odds were weighted toward intervention—narrowly—and saw inaction in the swirling regional circumstances of the spring of 2011 as potentially even more problematic.

With similar reservations, Obama opted for carefully calibrated military action to stop Qaddafi's forces short of Benghazi. In discussions at the White House on the evening of March 15, the president was displeased with the initial recommendations he received, dismissing the notion that a no-fly zone would block Qaddafi's tanks and artillery, the bigger threats to civilians in Benghazi. After his advisors regrouped, Obama approved what was basically a "no-drive" option, under which coalition aircraft could strike at Qaddafi's ground forces, now strung out along the coast road to Benghazi. In only two days, Susan Rice deftly maneuvered a resolution legitimizing the use of force through the Security Council—the first time in its history that the UN had authorized force to forestall an "imminent massacre"—and Obama emphasized publicly that the U.S. role would be limited. The United States would contribute "unique capabilities"—taking out Libyan air defenses, aerial refueling, intelligence support, precision strikes—at the front end of the mission, which would be led by our international partners. There would be no U.S. troops on the ground.

Although he was later pilloried for an unnamed White House official's inartful characterization of the U.S. strategy as "leading from behind," the president's actions looked strikingly successful at first. Benghazi was spared Qaddafi's attack, and his forces were beaten back. Rebel militias regained momentum, and by August had taken Tripoli. Almost inevitably, the civilian protection mission morphed into backing for the rebel ground forces, and Qaddafi's overthrow— precisely what Moscow had feared, and what we had assured them would not be the case. After Tripoli fell, Qaddafi went on the run. He was eventually captured and ignominiously killed in Sirte in October, near where I last met him, at a more hopeful moment, in 2005.

In the immediate aftermath of Qaddafi's downfall, the Libyan operation seemed a classic example of how Obama's "long game" strategy could limit American exposure in the Middle East and prod others to step up. It cost the Pentagon less than a billion dollars, half of what we were spending in Afghanistan every week. Our European and Arab partners carried out 90 percent of the air sorties. The UN sent a political mission into Tripoli to help a transitional government; oil production resumed; and we began to plan a training program for new Libyan security forces as militias demobilized. Chris Stevens, an intrepid Arabist who had been stationed in Tripoli before the revolution and had then taken a freighter into Benghazi during the revolt to lead our diplomacy with the opposition, became our first ambassador to post-Qaddafi Libya in the early summer of 2012.

I visited Chris and his team in Tripoli in July, just after Libya's remarkably smooth first postwar elections. Secular parties had done unexpectedly well, and Islamist groups had not fared nearly as impressively as they had in Egypt or Tunisia. I had grown to respect Chris immensely in his previous posts in the Middle East, where at different times he had been my "control officer," managing my visits to Jerusalem and Damascus, among other places. He had an easygoing professionalism that won over Arabs as well as American colleagues, and by now knew Libya better than anyone else in the Foreign Service, as well as the broader foreign policy bureaucracy.

At the end of a long day of meetings, we decompressed over beer at his modest residence on the makeshift embassy compound. In the wake of the elections, he was cautiously upbeat, recognizing all the troubles on the landscape but confident in his ability to connect with Libyans and play a useful role. He acknowledged that security was a difficult problem and would likely become the country's Achilles' heel. He stressed that he would be careful, not just for his own sake, but for the entire mission. But he knew that there was no such thing as zero risk in our profession. That conversation has haunted me ever since.

On a trip to Jordan in September, I received the kind of call you always dread in the middle of the night. It was the State Department Operations Center, informing me that there had been an attack on American diplomats in Benghazi. There was no further information. A few hours later, a somber senior watch officer told me that Chris Stevens and three of our colleagues had been killed. I was numb and horrified as I learned more of the details. Chris had been on a brief visit to Benghazi, where we kept a small diplomatic outpost—not a formal consulate, but a base from which we could keep in touch with developments in the political center of Libya's east, where the revolution had started. After a day of meetings in town, Chris and his security detail had returned for the night to our tiny compound. Shortly after 9 P.M., a group of Libyan extremists launched a coordinated attack, overwhelming the compound's defenses. Fierce fighting continued until after midnight at a second American compound, run by the CIA, located a mile or so away.

I spent that sleepless night in Amman and continued on to Baghdad in the morning, as scheduled. I cut short my trip there to accompany Chris's remains and those of our other colleagues back to the United States a couple days later. It was the longest plane flight I can remember, sitting in that cold, cavernous C-17 aircraft across from four flag-draped coffins. It was all surreal; I barely recall landing at Andrews Air Force Base, or the terribly sad arrival ceremony at which the president and Secretary Clinton spoke.

It didn't take long for the Benghazi attack to become a political football at home. Legitimate questions about what more we should have done on security were wrapped up in a set of investigations and hearings that were astonishingly cynical, even by the standards of modern Washington. When Secretary Clinton fell and suffered a concussion, and thus was unable to testify before Senate and House committees in December, I stepped in on short notice, along with my friend Tom Nides, the deputy secretary for management and resources.

We spent seven hours before the Senate Foreign Relations Committee and the House Foreign Affairs Committee. There is nothing like a high-profile hearing on a contentious, politically charged issue to focus your mind, or remind you just how brutal Washington politics can be. We did our best to project a calmness that neither of us felt. Nides leaned over before the House hearing began and whispered, "If you screw up, you're on your own, buddy." That broke the tension, and we soldiered on. We tried to be honest about our mistakes, and precise about the steps we were already taking to tighten security, while making clear that there could never be a risk-proof approach to diplomacy. Our colleagues overseas often operated in dangerous places, and that would remain the nature of our profession.

The Benghazi tragedy and the endless political circus around it substantially lessened the administration's appetite for deeper involvement in Libya. Preoccupation with security made it difficult for American, European, and UN personnel to function. Tensions among Libyan militias increased, and disorder mounted. Other Arab states began to support competing proxies, with the Egyptians and Emiratis backing some groups in the east, and the Qataris funneling money and arms to Islamists. ISIS and al-Qaeda affiliates sprung up. The fumbling authorities in Tripoli alternately clamored for and resisted Western help, complaining about lack of support but allergic to systematic advice or the practical requirements of signing memoranda of understanding or following through on their commitments.

Our embassy continued to perform valiantly, when it could operate in-country. On one visit in the spring of 2014, Deborah Jones, our ambassador, managed to corral all of the major rebel militia leaders to meet with me and discuss how they might coexist for the national good. It was a memorable scene, the motley crew of self-professed revolutionary heroes more suspicious of each other than they were of the Americans, with their bodyguards all standing just outside the room, fingers on triggers. We made little headway. I reported to Secretary Kerry that I had never seen Libya "in a more fragile state."[10] President Obama was less diplomatic in his *Atlantic* interview with Jeff Goldberg a couple years later. Libya, he said, had become "a shit show."

The president wasn't far off. Our intervention in 2011 had saved thousands of innocent lives, at relatively modest initial cost to the

United States. Without a strong post-intervention American hand, our neat "long game" coalition stumbled—the incapacity and irresolution of most of the Europeans painfully exposed, most of the Arabs reverting to self-interested form, and rival Libyan factions unified only by their ardent opposition to any meaningful foreign support and engagement. Libya became a violent cautionary tale, whose shadow heavily influenced American policy toward the far more consequential drama unfolding in the Levant—Syria's horrendous civil war.

* * *

HINDSIGHT NEITHER DIMINISHES the continuing pain and cost of Syria's civil war, nor illuminates any easy choices for policymakers. As I write this, more than half a million people have been killed. Thirteen million more, approximately two-thirds of the country's prewar population, have been driven out of their homes, at least half of them flooding across Syria's borders and unsettling political order and local economies in the Middle East and Europe. ISIS sprang out of the sectarian chaos of Syria and a still-wounded Iraq. Outside powers preyed on Syria's divisions, from Iran and Russia to the Gulf Arabs, settling scores and angling for advantage across its battered landscape. The Assad clan has clung to power with unyielding harshness, mowing down peaceful protestors and gassing civilians. Syria remains bloody and broken, its recovery a distant aspiration, its pathologies still threatening its neighborhood.

It is hard not to see Syria's agony as an American policy failure. Many see it as the underreaching analog to the disastrous overreach of the Iraq War a decade before. As someone who served through both, and shared in the mistakes we made, I am not persuaded by the analogy. There were times during Syria's protracted crisis when more decisive American intervention might have made a difference. Like many of my colleagues, I argued for more active support in 2012 for what was then still a relatively moderate, if ragtag, opposition, and for responding militarily to Assad's use of sarin gas in the summer of 2013. Neither step, however, would necessarily have turned the tide.

It was not only the shadow of Libya and its torment that hung over those choices, it was also the far darker shadow of Iraq. In terms of Obama's "long game" calculus, having the discipline to avoid getting sucked into another military entanglement in the Middle East, which would likely only underscore the limits of our influence in a world of predators for whom Syria's battles were existential, was paramount. It took cold-blooded rigor of the sort that Jim Baker and Brent Scowcroft would have admired to resist the clamor for direct military action against Assad, tempting as it was.

Yet again, where we ran into trouble was in our short game. We misaligned ends and means, promising too much, on the one hand—declaring that "Assad must go" and setting "red lines"—and applying tactical tools too grudgingly and incrementally, on the other. If you added up all the measures we eventually took in Syria by the end of 2014, including a more ambitious train and equip program for the opposition, and telescoped them into more decisive steps earlier in the conflict, their cumulative impact might have given us more leverage over Assad, as well as the Russians and Iranians. They wouldn't on their own have produced Assad's downfall, but they might have created a better chance for a negotiated solution. It was in many ways another lesson in the risks of incrementalism.

In the Assad family playbook, conciliation was a fatal weakness, suspiciousness a guiding principle, and brutishness an article of faith. Nevertheless, before 2011, the Obama administration tested with Assad whether some modest improvement in relations might be possible. Special Envoy for Middle East Peace George Mitchell had extensive discussions in Damascus about reviving the Syrian track of the peace process, and I visited Assad twice to gauge his seriousness about clamping down on cross-border support for extremists in Iraq and broader counterterrorism cooperation. After a long one-on-one conversation with him in February 2010, I reported to Secretary

Clinton that it made little sense to get our hopes up about the Syrians. "The safest bet," I said, "is that they will evade and obfuscate; that's generally their default position."[11]

When the Arab Spring began to break in early 2011, Assad showed none of the initial hesitation that, he believed, had unraveled Ben Ali and Mubarak. Their experiences cast their own shadows onto the young Syrian dictator's thinking, which was reinforced by reminders from his hard-edged family and advisors about Hafez al-Assad's rigid rulebook. In Dara'a, near the border with Jordan, a group of schoolchildren spray-painted antiregime slogans on the wall of their building. "It's your turn, Doctor," was their not-so-subtle message to the ophthalmologist turned president in Damascus. They were arrested and tortured, sparking demonstrations. Syrian security forces responded harshly, with two dozen civilians killed on April 9.

As protests mounted across the country, so did the death toll. An armed opposition began to emerge, fragmented but gradually more threatening to the regime. In July, our ambassador in Damascus, Robert Ford, visited Hama, a large city north of Damascus that Hafez al-Assad had leveled thirty years before to suppress Islamist dissent. Hama had become another scene of large, peaceful protests, and the demonstrators showered Ford with flowers. Assad dug in harder, stubbornly resistant to calls for dialogue with dissidents. President Obama had been careful in his rhetoric, but the explosion of violence over the summer and Assad's intransigence finally led him to conclude publicly that Assad had to go. "For the sake of the Syrian people," he said, "the time has come for President Assad to step aside."

There was still a widespread sense in the region, and in the administration, that Assad's demise was only a matter of time. King Abdullah of Saudi Arabia told me that Assad was "finished." King Abdullah of Jordan had a similar view. In Abu Dhabi, Crown Prince Mohamed bin Zayed was more nuanced; he thought Assad was on the ropes, but "could hang on for a long time" if the opposition didn't squeeze hard now. Fred Hof, the State Department's senior advisor on

Syria, said Assad was "a dead man walking." The U.S. intelligence community didn't push back against that assessment.

Following the president's judgment on Assad, the administration went through its own collection of tactical steps. Sanctions were enacted against senior Syrian regime officials; the European Union acted along similar lines; the Arab League spoke out against Assad; and an effort began to obtain UN Security Council authorization for tougher measures. With the bitter experience of the Libya resolutions and Qaddafi's overthrow fresh in their minds, however, neither the Russians nor the Chinese were interested in signing any more blank checks. They repeatedly vetoed even the mildest of resolutions condemning Assad's bombardment of unarmed civilians—undercutting international pressure and proving to Assad he would face no sanction for his war crimes. Their vetoes were callous and destructive, only exacerbating the human tragedy unfolding in Syria.

Despite setbacks at the UN, we engaged intensively with the Russians to try to find a pathway to a negotiated transition. In conversations with Secretary Clinton and me, Sergey Lavrov asserted that Russia was not "wedded" to Assad, but would not push him out, and worried about who or what might come after him. Obama and Putin had a testy exchange on Syria on the margins of a G-20 summit in Mexico in early June 2012. In Geneva at the end of the month, Clinton and Lavrov agreed to a formula brokered by former UN secretary-general Kofi Annan, who was serving as UN envoy on the Syria crisis. According to the Geneva Communiqué, Russia and the United States agreed to press for the formation of a transitional governing body in Syria, "with full executive powers," whose composition would be determined by "mutual consent" of the current Syrian authorities and the opposition. We believed "mutual consent" was effectively a veto for the opposition over Assad's continued authority; the Russians conceded no such thing, and insisted that they weren't going to lean on Assad to begin to transfer power. The communiqué was less an agreement than a neat summary of our differences.

I followed up in Geneva in December and then again in January 2013 with Lakhdar Brahimi, who succeeded a deeply frustrated Annan as UN envoy, and Mikhail Bogdanov, the Russian deputy foreign minister responsible for the Middle East. I had considerable respect for both of them. Brahimi was the UN's most accomplished troubleshooter, a former Algerian foreign minister with a sure feel for the Middle East and a passionate commitment to resolving conflicts. Bogdanov was the best of Russia's impressive cadre of Arabists, with long experience in Syria and an encyclopedic knowledge of its regime and personalities.

In the winter of 2012–13 the Russians were growing nervous about Assad's staying power. He had been steadily losing ground to opposition forces, regime morale was declining, and he was having trouble finding recruits for his military. In our private conversations, Bogdanov was candid about his concerns about Assad, and about the extent to which fighting in Syria was becoming a magnet for Islamic extremists. He was equally concerned about the difficulty of shaping a stable post-Assad leadership, and dubious about the political opposition, which was weakly led and divided. Bogdanov said he saw no signs of significant defections from Assad's inner circle or military and security leadership; Bashar's father had built a system around the notion that insiders would either hang together or hang separately, and that didn't seem to be cracking.

We went round and round with Brahimi about how to translate the Geneva Communiqué into practice, but spun our wheels. We simply could not convince the Russians that we had a plausible theory of the case for the day after Assad, and the Russians were uninterested in offering their own. By the early spring of 2013, the sense of Russian urgency and nervousness evaporated as a substantial influx of Hezbollah fighters from Lebanon and Iranian material support gave Assad a boost and his fortunes began to shift on the battlefield. I doubt the Russians were ever serious about pressuring Assad to leave, and they lacked the leverage to accomplish that unless the Iranians agreed, which was never going to happen.

Our own lack of leverage was a major diplomatic weakness. The argument for doing more in 2012 to bolster the opposition was never, at least in my mind, about victory on the battlefield. It was about trying to demonstrate to Assad and his outside backers that he couldn't win militarily, and that his political options were going to narrow the longer the fighting continued. It was a way to manage the opposition, and to use our provision of training and equipment to help make them a more coherent and responsive force. And it was a way to herd the cats among the other supporters of the opposition—to try to discipline the feuding Gulf Arabs, help ensure that we weren't acting at cross-purposes with one another, and keep their assistance away from the more extreme groups to which some of them were drawn. I hated the then-fashionable term "skin in the game," which always seemed too glib in the face of Syria's ugly realities, but that was essentially what this was about—giving greater weight and credibility to our political strategy.

Most of Obama's senior advisors advocated this approach. At the end of the summer of 2012, Clinton joined David Petraeus, now director of the CIA, and Leon Panetta, who had succeeded Gates the year before as secretary of defense, in a concerted effort to persuade the president to approve a more ambitious train and equip program. Obama was unconvinced. In the subsequent recollections of some of the protagonists, this debate and the pivotal NSC meeting in the Situation Room is portrayed as a kind of "Gunfight at the OK Corral," with the president alone against the passionate and ironclad arguments of his subordinates. I don't remember it in quite the same way.

It was like so many high-level deliberations among smart people about complicated problems—harassed by time pressures, domestic critics, and impatient allies. Clinton and Petraeus did argue carefully for doing more, and like most people in the room that afternoon, I agreed. The president asked penetrating questions, for which none of us had especially compelling answers. Our understanding of the capacity and makeup of the Syrian opposition was in truth quite limited. Predictions of Assad's fragile future were far more educated guesses than scientific conclusions, and no one really knew what it would mean when the Iranians and Russians doubled down in response to any increase in American support for the opposition. With the legendary success of its covert program in Afghanistan in the 1980s as the unspoken predicate, the intelligence community tended to overstate how fast and how effectively it could arm the Syrian rebels. And fears of what had later happened in Afghanistan, with the U.S.-armed mujahedeen morphing into the Taliban and embracing bin Laden, loomed large for Obama. It was not an easy call.

* * *

BY CONTRAST, I thought the choice to respond to Assad's later use of chemical weapons (CW) was more clear-cut. In unscripted public remarks in August 2012, Obama declared that Assad's use of chemical weapons would cross "a red line." Throughout the rest of 2012 and the first half of 2013, we became more and more convinced that Assad was employing sarin gas and other chemical weapons against his own people. He seemed to be testing the edges of our response, with fairly small-scale use gradually growing bolder. I had been asked by the White House twice in the spring and early summer to telephone Syrian foreign minister Walid Muallem, with whom I had dealt for decades, and make clear that we knew what his regime was doing and would not tolerate it. If it continued, there would be consequences. Muallem listened both times and smugly dismissed my claims. "We're not responsible," he said. "Maybe it's your Islamist extremist friends."

Then on August 21, the Syrian military used sarin against civilians in Ghouta, a rebel-controlled suburb of Damascus. More than fourteen hundred people were murdered, many of them children. The intelligence on this attack was solid, and gruesome video footage was shown around the world. Susan Rice, now national security advisor, convened a series of Principals Committee meetings to consider options. The overwhelming consensus of the group was that the issue was not whether to respond militarily, but how. American warships were positioned in the eastern Mediterranean, their cruise missiles well within range of a variety of potential targets—the airfields from which chemical attacks had been launched, suspected CW depots, and Assad's own palace and helicopter fleet. The French were ready to join in a strike. So were the British—at least until a disastrous, ill-prepared vote in Parliament on August 29 denied Prime Minister David Cameron the authority to act militarily.

At the request of the White House, John Kerry appeared in the State Department's Treaty Room on August 30 and made a forceful statement, which I helped craft, and which all but promised military action. Both the secretary and I went home that evening convinced that the president would order a strike over the weekend. I firmly believed, like Kerry, that it was the right call. Assad had not only crossed our red line, but had violated a crucial international norm.

There were obvious downsides. Striking at chemical weapons facilities risked plumes of poisonous materials, and we knew we couldn't locate or destroy all of their stockpiles. Assad might up the ante and lash out even more brutally, pushing us all down a very slippery slope. It seemed to me, however, that we were on firmer ground than proponents of the slippery-slope argument would admit. I sympathized with the president's cynicism about the Washington establishment's tendency to retreat behind the argument that "American credibility is at stake" as the all-purpose justification for the use of force. This was not just about our credibility. Our intelligence was incontestable, and a strong punitive strike in response to CW use would be aimed clearly at defending an international norm and deterring future use. It didn't

imply an effort at regime change, or direct intervention in the civil
war. It was the best case for using force that we'd have against Assad,
and the best near-term window to shape the conflict's trajectory.

Kerry called later that night to tell me that there had been a change
in signals. "I can't believe it," he said, "but the president just called to
say we're holding." The chain of events had unfolded rapidly. Early on
Friday evening, the president had gone for his customary end-of-the-
day walk around the South Lawn of the White House with his chief
of staff, Denis McDonough. Denis was as good a sounding board as
the president could hope for—thoughtful and whip smart. Obama
was uneasy about moving forward without congressional authorization; a strike in Syria could carry with it all sorts of unintended consequences, and Congress needed to take some ownership. If we were
going to use force, we should do it the right way and break the bad
habit of executive overreach (and congressional evasiveness) that had
proved so corrosive since 9/11. Cameron's parliamentary fiasco the
day before was a reminder of what could go wrong, but the president
was determined.

The following day, Obama made a brief public statement indicating that he would seek congressional authorization for a strike against
Assad. Prospects for approval were dim. Few Republicans wanted to
be helpful to Obama, and many Democrats were uneasy, afflicted by
2003 Iraq War déjà vu. The French felt abandoned. Our Arab partners were appalled, and saw the decision as another sign of American
wavering—one more sin in the litany that had begun with "abandoning" Mubarak.

Meanwhile, Jake Sullivan and I went off to Oman in early September to resume secret talks with the Iranians. We made significant
headway on the nuclear issue, certainly more than we had expected.
Some critics have alleged that it was the secret talks and preserving
their potential that caused Obama to hesitate about a strike against
Assad, whom the Iranians were fiercely backing. I never once heard
the president voice that concern. It always seemed to me that his

choices on Syria at this moment had much more to do with the risks of getting mired in another conflict there than the risks of jeopardizing the secret channel with Iran. In fact, Jake and I sent a note to the White House during that early September round in Oman arguing that a strike (which we both favored) would complicate but not blow up the talks. The Iranians were perfectly capable of compartmentalizing our relations, with Foreign Minister Javad Zarif beginning a nuclear negotiation while Quds Force commander Qassem Soleimani did his best to threaten our interests across the Middle East. We ought to be able to compartmentalize too.

Over the medium term, we thought, it would actually help—reminding a variety of audiences, including the Iranians—that there were circumstances in which we would use force to protect our most critical interests in the region. That would be an unsubtle signal of our determination to ensure, by whatever means necessary, that Iran did not develop a nuclear weapon. It would also demonstrate that even if we reached an agreement on the nuclear issue, we would not ease up on other contested areas. That was a message that would help manage some of the inevitable angst from regional friends.

While we were negotiating secretly in Oman, events moved quickly on the Syrian CW issue. The president saw Vladimir Putin, the recently reinstalled Russian president, at the G-20 meeting in St. Petersburg in the first week in September. Putin pitched a vague proposal for a diplomatic resolution of the CW problem, with Assad potentially agreeing to ship his remaining chemical stockpiles out of the country and end his program. It was hard to know how seriously to take the Russians. When Kerry was asked by the press in London on September 9 about what could be done to avoid military action in Syria, he responded offhandedly that the Syrians could turn over all their chemical weapons immediately, but expressed disbelief that they would. Lavrov called him right afterward and insisted that the Russians wanted to work with us on "our initiative." In one of diplomacy's stranger recent turns, Kerry, Lavrov, and their teams hammered out a framework agreement for the removal of Syrian CW, which they announced on September 14 in Geneva. It was a significant step, even though the Syrians concealed some remaining stocks from international inspectors. A diplomatic agreement to remove Assad's declared CW arsenal was in many ways a better outcome than a punitive military strike. The lingering impression, however, was that the Obama administration had blinked at the moment of military decision. It would leave an enduring mark.

Assad was willing to make a show of conceding chemical weapons to his Russian patrons, but his singular determination to stamp out the opposition never wavered. He was convinced that what he had bought for giving up chemical weapons, at least temporarily, was a "get out of jail free" card on future American use of force against him. Faced with significant manpower shortages, he was also able to count on the Iranians to fill the gap, principally by sustaining Hezbollah and other Shia militias.

Secretary Kerry was relentless in his pursuit of diplomatic openings, and logged endless hours on the phone and in meeting rooms with Lavrov. The Russians had neither the leverage nor the inclination to try to show Assad the door, however unseemly a client he might be. Putin's tolerance for unseemliness was high, and he enjoyed the emerging narrative in the Arab world that Russia was a more reliable partner than America. As King Abdullah of Saudi Arabia told me, "The Russians are wrong to back Assad, but at least they stand by their friends." Kerry was equally relentless in arguing in Washington for more support for the opposition, and later for targeted use of force against the Assad regime, to stem the tide of regime advances and bolster America's diplomatic hand. He didn't find much appetite in the White House, where the holes in the argument and the risks of setbacks always outweighed the potential gains.

I was invited to an informal afternoon discussion in the Oval Office between the president and his White House advisors in the summer of 2014, a two-hour session focused mainly on the Syria crisis.

We talked about how moderates were losing strength within the opposition, and Sunni extremists were gaining. This fit Assad's narrative that he was the last person standing between secular order in Syria and Islamic radicals. The Russians, I thought, were unlikely to engage in serious diplomacy, let alone throw their limited weight behind a political transition. I argued at one point that we needed to put "more pieces on the board" to reanimate diplomacy—to create a bigger and more effective train and equip program for the waning moderate opposition groups, and consider some form of "safe zones" in a few places in Syria along the borders of Jordan and Turkey. There the moderate opposition could train, safeguard displaced Syrians, and begin to develop habits of governance that could at least point in the direction of a future transition.

This was not the first time the president had heard these arguments. He listened carefully and didn't dismiss them out of hand, but it was not hard to sense his impatience with recommendations for safe zones, which begged much bigger questions of who exactly would help protect them and at what cost, not to mention the tangled issue of international legal justification.

As 2014 wore on, it was the dramatic and unexpected rise of ISIS, the fall of Mosul, and the grave risk to Iraq's stability that ultimately persuaded the White House to act more boldly. A $500 million Pentagon-led train and equip program was launched for the moderate Syrian opposition, aimed ostensibly at fighting ISIS, not Assad. It proved to be too cumbersome, too little, and too late to have any significant effect on the Syrian civil war. A coalition of Islamist fighters who benefited from some combination of CIA and Gulf Arab support was making notable gains, causing grave concern in Moscow.[12] As a result, in the early fall of 2015, Putin intervened more decisively in Syria, using a relatively modest military deployment to maximum political effect. Russian airstrikes steadied Assad's forces and helped them press their advantage on the ground. The American-led campaign against ISIS, accelerating as I was leaving government at the end of 2014, eventually rolled back the ISIS caliphate in Mosul and Raqaa. Bashar al-Assad remained in Damascus, having regained control of most of Syria's major population centers, refuted predictions of his demise, and devastated his country for generations to come.

*   *   *

THE COMPLICATED STORIES of Syria, Libya, and Egypt during the Obama administration were only parts of a larger American policy tableau in the Middle East. Obama's broad strategy—his long game—was to gradually break the region's decades-long psychological, military, diplomatic, and political hold on American foreign policy. He knew we couldn't detach ourselves entirely or neglect the festering risks; it was time, however, to shift the balance of tools we employed. For too long, the president thought, we had invested too much in an ill-considered combination of policy instruments, partners, and objectives. It was time to realign and rebalance—use our leverage where we could and solve the issues of biggest consequence to regional stability like Iran's nuclear program or the Arab-Israeli conflict; construct two-way streets where for too long U.S. policy was giving a lot and getting too little in return from its partners and allies; and finally make a significant effort to help the region fill the deficits in education and economic and political modernization on which extremists fed.

It made eminent sense. It just turned out to be much harder to execute than Obama expected. The distant promise of the long game was held hostage by the infinite complexities of the short game, by twists and turns that surprised him, and tactical choices and trade-offs that frustrated all of us. By the second term, the rhythm of White House principals and deputies meetings, well over half of them focused on the Middle East, made it difficult to see where the rebalance to Asia and other priorities had gone. Some of this, of course, was simply what international politics are all about. Assumptions don't always hold. The unexpected intrudes. Yet precisely because Obama and his closest advisors had such strong convictions about the wisdom of their long game, they were sometimes reluctant to adjust to unforeseen forces and new facts.

It was the Arab Spring that brought all this into sharpest relief. For all their drama and consequence, the Arab revolts during the Obama era were part of a much longer process, an early round in what will be a series of struggles to deal with the ills of a profoundly troubled part of the world. Egypt, Libya, and Syria were not the only societies affected, as Tunisians and Yemenis can attest, and they won't be the last. Theirs were just the most compelling for American policy. With all the inevitable tactical missteps, and things we might have done differently or better, the Obama administration's approach in Egypt was basically sound. We recognized the limits of our power, handled Mubarak's departure about as well as we could have, and preserved a security relationship that—warts and all—still mattered.

We made serious mistakes in Libya. They had less to do, in my view, with our initial decision to act, and more with our failure to plan for and sustain a realistic approach to security after Qaddafi's fall. We helped prevent a massacre, and played a critical role in a tactically successful military intervention. We got our medium-term assumptions wrong, however; we badly overestimated Libya's post-Qaddafi resilience and the staying power of our partners, and underestimated the ferociousness of the counterrevolutionary pushback, including from Egypt and some of our closest Gulf partners.

Syria is most troubling of all. A major American military intervention would not have solved the conflict, and would likely have made it worse for us. The mistake we made between 2012 and 2014 was that we regularly paired maximalist ends with minimalist means. More modest objectives (a much slower pace toward post-Assad governance, for example) and more concentrated means (such as an earlier, more robust train and equip program for the opposition) would have been a more coherent combination. We might have given ourselves more diplomatic leverage, and enhanced the chances for a negotiated transition, if we had acted sooner and stronger—particularly in the late summer of 2012 and over the CW red line a year later. Instead, we did plenty to escalate the conflict and far too little to end it.

Ultimately, Obama could not escape his inheritance in the Middle East. The array of problems facing him was much less susceptible to the application of American power in a world in which there was less of that power to apply. The events of the Arab Spring turned Winter overshadowed in many respects Obama's effort to reset America's role in the region and the world over the long term. His nuclear deal with Iran, however, would reinforce his convictions about the power of diplomacy and America's pivotal leadership role.

9

Iran and the Bomb: The Secret Talks

LATE ONE NIGHT in February 2013, I climbed into an unmarked U.S. government Gulfstream jet parked on the deserted tarmac at Andrews Air Force Base. Secretary Kerry's parting words, delivered with his characteristic optimism and self-assurance, still rang in my head: "We've got the diplomatic opportunity of a lifetime." I felt far more uncertain.

I spent much of that seventeen-hour flight to Oman reviewing briefing books, talking through strategy and tactics with our negotiating team, and trying to come to grips with the task before us. It had been thirty-five years since the United States and Iran had had sustained diplomatic contact. There was baggage on both sides, and massive mutual mistrust. The diplomatic stakes were high, with Iran's nuclear program accelerating and military conflict between us an increasing possibility. The politics in both our capitals were explosive, with little room for diplomatic maneuver. International diplomacy had run aground, its thus far desultory exchanges missing a key ingredient—a direct discussion between the two principal protagonists, the United States and Iran.

For all the anxiety, it was also hard not to feel a sense of possibility. Here was a chance to do what diplomats spend their whole careers trying to do. Here was a chance to apply tough-minded diplomacy, backed up by the economic leverage of sanctions, the political leverage of an international consensus, and the military leverage of the potential use of force. And here was a chance to demonstrate the promise of American diplomacy after a decade of America at war.

* * *

IRAN HUNG OVER much of my career, a country synonymous in American foreign policy terms with troubles, threats, and blunders. Iran seemed a menacing and impenetrable presence, too big and dangerous to ignore, but too intransigent to engage. It was a mine-field for diplomats, and nobody had a good map.

I took the Foreign Service entrance exam in November 1979, a few days after the seizure of our embassy in Tehran and the beginning of a hostage crisis that brought down a president. Iranian-backed terrorists twice bombed our embassy in Beirut, and killed more than two hundred Marines in another attack there. The Iran-Contra scandal nearly brought down a second president.

The sweeping success of Desert Storm in 1991 propelled American influence in the Middle East to its zenith. The Clinton administration worked hard to contain Iran, but also explored in the late 1990s a possible opening with the Khatami government. It never got very far. The post–9/11 landscape offered a similar opportunity, which we never seized. Instead, the U.S.-led overthrow of Iran's bitter historical adversaries in Kabul and Baghdad, and the chaos that ensued, delivered Iran a strategic opening that it was only too pleased to exploit.

In late 2001, the U.S. intelligence community began to track two clandestine nuclear sites in Iran: a uranium enrichment plant at Natanz and a facility in Arak that could eventually produce weapons-grade plutonium. These efforts, undeclared to the IAEA, built on

Iran's overt civilian nuclear energy program, which began during the shah's time—ironically, with the initial support of the United States.

The revelation of the covert sites in the summer of 2002 set off a diplomatic dance that continued for the next several years. The UN Security Council passed resolutions demanding that Iran suspend its enrichment work. Iran instead plowed stubbornly ahead. Given the unwillingness of the Bush administration to engage directly with Iran, our European allies (the United Kingdom, France, and Germany, or the "EU-3") began a negotiation with the Iranians that showed fitful progress, as Tehran sought both to preserve its enrichment program and the long-term possibility of weaponization and at the same time avoid economic sanctions. Russia and China later joined the EU-3, which was eventually rebranded as the P5+1 (the five permanent members of the UN Security Council plus Germany).

This all boosted the market for international diplomatic acronyms, but didn't make much of a dent in Iranian behavior. By the last year of the Bush administration in 2008, despite the imposition of several rounds of UN sanctions against Iran and growing international concern, the Iranians had accumulated half the amount of low-enriched uranium they would need to enrich further and make a single bomb. They were spinning more than four thousand primitive IR-1 centrifuges at Natanz, and were making halting progress toward more sophisticated models.

While the American intelligence community concluded famously in 2007 that the Iranian leadership had suspended its weapons work back in 2003, the fact that they were clearly determined to keep their options open in the face of mounting international pressure was deeply troubling. An unconstrained Iranian nuclear program or a regime clearly bent on a weapons program would add yet another layer of risk and fragility to an already unstable region. Our friends—the Gulf Arab states and, especially, Israel—had to take that threat seriously.

As the Bush administration grappled with the damage done by the Iraq War, some of its senior figures began to recognize that its stubborn insistence on not engaging directly in P5+1 diplomacy with Iran had become counterproductive. An early probe for direct talks in May 2003, orchestrated by the enterprising and well-intentioned Swiss ambassador in Tehran, was never pursued. I was traveling in the region when Tim Guldimann, about to complete his ambassadorial tour in Iran, came to Washington and met with my deputy, Jim Larocco, to present a short paper that he insisted had been drafted in cooperation with Iran's ambassador in Paris, the nephew of Iranian foreign minister Kamal Kharazi. Guldimann said the whole effort had been sanctioned at high levels of the Iranian government. The document itself was intriguing, offering a wildly ambitious dialogue across the whole range of U.S.-Iranian differences. Jim and my other NEA colleagues pressed Guldimann hard on who exactly in Tehran had endorsed the paper, and how explicitly that was conveyed. Guldimann was too vague for Jim's taste. The tangled history of ill-sourced messages and double-dealing cast a shadow on our deliberations.

We conveyed the document and an account of Jim's conversation to Secretary Powell and Deputy Secretary Armitage—noting our doubts that it bore the stamp of the highest level of Iran's leadership, but recommending that we test the proposition and reopen the contacts with Iran that had been suspended a year earlier. Powell and Armitage agreed. But in the heady immediate aftermath of the invasion of Iraq, there was little White House interest in talking to a charter member of the "axis of evil," and a conviction that direct engagement would be a reward for bad behavior. For Vice President Cheney and hardliners in the administration, the calculus was clear: If the Iranians were worried about being next on the American hit parade after Saddam, it wasn't a bad idea to let them stew a little.

Throughout the remaining two years of my time in NEA we continued to make the case for dialogue with Iran. I repeated the argument in my December 2004 transition memo to Secretary Rice. I also added a proposal—which was adopted—to restart a serious program of Persian-language training for a small cadre of American diplomats, and then station them in several posts on Iran's periphery to develop expertise and prepare for an eventual resumption of contacts. The "Iran Watchers" initiative had as its inspiration what we had done more than seven decades before in preparing Russian-language specialists for eventual reopening of diplomatic relations with the Soviet Union.

By the time I returned to Washington from Moscow in the spring of 2008, the mood had begun to shift a little. Chastened by the postwar mess in Iraq, President Bush had replaced Don Rumsfeld with Bob Gates at the Pentagon. The vice president's hawkish views were less dominant, and Rice was pressing on several fronts for more active American diplomacy.

In late May 2008, I sent Secretary Rice a long memo entitled "Regaining the Strategic Initiative on Iran." I began by arguing that "our Iran policy is drifting dangerously between the current muddle of P5+1 diplomacy and more forceful options, with all of their huge downsides." Our unwillingness to engage directly with Tehran was costing us more than the Iranians, and deprived us of valuable leverage. "The regime has constructed a narrative which portrays Iran as the victim of implacable American hostility," I wrote, "increasingly gaining the diplomatic upper hand regionally and globally, with the American administration—not Iran—increasingly the isolated party. Reviving significant pressure against Iran's nuclear program requires us to puncture that narrative."[1]

I had two practical suggestions. First, it was long past time for the United States to join our European, Russian, and Chinese partners at the negotiating table. I had few illusions that the government of Mahmoud Ahmadinejad, let alone the deeply suspicious Supreme Leader, was ready to negotiate seriously. By not engaging, we were giving them an easy out—allowing them to hide behind the pretext that they couldn't really be sure about P5+1 proposals, because the

Americans weren't there to back them up. Our physical presence would put us on the high ground, put the Iranians on the defensive, strengthen solidarity with our negotiating partners, and better position us to pivot to more sanctions if Tehran balked again.

My second idea would revive an initiative that had already been kicked around at lower levels in the administration. I suggested to Rice that we should propose quietly to the Iranians that we staff our interests section in Tehran with a few American diplomats, revising the arrangement that had been in effect since the assault on our embassy in Tehran in 1979, under which the Swiss represented our interests in Iran. We would reciprocate by allowing the Iranians to staff their interests section in Washington, managed by the Pakistani government, with a handful of Iranian diplomats. Like the argument for joining the P5+1 talks, the focus was on tactical advantages. I had little expectation that the Supreme Leader would actually agree to such a proposal. The last thing he wanted to see was a long line of Iranian visa applicants around a U.S. diplomatic facility in Tehran staffed by Americans; for the Ayatollah Khamenei, this would be the ultimate Trojan horse. The proposal, which would inevitably become public, would only further cement our grip on the high ground. I suggested that we pitch the idea to the Iranians through the Russians, who had good high-level channels in Tehran and whose support would be crucial if we had to go back to the UN Security Council for tougher sanctions.

I concluded with a broad argument, echoing the classic containment concept that Rice knew so well as a recovering Sovietologist. In dealing with a profoundly hostile adversary beset by its own serious internal contradictions, I said, "a successful strategy will require calculated risk-taking on our part…with the same combination of multiple pressure points, diplomatic coalition-building, wedge-driving among Iran and its uneasy partners, and selected contacts with the regime that animated much of Kennan's concept." Moreover, we should simultaneously explore "creatively subversive ways to accentuate the gap between the regime's deeply conservative instincts and popular Iranian desire for normalization with the rest of the world, including the U.S."[2]

Rice saw the possibilities immediately, and knew that we needed to inject some new American initiative into nuclear diplomacy with Iran. The proximate opportunity in the talks themselves was the presentation by Javier Solana, the de facto European Union foreign minister, of a renewed P5+1 proposal to Iran. The essence of his proposal was a freeze on Iranian nuclear activities, including enrichment, and a reciprocal freeze on new UN Security Council sanctions, which would allow space for negotiations on a comprehensive nuclear deal. Solana conveyed this plan in Tehran in June 2008, and the Iranians pledged to respond at a follow-up meeting in Geneva in July. Rice decided to seek the president's approval for me to attend the Geneva meeting—and to also get his blessing on the interests section idea.

One morning in early July, I rode over with the secretary to one of her regular sessions with President Bush to make our pitch. Now nearing the end of his tenure, he looked a little grayer, but his decency and good humor were undiminished.

"Burnsie," he said with a familiar smile as I walked in behind the secretary, "it's good to have you back in Washington." Vice President Cheney sat in an armchair next to the president, less visibly enthused about my homecoming. I joined Rice on a couch alongside Bush, and she quickly laid out our case. The president asked a couple questions about how the interests section proposal would work, and expressed skepticism about what impact joining the Geneva talks with the Iranians would have on their behavior, but saw the value of trying both. The vice president started to object, arguing that we shouldn't reward the Iranians by appearing at a meeting. Bush cut him off. "Dick," he said with a wave of his hand, "I'm okay with this, and I've made up my mind." A lot had changed since the first term and the run-up to the Iraq War, I thought to myself. Diplomacy had its uses after all.

On July 19 in Geneva, amid massive media attention, I broke the taboo on direct American participation in the nuclear talks. I joined my P5+1 colleagues around an oblong table in a cramped meeting hall in the old city. I had been reminded by the secretary and Steve Hadley to keep my game face on and look appropriately sober while the cameras filmed the opening of the first session. They had also both suggested that it might be best to remain silent during the talks and simply witness the Iranian reply to Solana. The first point made sense. The second did not. If the purpose of joining the talks was to emphasize our seriousness and tag Iran as the diplomatic problem child, the silent treatment would backfire. Looking across the table directly at Saeed Jalili, the head of the Iranian delegation, I made a simple statement. I said that I hoped the Iranians understood the significance of the signal we were sending by joining the talks. We knew what was at stake on the nuclear issue; we were determined to prevent Iran from developing a bomb and to hold it to its international obligations; and we were firmly behind the P5+1 proposal. I emphasized that Iran had a rare opportunity before it; we could only hope that it would take advantage of it.

Jalili took careful notes, and smiled faintly throughout. I got lots of sidelong glances from him and his colleagues, who seemed to find the American presence unnerving. Jalili then embarked on nearly forty minutes of meandering philosophizing about Iran's culture and history, and the constructive role it could play in the region. He could be stupefyingly opaque when he wanted to avoid straight answers, and this was certainly one of those occasions. He mentioned at one point that he still lectured part-time at Tehran University. I didn't envy his students.

Jalili wound up his comments by handing over an Iranian "non-paper." The English version was mistakenly headed "None Paper," which turned out to be an apt description of its substance. Solana and the rest of us looked at it quickly, at which point my French colleague helpfully groaned and muttered, "Bullshit," which caused Jalili to look somewhat startled—and me to lose my game face. Fortunately, the cameras were long gone.

In a quick note to Secretary Rice that evening, I reported that "five and a half hours with the Iranians today were a vivid reminder that we may not have been missing all that much over the years." Nevertheless, our P5+1 colleagues were delighted that the United States was now visible and engaged. The Russians and Chinese seemed particularly impressed. However disappointing the Iranian response, we were back on the high ground.[3]

Neither joining the Geneva meeting nor the interests section initiative produced any substantive breakthroughs as the Bush administration came to an end. I joined Rice for a quiet meeting with Sergey Lavrov in Berlin later in July, and pitched the interests section idea. Lavrov agreed readily that Russia would convey it to Ali Akbar Velayati, the Supreme Leader's foreign policy advisor. But then the war in Georgia intervened, the Russians lost interest in being the messenger, we lost interest in the Russians, and the idea never went any further. We had, however, laid some of the groundwork for Barack Obama's much more active and imaginative approach to the Iranian nuclear dilemma.

* * *

AS HE MADE clear during his campaign for president, Obama sought a mandate to wind down America's wars in the Middle East and to make diplomacy the tool of first resort for protecting American interests. He advocated direct, unconditional engagement with adversaries, embroiling him in an early disagreement with his hard-nosed rival in the Democratic primaries, Hillary Clinton. By the time he took office in January 2009, Iran loomed as the biggest test of both of those propositions—whether diplomacy backed up by economic and military leverage could produce results, and whether direct contacts with our toughest adversaries could pay off.

President Obama found an effective partner for his Iran diplomacy in Clinton. She was instinctively more cautious about engaging the Iranians, and more skeptical about the chances of ever reaching an agreement that would deny Tehran a bomb. She agreed, however, that direct engagement was both the best way to test Iranian seriousness and the best way to invest in the kind of wider international coalition that we'd need to generate more pressure on Iran if it failed those initial tests.

Three days after she was sworn in as secretary of state, I sent Clinton a memo entitled "A New Strategy Toward Iran." I began by trying to encapsulate our fundamental purpose:

> Recognizing that Iran is a significant regional player, our basic goal should be to seek a long-term basis for coexisting with Iranian influence while limiting Iranian excesses, to change Iran's behavior but not its regime. That means, among other things, preventing Iran from achieving nuclear weapons capability; channeling its behavior so that it does not threaten our core interests in a stable, unitary Iraq and an Afghanistan that is not a platform for the export of violent extremism; and gradually reducing Iran's capacity to threaten us and our friends through support for terrorist groups. We should also speak out consistently against human rights abuses in Iran.[*]

I argued for a comprehensive approach. As with China in the early 1970s, it made sense to employ careful and incremental tactics at the outset, but as part of a coherent long-term strategy. "We should set," I said, "an early tone of respect and commitment to direct engagement, however severe our differences." I added the obvious: "Dealing with Iran will require enormous patience, persistence and determination. Deeply conspiratorial and suspicious of American motives, and riven by factions especially eager to undermine one another in the run-up to Iran's Presidential elections in June, the Iranian elite will be prone to false starts and deceit." We shouldn't underestimate the reality that, especially for the Supreme Leader and the hard men around him, animus toward the United States was the core organizing principle for the regime. But, I continued, "we should deal with the Iranian regime as a unitary actor, understanding that the Supreme Leader (not the President) is the highest authority. We have failed consistently in the past when we tried to play off one faction against another."

I also emphasized that we shouldn't lose sight of Iran's vulnerabilities. "Iran is a formidable adversary . . . but it is not ten feet tall. Its economy is badly mismanaged, with rising rates of unemployment and inflation. It is vulnerable to the ongoing sharp decline in oil prices, and to its dependence on refined petroleum products. It has no real friends in the neighborhood, distrusted by the Arabs and the Turks, patronized by the Russians, and suspicious of the Afghans." Finally, I stressed that "we need to be always conscious of the anxieties of our friends, as well as key domestic constituencies, as we proceed with Iran." I warned that our Sunni Arab partners would be nervous that we were abandoning them for a new Persian love interest. The Israelis would be at least as worried, given the undeniable threat that Iran's proxies and nuclear and missile programs posed for them. We'd have a big challenge managing Congress and its widespread aversion to serious engagement with Iran. And, I argued, "we must make sure that the Administration speaks with one voice, and avoids the divisions which beset the last Administration."[5]

Convinced by the argument, Clinton brought discipline and skill to the task. President Obama was eager to begin, and he convened a series of meetings in early 2009 to hammer out a broad strategy, close to the one I had tried to lay out for the secretary. Obama's inheritance on Iran was difficult. When he told the Iranians in his inaugural address on January 20 that "we will extend a hand if you are willing to unclench your fist," Tehran had already stockpiled enough low-enriched uranium for a nuclear weapon. Its missile systems were advancing. And while we had no firm evidence of a revival of Iran's earlier weaponization efforts, we could never be entirely sure.

In March, the president sent a videotaped Nowruz message to the Iranian people and, in a subtle effort to signal his lack of interest in forcing regime change, referred to the government by its formal name—the Islamic Republic. He committed the United States to "engagement that is honest and grounded in mutual respect." The Iranian popular reaction was overwhelmingly positive. The regime, particularly the Supreme Leader, remained skeptical.[6]

In early May, the president sent a long secret letter to the Ayatollah Khamenei. The letter tried to thread a needle—the message needed to be clear, but written in a way that would not cause too much controversy if it was leaked. In the letter, Obama reinforced the broad points in the Nowruz message. He was direct about his unwavering determination to prevent Iran from acquiring a nuclear weapon, and his support for the P5+1 position that Iran was entitled to a peaceful civilian nuclear program. He also made clear that it was not the policy of his administration to pursue regime change, and indicated his readiness for direct dialogue. The Supreme Leader replied a few weeks later, trying to thread a similar needle. His message was rambling, but at least by the standards of revolutionary Iranian rhetoric not especially edgy or sharp. While it offered no explicit reply to the president's offer of direct dialogue, we understood it nevertheless as a serious indication of his willingness to engage. President Obama responded quickly, in a short letter that proposed a discreet bilateral channel for talks, naming me and Puneet Talwar, a senior NSC staffer, as his emissaries.

All this halting momentum, modestly encouraging given the usual tribulations of dealing with Iran, came to an abrupt stop when the Iranian presidential elections in June turned into a bloodbath. The regime's ballot stuffing and repression of a surprisingly potent Green Movement opposition led to violence in the streets, documented by cellphone-wielding Iranian citizens and broadcast around the world in dramatic fashion. The government cracked down with its customary brutality, with paramilitary militias beating demonstrators, thousands arrested, and dozens killed. The White House's public response was initially tepid, less because of concern that it would jeopardize the fledgling effort at talks and more because the message from Green Movement leaders was not to suffocate them with an American embrace and allow the regime to paint them as U.S. stooges. In hindsight, we should have politely ignored those entreaties and been sharper in our public criticism from the start. Such criticism, which we eventually made quite strongly, was not only the right thing to do, it was also a useful reminder to the Iranian regime that we weren't so desperate to get nuclear talks started that we'd turn a blind eye to threatening behavior, whether against Iran's own citizens or our friends in the region.

As the summer of 2009 wore on, we continued to invest systematically in our P5+1 partners. Part of this had to do with an intriguing new idea that had emerged from IAEA director General Mohamed ElBaradei. Near the end of his tenure, ElBaradei still smarted from his frequent clashes with the Bush administration, but was anxious to help the new American administration get off on a more positive footing. The Iranians had sent a formal request to the IAEA in early summer, notifying them that the Tehran Research Reactor (TRR), which produced medical isotopes, had nearly exhausted the supply of 20 percent enriched uranium fuel plates that the Argentines had supplied in the 1990s. The implication seemed clear: Either ElBaradei would produce an alternative supplier, or the Iranians would produce the material themselves—and move closer to weapons-grade enrichment.

ElBaradei had the beginnings of a creative proposal. Why not call the Iranian bluff and supply the fuel plates, which posed no risk of being used for enrichment or weapons purposes? Bob Einhorn, my Baker-era Policy Planning colleague and now a senior advisor on nonproliferation issues at State, and Gary Samore, his counterpart at the NSC staff, took this one very interesting step further. Why not offer to supply the fuel plates for the TRR, but insist in return that the Iranians "pay" with about twelve hundred kilograms of 5 percent enriched uranium, roughly the amount that it would take to produce a batch of 20 percent fuel plates (and roughly the amount for one bomb's worth of material) to replenish the original Argentine shipment? Subtracting it from the then Iranian stockpile of about sixteen hundred kilograms would leave only four hundred kilos, far less than what they would need if they wanted to try to break out toward a weapon. It would take the Iranians a year or so to get back to one bomb's worth of material. That would provide time and space for serious negotiations about both the interim "freeze for freeze" proposal and a comprehensive solution.

Another priority that spring and summer was to strengthen cooperation with Russia on the Iran nuclear problem. The Georgia war in August 2008 had cratered U.S.-Russian relations, and the Obama administration had begun its effort to "reset" the relationship. Cooperation with Russia was the key to making the P5+1 effective. If the Iranians realized that they couldn't separate Moscow and Washington, and that we and the Russians might actually work together on much tougher sanctions, there might be a chance of focusing minds in Tehran. President Obama's conversation with Dmitry Medvedev in London in April 2009 was an excellent start. Secretary Clinton stayed in close touch with Foreign Minister Lavrov, and I had several long, quiet meetings with Deputy Foreign Minister Sergey Ryabkov, my counterpart and Russia's representative in the P5+1 talks. Ryabkov and I discussed the TRR proposal, and began to outline a cooperative arrangement in which Russia might produce the fuel plates for the TRR and take the Iranian low-enriched material in return.

Events came to a head in September 2009. As the annual meeting of the UN General Assembly approached in New York, which would be followed shortly by a G-20 summit in Pittsburgh, U.S., British, and French intelligence uncovered damning evidence of a covert Iranian enrichment site, buried deep inside a mountain near Qom. What made the clandestine site especially alarming was its relatively modest scale; with a capacity of only about three thousand centrifuges, it was much too small to produce enriched uranium fuel for a civilian nuclear power plant, but big enough to produce material for one or two nuclear bombs a year. Apparently nervous that Western governments might be poised to expose them, the Iranians sent a brief, seemingly innocuous note to ElBaradei informing the IAEA (many months after they were obligated to) of vaguely described construction work near Qom, at a site they called Fordow.

ElBaradei walked into a previously scheduled meeting at the Waldorf Astoria hotel in New York with me, Samore, and Einhorn on the evening of September 20. A little jet-lagged, and unaware of what we already knew about Fordow, ElBaradei reached into his pocket and handed us the Iranian notification. As Gary, Bob, and I each took turns looking at it, struggling to seem nonchalant, we quickly realized that it referred to the covert enrichment facility at Qom. We now had a fair amount of leverage with the Iranians, and a powerful argument to use with the Russians. Medvedev was angered by the revelation, partly because the Russians had again been caught off guard, and partly because the Iranians had apparently deceived them too. When President Obama announced the breach we had uncovered a couple days later in Pittsburgh, it deepened the resolve of the P5+1 to push the Iranians hard at the meeting that had already been scheduled in Geneva on October 1, and left Tehran backpedaling.

Led again by Javier Solana, my P5+1 colleagues and I met with Saeed Jalili and the Iranian delegation at a chateau outside Geneva on a sunny day in early October. We spent a desultory three hours in the morning delivering familiar positions across the table. Impatient and concerned that we'd miss the moment, I took advantage of the break for lunch, walked up to Jalili, shook his hand, and said, "I think it would be useful if we sat down and talked." He agreed, having presumably gotten advance permission from Tehran. And so began the highest-level conversation between the United States and Iran since 1979.

We walked over to a small side room and sat down around a polished round table with seats for four. Bob Einhorn joined me, and

Jalili was accompanied by his deputy, Ali Bagheri. Puneet Talwar arrived a few minutes later and sat behind Bob. Jalili was more soft-spoken than in our prior encounter. There were no set pieces this time. This was the first bilateral talk we had ever had with the Iranians on the nuclear issue, and I didn't want to waste it with a long preamble. I was also mindful that Jalili, with or without bombast, remained deeply suspicious of this whole interaction. He was a true believer in the Islamic Revolution, and he had come by his convictions through bitter experience. Wounded fighting the Iraqis in the 1980s, he had lost part of his right leg and walked with a distinct limp. Like many in his generation, he had learned the hard way in the trenches that Iran could trust no one and could only rely on itself.

I laid out carefully the TRR swap concept that ElBaradei had already previewed to the Iranians. Bob added some details, to make sure Jalili and Bagheri understood precisely what we were proposing. Jalili asked a few questions, but seemed to accept the core concept, and to appreciate how Iran would benefit from such a reciprocal arrangement. I also made clear, in a straightforward tone, that the consequences of rejecting the proposal, especially in light of the Qom revelation, were certain to be substantially tougher sanctions. Jalili seemed confident that Tehran would approve. "Our viewpoint," he said, "is positive." After we broke up, I asked Bob to go through the TRR proposal one more time with Jalili's deputy. They produced a paragraph summarizing our understanding, which we agreed that Solana could make public. Our P5+1 partners were supportive, relieved that we finally seemed poised to make some headway.

While hopeful, I told Secretary Clinton on the phone later that afternoon that the chances were probably less than fifty-fifty that the deal would stick in Tehran. Unfortunately, my pessimism proved well founded. A follow-up meeting in Vienna, hosted by the IAEA later in October, collapsed when the Iranians tried to walk back key provisions, particularly the shipment of twelve hundred kilograms of material to Russia. That was the crucial confidence-building step. The irony was that President Ahmadinejad was the biggest booster of the TRR agreement in Tehran, anxious to improve his standing after the disastrous fixed election and show that he could "deliver" the Americans. I assumed that Jalili's positive response in Geneva reflected Ahmadinejad's eagerness, and perhaps also wider regime worries after the Qom revelation that they needed to find a way to ease tensions. The Iranian president's political rivals, some of whom had been involved in the nuclear negotiations before and might otherwise have taken more supportive positions, didn't want Ahmadinejad to get the credit for any breakthrough, however modest. Iranian politics are a brutal contact sport, and the TRR deal was one of its many casualties.

As we had warned Jalili, his rejection of the deal led us to pivot to greater pressure against Iran. Secretary Clinton played a particularly effective role in helping Susan Rice, our ambassador at the United Nations, cajole the members of the Security Council toward a much tougher sanctions resolution, finally passed as UN Security Council Resolution 1929 in early June 2010. The Iranians played their usual critical role in helping us to persuade key members of the council, announcing in February 2010, for example, that they were beginning to enrich to 20 percent, ostensibly for the TRR. Russia's position was crucial; among the permanent, veto-wielding members of the council, we could count on strong support from Britain and France for more substantial sanctions, and China tended on the Iran issue at least to defer to Russia. Frustrated by the Iranians after the Qom disclosures and the failed TRR experiment, and increasingly confident in the possibilities of selective cooperation with the United States as the "reset" evolved, Medvedev eventually came around to support Resolution 1929.

An improvised effort in May by Brazil and Turkey to rescue the TRR proposal and stave off a new round of sanctions was too little, too late. In mid-May, Presidents Luiz Inácio Lula da Silva and Recep Tayyip Erdoğan went to Tehran and announced with great fanfare that they had brokered a breakthrough. The problems with their vaguely worded declaration were manifold: Since the Iranians now had accumulated enough low-enriched uranium for two bombs, exporting half would still leave them with enough for a bomb, if they chose to enrich to weapons-grade; the arrangements for shipping the material out of Iran to be swapped for TRR fuel plates were unclear; and Iran had already started enriching to 20 percent, another new problem. The bigger issue was that we had put enormous effort into getting Russia and China on board for what became UN Security Council Resolution 1929, and it would have been foolish to turn back unless the Iranians had made a spectacular move. This wasn't.

Passage of Resolution 1929, aimed in part at isolating Iran from the international financial system, was an enormous relief. I was at the high school graduation of our younger daughter, Sarah, in Georgetown on the day the vote took place in New York. Much to the consternation of the watch officers at the State Department Operations Center who had been connecting me with calls to P5+1 counterparts and a variety of American colleagues earlier that day, I happily turned my cellphone off for a few hours to enjoy Sarah's moment.

Resolution 1929 provided a platform for additional U.S. sanctions against Iran, as well as significant new EU measures. The U.S. steps, adopted overwhelmingly by Congress two weeks later, were aimed in part at reducing international purchases of Iranian oil, the lifeblood of its crumbling economy. The EU followed in July with a stringent package of its own. Far more than any previous combination of sanctions, these took a serious toll on the Iranian economy. By the end of President Obama's first term, the value of Iran's currency and its oil exports had each declined by 50 percent.

Iranian nuclear advances, however, continued to move at a dangerous pace. By the end of 2012, it had a stockpile of nearly six bombs' worth of 5 percent enriched material, and probably half a bomb's worth of 20 percent material. It was spinning more and more centrifuges at its openly declared site at Natanz, installing centrifuge cascades at Fordow, experimenting with more advanced centrifuges, and continuing work on its heavy water plutonium-producing site at Arak. Its missile systems were increasing in range and sophistication.

The country most alarmed by these developments was Israel. Although appreciative of all the effort that had gone into stepping up sanctions, Prime Minister Netanyahu argued throughout the latter part of Obama's first term that sanctions and diplomacy would be too slow to curb Iran's nuclear ambitions, and that military action would likely be required. His clear preference was to press Obama toward U.S. military action, especially against the deeply embedded enrichment facility at Fordow. Obama was unconvinced by the logic or necessity of force at this stage, and deeply irritated by Netanyahu's heavy-handed attempts to manipulate him in the run-up to the 2012 presidential elections. The Israeli leader's efforts to badger and maneuver Obama into a more belligerent approach had the opposite effect, deepening and accelerating his commitment to finding a way short of war to stop the Iranians.

Even a sweepingly effective attack on the Iranian program, Obama believed, would only set back the Iranians by two or three years. They would undoubtedly regroup, take their program fully underground, and very likely make a decision to weaponize, with wide popular support in the aftermath of a unilateral U.S. or Israeli strike.

Obama and Clinton worked carefully to manage Netanyahu's pressure and demonstrate U.S. determination to ensure by whatever means necessary that Iran would not acquire a nuclear weapon. National Security Advisor Tom Donilon deepened consultations with the Israelis on intelligence, as well as on sanctions and diplomatic strategy. We stepped up the transfer of sophisticated military systems to Israel, and accelerated our own plans for a new, fifteen-ton bomb that could penetrate Fordow. The United States and Israel reportedly jointly developed and deployed a malicious computer worm dubbed Stuxnet to sabotage, at least temporarily, the Iranian program. This campaign helped deflect Netanyahu's push to bomb, but it was clear as President Obama began his second term that the drumbeat would

get louder again if we couldn't make diplomacy work. As Hillary Clinton would later describe it, "the table was set" for a renewed diplomatic push, with sanctions eating away at the Iranian economy and a
Supreme Leader in Tehran nervous about a repetition of the unrest
that had so unsettled his regime in the summer of 2009.[7] What was
still missing, however, was a direct channel with the Iranians.

* * *

THE STORY OF how the Omani back channel to Iran emerged
seems, like so many things in diplomacy, a lot neater in retrospect
than it did at the time. Sultan Qaboos, an engaging ruler of the old
Arab school, had navigated complicated currents at home and in the
region for more than four decades, and had maintained a good rapport with the Supreme Leader in Tehran. Eager to play the intermediary, and nervous about the dangers of conflict so close to home, Oman
sent the new U.S. administration a series of low-key overtures about
its readiness to establish a channel to Iran.

The principal messenger for the sultan was Salem Ismaily, a clever,
urbane, persistent, and resourceful advisor, who, in the ambiguous
way in which Middle East elites often function, moved easily between
the worlds of officialdom and private business, and was often used as
a trusted fixer and negotiator. Salem was supremely confident of his
ability to set up a reliable channel to Tehran, although sometimes
murky about who exactly he was dealing with on the Iranian side.
Given the checkered history of American-Iranian contacts, we were
always skeptical of new initiatives, which often turned out to be over-
enthusiastic at best, and duplicitous at worst.

But Salem's steady and upbeat insistence that he could deliver,
backed up by long-standing trust in Qaboos, set the Omani overtures
apart. What solidified my confidence in Salem and his relationships
in Tehran was his role in securing the release of three young American hikers who had strayed into Iran along the border with Iraqi
Kurdistan in the summer of 2009. They were arrested and thrown

into the dismal confines of Evin Prison in downtown Tehran, where American embassy hostages had been held many years before. The hikers faced deep uncertainty. We tried through a variety of channels to secure their release, with no luck—until Salem got involved. Using his contacts in Tehran and the sultan's reputation and resources, he managed over the next two years to negotiate the release of all three Americans.

In October 2011, shortly after the hikers had returned home, Secretary Clinton met with Qaboos in Muscat, and concluded that the Omani channel was our best bet. President Obama spoke a couple times by phone with the sultan, and was similarly impressed, especially by Qaboos's conviction that he could deliver contacts with Iranians fully authorized by the Supreme Leader. I shared the view that the Omanis offered a promising opening, although I always wondered whether their relative success with the Iranians was a matter of their influence and ingenuity, or perhaps simply that they were a convenient vehicle for the Iranian regime when it decided to unburden itself of problems (like the hikers) or test channels with some plausible deniability. It also always appealed to the Iranians to sow dissension among the Gulf Arabs and use the Omanis to irritate the Saudis.

Even more energetic in his promotion of the Oman channel was Senator John Kerry, chairman of the Senate Foreign Relations Committee. Kerry had long been persuaded that the United States had to come to terms with Iran's nuclear progress and engage directly. Coordinating with Clinton and Donilon, he had a series of meetings and phone calls with the sultan and Ismaily in late 2011 and 2012, which made him a passionate advocate of the Oman channel. He made clear his commitment to exploring a dialogue with the Iranians, and his interest in playing a personal role.

At around the same time, Salem came to us with a new proposal, which he and the sultan were certain bore the approval of the Supreme Leader. He suggested a direct U.S.-Iranian meeting in Muscat, quietly facilitated by the Omanis. He asserted that the Iranians would be prepared to address any issue, but wanted to focus in particular on the nuclear problem. He was uncertain who would lead the Iranian team, but thought it might be Ali Velayati. After some debate in Washington, we decided to suggest a preliminary, preparatory meeting at a lower level. We had been burned so many times in the past few decades that caution seemed wise.

Jake Sullivan, still serving as Secretary Clinton's Policy Planning director, and Puneet Talwar were natural choices to represent the United States at this exploratory session. Puneet had joined me for innumerable P5+1 rounds, and was a key player in the TRR initiative. Jake was Hillary Clinton's closest policy advisor. He had her full confidence, and the president's trust.

In early July, Jake was off on yet another overseas trip with the secretary when I called him and asked if he could break off for a couple days in Oman. He didn't hesitate, and made his way from Paris to Muscat, where, hosted by Salem, he and Puneet spent a long and not particularly encouraging day with a mid-level Iranian delegation. Jake reported that the Iranians had been almost entirely in "receive mode," and seemed intent on securing some kind of substantive down payment for any future talks. They were particularly focused on the thorny issue of their "right" to enrichment—something that the Treaty on the Non-Proliferation of Nuclear Weapons did not explicitly convey, and that their continuing violation of successive IAEA and UNSC resolutions did little to promote. With his usual candor, an unusually effective mix of Minnesota politeness and East Coast hardheadedness, Jake made clear that the issue was what the Iranians would do to satisfy powerful international concerns, not the other way around.

Over the next few months, as the American elections approached in November, both sides regrouped. We made clear, through Salem, that we were ready for further meetings but weren't in any rush. Sanctions pressure was building, and we wanted the Iranian government to feel the pain.

Following President Obama's second inauguration, John Kerry succeeded Hillary Clinton as secretary of state. On the same day his nomination was announced, Kerry asked me to stay on as deputy secretary. I had planned to retire, but I was glad to accept.

It was obvious that Secretary Kerry, like the president, wanted to make Iran negotiations a priority for the second term. Sensing an opening, Salem conveyed renewed interest from the Iranians in meeting again, this time at a higher level, with a deputy foreign minister heading their delegation. We eventually settled on March 1, 2013, in Oman. I would lead the American team, with Jake as my alter ego. He had already become my closest collaborator in the Obama administration—the best of his generation of foreign policy thinkers and practitioners, strategically creative as well as tactically adept. We'd be joined by Puneet and Bob Einhorn; Jim Timbie, whose encyclopedic knowledge of nuclear issues and four-plus decades of negotiating experience made him a quiet national treasure; Richard Nephew, a specialist on sanctions; and Norm Roule, the senior advisor on Iran in our intelligence community.

The president convened several meetings in February to review our approach. In all my three decades in government, this was—along with the bin Laden raid in 2011—the most tightly held effort. The White House Situation Room, usually crowded with cabinet officials and backbenchers, was unusually spare. Only a handful of people in the White House and the State Department knew of the secret talks, and we went to great lengths to preserve their discretion. Meetings on this issue didn't go on our public calendars, or bore innocuous titles; documents related to the talks were kept only on the ultra-secure White House communications systems.

By this point, the president's grasp of the Iranian nuclear issue and his policy sense were both well developed. His expectations were realistic; he knew the odds that the Iranians would be willing or able to accept sharp limitations on their nuclear program were low. He also knew the dangers of being played by Tehran, as had happened too many times before. Yet he was determined to test the proposition, and secure in the investment he and Secretary Clinton had made in the first term on sanctions and international solidarity. "We're as well positioned to negotiate as we've ever been," Obama said in one session in the Situation Room. "We've set this up right. Now we'll see if we can make this work."

President Obama laid out the framework for our effort crisply. First, our direct channel wasn't a substitute for the wider P5+1 channel, but a pragmatic complement. Agreements on the nuclear issue could only come through that broader group, since it was the source of much of the international pressure that was starting to weigh on Tehran.

Second, we would have to keep the bilateral channel secret. The Iranians, facing enormous internal pressures, and filled with suspicion of American motives, warned that any premature disclosure would make it impossible to continue. Secrecy would help prevent opponents in both capitals from smothering the initiative in its crib—but it would carry future costs, feeding stab-in-the-back criticisms from some of our closest partners, particularly the Israelis, Saudis, and Emiratis. We knew that secret talks would be hard to sustain. In the age of omnipresent information technology and never-ending media scrutiny, it was unlikely that we could avoid disclosure for long. Oman was a relatively quiet and off-the-beaten-path place, but it was also a fishbowl in its own way, under the intermittent scrutiny of a variety of intelligence services.

We also knew that transitioning from a direct channel back into multilateral talks would be complicated and awkward. Some of the best foreign diplomats with whom I had ever worked had been or remained part of the P5+1. I didn't much enjoy the idea of keeping our efforts from them. But we would never have gotten as far as we later did, as relatively fast as we did, if we had been trying to negotiate with the Iranians in the glare of international publicity, and solely in the inevitably more cumbersome P5+1 process.

The president stressed a third point. We would focus the back-channel talks on the nuclear issue, which was the most pressing and explosive of our many problems with Iran. It was the concern around which we had united the international community and built such powerful pressure, and the one on which the Iranians seemed prepared to engage. Moreover, our Gulf Arab partners were adamant that we not widen the aperture of the nuclear talks and address Iran's non-nuclear transgressions, unless they were in the room. The purpose of the secret bilateral talks would be to test Iranian seriousness on the nuclear issue, and jump-start the broader P5+1 process.

This was a fairly transactional and unsentimental view of the nuclear negotiations, without any grand illusions of overnight transformations in Iranian behavior or U.S.-Iranian relations. I was a short-term pessimist about the prospect for such changes, given the cold-blooded nature of that regime, its resilience and practiced capacity to repress, and the opportunities before it to meddle in a troubled Arab world. We knew we'd have to embed any progress on the nuclear issue in a wider strategy to push back against threatening Iranian behavior in the region, and preserve leverage and non-nuclear sanctions to draw on.

The president's fourth bit of guidance cut right to the core of the transactional challenge. We would indicate to the Iranians, carefully, that if they were prepared to accept tight, long-term constraints on their nuclear program, with heavily intrusive verification and monitoring arrangements, we would be prepared to explore the possibility of a limited domestic enrichment program as part of a comprehensive agreement. There had been considerable internal back-and-forth on this issue, beneath the president's level, less over whether to play this card than when. I thought it was best to do it at the outset, as a sign of our seriousness and a test of theirs, putting the burden squarely on the Iranians to show that they would accept tough constraints, and make clear in practical terms that they wouldn't be able to break out to a bomb. Tom Donilon was a little uneasy about that tactic. He wanted to see more tangible evidence of Iranian seriousness before playing a card that—however carefully framed the proposition— would be hard to put back in the deck.

The president was convinced that we'd never get an agreement with the Iranians without some limited form of domestic enrichment. They had the knowledge to enrich, and there was no way you could bomb, sanction, or wish that away. Maybe we could have gotten to a zero enrichment outcome a decade earlier, when they were spinning a few dozen centrifuges. That was extremely unlikely to happen in 2013, with the Iranians operating some nineteen thousand centrifuges, and with broad popular support across the country for enrichment as part of a civilian program. The president wanted to cut to the chase in the back-channel talks, and that made sense to me. He approved the caveated formula we suggested, but placed heavy emphasis on the verb "explore." This was not a promise or a guarantee.

Finally, the president reminded all of us that the chances of success were "well under fifty-fifty." We'd keep all our other options open. We'd keep developing the "bunker buster" bomb we'd need to strike Fordow. The Pentagon would "set the theater" and demonstrate through regular deployments and thorough preparations that our military was prepared to act. We'd keep up other efforts to slow and obstruct the Iranian program. And we'd be ready to pivot again from a failed negotiating effort to even stronger sanctions. If direct talks went nowhere, it would be harder to blame the United States, and easier to build more pressure against a recalcitrant Iran.

At the end of our last meeting, the president shook hands with Jake and me and said simply, "Good luck." Obama was staking a lot on this uncertain enterprise, and we were determined to do all we could to make it work.

* * *

WE WOULD SOON get used to long flights to Oman in unmarked planes with blank passenger manifests, but I was too restless on that first trip at the end of February 2013 to sleep, wondering what lay ahead. Salem met us on arrival at a military airfield in Muscat, upbeat as always, and confirmed that the Iranian delegation, led by Deputy Foreign Minister Ali Asghar Khaji, had arrived just before us.

We drove about thirty minutes outside Muscat, to a secluded military officers' club on the Arabian Sea. Its four walls became the boundaries of our little universe for the next few days. Our team spent that first evening reviewing our approach to the start of talks the next morning and hashing out roles and responsibilities. Our expectations were modest, but after many months of internal debate and planning, we were just glad to finally get started.

The next morning was typically hot and humid. I went out on an early-morning stroll, but the sauna-like conditions did little to cure me of my jet lag. Salem, the chief of the royal court, and the head of Omani intelligence greeted both delegations as we walked into the meeting room, which offered a panoramic view of the sea. I shook hands with Khaji and his colleagues, who included Reza Zabib, the chief of the Iranian Foreign Ministry's North America division; Davoud Mohammadnia, from the Ministry of Internal Security, or MOIS; representatives of Iran's atomic energy agency; a capable Iranian interpreter; and what I always assumed were a number of listening devices to record our conversations. We sat on opposite sides of a long table, too weighted down by history to enjoy the view or the moment. The Omanis, clustered around the head of the table, offered a few brief words of welcome and then departed. There was then an awkward pause.

I broke the silence by asking Khaji if he wanted to speak first. In what was an early indication that the Iranians were mostly on a reconnaissance mission, he deferred to me. I then made a brief presentation, along the lines the president had approved in the Situation Room a few days before. I tried to strike a respectful but candid tone. This was an important moment for both of us, a rare chance to talk directly and privately. We had no illusions about how hard this would be. While it was not our purpose to point fingers or lecture, there were profound mutual suspicions, and a long record of Iranian defiance of its international obligations that had provoked widespread concern. There were too many unanswered questions; too many obvious disconnects between the requirements of a realistic civilian nuclear energy program and the pace and lack of transparency of Iran's efforts; and too much disregard for the clear requirements of a series of UN Security Council resolutions. There was a serious and growing risk that Iran's domestic enrichment capacity could be quickly and covertly converted to produce weapons-grade, highly enriched uranium. That concern cut right to the core of what was at stake and the dilemma we faced.

The nuclear issue was not just a dispute between Iran and the United States, but between Iran and the P5+1, and the broader international community. I repeated the president's message in his earlier letters to the Supreme Leader—it was not the policy of the United States to seek regime change in Iran, but we were absolutely determined to ensure that Iran did not acquire a nuclear weapon. Any hope for a diplomatic resolution would require Iran to understand the depth of international concerns and act upon them. I repeated bluntly that failure to take advantage of the uncertain window before us would certainly increase the costs to Iran, and the risk of military conflict.

The key to any diplomatic progress would be Iran's willingness to take concrete, substantial measures to give the rest of us confidence that a peaceful program could not be converted into a weapons program. If Iran were ready to do that, I continued, we would be willing to explore whether and how a domestic enrichment program could be pursued in Iran, as part of a comprehensive settlement of the nuclear issue. That settlement would require many difficult, long-term Iranian commitments, and intense verification and monitoring provisions. Should we eventually reach a satisfactory agreement, the United States would be prepared to call for an end to all United Nations and unilateral sanctions against the Iranian nuclear program. Such a process would likely have to unfold in phases, with early practical steps to build confidence, leading to a comprehensive agreement.

There was enormous skepticism in both our capitals, I concluded. I shared much of that skepticism, but if the Supreme Leader's fatwa against nuclear weapons was serious, then it shouldn't be impossible to find a diplomatic path forward and prove the skeptics wrong. We were certainly prepared to try.

As I went through this presentation, Khaji and his colleagues listened and took copious notes. There were a few cold stares, and some head-shaking, but no interruptions. The Iranians in Oman were a welcome change and stark contrast to the doctrinaire, obstructionist Jalili-led delegation in the P5+1 talks. They were professionals, mostly career diplomats, and it wasn't hard to sense a shift in style and seriousness of engagement.

When I was done, Khaji took the floor. His tone was measured, even when he recited a long and predictable list of grievances about American policy. He spoke sharply about the unfairness of UN Security Council resolutions, the assassinations of Iranian nuclear scientists, and the U.S. public emphasis that "all options are on the table." He objected to American references over the years to the use of "carrots and sticks" against Iran. Raising his voice, he exclaimed, "Iranians are not donkeys!"

Khaji had little of substance to offer, although he stressed that he "wanted to look to the future." The Iranian delegation had clearly taken note of my heavily caveated comment about domestic enrichment, but they were looking for (and probably expecting) more. Khaji asserted that Iran would defend its "right" to the whole nuclear fuel cycle, including enrichment, "at any cost." We went back and forth over this argument, emphasizing our conviction that no such explicit "right" was granted by the NPT. The problem that Iran's defiant behavior had created was simply that there were serious and growing international doubts about whether it wanted only a civilian program, or might pursue a military one. The onus was on Iran to disprove those doubts. Constant reassertion of imaginary rights was not going to get anywhere.

In the first of several one-on-one conversations, Khaji and I sat privately after the opening plenary meeting. He was approachable but guarded, and acknowledged that he was encouraged that we were finally talking to each other directly. He appealed almost plaintively for acceptance of Iran's right to enrich, implying that it would be hard to engage without it. At one point he pulled out a bulky file of papers, which appeared to be Omani notes from alleged conversations with various Americans, including members of Congress, acknowledging Iran's right to enrich. I explained that in our political system, members of Congress did not speak for the president. I repeated our position, said I was sure those conversations were taken out of context or were well-meaning Omani garbles, and stressed that we needed to focus on what was practical if we were going to get this process off the ground.

We spent the next couple days covering essentially the same terrain over and over. I took evening walks with Khaji around the officers' club compound, and Jake and my other colleagues had similar chats with their counterparts. There was a powerful cognitive dissonance at the heart of our discussions at this stage, which never entirely disappeared throughout the secret talks. The Iranians would maintain, in a tone of wounded pride, that the nuclear problem was all a big misunderstanding, that they had done nothing wrong, never had explored steps toward a bomb, and had acted within their international rights. Sanctions were unjust and should be lifted. We responded firmly that the Iranians would never get anywhere in nuclear negotiations if they didn't realize that they had a gaping credibility problem—not just with the United States but with the wider international community.

Near the end of our final session on March 3, Jake and I told the Iranians bluntly that there wasn't much point in continuing the secret talks if they weren't going to think much more seriously about the tangible steps they would need to take. The Iranians were wildly unrealistic in their expectations; they weren't in the same ballpark, or even playing the same sport, as an increasingly determined international community.

Zabib made an impassioned plea as we wrapped up the last meeting. He recounted a trip to New York years before, and a large sign he had encountered at JFK airport on his arrival. Torturing his English syntax a bit, he recalled that it read "Think the Big." "That's what you Americans must do," he said. "Think the big. If you do, everything will become better." I smiled at Jake. Neither of us could think of a succinct way to explain that the issue here was not the elasticity of our thought process, but the seriousness of Iran's commitment. So we simply urged them to think about everything we had discussed over the previous three days in Oman, and to consider the choices that lay before them.

It was an incongruous conclusion to an incongruous first round. We reported back to Washington that we were "miles apart on substance." Khaji was an able diplomat, but not empowered. None of that was unexpected, after so many years of not talking to one another directly. The atmospherics were significantly better than the more sterile P5+1 process had been, with at least the possibility of less polemical and more practical conversations, and maybe more room for creativity. Zabib's plea to "think the big" did not exactly fill us with confidence, but it was at least a start.

We retraced our seventeen-hour journey and arrived back in Washington on March 4, our secret still intact. The next day, with Secretary Kerry out of the country, the president asked to see Jake and me in the Oval Office so we could report directly on our discussions in Oman. The president was sitting in his usual chair in front of the fireplace, having just finished his regular morning intelligence briefing. He listened attentively. We went through our impressions, careful not to oversell what was just a first step on a long road. "I never expected immediate progress," the president said. "This may or may not work. But it's the right thing to do. Let's just hope we can keep it quiet, and keep it going."

* * *

WE HAD LEFT that Omani beach compound still not convinced that our secret initiative had a future. Events over the rest of the spring were not reassuring. The P5+1 met with Jalili and the Iranians in Almaty in early April, but made no headway. We had made clear through Salem Ismaily and the Omanis that we were ready to resume the back-channel talks, but the Iranians were consumed by the run-up to their presidential elections in June. There was no point in running after them; we had no idea who would succeed Ahmadinejad, and it made sense to wait and see.

The unexpected election of Hassan Rouhani in June 2013 created a modest new sense of possibility. A former lead nuclear negotiator and a wily survivor in the unsentimental world of revolutionary Iranian politics, Rouhani saw the toll that international sanctions (as well as Ahmadinejad's erratic populist mismanagement) had taken on the country's economy. He managed to persuade the Supreme Leader that Iran needed to explore a more serious nuclear negotiation and consider some real compromises, or face a resurgence of the internal political unrest that had jarred the regime in the summer of 2009. In hindsight, it was useful to have launched the secret channel while Ahmadinejad was still president and before Rouhani was elected. Had we waited until after the election, it might have appeared to the ever-suspicious Khamenei that we were fixated on Rouhani and neglecting the ultimate decision-maker. It also cost Rouhani far less political capital to push for direct talks with the Americans when the more hawkish Ahmadinejad government had already crossed that Rubicon.

Rouhani had a resourceful partner in his new foreign minister, Javad Zarif, who emerged as the new face of Iranian diplomacy. With a doctorate from the University of Denver, where he (like Condi Rice) had studied under Madeleine Albright's father, Zarif had served for many years as Iran's permanent representative to the United Nations in New York. He was a formidable diplomat. He knew how to navigate his own treacherous political system and squeeze the most out of his instructions—and he knew how to use his talents and sympathetic image, as well as a sometimes frustrating gift for melodrama, to cajole and maneuver the rest of us.

President Obama's short congratulatory message to Rouhani received a rapid and positive reply. Rouhani was inaugurated on August 4, and two days later announced publicly his readiness to resume the P5+1 talks. The Iranians also told the Omanis that they wanted to restart the back-channel process, and Salem came away from conversations in Tehran that summer convinced of newfound seriousness. We agreed to meet again at the beach compound in early September.

In preparation, we took stock of our approach. Our long-term challenge remained the same: to cut off the pathways that the Iranians might use to develop a nuclear weapon. By the time of Rouhani's inauguration, they had accumulated a substantial stockpile of enriched uranium. Meanwhile, they were continuing construction of their heavy water plant at Arak, moving steadily to create a potential plutonium pathway to a bomb. A covert effort remained our biggest concern.

We had substantial negotiating assets. UNSC sanctions, as well as U.S. and EU measures, were having a major impact. Markets for Iran's oil exports were rapidly contracting, and Tehran was starved for hard currency, with over $100 billion in oil revenues frozen and inaccessible in overseas banks.

We were determined to get the most out of that leverage. A two-stage process still made the most sense, given the mistrust between us, and the urgency of freezing their nuclear progress to give us time to try to negotiate a comprehensive deal. We'd seek in an initial phase to stop the advance of the Iranian nuclear program, across all of its fronts, in return for no further nuclear sanctions. In addition, we'd try to roll back key aspects of their program, especially their 20 percent enrichment effort, in return for limited sanctions relief. We'd also seek initially to apply the most intrusive inspection procedures possible, across the entire supply chain, from uranium mines and mills to centrifuge production and storage. That would create a solid precedent for longer-term verification provisions in a comprehensive agreement.

The president convened a session shortly before we returned to Oman to give us our final guidance. Vice President Biden, Secretary Kerry, and Susan Rice, who had recently succeeded Tom Donilon as national security advisor, were there too, along with a tiny circle of officials who knew of the back channel. All the principals by this point knew the details of the nuclear issue and our approach. The president's grasp of arcane technical details was impressive, as was John Kerry's, who was eager to dive in himself at the right time.

As the president concluded the meeting, he motioned Jake and me over as he walked out the door of the Situation Room. "You guys know what needs to get done," he said. "I trust you. So don't screw it up." He smiled slightly, but we couldn't decide whether to feel buoyed by his confidence, anxious about his warning, or some of both. Those are the moments when you'd almost prefer the comfortable straitjacket of fourteen pages of single-spaced instructions.

The Iranian delegation this time was led by two deputy foreign ministers, Majid Takht-Ravanchi and Abbas Araghchi. In Zarif's mold, both had done graduate degrees in the West, Ravanchi at the University of Kansas and Araghchi at the University of Kent in the United Kingdom. Both were tough Iranian patriots, skeptical of doing business with Americans and dogged in arguing their positions. We discovered that they could also be creative problem-solvers. In the hours and hours of conversations that followed, we exhausted the whole range of emotions, searching for practical solutions, occasionally pounding the table or walking out of the room, and sometimes even finding a little bit of humor in our shared predicament. While trust was always in short supply between Iranians and Americans, I developed considerable professional respect for Ravanchi and Araghchi, although I doubted that expressing that publicly would be career-enhancing for either of them.

Ravanchi and Araghchi were professional diplomats, not ideologues, but they were no less committed to Iran, no less proud of the revolution, no less determined to show that they could hold their own in the diplomatic arena. They were often guarded about the difficulties they faced at home, although they would sometimes confide that they had a Supreme Leader who was just waiting to say "I told you so" and prove that the Americans could not be trusted and that Obama was just as bent on regime change as Bush.

From the start, the atmosphere in the September round was much different, and more encouraging, than what we had experienced in March. We conducted the negotiations in English, without translation, which made for much easier and more informal discussions. Ravanchi and Araghchi were comfortable in their interactions with us, always careful to stay within the bounds of their instructions, but uninhibited in going back and forth in more formal plenary sessions or smaller conversations. They agreed that first day that a two-phase approach was best. We talked about the broad outline of a comprehensive deal, but agreed quickly that we'd get stuck if we tried at this early stage to get much beyond general principles. We spent most of our time on what it would take to put together a six-month interim accord. They had thoroughly digested our exchanges with Khaji. While they would regularly come back at the issue of a "right" to enrichment, they understood our position and didn't belabor the point, at least at this stage.

The pattern for our meetings in the back channel soon took shape. We would begin with a five-on-five plenary session, and then break for separate conversations, sometimes one-on-one and often Araghchi and Ravanchi with Jake and me, while our colleagues would get into more detail on the limitations and verification measures we had in mind, and the sanctions relief at the front of the Iranians' mind.

Our biggest challenge was countering Iranian expectations of the magnitude of sanctions relief that we could offer for the interim phase. We believed that the best tool we had for providing limited relief was the frozen oil revenue that was gradually building up in foreign banks, at a rate of roughly $18 billion every six months. Metering out a fraction of those funds would allow us to preserve the overall architecture of sanctions, and keep all the leverage we'd later need for comprehensive talks. Not surprisingly, the Iranians had a vastly different definition of what "limited" relief meant. They insisted stubbornly that all $18 billion should be released in return for their acceptance of six-month limitations on their program. We indicated early on that we could consider no more than about $4 billion.

Another problem was Iranian concern about how much they could count on a commitment by the U.S. administration not to enact new sanctions for six months, given the role of Congress. It was not an unreasonable worry. We explained at length how our system worked, and why we believed an administration commitment would hold up, assuming that Iran limited its program substantially along the lines we were discussing. But the Iranians were never entirely reassured by the formulas we offered, and the truth is that we weren't either, given the uncertain state of American politics. "The best thing we can do," I told Araghchi, "is make a solid agreement, and then live up to it scrupulously." Those words would ring hollow a few years later.

While it was clear after this session that we still had a tough slog ahead of us, we could now see that a first-step understanding was possible. With relatively modest sanctions relief, we could freeze their program, and roll it back in some important respects. Rouhani and Zarif seemed to want to show their own critics at home that they could produce early progress and begin to ease sanctions pressure. We reported all this to the White House and Secretary Kerry, conscious of the value of underpromising and overdelivering. We also stressed the Iranians' concern that we keep this channel secret. In our side conversations, both Ravanchi and Araghchi had worried that premature disclosure would torpedo the talks at home.

We agreed with the Iranians to meet next in New York later in September, when the annual UN General Assembly session would provide good cover for Ravanchi and Araghchi to come with Zarif, as well as Rouhani, who was making his first visit to the UN as Iran's president. We had four rounds of talks over nearly two weeks in New York, and made considerable progress. Jake and I put an initial draft text on the table in our first discussion with Ravanchi and Araghchi on the evening of September 18, in a room at the Waldorf Astoria. We were acutely aware of the danger of negotiating with ourselves as time wore on, but it quickly became apparent that we could much more effectively drive the process by taking the pen. We also realized that the only way we could really be sure that we were making progress was to put notional understandings on paper. Araghchi in particular bristled at our continuing insistence that we couldn't provide more than a small fraction of frozen Iranian oil revenue during the initial six-month period, and at our emphasis on mothballing nuclear infrastructure to reassure us that frozen centrifuges could not simply be reactivated. We kept at it, and over the next week painstakingly removed brackets around contested language and agreed on significant portions of the interim agreement.

As productive as the New York rounds were, they had their moments of minor drama too. Just as the Iranians were walking down the hall to our meeting room at the Waldorf, Jake and I noticed that hanging on the wall across from the room was a large framed photo of the shah visiting the Waldorf in the 1970s. We tried to take it down quickly, but it was firmly attached to the wall. Ravanchi and Araghchi didn't seem to notice as we hurriedly ushered them through the door. The last thing we wanted was to offend our counterparts or inspire a forty-minute recitation about America's support for the ancien régime.

We conducted several more rounds later in the week across town, away from the hustle and bustle of the United Nations meetings, at a hotel on Manhattan's West Side. The Iranian delegation had no trouble moving in and out of the hotel quietly. With its kaleidoscope of humanity, Manhattan was one place where five guys with white shirts buttoned all the way up and no ties could blend in easily.

Our progress in the direct bilateral talks set the stage for Secretary Kerry's first encounter with Zarif, on the margins of a P5+1 ministerial meeting at the UN on September 26. In their thirty-minute tête-à-tête, Kerry and Zarif reviewed the encouraging results of the back channel so far, and agreed that we should keep at it. It was the first half hour of what would be endless hours of face-to-face meetings, texts, and telephone calls between them; their relationship and drive was at the heart of everything that was later achieved.

Meanwhile, Jake was trying to explore the possibility of a meeting between Rouhani and Obama. The initial signals we received from Zarif and the Iranian negotiators were positive, but Rouhani and his political advisors got more concerned about the potential backlash in Tehran the more they considered the idea. Rouhani had already made quite a splash at the UN, sounding decidedly unlike Ahmadinejad as he acknowledged the Holocaust, and working with Zarif in a flurry of meetings and interviews to put a much different face on Iranian diplomacy. Once the Iranians began to press us to agree to preconditions for even a brief pull-aside encounter, invoking the familiar plea for some recognition of a "right" to enrich, it was apparent that the effort to engineer a meeting was not worth it.

Somewhat to our surprise, the Iranians came back to us with a proposal for a phone call between the two presidents on Rouhani's last day in New York. There were no preconditions. The call was connected as Rouhani was in his car on the way to the airport. The brief silence during the connection felt like a lifetime. Not surprisingly, Jake was anxious—about whether he had been given the right number, or whether this was all a setup in which some radio host in Canada would pop up on the line in an elaborate prank. Finally, the call connected. Obama and Rouhani had a cordial fifteen-minute conversation. Obama congratulated Rouhani on his election, and stressed that they now had an historic opportunity to resolve the nuclear issue. Mindful that a variety of foreign intelligence services might be listening, Obama made only an oblique reference to the secret bilateral talks. Rouhani responded in the same constructive tone, closing with a somewhat surreal "Have a nice day" in English. The glimmer of possibility was steadily getting brighter.

We met twice more in October in the familiar confines of the Omani beach club. Sanctions relief remained a source of great irritation to the Iranians. We wouldn't budge from our position of roughly $4 billion in relief over six months, far short of the $18 billion that the Iranians sought. We still had sharp differences over restrictions on the Arak heavy water facility, as well as over the continuing Iranian insistence on language about their "right" to enrich. Trying to anticipate some of the main lines of concern expressed by critics of the P5+1 process, we pressed relatively late in the game for a freeze on new centrifuge production, not just their installation. That set Araghchi off. "What are you going to demand next?" he asked, with an air of deep exasperation.

We talked at length with the Iranians about how best to handle the resumption of P5+1 meetings in Geneva in mid-October, in the middle of our extended back-channel talks that month. We both recognized that we were approaching the point where we would merge the two processes, but we had made surprising strides in the secret bilateral talks, and thought it was worth seeing how far we could get by the end of October. Araghchi suggested that Iran make a general presentation to the P5+1, laying out the broad contours of a two-phase approach, including interim and comprehensive agreements. The Iranians left out the details to which we had tentatively agreed, as well as the areas of continuing disagreement, but it was useful to introduce the framework. By the time we completed an intensive two-day back-channel session on October 26–27, we had a draft text that still had five or six contested passages, but that was beginning to resemble a solid step forward after so many years of tension on the nuclear issue. In a meeting with Sultan Qaboos just before we flew home from Muscat, I again expressed our appreciation for everything he had done to make this channel work. "We're getting close," I assured him.

* * *

THE PRESIDENT WAS pleased with the progress we had made, but intent in his lawyerly way on "buttoning it down tight." We were genuinely surprised that we had come such a long way in such a short time. We were equally surprised that the back channel had stayed secret through eight rounds. We realized that that would not last much longer, with at least two journalists already beginning to put some of the pieces together.

A new P5+1 round under the leadership of EU high representative Cathy Ashton was scheduled to begin on November 7 in Geneva. With Wendy Sherman, my exceptional successor as undersecretary for political affairs and as head of our P5+1 delegation, joining us for the late October back-channel talks in Oman, we had told the Iranians that we would inform our multilateral partners of our direct bilateral meetings before the November session. They were a little nervous, but understood that the time had come. We scheduled another back-channel round on November 5–7 to see if we could remove another bracket or two in the draft text, before turning it over to our P5+1 partners for their consideration as the basis for rapid completion of an interim agreement.

Wendy had the unenviable task of briefing our P5+1 colleagues on the back-channel effort. The debate about when to tell our closest allies about the secret talks had been extensive. I was torn, having spent years as undersecretary working with my P5+1 counterparts, and understanding the very real concerns of the Israelis and our Gulf Arab partners, but also acutely aware of the risks of leaks and premature public disclosures. The White House preferred, in any case, to hold off as long as we could in the fall of 2013, but by the end of October there was no longer any good reason to wait.

Starting with Ashton, who knew as well as anyone that bilateral U.S.-Iran talks were essential, Wendy laid out the quiet effort we had been making, and the main areas of agreement and disagreement with the Iranians. Some of our partners were not entirely surprised. The British government, for example, had excellent contacts in Oman, and was generally aware of our progress. The president had also taken Prime Minister Netanyahu into his confidence at the end of September, in a one-on-one conversation at the White House. Netanyahu was not surprised either, since the Israelis had their own sources in the region, but he was decidedly less understanding than the Brits. He saw our back channel as a betrayal.

On November 5, we met with the Iranians at the Mandarin Hotel in Geneva, on the other side of town from the InterContinental, where the P5+1 session would take place a couple days later. The president and Secretary Kerry told us to make a final push to improve the draft text, which now bore the suitably anodyne title "draft joint working document." We made a little more progress on defining a "pause" on Arak, but still had bracketed language there. We had made quite a bit of headway on specifying the elements of a freeze on enrichment at Natanz and Fordow, and on conversion and dilution of Iran's existing stockpile of 20 percent enriched material. We were close to an understanding on sanctions relief in return, at roughly the $4 billion figure over six months that we had set out at the start of the back-channel talks. We also settled on an unprecedented set of verification and monitoring measures that would serve as a solid foundation for much more detailed arrangements in an eventual comprehensive agreement. The draft text we produced with Ravanchi and Araghchi still had three or four difficult brackets to resolve in its four and a half single-spaced pages.

It was probably inevitable that the handover to the P5+1 would have its awkward moments. Some of our European colleagues were impressed by our progress, but not happy about being kept in the dark. Ashton did a superb job of focusing the group on the opportunity the draft text offered. With Zarif already in Geneva to take charge of the Iranian team, John Kerry flew in on November 8. French foreign minister Laurent Fabius was close on his heels, bringing both considerable Gallic ego, a bit bruised over the back channel, and some solid ideas on how to tighten language, especially on Arak. Sergey Lavrov and the other ministers flew in too.

The next couple of days had lots of drama, some contrived and some reflecting real frustration, emotion, and exhaustion. Pressures were building in Washington for another round of sanctions, and Zarif faced his own share of domestic suspicions and second-guessing. Some of our P5+1 partners were still smarting over the back channel. Ashton and Kerry skillfully defused most of the tensions within the P5+1, and we developed a revised text that the group supported. It built on the back-channel draft, filling in new proposed language in some of the bracketed areas, and adding a few new sentences.

Zarif was not thrilled to see this updated text on November 9. The Iranians knew that the bilateral draft we had been working on for months still had brackets with unresolved differences over language. They also knew that it would have to be reviewed and accepted by the rest of the P5+1, who would undoubtedly want to put their own stamp on it. As Zarif reminded Kerry, he faced a tough audience in Tehran, and any shifts in language, however minor, were troublesome. Like other accomplished diplomats, Zarif was also a gifted thespian, and his head-in-hands expressions of gloom and duplicity unsettled some of the other ministers.

After a long day and night of discussions, the ministers agreed to consult in their capitals and convene another, hopefully final, round of talks in Geneva on November 22. The back channel had still not become public, and we worried that their revelation would complicate completion of an interim agreement. Jake and I arrived back in Geneva on November 20 to help bridge the final gaps with the Iranians. Coordinating closely with Ashton, and joined by Sherman, we met with Araghchi and Ravanchi on the twenty-first. We further narrowed our differences. The Iranians seemed more relaxed about preambular language on enrichment, in which we had carefully separated the words "right" and "enrichment," using the first to refer explicitly to NPT language on the widely acknowledged right of members in good standing to peaceful nuclear energy, and the second in the much more conditional sense of an Iranian demand that might be applied if mutually agreed, long-term limitations on its program were developed. We made some headway on Arak, as Araghchi and Ravanchi grudgingly accepted French edits to more tightly define a cessation of construction activity at the site.

We also pinned down an excellent set of verification measures, including 24/7 surveillance arrangements at Natanz and Fordow, and access to each step along the nuclear supply chain. On sanctions relief, we wound our way toward the formula that Kerry and Zarif eventually agreed upon. Its core was $4.2 billion in unfrozen Iranian oil revenue, metered out in six monthly installments. It had a few additional provisions, notably a relaxation of sanctions on the auto industry, whose main beneficiary was French automaker Renault. Zarif recounted to us with a mischievous glint in his eye that Fabius had spent most of their bilateral sessions in Geneva on this issue, not on Arak and the other questions on which he had been so voluble in public.

Throughout November 22 and 23, John Kerry was his usual relentless self, nudging Zarif toward the finish line, working with Ashton to manage the P5+1, and staying in close touch with the president by secure phone. Jake and I came over to the InterContinental Hotel for the final push, using service elevators and stairwells to get up to the secretary's suite. Our cloak-and-dagger seemed a little silly at this stage, but it had become habitual over the past eight months, and we figured it was worth it if we could keep the back channel under wraps until an interim agreement, now termed the "Joint Plan of Action," could be reached.

We could sense that the Iranians were in a hurry to finish the deal, before their own politics became an even bigger impediment. We didn't think we needed to concede anything further on sanctions, and were confident that we had succeeded in preserving most of our leverage for the much more complex task of negotiating a comprehensive accord. Borrowing a famous Mel Gibson line from the movie *Braveheart*, as he urged his Scottish compatriots to stand firm in the face of charging English cavalry—and with a little of the giddiness that comes from high stakes and little sleep—Jake and I kept repeating to each other "Hold, hold, hold" as the Iranians kept probing for concessions.

By 2 A.M. on November 24, we were nearly there. The ministers were straining one another's patience by this point, and I met with Ravanchi to iron out the last bits of language. Tired and relieved, we quietly congratulated one another. Ashton mobilized all the ministers for a signing ceremony at 4 A.M. Araghchi called me thirty minutes before the ceremony to say that he had "just two or three more changes to make" in the text. The Iranians were never entirely satisfied until they had overreached on nearly every issue and tested every last ounce of flexibility. I laughed politely. "It's a little late for that," I said. "We're done."

The Joint Plan of Action (JPOA) was a modest, temporary, and practical step. Iran froze its nuclear program for an initial six months, and rolled it back in key respects, especially in disposing of its existing stockpile of 20 percent enriched uranium. It accepted intrusive monitoring arrangements. In return it got limited sanctions relief, and a commitment not to increase sanctions for six months.

The JPOA aroused more than a little controversy. Prime Minister Netanyahu said publicly on November 24 that it was "the deal of the century" for Iran. I told Ravanchi that hyperbolic statements like that should help his selling job at home, and he smiled with some satisfaction. Then the congressional critics joined in, predicting that the Iranians would cheat and the whole edifice of sanctions that we had so painstakingly put together over the years would collapse, long before a comprehensive deal could be negotiated. None of that turned out to be true. The JPOA was a solid agreement, in many ways better for us than for the Iranians, who still faced huge economic pressure. It offered us and the Iranians an opportunity to show that we could actually each live up to our sides of a fair bargain, and it gave the president and Secretary Kerry the time and space to negotiate a final agreement.

* * *

NEWS OF OUR back channel broke a few hours after the signing of the JPOA, helping to explain how the P5+1 and Iran had concluded the interim deal so quickly. Spent after this long effort and more than three decades in the Foreign Service, I intended to retire at the end of 2013. I had promised John Kerry when he asked me to remain as deputy secretary that I'd stay on for his first year. In the end, encouraged by him and the president, and admiring them both immensely, I would keep at it for an additional year, until late 2014.

I was especially touched when President Obama invited me to lunch at the White House to reinforce the case for continuing at State. He was an adroit closer. We sat in his small private dining room just off the Oval Office, with tall windows looking out onto the Rose Garden. Over a relaxed conversation, we covered everything from our daughters and the current NBA season to the Iran negotiations and the state of the State Department. "I don't want to play on your Irish Catholic guilt," he said, "but I consider you to be the ultimate professional, and it would mean a lot to me if you would stay for another year." I noted that he was doing a pretty good job on the Irish Catholic guilt part—and that he had had me at the lunch invitation.

With the back channel now history, Jake and I played a supporting and episodic role in the negotiations for a comprehensive nuclear agreement that consumed 2014 and the first half of 2015. In all those hours and days of secret talks, we had built some rapport with Araghchi, Ravanchi, and their other colleagues, as well as with Zarif. While the Iranians knew that the road to a comprehensive deal went through the P5+1, it was also clear that what were now overt and frequent U.S.-Iran contacts were the core of the effort. Even the distinctly unsentimental Iranians could get a little nostalgic sometimes about the seemingly simpler days of the back-channel talks in 2013.

Secretary Kerry threw himself into the comprehensive process, and he and Zarif were its prime movers. Wendy was tireless, and a deft leader of a vastly expanded negotiating team, including Timbie and Roule and terrific experts from Treasury, Energy, and other departments. Energy Secretary Ernie Moniz's nuclear expertise and creativity helped to bridge gaps with his Iranian counterpart, Ali Salehi, a fellow MIT alum. I joined our team a few times in the cramped confines of the Palais Coburg hotel in Vienna, where both the slow rhythm of multilateral negotiations and the buffet menu became very familiar. At Kerry's request, I saw Zarif privately a couple times in the second half of 2014. Before marathon talks in Lausanne in the spring of 2015, I met quietly in Geneva with Araghchi and Ravanchi. With congressional impatience and appetite for new sanctions growing, and the Iranians backtracking on key issues, I told them bluntly, "We have come so far, but maybe we should start thinking about a world without an agreement." That helped get their attention.

Kerry's talks with Zarif and Ashton in Lausanne in late March and early April 2015 were the longest continuous negotiation that a secretary of state had engaged in since Camp David in 1978. A framework for a Joint Comprehensive Plan of Action (JCPOA) was announced on April 2, and the final deal emerged in July. In return for the gradual lifting of sanctions, Iran made a permanent commitment never to develop a nuclear weapon, and accepted substantial, long-term limitations on its civilian nuclear program. Ninety-eight percent of Iran's stockpile of enriched material was removed, and so were nearly two-thirds of its centrifuges. The deal also cut off Iran's other potential pathways to a bomb, eliminating the heavy water reactor core at Arak and the capacity to produce weapons-grade plutonium. Extensive verification and monitoring measures were put in place, some of them permanent. For the next decade, at least, Iran's "breakout time"—the time it would theoretically take to enrich enough weapons-grade uranium for a bomb—was extended from the two or three months frozen in the JPOA to at least one year. We had achieved our objective, and we diverted a potential path to war.

* * *

IT WAS HARD to imagine when we embarked on that first secret flight to Oman in early 2013 that diplomacy could resolve the Iranian nuclear issue, at that time the most combustible challenge on the international landscape. The even longer history of grievance and suspicion in America's relations with Iran was another massive obstacle. The politics in Tehran and Washington were corrosive, offering little room for maneuver or incentive for risk-taking. The nuclear problem itself was maddeningly complicated and opaque. There was little reason to think that we could overcome any one of those obstacles, let alone all of them.

Neither the JPOA nor the JCPOA were perfect agreements. In a perfect world, there would be no nuclear enrichment in Iran, and its existing enrichment facilities would have been dismantled. But we don't live in a perfect world, and perfect is rarely on the diplomatic menu. We couldn't neatly erase by military or diplomatic means Iran's basic know-how about enrichment. What we could do was to sharply constrain it over a long duration, monitor it with unprecedented intrusiveness, and prevent its leadership from building a bomb.

For all its trade-offs and imperfections, this was a classic illustration of how diplomacy can work. We set out at the beginning of the Obama administration, building on tentative steps taken at the end of the Bush administration, to test Iranian seriousness directly and invest in a wider coalition, and to build a stronger sanctions program. Our willingness to engage in direct talks and think creatively was a critical ingredient. It put the Iranians on the defensive, removed a pretext for their inaction, and solidified our coalition. When Tehran proved unwilling or incapable, it gave us the opportunity to build substantial economic leverage. Always lurking just over the horizon was the reality of American military power, backing up our determination to ensure that, by one means or another, Iran would not develop a nuclear weapon.

When our leverage had reached a kind of critical mass, we had to use it or risk losing it. Sanctions had so much impact on Iran because they were international, and widely, if often grudgingly, supported. Once Rouhani and Zarif took office and portrayed Iran in a more pragmatic and sympathetic light, it was time to put diplomacy to a rigorous test. Framing the issue as a question of whether Iran could accept sufficiently tough, long-term constraints in return for sanctions lifting and the possibility of limited domestic enrichment was key. There would have been no agreement without sharp constraints and strong monitoring—but there would also have been no agreement if we had insisted on zero enrichment. As Araghchi once put it to us, a civilian nuclear program, including enrichment, was "our source of national pride, our moon shot."

In the first few years after completion of the JCPOA, contrary to the prediction of its opponents that Iran would cheat, the IAEA and the U.S. intelligence community repeatedly affirmed Iranian compliance. Iran's economy did not become a juggernaut as a result of sanctions relief. The agreement deprived the regime of the argument that outside pressure—not chronic mismanagement, corruption, and misallocation of resources—was the source of the grim economic circumstance of most Iranians. Widespread protests in the summer of 2017 demonstrated that the clerical leadership was not sitting comfortably in Tehran. Much as the Supreme Leader feared during the nuclear negotiations, the deal had exposed the regime's vulnerabilities, not erased them.

Meanwhile, Iran continued to export instability across the Middle East, exploiting and accelerating chaos in Syria and Yemen, its forces and proxies locked in a bitter regional competition with Saudi Arabia and other Sunni Arab states. President Obama had always understood that the nuclear agreement would have to be embedded in a wider strategy for reassuring our friends and partners, who were unnerved by the prospect that dialogue with Tehran might someday temper our support for them. The nuclear deal explicitly reserved the option for the United States and its partners to take measures against the Iranian government for non-nuclear transgressions; but it was still tempting for critics to caricature the administration's approach as constraining Iran's nuclear ambitions but enabling its regional troublemaking.

Donald Trump came into office with visceral contempt for the JCPOA, which he called "the worst deal ever." He was dismissive of its practical merits in limiting Iran's nuclear program, and of the whole notion that there was value in the classic diplomacy of building coalitions and hammering out negotiated solutions, with all the give-and-take they required. His was a much more unilateralist impulse, aimed not so much at a better deal with the Iranians as at squeezing them so hard that they'd either capitulate or implode. Despite the entreaties of other P5+1 players, and despite zero evidence of Iranian noncompliance, Trump pulled the United States out of the JCPOA in May 2018.

I was surprised only that he had taken so long to withdraw, given the vehemence of his views. It was nevertheless a dispiriting moment, after years of effort to produce an agreement in which I continued to believe firmly. I wondered what we might have done differently to better insulate the deal. Perhaps we could have pressured the Iranians longer through the interim accord, the JPOA, and extracted more concessions from Tehran—on the duration of certain enrichment restrictions, for example. But the reality was that politics in both the

United States and Iran were tortured and impatient, and it was always a lot harder than it looked from the outside to hold the P5+1 together, especially after serious rifts began to emerge over other problems, like Ukraine or the South China Sea.

We could have done a better job, both before and after the comprehensive nuclear agreement was reached, of confronting the wider challenge of Iran in the Middle East. A willingness to take more risks against the Assad regime after the Syrian civil war began in 2011 would have sent a strong signal to Iran, and cushioned the disquieting effect of the nuclear deal for the Saudis and our other traditional friends. Some of their angst, however, was simply unavoidable. They were deeply worried by the tumult of the Arab Spring, and the prospect of an eventual regional order in which Iran couldn't be denied a place. But we could have done more to show that the nuclear agreement was the start, not the end, of a tough-minded policy toward Iran.

It certainly would have helped shield the JCPOA from Trump's decision to withdraw if we had been able to anchor it better politically at home. It would have been harder to undo as a formal treaty than as an executive agreement. In a deeply polarized Washington, however, the two-thirds affirmative vote in the Senate required for a treaty was virtually impossible. The fact that public opinion polls showed 60 percent of Americans were opposed to withdrawing from the nuclear agreement was not a sturdy enough defense.

Trump's abrogation was another reminder of how much easier it is to tear down diplomacy than to build it. Pulling out of the nuclear deal alienated allies who had joined us in the effort for many years. Reimposition of U.S. sanctions in the face of opposition from partners further damaged a tool of policy already suffering from abuse, driving other countries to lessen reliance on the dollar and the U.S. financial system. It also betrayed an obsession with Iran that exaggerated its strategic weight and undermined larger priorities like rebuilding alliances or managing great power rivals.

Trump's demolition of the Iran deal was a further blow to our own credibility, to international confidence that we could keep our end of a bargain. "Credibility" can be an overused term in Washington, a town sometimes too prone to badger presidents into using force to prop up our currency and influence around the world. But it matters in American diplomacy, especially at a post-primacy moment when our ability to mobilize others around common concerns is becoming more crucial. With its echoes of the muscular unilateralism on the road to the Iraq War in 2003 and the seductive appeal of remaking regional order through American power, the decision to abandon the JCPOA signaled anew a dangerous dismissiveness toward diplomacy. It was exactly the kind of risky, cocky, ill-considered bet that had shredded our influence before, and could easily do so again.

10

Pivotal Power: Restoring America's Tool of First Resort

DEPARTURES COMPEL US to look backward as well as forward. I was doing a little of both as I stood onstage in the State Department's ornate Benjamin Franklin Room at my retirement ceremony in the fall of 2014. It was an extraordinarily generous send-off, which left my ego straining at its moorings. The room was packed with family, friends, colleagues, and diplomatic counterparts. There was a video compilation of congratulatory messages from all the living secretaries of state going back to Henry Kissinger.

President Obama made a surprise appearance and spent time with my family. In his remarks, he reminded the audience of his confinement in Perm as a freshman senator a decade before, of some of our other, more productive adventures in the years that followed, and of the unheralded sacrifice of Lisa and the girls and all Foreign Service families. Vice President Biden was his usual bighearted self, working the room with infectious enthusiasm. Secretary Kerry announced the naming of one of the department's auditoriums in my honor. I was touched by his thoughtfulness—and amused by several condolence messages that my staff subsequently received from colleagues overseas assuming the worst.

As the ceremony continued and the kind words multiplied, I realized that the sense of detachment I had developed as a military brat, and refined during all those years on the move from one post and assignment to another, was fading fast. Lisa and I had taken our oaths of office in this very room thirty-three years earlier—I had known one employer, one institution, and one profession ever since. It was hard to say goodbye, but I was proud of the modest role I played in the larger drama of American diplomacy.

My mind wandered to an even more elegant, and certainly more consequential, setting a quarter century before, to that massive hall in Madrid's royal palace where I had glimpsed the centrality and power of American diplomacy on full display. It was a memory that seemed increasingly distant, dulled by the realities of a changing international landscape. America's unipolar moment was, by definition, temporary. Inevitably, our relative power would diminish as other players became wealthier, stronger, and more assertive. In the midst of these dramatic geopolitical shifts, some of which we accelerated with our own mistakes, we also lost our way in diplomacy. At first lulled by the experience of post–Cold War dominance and then shocked by 9/11, we gradually devalued diplomatic tools. All too often, we overrelied on American hard power to achieve policy aims and ambitions, hastening the end of American dominance, deepening the desire and capacity of adversaries to upend the American-led international order, and disillusioning the American public.

As that lovely retirement ceremony and my own career drew to a close, I could see that the next generation of American diplomats would have a difficult hand to play. Their challenge, however, became exponentially more severe two years later with the election of Donald Trump. During his presidency, our relative influence diminished further and faster, as did our capacity and appetite to lead. Our role withered, leaving our friends confused, our adversaries emboldened, and the foundations of the international system we built and preserved for seven decades alarmingly fragile.

The administration's profoundly self-destructive shock and awe campaign against professional diplomacy only compounded the challenge. Its early unilateral diplomatic disarmament, born of equal parts ideological contempt and stubborn incompetence, was taking place at precisely the moment when diplomacy mattered more than ever to American interests, in a world where we were no longer the only big kid on the block but still a pivotal power best positioned to lead the world in managing the problems before us.

The window for defining a strategy for a changing international landscape, and America's pivotal role, is slowly closing—but it is by no means shut. That strategy will require a new compact on diplomacy, one that reinvests in diplomacy's core functions and roles, adapts smartly to new challenges and realities, and reinforces the connection between leadership abroad and rejuvenation at home.

* * *

WHOEVER WAS ELECTED president in 2016 would have had to contend with a complicated set of dilemmas rooted in both a rapidly shifting international environment and a disaffected domestic mood. Donald Trump didn't invent them, nor could Hillary Clinton have avoided them. As Americans went to the polls in November 2016, theirs was a world in the midst of historic transformations, which would strain the capacity and imagination of any new administration.

The reemergence of great power rivalry was in some ways a return to a more natural state of international affairs than the bipolar contest of the Cold War or the moment of American dominance that followed. Yet it carried complex risks and trade-offs, for which American statecraft was out of practice. China's ambition to recover its accustomed primacy in Asia had already upended many of our comfortable post–Cold War assumptions about how integration into a U.S.-led order would tame, or at least channel, Chinese aspirations. President Xi Jinping was flexing his muscle not only in Asia but all the way to the gates of Europe and the Middle East. Our traditional allies in Asia, as well as new partners like India, were taking notice and adjusting their strategic calculations—raising regional temperatures and increasing uncertainties.

China's dynamism, and that of the broader Asia-Pacific region, only highlighted further the struggles of Europe—beset by internal political crises and external pressures, including from a resurgent Russia. Putin continued to punch above his weight, exploiting divisions within Europe, settling scores in Ukraine and Syria, and sowing chaos beyond his wildest ambitions in the American elections.

Alongside these great power frictions, crises of regional order continued to bubble, products of both the strengths of local competitors and the weaknesses of failing states. The Middle East remained best in class in dysfunction and fragility. No longer the global energy player it once was, no longer able to sustain its rentier economies, no longer able to camouflage its deficits of opportunity and dignity, much of the Arab world teetered on the edge of more domestic upheavals, with extremists eager to prey on its vulnerabilities. Africa's future carried both promise and peril, with a population likely to double to two billion by the middle of the twenty-first century and unresolved problems of regional conflict, poor governance, and food, water, and health insecurity all looming large. The Americas remained the natural strategic home base for the United States, poised to benefit from the possibilities of a "Pacific Century," but burdened by inequalities and a limited U.S. attention span.

Beyond the unsettled rivalries of states, and the decaying foundations of regional stability, the old postwar order groaned and creaked, its institutions overdue for adaptation. The five permanent members of the UN Security Council were jealous guardians of an outdated system, and the international financial and trade institutions struggled with serious reform. Meanwhile, the transformative effects of climate change were becoming more evident with each passing season. With polar ice caps melting, sea levels rising, and weather patterns swinging wildly, the implications of an environment badly damaged by human behavior grew more dangerous and immediate. The prospect of half the world's population facing significant water shortages was a mere two decades away.

The pace of the revolution in technology made the impact and dislocations of the Industrial Revolution look plodding by comparison. Advances in machine learning, artificial intelligence, and synthetic biology moved at breathtaking speed, outstripping the ability of states and societies to devise ways to maximize their benefits, minimize their downsides, and create workable international rules of the road. More broadly, authoritarian regimes used the apparently decentralizing power of technology to consolidate control of their citizens.

The competition, collisions, and confusion that all these forces produced had been building for some time, and their contours were faintly apparent even in the heady aftermath of the Cold War. In the memo for incoming secretary of state Christopher in January 1993, I highlighted the schizophrenia of the emerging international system, with the globalization of the world economy unfolding alongside the fragmentation of international politics. Power balances and relative positions were bound to be fluid, and often profoundly disorienting. "The resulting chaos," I added, "is enough to almost—almost—make one nostalgic for the familiar discipline and order of the Cold War."[1] A quarter century later, my nostalgia was still under control, but the problem loomed much larger.

The diplomatic profession, like other endangered vocational species during this period of profound disruption, was overwhelmed by existential angst. I witnessed firsthand during the course of my career how the near monopoly on presence, access, insight, and influence that diplomats used to have in foreign capitals and societies was eroding. As a young diplomat in the Middle East in the early 1980s, I wrote "airgrams"—deliberate, long-form analyses that took several days to reach Washington by diplomatic pouch. Senior officials traveled with increasing frequency to foreign capitals, but the unhurried nature of communication kept diplomatic channels in the forefront and diplomats on the front lines, with considerable reach and autonomy.

A decade later, the "CNN effect" during the Gulf War demonstrated the ubiquity of real-time information, and in the years that followed the Internet tore down the remaining barriers to information and direct communication. Heads of state and senior officials across government departments could interact easily and directly, leaving foreign ministries and embassies feeling anachronistic. Nonstate actors—heads of massive philanthropic foundations, civil society activists, and corporate CEOs, among many others—wielded increasing international influence, shaping and funding a wide array of policy agendas. WikiLeaks displayed the vulnerabilities of "confidential" reporting, and social media muddied what once seemed like clear channels for shaping public opinion.

Despite considerable efforts by secretaries of state from both parties, we often failed to adapt wisely to this new reality, letting core skills atrophy while falling behind the curve as new policy challenges, players, and tools emerged. Budgets dropped precipitously after the Cold War, with a 50 percent cut in real terms for the State Department and foreign affairs budget between 1985 and 2000. Secretary Baker opened a dozen new embassies in the former Soviet Union without asking Congress for more money, and under Secretary Albright intake into the Foreign Service ground to a halt. More broadly, the steady militarization and centralization of policy turned into a gallop after 9/11, inverting the roles of force and diplomacy, diverting American power down the tragic dead end of the Iraq War, and distorting both strategy and tools.

It is of course true that the chances for successful diplomacy are vastly enhanced by the potential use of force. There is often no better way to focus the minds of difficult customers at the negotiating table than to have those remarkable tools on full display in the background. That was what gave force to Baker's persuasive skills in the run-up to Madrid, and to Kerry's diplomacy with the Iranians. "You have no idea how much it contributes to the general politeness and pleasantness of diplomacy," mused George Kennan, "when you have a little quiet armed force in the background."[2]

Overreliance on military tools, however, leads into policy quicksand. That was the lesson of the battleship *New Jersey* lobbing shells into Lebanon in the early 1980s, unconnected to workable strategy or diplomacy. And it was the lesson, on a far more disastrous scale, twenty years later in Iraq.

The militarization of diplomacy is a trap, which leads to overuse—or premature use—of force, and underemphasis on nonmilitary tools. "If your main tool is a hammer," as Barack Obama liked to say, "then every problem will start to look like a nail." Even Pentagon and military leaders went out of their way to highlight the perils of the imbalance between force and diplomacy. Secretary of Defense Bob Gates regularly reminded Congress that U.S. military band members outnumbered foreign service officers, and one of his successors, Jim Mattis, famously noted that cutting funding for diplomacy would require him "to buy more ammunition."

Gates and Mattis understood that the weight of the military's mission and capabilities can erode a focus on diplomacy, or distort its central tasks. In Iraq and Afghanistan, diplomats found themselves slipping into supporting roles in the military's counterinsurgency strategy, preoccupied with local social engineering and the kind of nation-building activities that were beyond the capacity of Americans to accomplish. It sometimes seemed as if we were trying to replicate the role of the nineteenth-century British Colonial Service, not play the distinctive role of the American Foreign Service. We were being challenged to pour increasingly limited civilian resources into long-term efforts to build governance and economic structures that could only be constructed by Iraqis and Afghans themselves. The more immediate and consequential function of diplomats on the ground was the persistent, head-banging work of persuading senior national leaders to bridge sectarian divides, minimize corruption, and slowly create some sense of equitable political order. In wider terms, it was the job of diplomats to try to build regional support for fragile national governments in conflict zones, and to limit external meddling.

If the militarization of diplomacy was one post–9/11 trap, over-centralization and micromanagement by a swollen NSC staff was another. There was no way that the five dozen or so professionals on the NSC staff of Colin Powell in the late 1980s, or the similarly sized staff of Brent Scowcroft under Bush 41, would suffice in the post–9/11 era. The tempo of counterterrorism activities and the demands of a global economy meant that the White House had to expand its coordinating capacity. But the fivefold growth over a quarter century was a classic case of overreach. The NSC staff continued to attract the most seasoned political appointees and many of the very best career officers from cabinet agencies. Their natural temptation was to take on more operational roles. Their proximity to the Oval Office deepened their sense of mission, and their energy and talent fueled their enthusiasm for not only coordinating but also shaping and executing policy.

The problem was that this made a self-fulfilling prophecy of complaints about lack of initiative and drive from other agencies, particularly State. On the rugged playing fields of Washington bureaucratic politics, State has often found itself elbowed to the sidelines. Assistant secretaries responsible for critical regions would be squeezed out of meetings in the Situation Room, where back benches were filled with NSC staff. With a dwindling sense of being in on the takeoff of policy deliberations or decisions, it was in some ways natural for even fairly senior State personnel to feel disconnected from responsibility for the landing, for policy execution. None of that is an excuse for the failure of the department to show more drive and ingenuity, get out of our own way bureaucratically, streamline our structure, and energize our culture. But overcentralization and overmilitarization made it a lot harder than it needed to be.

In the midst of too many aborted takeoffs and crash landings, as the international arena grew more threatening, and as the blood, treasure, and opportunity costs of America's misadventures grew more obvious, a yawning gap emerged between a Washington establishment deeply committed to American global leadership and a less convinced American public. Making the case for American leadership in an emerging global order was becoming harder by the day.

The Clinton administration faced an early version of this challenge after the Cold War. As we wrote to incoming secretary Christopher, the post–Cold War transition "leaves you and the President with a very tough task. It was relatively easy during the Cold War to justify national security expenditures and build support for sustained American engagement overseas. It is infinitely harder now." By 2016, ritual incantations of terms like "liberal international order" failed to resonate beyond the Beltway "blob," and the disconnect between our easy conceits about American indispensability and a citizenry's doubts that we had our priorities in the right order continued to grow.

The legacy of the first decade of this century, of two massively expensive and debilitating wars and a global financial crisis, reinforced a sense not only of fatigue about foreign entanglements, but also genuine resentment. Much of the American public had a visceral understanding of the widening gaps in wealth and opportunity across our society, and of the failure of successive administrations to address serious infrastructure problems. And much of the public understood instinctively that we had made some poor choices about overseas commitments, at a time when we were probably less exposed to anything resembling an existential foreign danger than at any point in recent decades. Their mistrust and doubts were aggravated by the perceived success of rivals and adversaries on the back of America's sacrifices and missteps. Bureaucratic reforms and legislative fixes wouldn't matter unless this fundamental rift was healed.

* * *

THE TRUMP ADMINISTRATION took these inherited challenges, accumulated over three post–Cold War decades, and made them much worse. It diminished American influence on a shifting international landscape, hollowed out American diplomacy, and only deepened the divisions among Americans about our global role.

Like Barack Obama, Donald Trump recognized that America's approach to the world needed to change significantly. Like Obama, Trump focused on the right question: How should the United States reshape its strategy at a moment when the unipolar dominance of the post–Cold War era was passing, and popular support for active American leadership was fraying? Both saw the need for rebalancing security relationships with allies who had long borne too small a share of the burden, and economic relationships with rivals like China, who had enjoyed protectionist trade advantage long after their "developing country" rationale had faded. Both were willing to break with convention in dealing directly with adversaries, and both were innately skeptical of foreign policy orthodoxy. Their answers to the core question of reshaping American strategy, however, were vastly different.

President Obama sought to adapt American leadership and the international order that we had largely shaped and preserved for seven decades. He sought to apply the sense of enlightened self-interest that had animated American foreign policy, at its best, since the days of the Marshall Plan in Europe—a commitment to enlarge the circle of people and countries around the world with a shared stake in rules and institutions that enhanced our security and prosperity. His attitude was grounded in realism about the limits of American influence. Obama's concern for avoiding overreach and commitment to playing the long game in the face of short-game crises could sometimes come across as diffidence. But he had a fundamental optimism about where the arc of history would carry a United

States that carefully cultivated a model of political and economic openness and updated the alliances and partnerships that set us apart from lonelier powers like China and Russia.

There was nothing diffident about President Trump. His aim was not to adapt, but to disrupt. He came into office with a powerful conviction, untethered to history, that the United States had been held hostage by the very order it created; we were Gulliver, and it was past time to break the bonds of the Lilliputians. Alliances were millstones, multilateral arrangements were constraints rather than sources of leverage, and the United Nations and other international bodies were distractions, if not irrelevant.

Instead of the enlightened self-interest that drove Obama and most of post–World War II American foreign policy, the Trump administration took office more focused on the "self" part than the "enlightened." Trump's "America First" sloganeering stirred a nasty brew of belligerent unilateralism, mercantilism, and unreconstructed nationalism. On the international stage, the new administration often used muscular posturing and fact-free assertions to mask a pattern of retreat—abandoning in rapid succession the Paris climate accords, the Trans-Pacific Partnership, the Iranian nuclear agreement, and a slew of other international commitments. Disruption seemed to be its own end, with little apparent thought given to "plan B" or "what comes next." Trump's approach was more than an impulse; it was a distinct and Hobbesian worldview, but far less than anything resembling a strategy. Not surprisingly, adversaries took advantage, allies hedged, and already strained institutions teetered.

The image of possibility and respect for human dignity that attracted so many around the world, despite all our flaws, grew more and more tattered. Many years of representing the United States abroad had taught me that the power of our example mattered more than that of our preaching. Now our example was increasingly one of incivility, division, and dysfunction, and our preaching had less to do with highlighting human rights abuses wherever we saw them and more to do with insulting allies and indulging autocrats.

The Trump administration's hollowing out of the State Department embodied its ideological convictions and temperamental instincts. To be fair, American diplomacy was unsettled before Trump. Decades of unbalanced investment in defense and intelligence had taken its toll. The department's failure to rein in its counterproductive bureaucratic and cultural habits did not help. But the new president's dismissiveness toward professional diplomats, like his wider approach to America's role in the world, took a complicated situation and made it a crisis.

In July 2018, President Trump asserted at a press conference in Finland with President Putin that he was an advocate of "the powerful tradition of American diplomacy," but his behavior bore no resemblance to thoughtful, well-prepared exemplars of that tradition like Jim Baker.[3] Trump's view of diplomacy was narcissistic, not institutional. Dialogue was unconnected to strategy; the president seemed oblivious to the reality that "getting along" with rivals like Putin was not the aim of diplomacy, which was all about advancing tangible interests. And "winging it" in crucial high-level encounters was a prescription for embarrassment—especially when dealing with experienced autocrats like Putin, who rarely winged anything.

For the Trump White House, the Department of State was a realm of "deep state" heresy, of closet Obama and Clinton supporters bent upon resisting the new administration. That was a major, if convenient, misapprehension. If anything, career foreign and civil service officers at State are almost loyal to a fault, eager for the opportunity to deliver for a new administration, and hopeful that their expertise will be valued, if not always heeded. What they got from the White House was an attitude of open hostility, reflecting the distrust of convention and professional expertise that fueled the Trump political phenomenon and energized the new president.

Trump's first secretary of state, Rex Tillerson, just dug the hole deeper. An accomplished former head of Exxon, Tillerson had an insular and imperious style, a CEO's skeptical view of the public sector, and an engineer's linear view of how to remold diplomacy. He embraced the biggest budget cuts in the modern history of the department; launched a terminally flawed "redesign process"; cut himself off from most of the building; drove out many of the most capable senior and mid-level officers; cut intake into the Foreign Service by well over 50 percent; and reversed what were already painfully slow trendlines toward better gender and ethnic diversity. Most pernicious of all was the practice of blacklisting individual officers simply because they had worked on controversial issues in the previous administration, like the Iran nuclear deal.

The savaging of American diplomacy as the Trump administration consolidated its grip was not the first such assault in our history, but it was in many ways the worst. There is never a good time for diplomatic malpractice. This just happened to be a particularly dangerous moment.

* * *

ALEXIS DE TOCQUEVILLE once wrote, "The greatness of America lies not in being more enlightened than any other nation, but rather in her ability to repair her faults."[4] The Trump era poses a test of our capacity for self-repair beyond even Tocqueville's imagination. It would be foolish to underestimate the damage to our standing and influence, and to the prospects for shaping a stable international order for a challenging new age. Nevertheless, our recuperative powers and underlying strengths are still formidable.

No longer the dominant player that we were after the end of the Cold War, no longer able to dictate events as we may sometimes have believed we could, we nevertheless remain the world's pivotal power— able to update international order in a way that reflects new realities but sustains our interests and values. Over the next several decades, assuming we don't keep digging the hole deeper for ourselves, no other nation is in a better position to play that pivotal role, or to navigate the complicated currents of twenty-first-century geopolitics.

Our assets are substantial. We still spend more every year on defense than the next seven countries combined. Our economy, despite risks of overheating and persistent inequalities, remains the biggest, most adaptable, and most innovative in the world. Energy, once a vulnerability, now offers considerable advantages, with technology unlocking vast natural gas resources, and advances in clean and renewable energy accelerating. Demography is another strength. Compared to our peer competitors, our population is younger and more mobile, and if we could stop doing so much practical and moral damage to ourselves on immigration issues we could lock in that strategic edge for generations. Geography sets us apart, with our two liquid assets—the Pacific and Atlantic oceans—insulating us to some extent from the kinds of security threats that expose other major powers. Diplomacy ought to be another advantage. We have more allies and potential partners than any of our peers or rivals, with greater capacity for coalition-building and problem-solving.

Our advantages are not permanent or automatic. To maintain them, we have to do a far better job of husbanding them wisely and applying them with care and purpose. It is a truism that effective foreign policy begins at home, with sustained attention to the domestic foundations of American power. And yet for all the injuries we've inflicted on ourselves in recent years—for all the unforced errors, for all the hollowing out of both diplomacy as a tool of policy and of the American idea as a source of global influence—we still have a window before us in which we can help shape a new and more durable international order before it gets shaped for us.

Fashioning a strategy for America in a post-primacy world is no easy task. The most famous American strategy of the postwar era, Kennan's containment doctrine, went through a number of significant variations during the decades before the end of the Cold War.[5] At its core was a commitment to invest in the resilience of the community of democratic, market-based states that the United States led, and a cold-eyed recognition of the weaknesses that would eventually unravel the Soviet Union and its unwieldy Communist bloc. A balance of military strength, economic vigor, and careful diplomacy helped avoid direct conflict, avert nuclear war, and manage competition in the post-colonial world.

In the post–Cold War era, none of us had the intellectual dexterity to fashion a simple slogan to match Kennan's concept. As we tried to suggest in the January 1993 memo to Christopher, a strategy premised on the "enlargement" of the coalition and ideas that had won the Cold War was enticing, but had inherent limits in a world in which challenges to regional order were bound to emerge, globalization would produce its own contradictions and collisions, and America's temporary dominance would inevitably be contested by the rise of others. As enlargement encountered constraints, and as we compounded them in Iraq in 2003 and in the financial crisis several years later, we struggled to shape a post-primacy alternative.

A successful American strategy beyond Trump will likely have to return to Obama's central propositions about rebalancing our portfolio of global investments and tools, sharpening our attention on managing competition with great power rivals, and using our leverage and our capacity to mobilize other players to address twenty-first-century challenges. That ought to be infused with a bold and unapologetic vision for free people and free and fair markets, with the United States as a more attractive exemplar than it is today.

Asia continues to loom as our first priority, with China's rise the most consequential geopolitical trend of our time. President Trump's unpredictability and detachment have opened the playing field for China, offering an unexpectedly early path to dominance in Asia. That China and its neighbors, as well as the United States, are entangled economically, their future prosperity wrapped up in one another's success, is a brake on conflict, but not a guarantee against it.

The unease among other players across Asia about Chinese hegemony creates a natural opportunity for Washington to knit together relationships with traditional allies like Japan and emerging partners like India. That was the origin of the Bush 43 administration's long-range bet on India, which meant bending the rules on nonproliferation for an even wider strategic gain.

A deeper American focus on Asia makes transatlantic partnership more, not less, significant. It implies a new strategic division of labor with our European allies, where they take on even more responsibility for order on their continent, and do even more to contribute to possibilities for longer-term order in the Middle East, while the United States devotes relatively more resources and attention to Asia. It also demands a sustained effort at a trade and investment partnership that addresses new economic realities, expectations, and imperatives. That argues for a renewed Atlanticism, built on shared interests and values, in a world in which a rising China, a resurgent Russia, and persistent troubles in the Middle East ought to cement a common approach. Our main security challenge now is to consolidate, not expand, NATO—bolstering the sovereignty and political and economic health of Ukraine outside anyone's formal military structures, and deterring Russian aggression. We have a deep interest in encouraging a vibrant, post-Brexit European Union.[6]

A more durable twenty-first-century European security architecture has eluded us in nearly three decades of fitful attempts to engage post–Cold War Russia. That is not likely to change anytime soon—certainly not during Putin's tenure. Ours should be a long-game strategy, not giving in to Putin's aggressive score-settling, but not giving up on the possibility of an eventual mellowing of relations beyond him. Nor can we afford to ignore the need for guardrails in managing an often adversarial relationship—sustaining communication between our militaries and our diplomats, and preserving what we can of a collapsing arms control architecture. Over time, Russia's stake in healthier relations with Europe and America may grow, as a slow-motion collision with China in Central Asia looms. With the return of great power rivalry, we'll have an increasing interest in putting ourselves in the pivotal position, able to manage relationships and build influence in all directions.

Disorder in the Middle East will remain that troubled region's default position for years to come. Pessimists are hardly ever wrong there, and they rarely lack for company or validation. A hard-eyed look at our own interests argues for less intensive engagement. We are no longer directly dependent on Middle East hydrocarbons. Israel is more secure than ever before from existential threats. Iran is a danger, but an opportunistic power, its ambitions bounded in a Sunni-majority region, as well as by simmering domestic discontent and a moribund economy. Despite Russia's resurgence, there is no external adversary to compel our attention, as there was during the Cold War.

As President Obama discovered, however, deleveraging in the Middle East is sometimes destabilizing in its own right. Insecurity in the region is a powerful contagion, and threats regularly metastasize beyond its boundaries. The United States can't afford to neglect its leadership role—while applying a massive dose of humility and rejecting the large-scale military and nation-building efforts of the recent past, which were doomed to failure in a region that has often been a graveyard for military occupiers and social engineering projects by outsiders, however well intentioned. As part of a long-term strategy, we should reassure our traditional Arab partners against the threats they face, whether from Sunni extremist groups or a predatory Iran. But we should insist in return that Sunni Arab leaderships recognize that regional order will ultimately require some modus vivendi with an Iran that will remain a substantial power even if it tempers its revolutionary overreach. We should also insist that they address urgently the profound crisis of governance that was at the heart of the Arab Spring. Genuine friendship with Israel should impel us to push for the two-state solution with Palestinians that is already past its expiration date, but without which Israel's future as a Jewish, democratic state will be in peril.

President Trump's disregard for Africa and Latin America has been foolish, as demography and a variety of uncertainties and possibilities reinforce their strategic significance for the United States. Similarly, his antipathy for multilateral agreements and international institutions will leave his successors with a huge rebuilding task, especially since renovation and adaptation were already long overdue. It was an historic mistake to walk away from the Trans-Pacific Partnership; with a subsequent effort in Europe, we could have anchored two-thirds of the global economy to the same high standards and rules as our own system, helped emerging markets join the club over time, and shaped China's options and incentives for reform. None of that is to suggest that we don't have to do a much better job of insisting on fair, two-way-street provisions in trade agreements, and of cushioning their effects on important sectors of our own economy and labor force. Walking away from imperfect agreements, however, is rarely better than addressing their imperfections over time.

Trump's rejection of the Paris climate accords and spectacular backtracking on our global commitments on migration and refugees were also devastating, deepening mistrust of our motives and reliability. There has been no hint of American leadership on a host of accelerating technology questions, from cyber threats to the impact of rapid advances in artificial intelligence, that are likely to transform geopolitical competition in the twenty-first century in the way that the Industrial Revolution transformed it in the nineteenth and twentieth centuries. In the emerging power configuration, American resources and influence are relatively less substantial than they were a decade ago, and even more damaged as a result of the Trump administration's policies. Nevertheless, in all these areas, the United States has a pivotal role to play, and the quality of its diplomacy will be the key to playing that role well.

* * *

"MY GOD, THIS is the end of diplomacy," sighed Lord Palmerston, Britain's foreign secretary, a century and a half ago when he was handed his first telegram. It was not the first time that diplomacy's demise seemed imminent, and it was not the last. As the second decade of the twenty-first century draws to a close, the notion of American diplomacy as a tool of first resort seems quaint, if not naïve, like pining for the return of the village watchmaker in a smartwatch world.

Selling the practical virtues of diplomacy is a complicated undertaking. For all the debate about "hard power," "soft power," and "smart power" in recent years, diplomacy is most often about quiet power, the largely invisible work of tending alliances, twisting arms, tempering disputes, and making long-term investments in relationships and societies. Diplomacy is punctuated only rarely by grand public breakthroughs. Its benefits are hard to appreciate. Crises averted are less captivating than military victories; the lower costs to consumers that come from trade agreements are less tangible and direct than a closing factory; the preventive care that occupies most diplomats is less compelling than the military's dramatic surgical triumphs. In the new era of disorder before us, however, the quiet power of American diplomacy has never mattered more.[7]

There is no neat alchemy for renewing American diplomacy, but there are at least three imperatives: reinforcing the core roles and qualities that continue to sustain successful diplomacy; adapting diplomatic tradecraft to manage new challenges; and revitalizing a compact with an American public less certain of the purpose and importance of American leadership.

Over the course of my career, we struggled and often failed on all these counts. Lulled into complacency by a seemingly more benign post–Cold War international environment and our unipolar dominance, we let atrophy the essence of diplomacy—the ability to cajole, persuade, browbeat, threaten, and nudge other governments and political leaders in directions consistent with our interests and values. Stunned by the earthquake of 9/11 and its aftershocks, we entered a prolonged period of strategic and operational distraction. Stabilization, counterinsurgency, countering violent extremism, and all the murky concepts that mushroomed in the era of the great inversion proved to be flawed guideposts for the adaptation of American diplomacy. We tended to oversell the merits of diplomats as social workers and undersell the core role of diplomats in hammering out the best relations we could between states, from the like-minded to the nastily adversarial.

Even as funding and State's relative role diminished, we spread our diplomatic wings further and took on issues and missions for which we lacked expertise and the means to make a meaningful difference. We compounded the problem by failing to build the expertise and operational agility that we'd need to confront the increasingly urgent challenges of this century, from the revolution in technology to climate change. That all combined to make it infinitely harder to demonstrate the power and purpose of American diplomacy at its best, precisely at the moment when we needed it most, and at a time when the political foundations at home critical to effective leadership abroad were collapsing.

* * *

THE CORE ROLES and qualities of good diplomats are not fundamentally different today from what they were in earlier eras. George Kennan and George Shultz both described diplomats as "gardeners," painstakingly nurturing plants and partners and possibilities, always alert to the need to prune, weed, and preempt problems. Their prosaic description may not fit well on a recruiting poster, but it still rings true today.

Others have referred to diplomats as conductors or organizers. In music, conductors ensure that all the instruments of an orchestra come together as one. In foreign policy, diplomats similarly harness all the tools of American statecraft—from the soft power of ideas, culture, and public diplomacy, to economic incentives and sanctions, intelligence-gathering and covert action, and military assistance and the threat of force—to achieve policy aims. Diplomats are classic organizers, whether in mobilizing the levers of American influence, shaping international alliances, or bridging divides with adversaries. Jim Baker played all of these roles in helping George H. W. Bush build the Desert Storm coalition, less a gardener than a herder of geopolitical cats. A political animal at heart, he understood instinctively how important it was to "remember your base"—to tend to international alliances, the great force multiplier of U.S. influence.

Effective diplomats also embody many qualities, but at their heart is a crucial trinity: judgment, balance, and discipline. All three demand a nuanced grasp of history and culture, mastery of foreign languages, hard-nosed facility in negotiations, and the capacity to translate American interests in ways that other governments can see as consistent with their own—or at least in ways that drive home the costs of alternative courses.

Judgment is essential to navigating foreign terrain in America's best interest. I have yet to find a better frame for the basic challenge of diplomatic judgment than Reinhold Niebuhr's "serenity prayer": "God grant me the serenity to accept the things I cannot change, the courage to change the things I can, and the wisdom to know the difference." Like any aphorism, Niebuhr's insight can be twisted in lots of different ways. Neoconservatives cited his "courage" to justify the invasion of Iraq in 2003; critics of the war pointed to his "wisdom" as the most compelling argument for restraint. What cannot be overstated, however, is the importance of sound judgment in a world of fallible and flawed humans—weighing ends and means, anticipating the unintended consequences of well-intentioned actions, and measuring the hard reality of limits against the potential of American agency.

When diplomacy succeeds, it is usually because of an appreciation of its limits, rather than a passion for stretching beyond them. Durable agreements are rooted in mutual self-interest, not one-sided imposition of will, and they frequently carry the baggage and imperfections of compromise, the inevitable consequences of the give-and-take of even the most fruitful negotiations. That was the story of the Iran nuclear agreement, and Qaddafi's negotiated abandonment of terrorism and weapons of mass destruction. It was an appreciation of the limits of power that encouraged George H. W. Bush and his team to stop short of overthrowing Saddam in 1991, after the rapid success of Desert Storm in expelling Iraq from Kuwait. Bush, Baker, and Scowcroft were patient practitioners of Hippocratic diplomacy, intent on doing no harm in uncertain circumstances, guided by prudence and judicious use of America's power and tools.

When circumstances offer rare openings for diplomatic agency, diplomats have to be able and willing to make big bets. That was the genesis of the Bush 41 administration's masterful management of German reunification, and of Jim Baker's brilliance in translating military victory in Iraq into a diplomatic triumph in Madrid. American leverage was at its zenith in that period, but it took sound diplomatic judgment to apply it skillfully and seize historic openings.

Professional diplomats have an obligation to offer their honest judgments, however inconvenient. To policymakers and elected officials predisposed to "do things," career diplomats and their broken-record warnings about potential consequences or pitfalls can seem terminally prudent. Americans see themselves as problem-solvers, and the notion that some actions are best avoided can seem almost un-American to political leaders. Ambassadors in the field always face a tension between warning of possible policy failures and recognizing that gloomy analysis is not a policy.

Secretary of State Dean Acheson once complained that senior diplomats tended to be "cautious rather than imaginative."[8] Most of his successors, including the ten I served directly, have harbored similar concerns, some more openly than others. It is true that career officers sometimes seem to take particular relish in telling a new administration why its big new idea is not so big or so new, or why it won't work. It is also true that the increasing roles in foreign policymaking of both the NSC staff and other agencies over successive administrations have tended to bring out the more passive (or passive-aggressive) side of the State Department.

From Joe McCarthy to Donald Trump, American demagogues have doubted the loyalty and relevance of career diplomats, seeking to intimidate and marginalize them. Those are the most extreme circumstances, in which good people are forced out of the Foreign Service or muzzled. In my own career, I never had to face those extremes. I learned from remarkable professionals like Tom Pickering that policy initiative and a willingness to provide candid views were an essential part of being a career diplomat, especially as you became more senior. It never made sense to him, or to many in my generation, simply to serve as a postman for Washington decisions, or to wait for White House choices without first trying to shape them. I always admired the way Secretary Rice encouraged me to continue to provide my warnings of the looming trainwrecks with Putin's Russia and argue alternative policy courses, even though she had her own views, and the White House theirs. Never once did I feel that my two rubles from Moscow were unwelcome or irrelevant.

I have nothing but admiration for colleagues who in recent decades decided that they could no longer serve policies in which they did not believe. More than a dozen Foreign Service professionals resigned over American nonintervention in the Balkans in the early 1990s. Several others left over the Iraq intervention a decade later. Many more have resigned in protest of the Trump administration's assault on American diplomacy and the values that sustain it. Short of resignation, officers are obliged to exercise discipline and avoid public dissent. But they also have a parallel obligation to express their concerns internally and offer their best policy advice, even if the truths they perceive are unpalatable. A State Department in which officers are bludgeoned into timidity, or censor themselves, or are simply ig- nored, becomes a hollow institution, incapable of the disciplined dip- lomatic activism that this moment in history demands of the United States.

Balance is an equally important diplomatic trait, for diplomats are constantly called to manage inevitable trade-offs—among tactical choices, between short- and long-term goals, of practical interests and less tangible values. Diplomacy is often unavoidably transac- tional. It is a mistake, however, to lose sight of the enlightened self- interest that connects immediate choices to strategic possibilities, and embeds short-term interests in wider questions of principle.

The problem of promoting respect for human rights in authori- tarian societies, where we also have important security interests, is particularly complicated, and sometimes particularly painful. There is no perfect diplomatic playbook for managing this dilemma. The Trump administration has tended simply to abdicate, reserving its condemnation only for those autocracies with whom we are sharply at odds, like Iran. Much as I am convinced of the flaws of that ap- proach, which just feeds the arguments of Putin and other autocrats that the United States is fundamentally hypocritical and only pro- motes democracy and human rights to suit its own strategic purposes, our record in other administrations is hardly pristine.

Tone certainly matters. I have yet to meet the foreign leadership, or society, that responds well to being lectured to or patronized by Americans. Nor is ritual invocation of American exceptionalism espe- cially compelling against the backdrop of our current exceptionally unappealing domestic landscape. Yet there is also no substitute for raising human rights concerns directly and plainly. Addressing them is a matter of any state's long-term self-interest, not a favor to the United States or anyone else. Pressing those concerns is also a matter of who we are as Americans, and of our commitment to ideas of political tolerance, pluralism, and respect for diversity that remain a source of enduring strength.

I admired the way Hillary Clinton stepped up in the case of the blind Chinese dissident Chen Guangcheng. She took real risks, for the right reasons. In other cases over the years, however, we often had far less satisfying outcomes. I had countless conversations over the past couple decades with dictators in the Middle East and Central Asia and other hard places, pushing for a specific prisoner to be released, or to consider some general easing of repression. I also had countless conversations with local human rights activists, listening to their concerns and explaining as honestly as I could that we would continue to try to help, but also had interests in military access or counterterrorism cooperation that we couldn't easily jettison. Those were the trade-offs that were hardest to swallow.

Pulling off the myriad balancing acts of diplomacy demands discipline—the self-awareness to be humble and question assumptions. Too often, we've lulled ourselves into diplomatic wishful thinking, an almost willful cluelessness about what's really driving events abroad and the long-term consequences of our actions. After the Gulf War, many of us assumed naïvely that Saddam Hussein's regime would collapse of its own contradictions. However skeptical we may have been about much of the intelligence suggesting that Saddam possessed weapons of mass destruction in the run-up to the 2003 war, it didn't occur to us that the Iraqi dictator would manufacture the illusion that he retained them to ward off external and internal foes. Our failure of imagination obstructed more honest debate about the core rationale for war and our judgments about the risk of alternative courses. The wider tragedy, of course, was stubborn refusal to see clearly the inexorable complexities of the day after.

After the uprising of 2011 in Syria, many assumed mistakenly that the popular momentum that had swept away Ben Ali and Mubarak so quickly was bound to make short work of Assad. Even after the

Syrian president demonstrated his staying power, there was a similarly flawed assumption that Syria's bloodletting could be contained within its borders. Millions of refugees flooding neighboring countries, and eventually Europe, soon exposed the shortsightedness of that proposition. During the same period in Libya, there was too much wishful thinking about the independent capacity and will of our closest European allies, and too little appreciation of how hard it would be to put together any semblance of political order in a society that Qaddafi had stripped bare of modern institutions.

It proved especially hard to imagine the pace of events in Russia after the end of the Cold War. Yeltsin's Russia had shown the limits of American agency, but there was still a presumption that Moscow had little alternative to accepting a subordinate, if grudging, role in Europe. The expansion of NATO membership stayed on autopilot as a matter of U.S. policy, long after its fundamental assumptions should have been reassessed. Commitments originally meant to reflect interests morphed into interests themselves, and the door cracked open to membership for Georgia and Ukraine—the latter a bright red line for any Russian leadership. A Putin regime pumped up by years of high energy prices and wounded pride pushed back hard. And even after Putin's ruthless annexation of Crimea, it proved difficult to imagine that he would stretch his score-settling into a systematic assault on the 2016 American presidential elections.

Clairvoyance is an unattainable quality for any diplomat, but it pays to encourage rigorous questioning of assumptions. Informed by history and experience, diplomats have to be more unconventional in their thinking, and more assertive in testing accepted wisdom. Judgment, balance, and discipline remain the core qualities of diplomatic practice.

* * *

IN TODAY'S WORLD of digital and virtual relationships, there is still no good substitute for old-fashioned human interactions—not in business, romance, or diplomacy. The ability to build personal relationships, bridging what the legendary CBS journalist Edward R. Murrow called the "most critical link in the chain of international communication, the last three feet," remains at the heart of effective diplomacy.

A reaffirmation of the core of American diplomacy, a business of human relationships, is necessary but not sufficient to make it effective for a new and demanding era. We also need to build modern capabilities and skills on top of that traditional foundation. Our efforts at transformation to date have tended to focus on the capillaries of institutional change, rather than the arteries—more on how we look than how we work. That has to change.

We can begin by developing a clearer sense of diplomatic strategy, with a more rigorous operational doctrine.[9] The U.S. military has long embraced the value of systematic case studies and after-action reports. Career diplomats, by contrast, have tended to pride themselves more on their ability to adjust quickly to shifting circumstances than on more systematic attention to lessons learned and long-term thinking. As part of a post-Trump reinvention of diplomacy, there ought to be new emphasis on tradecraft, rediscovering diplomatic history, sharpening negotiation skills, and making the lessons of negotiations like the Dayton Peace Accords or the Iranian nuclear talks accessible to practitioners.

A reinvention of diplomacy would also mean updating American diplomatic priorities, with sharper focus on issues that matter more and more to twenty-first-century foreign policy, particularly technology, economics, energy, and climate. My generation and its predecessor had plenty of specialists in nuclear arms control and conventional energy issues; throw-weights and oil pricing mechanisms were not alien concepts. In my last few years in government, I spent too much time sitting in meetings on the seventh floor of the State Department and in the White House Situation Room with smart, dedicated colleagues, collectively faking it on problems and opportunities flowing from the technology revolution. The department, and the executive branch in general, should be more flexible and creative in order to attract tech talent, including through temporary postings and mid-level entry, just as we did at the dawn of the nuclear age.

The same is true in matters of commerce and economics. In our memo to Warren Christopher a quarter century ago, I wrote that it was already increasingly "hard to separate economic security from national security."[10] It is impossible today. In that paper, we argued that economic diplomacy "has to be a central feature of almost every aspect of our policymaking; nothing will affect our prospects in the world over the rest of this decade more significantly than the skill with which we shape the international economic environment and compete in it."[11] Since George Shultz's tenure, across my whole career as a diplomat, the State Department has been trying fitfully to step up its game on economic statecraft and commercial diplomacy. As an ambassador abroad, I spent a substantial amount of my time promoting American businesses and working to create a level playing field on which they could compete. There is much more that can be done.

Updating our knowledge and skills is a critical factor in molding a new diplomatic doctrine. Applying that doctrine successfully, and building a stronger sense of strategic purpose, also means making State a more dexterous institution. Individual American diplomats overseas can be remarkably innovative and entrepreneurial. As an institution, however, the State Department is rarely accused of being too agile. We have to apply our gardening skills to our own messy plot of ground, and do some serious institutional weeding.

State's personnel system is far too rigid and anachronistic. The evaluation process is wholly incapable of providing honest feedback and incentives for improved performance. Retention, especially of the most promising junior and mid-level officers, is becoming tougher. Promotion is too slow, tours of duty too inflexible, and mechanisms to facilitate careers of families with two working parents insufficient and outdated.

State's internal deliberative process is just as lumbering and conservative, with too many layers of approval and authority. During my last months as deputy secretary, I received a one-page memo on a mundane policy issue—with a page and a half of clearances attached to it. Every imaginable office in the department had reviewed it, and a few that severely strained my imagination. Like a number of my predecessors, I failed in my efforts to streamline the clearance process. The problem was not just the time-consuming nature of the process, but also the tendency to homogenize judgments. If you're the mid-level desk officer responsible for relations with Tunisia, for example, your sense of accountability for the quality of both the prose and the policy recommendations naturally tends to diminish in direct proportion to the number of other layers and officials involved. Responsibility needs to be pushed downward in Washington, and ambassadors in the field need to be empowered to make more decisions locally.

Delayering is long overdue—in Washington and in our embassies. If the right people are put into the right places in a tighter organizational structure, the result can be a more nimble, more responsive institution, better able to make the case for a more central role for diplomacy. And if greater authority is pushed to the field and personnel allocated more strategically to critical posts, State ought to become more quick-footed, and chiefs of mission more adept at directing the work of their interagency country teams. Embassy reporting and analysis will still matter—but less for its volume and more for its distillation of meaning and policy implications from the avalanche of information that flows into the U.S. government.

Smart adaptation to the realities of today's world and policymaking environment will require diplomats to become even more effective at managing physical risk. Diplomacy is a dangerous business. As the walls in the entrance hall of the State Department remind us, with their long lists of names of diplomats who died while serving overseas, physical risks are not new. In the 1970s alone, four U.S. ambassadors were killed at their posts. At the end of the decade, the entire embassy staff in Tehran was taken hostage. Since the Beirut embassy bombings in the early 1980s, and even more so after the East Africa embassy bombings of 1998, American diplomatic facilities have been constructed to strict, often fortresslike specifications. Over the past two decades, the diplomatic security budget increased by roughly 1,000 percent.[12]

Managing physical risk has become progressively more complicated in recent years, as policy choices have put diplomats in greater danger while absence of political courage at home has left them with less backing and support. With many members of Congress alternating between dismissiveness of diplomacy and political scapegoating when attacks occur, the department has inevitably become more risk-averse. As Chris Stevens knew, however, demanding zero security risk can mean zero diplomatic achievements. We have to learn and apply the painful lessons of Benghazi, and take every prudent precaution, but we cannot hole up behind embassy walls and still do our jobs.

* * *

WHAT THIS MOMENT also requires—alongside the refinement of core skills and the adaptation to new realities—is a new domestic compact, a broadly shared sense of American purpose in the world, and of the relationship between disciplined American leadership abroad and middle-class interests at home.

When I was a junior diplomat, George Shultz used to invite outbound U.S. ambassadors into his office for a farewell chat. He would walk over to a large globe near his desk (which many years later I had in my own office as deputy secretary) and ask each ambassador to point to "your country." Invariably, the ambassador would put a finger on the country of her or his assignment. Shultz would then gently move their finger across the globe to the United States—making the not-so-subtle point that diplomats should always remember who they represent and where they come from. Not a bad lesson to reinforce today.

As the 2016 U.S. presidential elections made vivid, the pews in the church of American global leadership have grown deserted. The preaching of the gospel by the foreign policy "blob" continues unabated—often unpersuasive and sometimes a little self-righteous. It's time for some honest stocktaking and a more concerted effort to ensure that American diplomacy is more intimately connected and responsive to the needs and aspirations of the American people.

This is not a novel challenge. One of the most significant, if least noted, passages in Kennan's "Long Telegram" comes at the very end. After elegantly analyzing the sources of Soviet conduct and making the case for containment, Kennan emphasizes in a few dozen words at the conclusion of his fifty-three-hundred-word message that the key to success would be "the point at which domestic and foreign policies meet"—the resilience of our society, and its connection to a disciplined, fundamentally optimistic approach to America's engagement in the world.

The last four administrations have all begun their terms with a similarly sharp focus on "nation-building at home," and a self-conscious determination to be rigorous about overseas commitments. Secretaries of state as different in their backgrounds and styles as Henry Kissinger and Jim Baker had a shared appreciation of the critical value of connecting with the American public, and constantly renewing a workable domestic compact. Kissinger spent much of his last two years as secretary delivering a series of a dozen "heartland" speeches around the country, laying out the case for careful international engagement to safeguard American security and prosperity. Baker understood that politics was as crucial an element of successful diplomacy as geopolitics. Every one of their successors has at one time or another emphasized the tight link between economic security and national security. Our transition memo to the Clinton administration stressed that the new administration would need to "spend considerable time and effort selling the inter-relationship of foreign and domestic policy to the American people. Few people will take that argument for granted any more."[13]

The challenge is that each successive administration often failed to marry its words with deeds, seemingly taking on more and more global responsibility and risks at greater expense and sacrifice for American society, with little obvious, direct benefit. If Martians landed in Washington and discovered that we are nearing our second decade of a military campaign in Afghanistan—despite all the issues elsewhere in the world and all the turbulence at home—they would likely get back on their spacecraft and look for alternative habitat. Most Americans share that sense of disbelief and exasperation about where and how we've invested our blood and treasure in recent decades.

As a result, making the basic argument for diplomacy as a tool of first resort, as a key to realizing the promise of America's pivotal role, will remain an uphill battle. Nevertheless, its main ingredients are straightforward. The starting point is candor and transparency about the purpose and limits of American engagement abroad. It's more effective to level with the American people about the challenges we face and the choices we make than to wrap them in the tattered robe of untempered exceptionalism or fan fears of external threats. Overpromising and underdelivering is the surest way to undermine the case for American diplomacy.

Another ingredient is demonstrating that diplomacy and international influence are aimed as much at facilitating and accelerating domestic renewal as they are at shoring up global order. That does not mean embracing narrow-minded, art-of-the-deal mercantilism. What it does mean is ensuring that the American middle class is positioned as well as possible for success in a hypercompetitive world, that we build open and equitable trading systems, and that we don't shy away from holding to account those who do not play by the rules of the game.

Our challenge is simply to underscore the powerful connection between smart American engagement in the world and our success at home. When the State Department plays a valuable role in nailing down big overseas commercial deals, as we did in a $4 billion Boeing sale in Russia more than a decade ago, it rarely highlights the role of diplomacy in creating thousands of jobs in cities and towns across the United States. There are growing opportunities to work closely with American governors and mayors, many of whom are increasingly active in promoting overseas trade and investment.

A workable domestic compact also depends upon a healthy relationship with Congress. With rare exceptions, members of Congress do not see advocacy for diplomacy as a political asset. The State Department does not have military bases or defense production plants in their states or districts, and includes relatively few constituents among its seventy thousand employees—the majority of whom are in any case foreign nationals working at posts overseas.

Members of Congress are mostly ambivalent about diplomats and diplomacy, although there are still probably a handful who sympathize with the unbridled hostility of Otto Passman, the legendary postwar congressman from Louisiana. "Son," Passman told one of my State Department predecessors a couple generations ago, "I don't smoke and I don't drink. My only pleasure in life is kicking the shit out of the foreign aid program of the United States of America."[14]

I never had the pleasure of dealing with Passman, and most of my encounters with Congress were relatively positive (the Benghazi hearings in 2012–13 were a notable exception, a thoroughly politicized circus aimed less at thoughtful oversight and more at partisan score-settling). As a diplomat, I testified before congressional committees off and on for nearly two decades, never wildly enthusiastic about the experience, but always mindful of its significance.

Like my senior colleagues at State, I also often briefed members informally. While serving as ambassador in Amman following the death of King Hussein, I returned to Washington regularly to lobby for increased financial assistance and support for the bilateral free trade agreement. Those trips always paid important dividends, and I found that ambassadors returning from the field had particular credibility with members of Congress and their staffs. That was particularly true as members traveled abroad less frequently, which was more and more the case in my last decade or so in government, with a few deeply committed exceptions like Senator John McCain.

Compared to the Pentagon and the CIA, however, State was generally far less persistent and systematic in making its case on the Hill. Defense and CIA would deploy significant numbers of personnel to troll the corridors of Congress and seek out opportunities to brief or answer questions. We were more cautious, reactive, and detached at State, and paranoia about missteps led the department to discourage young diplomats from building relationships with congressional staff. Building more effective ties to the Hill is tougher and more labor-intensive now than it was when I entered the Foreign Service, at a time when a relatively small number of senior members, in the congressional leadership and among committee chairs, could command the movement of legislation and budget resources. Power is more diffuse now, just like on the wider international landscape, but that makes congressional outreach all the more important.

A new domestic compact on diplomacy involves reciprocal responsibilities. The State Department and the executive branch have an obligation to follow through on serious reform, streamlining structure, modernizing communications, and finding a rational balance for budgets and roles across the national security community. To make it a two-way street, Congress will need to provide more resources for diplomacy, and offer more flexibility in pooling funds and maximizing their utility. This partnership will only take hold if it's embedded in a wider compact with citizens that restores their faith in the wisdom of American leadership and the significance and utility of diplomacy.

* * *

AS AMERICA ACCELERATED its rise to global power more than a century ago, Teddy Roosevelt took the stage at the Minnesota State Fair and drew new attention to an old proverb. "Speak softly and carry a big stick," he reminded the audience, "and you will go far." His point was not about belligerence, but balance, as the United States launched itself into a complicated and competitive world. Roosevelt saw clearly the interconnected value of force and diplomacy, the need to invest wisely in both to best serve America's interests. The international successes of the next century would not have surprised him, nor would he have been surprised when imbalances between force and diplomacy caused some of our most serious failures.

Of course we ought to ensure that our military's big stick is more imposing than anyone else's, that our tool of last resort is potent and durable. But big sticks will only take us so far, and we need urgently to renovate diplomacy as our tool of first resort. Its importance in a post-primacy world is only growing, and we isolate only ourselves, not our rivals, by its deeply misguided disassembly. Calculated neglect has already done permanent damage, and the sooner we reverse course, the better.

That will be much easier said than done. While there is much that America's diplomats can do to prove their value and relevance, they ultimately depend on wise leadership—in the White House and in Congress—to make the policy and resource decisions and provide the political backing that will unlock the promise of American diplomacy.

The good news is that there are plenty of reasons to be optimistic about the potential of American diplomacy. As I hope the pages of this book have helped to illustrate, it is an honorable profession, filled with good people and strong purpose. Another of Teddy Roosevelt's well-known sayings was that "life's greatest good fortune is the chance to work hard at work worth doing." By that standard, my long experience as an American diplomat was incredibly fortunate. While it may sometimes not seem so apparent in the age of Trump, the experience of the next generation of diplomats holds just as much promise. The image and value of public service is scarred and dented right now, but the diplomatic profession has never mattered more, or been more consequential for our interests at home and abroad.

The rebuilding process will be daunting, but we have a lot going for us—enduring sources of national strength, a pivotal role to play in a competitive world, and no existential threats before us. If we can recover a sense of diplomatic agility out of the muscle-bound national security bureaucracy that we've become in recent years, we can help ensure a new generation of security and prosperity for Americans.

One of the benefits of serving overseas, of a life in diplomacy, is the chance to see your own country through the eyes of others. From that first visit to Egypt at eighteen, to my years at Oxford and postings abroad, to constant travels in senior State Department jobs, I certainly became accustomed to the hostility with which particular American policies are viewed. I knew all too well the resentments that come with our weight in the world and how we have sometimes thrown it around. Through all that mistrust and suspicion, however, I also saw what people expected of us—a sense of possibility, of pragmatism, of recognizing problems and flaws and trying to fix them. That's who we still are—limping from self-inflicted political injury, challenged increasingly in a world of rising powers and shifting currents, but with a resilience that has always set us apart. "You're testing our faith like never before," a longtime European diplomat told me recently, "but I wouldn't bet against you—at least not yet." I wouldn't bet against us either. My faith in our resilience, like my pride in American diplomacy, remains unbounded.

Acknowledgments

My greatest good fortune as a diplomat was the extraordinary company in which I served. While never seeking or getting the credit they deserve, the friends and colleagues who shared this diplomatic journey enriched my life and honored our country with their skill and sacrifice. I could never acknowledge them all in these pages, but I am forever in their debt.

This book was a different kind of journey, but it benefited no less from the thoughtful support of many friends and colleagues.

At the Carnegie Endowment for International Peace, my new professional home, I have been blessed with an exceptional team. Matan Chorev, my chief of staff at the State Department and now at Carnegie, embodies the very best of his generation of foreign policy thinkers and practitioners. Utterly selfless, an elegant writer and editor, and a terrific friend, Matan has been indispensable to this project from its inception. He and Seth Center, a gifted diplomatic historian at the State Department, did a superb job of organizing more than thirty years' worth of memos, cables, and other archival documents and helping me think through how best to structure the book and its arguments.

My treasured friend, Mary Dubose, has put up with me and deftly organized my professional life for nearly three decades, and made sure to keep me focused and on track. Three exceptionally talented James C. Gaither Junior Fellows, Miles Graham, Rachel Mitnick, and Austin Owen, were invaluable research assistants. Kathleen Higgs, Carnegie's library director, could not have been more helpful. Tim Martin, Carnegie's digital director, imagined and built a beautiful website for the book and the digital diplomatic archive. I am especially lucky to have worked closely at Carnegie with two wonderful board chairs, Harvey Fineberg and Penny Pritzker, whose encouragement for this undertaking has been unstinting.

I am deeply grateful to the many indefatigable readers who plowed through all or parts of the draft manuscript. They include: Salman Ahmed, Rich Armitage, Tom Carothers, Derek Chollet, Ryan Crocker, Liz Dibble, Bob Einhorn, Mohamed el-Erian, Jim Fallows, Jeff Feltman, John Lewis Gaddis, Frank Gavin, Jeff Goldberg, Tom Graham, Dan Kurtz-Phelan, Dan Kurtzer, Jim Larocco, Neil MacFarlane, Jef McAllister, Denis McDonough, Aaron Miller, Nader Mousavizadeh, Marwan Muasher, Evan Osnos, Jen Psaki, Philip Remler, Rob Richer, Dennis Ross, Norm Roule, Eugene Rumer, Dan Russell, Karim Sadjadpour, David Satterfield, Jake Sullivan, Ashley Tellis, Dmitri Trenin, Andrew Weiss, and Alice Wells. A presentation of an early draft at Carnegie's "Research in Progress" seminar was particularly useful, and I'm grateful to Milan Vaishnav for the opportunity and to my colleagues for their frank and constructive feedback.

I owe a special debt of gratitude to a first-rate team at the Department of State who made possible the declassification of over one hundred documents and diligently reviewed the manuscript. Behar Godani is a gem, as are her colleagues—Kathy Allegrone, Anne Barbaro, Geoffrey Chapman, Alden Fahy, Paul Hilburn, and Daniel Sanborn. The State Department could not ask for more skilled and committed professionals.

I am also indebted to two remarkable institutions for providing ideal settings for extended periods of writing. Sir John Vickers and the fellows of All Souls College, Oxford, graciously hosted me as a visiting fellow in the autumn of 2017. The Rockefeller Foundation gave me a similar opportunity at its spectacular Bellagio Center in the spring of 2018, where my main challenge was not getting too distracted by the perfect view of Lake Como out my study window.

Andrew Wylie, my literary agent, has been an enthusiastic advocate and marvelous guide, as he has been for so many other lucky authors. I could not have been in better hands than at Random House. Andy Ward is the perfect editor—confident in his craft, and a rigorous and exacting partner. Chayenne Skeete did a wonderful job coordinating the all-star Random House team of Anna Bauer, Debbie Glasserman, Greg Kubie, Beth Pearson, and Katie Tull. Their support meant the world to me, and to the success of this project.

This book, like the rest of my professional life, is built on the bedrock of a loving family. I never had to look any further than my parents for the best role models I could hope to find. With his intellect and integrity, my father epitomized public service. My mother set an impossibly high standard of faith, decency, and compassion. My three brothers have inspired me by their own examples, kept me grounded, and embarrassed me year after year in fantasy football.

Dedicating this work to Lisa barely scratches the surface of what I owe her, and what her love and sacrifice have made possible for me. From that first day in the A-100 entry class almost forty years ago, she has been my best friend and most caring and constructive critic. By far our greatest accomplishments together are our two daughters, Lizzy and Sarah. Now remarkable young adults, they are a source of immense pride and joy. The diplomatic life that unfolds on the pages of this book is full of boldface personalities and dramatic events, but it was family that made it whole.

Appendix

The declassified documents in the pages that follow are a small sample of one diplomat's imperfect efforts to provide ground truths, strategic advice, and—on occasion—disciplined dissent. Nearly one hundred additional cables, memos, and emails from my thirty-three-year career in the Foreign Service are available at burnsbackchannel .com. My hope is that this memoir and archive make vivid the power and purpose of American diplomacy—both in our recent past, and in the era unfolding before us.

Excerpt: Memo to Secretary of State-Designate
Warren Christopher, January 5, 1993, "Parting Thoughts:
U.S. Foreign Policy in the Years Ahead"

In Policy Planning, our task was to look over the horizon and prepare American diplomacy to seize new opportunities and manage emerging challenges. The transition memo excerpted below offered the incoming Clinton administration a strategy for navigating the post–Cold War international landscape.

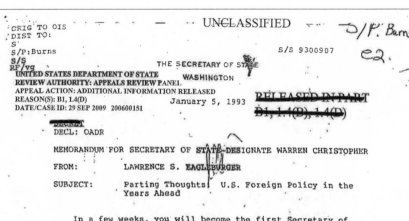

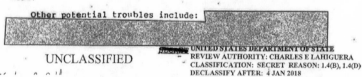

CRIG TO OIS   ·· UNCLASSIFIED   ⊃/F. Burns
DIST TO:
S'
S/P:Burns   S/S 9300907   e2.
S/S
RF/vg   THE SECRETARY OF STATE
UNITED STATES DEPARTMENT OF STATE   WASHINGTON
REVIEW AUTHORITY: APPEALS REVIEW PANEL
APPEAL ACTION: ADDITIONAL INFORMATION RELEASED
REASON(S): B1, 1.4(D)   RELEASED IN PART
DATE/CASE ID: 29 SEP 2009 200600151   January 5, 1993
                                                       B1, 1.4(B), 1.4(D)

          SECRET
          DECL: OADR

     MEMORANDUM FOR SECRETARY OF STATE-DESIGNATE WARREN CHRISTOPHER

          FROM: LAWRENCE S. EAGLEBURGER

          SUBJECT: Parting Thoughts: U.S. Foreign Policy in the
                         Years Ahead

               In a few weeks, you will become the first Secretary of
          State confirmed by the Senate in the post-Cold War era. The
          world that awaits you is a much different place than the one
          you and I have known through many years of government service.
          It is a world in the midst of revolutionary transition, in
          which you will have both an historic opportunity to shape a new
          international order and a sobering collection of problems to
          contend with.

               During your tenure, many achievements are possible: a
          genuine new partnership with Japan for global economic growth
          and security; a new trans-Atlantic compact linking us to the
          European democracies; the gradual incorporation of a reforming
          Russia and the East Europeans into a stable European system;
          peaceful reunification of the Korean peninsula; normalization
          of relations with a reforming Vietnam; the departure of Castro
          and the peaceful emergence of a free Cuba; expansion of free
          trade arrangements and consolidation of democratic institutions
          throughout the Hemisphere; nonracial democracy in South Africa;
          the invigoration of UN peacekeeping and peacemaking
          capabilities; and, not least, a whole series of Arab-Israeli
          peace agreements.

               That's the good news. The bad news is that there are at
          least as many troubles awaiting you as opportunities. Three
          immediate problems top the list, in my view: (1) the possible
          outbreak of a general Balkan war; (2) a breakdown of reform in
          Russia and a reversion to some form of authoritarian rule; and
          (3) the continuing threat of deepening global recession and
          trade wars between regional blocs, fueled by a collapse of the
          Uruguay Round and domestic political weaknesses throughout the
          West.

               Other potential troubles include: B1

UNCLASSIFIED   UNITED STATES DEPARTMENT OF STATE
                                      REVIEW AUTHORITY: CHARLES E LAHIGUERA
                                      CLASSIFICATION: SECRET REASON: 1.4(B), 1.4(D)
                                      DECLASSIFY AFTER: 4 JAN 2018

UNCLASSIFIED

- 2 -

continued trade tensions with the Japanese and perhaps

the lingering danger of nuclear war on either the Korean peninsula or in South Asia; a revived threat to Western interests in the Persian Gulf, from either a rearmed Iran or an unrepentant Saddam; or a breakdown in the Middle East peace process.

With the humility born of recent experience, let me offer a few personal thoughts on the post-Cold War world, and then on what I see to be the main policy challenges before you. To flesh out these questions, I am also sending you a more detailed collection of papers prepared by the Policy Planning Staff. I don't necessarily agree with every argument made in them, but they are a useful and provocative way to think about what lies ahead.

The Post-Cold War Setting

My starting point is a simple one. It seems to me that the basic purposes of American foreign policy are still to ensure the physical security and economic prosperity of our people, and to promote our values wherever we can -- at least in part for the common sense reason that democracies are less likely to threaten us and healthy free market economies are more likely to enhance our own economic well-being. As I look at prospects for advancing those core purposes over the next few years, a number of trends and developments in the post-Cold War world strike me as especially critical.

First, the most obvious consequence of the demise of the Soviet Union is that for the first time in fifty years we do not face a global military adversary. It is certainly conceivable that a return to authoritarianism in Russia or an aggressively hostile China could revive such a global threat, but that is not likely in the short term. We retain a vital stake in preventing domination of four key regions -- Europe, East Asia, the Persian Gulf, and Latin America -- by a hostile, non-democratic regional power. But it is hard to see any immediate regional threats of this nature with the end of the Cold War and the defeat of Iraq.

Second, in the absence of a global military threat, the most important global challenge we face is the emergence of an increasingly interdependent and competitive international economy. Creating and sustaining jobs at home depends more and more on exports, which in turn depend upon both renewed growth in the world economy and improved American competitiveness. We

UNCLASSIFIED

face stiffer and stiffer competition from our closest allies,
continued obstacles in protected markets in Europe and Asia, as
well as the danger of a collapse of order in the global trading
system. We retain substantial internal strengths -- a massive
domestic market, a flexible work force, high productivity, and
traditions of ingenuity and entrepreneurship -- but our
domestic economic shortcomings undercut our competitiveness.
They devalue U.S. leadership and, perhaps more importantly,
threaten domestic support for strong international engagement.

Third, the broadest systemic challenge that we face is the
deconstruction of the system of states that emerged as a result
of World War II and postwar decolonization, and that was held
in place by the Cold War. Alongside the globalization of the
world economy, the international political system is tilting
schizophrenically toward greater fragmentation. Most
dramatically in the former Soviet empire, but more generally
wherever state boundaries and racial, national, ethnic or
religious identities do not coincide, the old state system is
being transformed or is at least under strain. The resulting
chaos is enough to almost -- almost -- make one nostalgic for
the familiar discipline and order of the Cold War. Our basic
stake is in peaceful processes of change rather than in
clinging blindly to existing maps; but promoting such processes
is going to require great patience and skill, and creative ways
of safeguarding human and minority rights. Chaos in the
international political system is also going to confront us
increasingly with the dilemma of whether to take part in
limited military interventions in situations which do not
directly threaten our vital interests, but which endanger
innocent civilian populations and pull hard on our values and
humanitarian traditions. Somalia is only the first of these
kinds of challenges.

Fourth, as peoples reorganize themselves in the wake of the
Cold War, ideological competition continues. The collapse of
Communism represents an historic triumph for democracy and free
markets, but it has not ended history or brought us to the
brink of ideological uniformity. A great wave of democratic
institution-building is taking place, driven by a surging
post-Communist interest in the political and economic
empowerment of individuals. But democratizing societies that
fail to produce the fruits of economic reform quickly, or fail
to accommodate pressures for ethnic self-expression, may slide
back into other "isms", including nationalism or religious
extremism or some combination of the two. In much of the
world, including parts of it that are very important
strategically for us, Islamic conservatism remains a potent
alternative to democracy as an organizing principle.

Fifth, the proliferation of weapons of mass destruction and
advanced delivery systems is likely to be the central security
challenge of the 1990s. It is entirely possible that as many
as eight or ten new powers, many of them authoritarian and

SECRET
- 4 -

anti-Western, could acquire ballistic missiles equipped with
nuclear or biological warheads by the end of the decade. Such
a development would dramatically destabilize important parts of
the world, and could even threaten the physical security of the
United States. Proliferation becomes an even more dangerous
phenomenon when it intersects with fragmentation in the
international political system, increasing the number of
unstable actors with an incentive to acquire weapons of mass
destruction.

Sixth, a variety of new transnational threats have
appeared, particularly environmental degradation, drugs, and
the spread of deadly diseases like AIDS. Such dangers demand
collective action rather than purely national responses. They
also require an aggressive, new international scientific
agenda, in which American leadership will be critical.

Seventh, and perhaps most importantly, you will be tackling
all these challenges at a moment in our history when many
Americans will be preoccupied with domestic problems, and when
budgetary constraints on the conduct of American foreign policy
are likely to be tighter than at any point in the last
half-century. This leaves you and the President with a very
tough task. It was relatively easy during the Cold War to
justify national security expenditures and build support for
sustained American engagement overseas. It is infinitely
harder now. More and more, you will need to link our
involvement clearly and directly to American ideals, and
particularly to American economic needs. And more and more,
you will need to point clearly to what other governments are
doing to bear their fair share of the cost and burden. These
tasks will require a radical restructuring of our national
security institutions, most of which were designed for the Cold
War. And they will require that you and other senior
Administration officials -- and especially the President
himself -- spend considerable time and effort selling the
inter-relationship of foreign and domestic policy to the
American people. Few people will take that argument for
granted any more.

The Importance of American Leadership and Five Key Policy Tests

Against that backdrop, I am convinced absolutely that
American leadership is as important in this period of
revolutionary transition in the international system as it was
during the Cold War. Our self-interest, especially our
economic self-interest, requires it. And for better or worse,
peoples and governments still look to us to make sense of the
changes swirling around them and show some initiative and
purpose. No one else can play that role. The Communist
regimes have collapsed or are discredited. The European

SECRET

UNCLASSIFIED

- 5 -

Community is consumed with its own problems, and by no means as
monolithic in its view of political issues as we once hoped (or
feared) it would be. And the Japanese are neither ready nor
willing for such a task now. The bottom line is that in this
time of uncertainty, the United States has a unique role to
play -- as a provider of reassurance and architect of new
security arrangements; as an aggressive proponent of economic
openness; as an exemplar and advocate of democratic values; and
as a builder and leader of coalitions to deal with the problems
of a chaotic post-Cold War world.

I have yet to see a term or phrase which captures the
essence of America's new role and strategy as neatly as Kennan
did with "containment" at the outset of the U.S.-Soviet
confrontation. While this may simply reflect my own lack of
creativity, I suspect that it may be some time before such a
term emerges, perhaps after the contours of what lies beyond
this transitional period are clearer. In the meantime, I
believe the major challenges you face will fall into five
broad, interconnected categories:

- Renewing the adhesion -- the cement -- that held the
  democratic community together and won the Cold War;

- Promoting long-term expansion of that community to
  include our former Cold War adversaries, while coping
  in the meantime with the massive uncertainties and
  instabilities left in the wake of the collapse of
  Communism;

- Pressing a new regional agenda in what used to be the
  "Third World", composed of conflict resolution,
  nonproliferation, democratic institution-building, and
  economic growth;

- Competing aggressively in an open international
  economic system, while protecting the environment;

- Restructuring our national security institutions for
  the post-Cold War world.

1995 Moscow 883, January 11, 1995,
"Sifting Through the Wreckage: Chechnya and Russia's Future"

Following the collapse of the Soviet Union, violent separatism in the North Caucasus posed an enormous challenge for President Boris Yeltsin: His military's botched attempt to put down the Chechen insurrection during the winter of 1994–95 was emblematic of the "slow crumbling" of the new Russian state. This cable conveyed to Washington the depth of the crisis in Chechnya and its consequences for Russia and U.S. policy.

UNCLASSIFIED U.S. Department of State Case No. MR-2015-07420 Doc No. C06317048 Date: 05/03/2017
SECRET

PTQ3213

RELEASE IN FULL

DECLASSIFIED

SECRET   PTQ3213

PAGE 01   MOSCOW 00883 01 OF 04 111657Z
ACTION SS-00

INFO LOG-00 QASY-00 ADS-00 /000W
————————9ABC4B 111657Z /38
O 111652Z JAN 95
FM AMEMBASSY MOSCOW
TO SECSTATE WASHDC IMMEDIATE 9782
MOSCOW POLITICAL COLLECTIVE
INFO AMEMBASSY TALLINN
AMEMBASSY VILNIUS
AMEMBASSY RIGA
CIS COLLECTIVE

SECRET SECTION 01 OF 04 MOSCOW 000883

EXDIS   DECAPTIONED

E.O.12356: DECL:OADR
TAGS: PREL, RS
SUBJECT: SIFTING THROUGH THE WRECKAGE: CHECHNYA AND RUSSIA'S FUTURE

1. SECRET- ENTIRE TEXT.

SUMMARY AND INTRODUCTION
----

2. THE CHECHEN CRISIS IS FAR FROM OVER, BUT IT HAS
SECRET

SECRET

PAGE 02   MOSCOW 00883 01 OF 04 111657Z
ALREADY LAID BARE THE WEAKNESS OF THE RUSSIAN STATE
AND THE TRAGIC FLAWS OF ITS FIRST DEMOCRATICALLY-
ELECTED PRESIDENT. YELTSIN'S BLUNDERS, BORN IN LARGE
PART OF AN INCREASINGLY INSULAR STYLE OF DECISION
MAKING, HAVE RAISED A NUMBER OF FUNDAMENTAL QUESTIONS.
WHAT ARE THE CONSEQUENCES OF THE CHECHEN DEBACLE FOR
RUSSIA? IS YELTSIN IN CONTROL? WHAT IS HIS FUTURE?

Declassification Authority: Geoffrey W. Chapman, OCA, Senior Reviewer,
A/GIS/IPS

UNCLASSIFIED U.S. Department of State Case No. MR-2015-07420 Doc No. C06317048 Date: 05/03/2017
SECRET

SECRET

WHAT IS THE FUTURE OF REFORM? WHAT ROLE WILL THE
MILITARY PLAY IN RUSSIAN POLITICS? IS A BREAK UP OF
THE RUSSIAN FEDERATION LIKELY? HOW WILL RUSSIAN
FOREIGN POLICY BE AFFECTED? WHAT ARE THE IMPLICATIONS
FOR U.S. POLICY?

3. NOT SURPRISINGLY, THERE ARE NO NEAT ANSWERS TO ANY
OF THESE QUESTIONS. LIKE MOSCOW IN MID-WINTER, THE
RUSSIAN POLITICAL LANDSCAPE TODAY IS MOST ACCURATELY
PORTRAYED IN VARYING SHADES OF GRAY, NOT BLACKS OR
WHITES. NEVERTHELESS, WHAT FOLLOWS IS AN ATTEMPT·TO
PROVIDE SOME VERY PRELIMINARY ANSWERS, OR AT LEAST TO
BETTER FRAME THE QUESTIONS. PARAS 17-23 OFFER SOME
BROAD GUIDELINES FOR US. POLICY. END SUMMARY AND
INTRODUCTION.

THE EMPEROR HAS NO CLOTHES
----

4. THE CHECHEN CRISIS HAS LAID BARE THE WEAKNESS OF
THE RUSSIAN STATE AND THE TRAGIC FLAWS OF ITS FIRST
DEMOCRATICALLY-ELECTED PRESIDENT. MOST RUSSIANS HAVE
BEEN SHOCKED BY THE ABYSMAL PERFORMANCE OF THEIR
                        SECRET

                        SECRET

PAGE 03   MOSCOW 00883 01 OF 04 111657Z
MILITARY, A KEY SYMBOL OF STATE POWER AND ONE OF THE
FEW REMAINING NATIONAL INSTITUTIONS TO HAVE ENJOYED
WIDESPREAD RESPECT. THE MILITARY MACHINE THAT ONCE
BOASTED IT COULD REACH THE ENGLISH CHANNEL IN FORTY-
EIGHT HOURS HAS BEEN UNABLE TO SUBDUE "BANDIT
FORMATIONS" IN A TINY REPUBLIC WITHIN RUSSIA IN OVER A
MONTH. THIS INEPTITUDE -- PROBABLY EVEN MORE THAN THE
LOSS OF CIVILIAN LIVES WHICH HAS SO EXERCISED MOSCOW'S
LIBERAL INTELLIGENTSIA -- HAS LED RUSSIANS, AND
ESPECIALLY ELITES, TO QUESTION BORIS YELTSIN'S
COMPETENCE TO GOVERN.

5. WHAT RUSSIANS ARE WITNESSING IN CHECHNYA IS THE
FURTHER SLOW CRUMBLING OF THEIR STATE. DECAY AND
GOVERNMENTAL INADEQUACY ARE EQUALLY, IF LESS
GRAPHICALLY, APPARENT ELSEWHERE -- IN PUBLIC HEALTH,
THE ENVIRONMENT, ECONOMIC INFRASTRUCTURE, PUBLIC
MORALITY, AND PUBLIC SAFETY AND ORDER. THE POPULAR
MOOD SEEMS AS DOWNBEAT AS MOSCOW'S MID-WINTER GLOOM;
RECENT POLLS SUGGEST THAT OVER TWO-THIRDS OF VOTERS
THINK THE COUNTRY IS GOING IN THE WRONG DIRECTION.

SECRET

6. WHERE DID YELTSIN GO WRONG? HIS EFFORTS OVER THE
PAST YEAR BROUGHT A PERIOD OF RELATIVE STABILITY
WELCOMED BY MOST RUSSIANS, WHO WERE EXHAUSTED BY THE
TUMULTUOUS CHANGES OF RECENT YEARS. BUT YELTSIN MADE
LITTLE HEADWAY IN USING THAT COMPARATIVE POLITICAL
CALM TO CONSOLIDATE STATE, AND PARTICULARLY
DEMOCRATIC, INSTITUTIONS. INSTEAD, HE DREW BACK EVEN
FURTHER FROM THE TIME-CONSUMING AND MESSY PROCESS OF
FORGING A CONSENSUS AMONG DISPARATE POLITICAL FORCES.
SECRET

SECRET

PAGE 04   MOSCOW 00883 01 OF 04 111657Z
HE HAS RELIED INCREASINGLY ON A SMALL, NARROWING
CIRCLE OF ADVISORS WHOSE DISTINGUISHING FEATURE IS
THEIR POLITICAL DEPENDENCE ON YELTSIN HIMSELF.

7. SOME OF THOSE IN THIS INNER CIRCLE -- FIRST
PRESIDENTIAL ASSISTANT ILYUSHIN, SECURITY COUNCIL
SECRETARY LOBOV, AND FIRST BODYGUARD KORZHAKOV COME
IMMEDIATELY TO MIND -- HAVE NEVER BEEN NOTED FOR THEIR
REFORMIST INSTINCTS. OTHERS MAY HAVE MORE LIBERAL
INCLINATIONS, BUT IN WHAT SEEMS THE PREVAILING
SYCOPHANTIC ATMOSPHERE OF KREMLIN COURT POLITICS IT IS
HARD TO KNOW WHETHER THE PRESIDENT IS OFTEN TOLD WHAT
HE DOESN'T WANT TO HEAR. WHILE IT IS IMPOSSIBLE TO BE
CERTAIN, A NUMBER OF OUR CONTACTS HAVE TOLD US
RECENTLY THAT YELTSIN HAS ACCESS TO A VARIETY OF
SOURCES OF INFORMATION (AN OBSERVATION THAT KREMLIN
IRE WITH MEDIA COVERAGE OF CHECHNYA TENDS TO
REINFORCE), BUT TENDS TO RELY ON INACCURATE AND SELF-
SERVING ACCOUNTS FED HIM BY THE POWER MINISTRIES AND

SECRET

SECRET

NNNNPTQ3214

SECRET   PTQ3214

PAGE 01   MOSCOW 00883 02 OF 04 111657Z
ACTION SS-00

INFO LOG-00 OASY-00 ADS-00 /000W
----------------9ABC5B 111657Z /38
O 111652Z JAN 95
FM AMEMBASSY MOSCOW
TO SECSTATE WASHDC IMMEDIATE 9783
MOSCOW POLITICAL COLLECTIVE
INFO AMEMBASSY TALLINN
AMEMBASSY VILNIUS
AMEMBASSY RIGA
CIS COLLECTIVE

S E C R E T SECTION 02 OF 04 MOSCOW 000883

EXDIS

E.O.12356: DECL:OADR
TAGS: PREL, RS
SUBJECT: SIFTING THROUGH THE WRECKAGE: CHECHNYA AND
RUSSIA'S FUTURE

THE INTELLIGENCE SERVICES. IT IS ALSO IMPOSSIBLE TO
BE CERTAIN TO WHAT EXTENT YELTSIN IS MANIPULATED BY
THOSE AROUND HIM; WHAT SEEMS CLEAR IS THAT THE CLOSED
DECISION MAKING SYSTEM WHICH HE HAS OPTED FOR OFFERS
FEW BRAKES ON BAD ADVICE OR BAD INSTINCTS.

8. THE CHECHEN DISASTER IS IN SOME WAYS A LOGICAL
            SECRET

SECRET

PAGE 02   MOSCOW 00883 02 OF 04 111657Z
OUTGROWTH OF THIS INSULAR STYLE. STEP BY STEP OVER
RECENT MONTHS, YELTSIN AND HIS ADVISORS HAVE BLUNDERED
FURTHER INTO A QUAGMIRE, WITH BAD POLICY CHOICES
BEGETTING WORSE ONES. THE TRAGIC IRONY IS THAT THE

SECRET

SAME MULISH STUBBORNNESS THAT PRODUCED YELTSIN'S
GREATEST TRIUMPHS MAY NOW PROVE TO BE HIS UNDOING.

9. YELTSIN'S MISMANAGEMENT OF THE CHECHEN CRISIS,
COUPLED WITH HIS INCREASINGLY DISTANT LEADERSHIP STYLE
AND THE CONTINUING PAIN OF ECONOMIC TRANSITION, HAS
LED TO A COLLAPSE OF HIS POPULAR SUPPORT. IN A RECENT
NATIONWIDE POLL, ONLY 18 PERCENT OF RUSSIANS EXPRESSED
CONFIDENCE IN HIS LEADERSHIP -- AND THAT WAS BEFORE
THE ASSAULT ON GROZNYY WAS LAUNCHED. MORE IMPORTANT,
THE CHECHEN FIASCO HAS RESULTED IN A PROFOUND LOSS OF
RESPECT FOR YELTSIN AMONG KEY POLITICAL ELITES --
INCLUDING THE MILITARY, SECURITY FORCES, AND THE
MEDIA. HE CAN NO LONGER UNIFY THE COUNTRY AS HE ONCE
DID IN THE WAKE OF THE FAILED AUGUST 1991 PUTSCH. TO
RESTORE HIS SAGGING FORTUNES, HE IS RESORTING TO MORE
NATIONALISTIC RHETORIC AND POLICIES. INDEED, MANY OF
HIS CRITICS -- BOTH RADICAL REFORMERS AND HARDLINE
OPPONENTS -- ARE ARGUING THAT HE HAS ALREADY STARTED
DOWN THE PATH OF AN AUTHORITARIAN RESTORATION.

THE FUTURE OF REFORM
----

10. WHILE IT WOULD BE A MISTAKE TO DISCOUNT THIS
POSSIBILITY, THE CURRENT SITUATION DOES NOT LEND
                    SECRET

                    SECRET

PAGE 03   MOSCOW 00883 02 OF 04 111657Z
ITSELF TO NEAT CONCLUSIONS, EITHER ABOUT YELTSIN'S
FUTURE OR THE FATE OF POLITICAL AND ECONOMIC REFORMS.
LIKE MOSCOW IN MID-WINTER, THE RUSSIAN POLITICAL
LANDSCAPE TODAY IS MOST ACCURATELY PORTRAYED IN SHADES
OF GRAY, NOT BLACKS OR WHITES. WHILE IT IS NOW TOO
LATE FOR YELTSIN TO RECOVER THE HEROIC DEMOCRATIC
MANTLE HE ONCE WORE, IT IS STILL NOT TOO LATE
(ASSUMING NO CATASTROPHIC DETERIORATION OF HIS HEALTH)
FOR HIM TO MAINTAIN ENOUGH OF HIS AUTHORITY TO LIMP
ALONG TO THE SCHEDULED PARLIAMENTARY ELECTIONS AT THE
END OF THIS YEAR AND PRESIDENTIAL ELECTIONS IN JUNE
1996, AVOIDING AN EXTRA-CONSTITUTIONAL UPHEAVAL. HE
STILL APPEARS TO RETAIN SUPPORT AMONG POLITICAL ELITES
IN RUSSIA'S REGIONS, WHERE THE CHECHEN CRISIS HAS SO
FAR NOT HAD THE RESONANCE THAT IT HAS HAD IN THE
CAPITAL. BLUNDERING IN CHECHNYA HAS SEVERELY TESTED
MILITARY DISCIPLINE, BUT IT DOES NOT YET APPEAR TO BE
AT THE BREAKING POINT.

SECRET

11. THAT ASSUMES THAT YELTSIN "TAKES" GROZNYY SHORTLY
AND KEEPS THE VIOLENCE THAT WILL INEVITABLY CONTINUE
IN CHECHNYA AT A MORE MANAGEABLE AND LESS VISIBLE
LEVEL. IT ALSO ASSUMES THAT HE CHANNELS DISCONTENT
WITHIN THE MILITARY BY PLEDGING REAL REFORM AND MORE
RESOURCES FOR THE MILITARY, AND SHAKES UP THE SENIOR
LEADERSHIP -- WHICH IS A QUESTION NOT JUST OF FIRING
GRACHEV BUT OF FINDING THE RIGHT PERSON TO REPLACE
HIM. THE RESULT WILL NOT BE PRETTY, BUT IT WOULD BE
ENOUGH TO SUSTAIN YELTSIN IN POWER UNTIL THE END OF
HIS PRESIDENTIAL TERM, AND IN THE PROCESS BUY MORE
TIME FOR RUSSIA'S HALTING EXPERIMENT WITH POLITICAL
SECRET

SECRET

PAGE 04   MOSCOW 00883 02 OF 04 111657Z
PLURALISM.

12. IT IS IMPORTANT TO KEEP IN MIND THAT THE CHECHEN
TRAGEDY HAS THUS FAR DEMONSTRATED THE RESILIENCE OF AT
LEAST SOME OF THE POLITICAL CHANGES OF RECENT YEARS.
PUBLIC INDIGNATION OVER CHECHNYA HAS BEEN FUELED BY
THE RUSSIAN MEDIA'S INDEPENDENT, VIGOROUS, AND
CRITICAL REPORTING, REINFORCED BY WESTERN MEDIA
BROADCASTS, TO WHICH RUSSIANS HAVE REGULAR AND
UNIMPEDED ACCESS. THE FAILURE TO CRACK DOWN ON THE
MEDIA MAY BE ONLY FURTHER EVIDENCE OF THE STATE'S
WEAKNESS, BUT IT COULD ALSO MEAN THAT RESPECT FOR
PLURALISM IS TAKING ROOT.

13. ANY EFFORT TO RESTORE AUTHORITARIAN RULE IN
RUSSIA WOULD ALSO BE TEMPERED BY CONTINUING DEVOLUTION
OF POWER AND AUTHORITY TO RUSSIA'S REGIONS. AGAINST
THE BACKGROUND OF THE CENTRAL GOVERNMENT'S DECLINE,
REGIONAL ELITES ARE CONSOLIDATING POWER LOCALLY. MOST

SECRET

~~SECRET~~

NNNNPTQ3216

SECRET   PTQ3216

PAGE 01   MOSCOW 00883 03 OF 04 111658Z
ACTION SS-00

INFO LOG-00 OASY-00 ADS-00   /000W
------------------9ABC6D 111658Z /38
O 111652Z JAN 95
FM AMEMBASSY MOSCOW
TO SECSTATE WASHDC IMMEDIATE 9784
MOSCOW POLITICAL COLLECTIVE
INFO AMEMBASSY TALLINN
AMEMBASSY VILNIUS
AMEMBASSY RIGA
CIS COLLECTIVE

S E C R E T SECTION 03 OF 04 MOSCOW 000883

EXDIS

E.O.12356: DECL:OADR
TAGS: PREL, RS
SUBJECT: SIFTING THROUGH THE WRECKAGE: CHECHNYA AND
RUSSIA'S FUTURE

ENJOY THEIR NEWFOUND PREROGATIVES AND WILL BE LOATHE
TO CEDE THEM BACK TO MOSCOW UNDER ANY CONDITIONS.
THIS IS A HEALTHY DEVELOPMENT, FROM OUR PERSPECTIVE,
AS LONG AS IT DOES NOT PROCEED TO THE POINT WHERE IT
THREATENS RUSSIA'S UNITY. IF IT DOES, THAT IS MORE
LIKELY TO BE THE RESULT OF DECAY AND DISARRAY IN
MOSCOW THAN OF ANY REGIONAL URGE TO SEPARATISM, WHICH
                    SECRET

SECRET

PAGE 02   MOSCOW 00883 03 OF 04 111658Z
REMAINS GENERALLY WEAK.

14. EVEN IN THE BEST SCENARIO, HOWEVER, RUSSIA'S
POLITICAL EVOLUTION WILL REMAIN A LONG, UNEVEN, AND
VOLATILE PROCESS. UNDER YELTSIN AND HIS SUCCESSORS,
THERE IS LIKELY TO BE A CONSTANT, INTENSE
PREOCCUPATION WITH RESTORING EFFECTIVE STATE POWER AND
RECOVERING RUSSIAN NATIONAL PRIDE, NOW FURTHER
TARNISHED BY THE SELF-INFLICTED WOUND OF CHECHNYA.
THAT WILL MEAN A CONSTANT RISK FOR THE FORESEEABLE
FUTURE THAT RUSSIA'S EXPERIMENT WITH POLITICAL
PLURALISM WILL BE UNDERMINED OR OVERTURNED BY A MORE
FUNDAMENTAL DESIRE TO ENSURE ORDER IN SOCIETY. MUCH
WILL OF COURSE DEPEND ON THE ECONOMY; IF THE 1995
BUDGET FALLS APART AS A RESULT OF CHECHNYA
EXPENDITURES AND BROADER INDISCIPLINE, AND THUS
INFLATION CONTINUES TO RISE, THE POLITICAL
CONSEQUENCES COULD BE SEVERE.

MASKING RUSSIA'S WEAKNESS IN FOREIGN POLICY

15. IN FOREIGN POLICY TERMS, MILITARY INTERVENTION IN
CHECHNYA HAS BEEN A DISASTER FOR RUSSIA -- ISOLATING
IT INTERNATIONALLY, EXPOSING ITS WEAKNESS TO OTHER
FORMER SOVIET STATES OVER WHICH IT SEEKS INFLUENCE AS
WELL AS TO ATTENTIVE REGIONAL POWERS LIKE IRAN, CHINA,
AND TURKEY, AND PLAYING INTO THE HANDS OF FORMER
WARSAW PACT STATES WHO WILL SEEK TO ACCELERATE THE
PROCESS OF NATO EXPANSION. RUSSIANS ACROSS THE
SECRET

SECRET

PAGE 03   MOSCOW 00883 03 OF 04 111658Z
POLITICAL SPECTRUM ALREADY FEEL AN ACUTE SENSE THAT
THE WEST IS TAKING ADVANTAGE OF RUSSIA'S WEAKNESS, AND
THAT IS LIKELY TO BECOME MORE RATHER THAN LESS
PRONOUNCED AS A RESULT OF THE DEEPLY EMBARRASSING
EXPERIENCE IN CHECHNYA. IN A CHAOTIC DOMESTIC
POLITICAL SETTING, ASSERTIVE POLICIES ABROAD REMAIN
ONE OF THE FEW THEMES WHICH UNITE RUSSIANS.

16. ARMED WITH A VERY WEAK HAND, AND INCREASINGLY
ESTRANGED FROM RADICAL REFORMERS AND DEPENDENT ON
YELTSIN HIMSELF, ANDREY KOZYREV WILL CONTINUE TO
SEARCH FOR TACTICAL OPPORTUNITIES TO ASSERT RUSSIA'S
GREAT POWER STATUS, WITH AN EYE TO FORM (A SEAT AT THE
TABLE OF THE "POLITICAL G-8") AS MUCH AS SUBSTANCE.
RUSSIAN DIPLOMACY IS LIKELY TO REMAIN PRIMARILY
FOCUSED ON THE NEAR ABROAD AND EUROPEAN SECURITY. ON

SECRET

THE FORMER, THE GOVERNMENT OF RUSSIA WILL AIM AT A
MINIMUM TO PREVENT "OUTSIDE POWERS" FROM GAINING
INFLUENCE AT RUSSIAN EXPENSE, MINDFUL OF GROWING
ECONOMIC CONSTRAINTS ON RUSSIAN AMBITIONS. ON THE
LATTER, DRIVEN BY A FEAR OF EXCLUSION AND A PROFOUND
SENSE OF STRATEGIC WEAKNESS, KOZYREV WILL SEEK TO BUY
TIME ON NATO EXPANSION AND STRETCH OUT THE PROCESS FOR
AS LONG AS POSSIBLE.

COPING WITH UNCERTAINTY: U.S.-RUSSIAN RELATIONS IN
THE MONTHS AHEAD

17. AGAINST THE BACKDROP OF MOUNTING DISARRAY IN
SECRET

SECRET

PAGE 04   MOSCOW 00883 03 OF 04 111658Z
RUSSIA AND CONTINUING RUSSIAN ASSERTIVENESS IN FOREIGN
POLICY, MANAGING THE U.S.-RUSSIAN RELATIONSHIP WILL BE
MORE DIFFICULT, MORE FRUSTRATING, AND LESS PREDICTABLE
THAN AT ANY TIME SINCE THE FALL OF THE SOVIET UNION.
GIVEN THE INCREASINGLY CLOSED AND UNSTABLE STYLE OF
THE CURRENT LEADERSHIP, AND THE ABSENCE OF REAL
INSTITUTIONS TO ABSORB POLITICAL PRESSURES, SUDDEN
TURNS ARE INEVITABLE, AND WE WILL NEED TO LEARN TO
XPECT THE UNEXPECTED. OUR INFLUENCE OVER EVENTS IN
RUSSIA WILL REMAIN MARGINAL, AND OUR RANGE OF POLICY
CHOICES WILL OFTEN BE UNSATISFYING. NEVERTHELESS,
SEVERAL KEY POINTS ARE WORTH BEARING IN MIND AS WE
FRAME OUR POLICY.

18. FIRST, WE NEED TO KEEP A SENSE OF PERSPECTIVE.
RUSSIA IS EMBARKED UPON A LONG-TERM, REVOLUTIONARY
PROCESS OF RE-DEFINITION, WHOSE ULTIMATE OUTCOME WILL
REMAIN UNCERTAIN FOR YEARS TO COME. RUSSIA'S
AUTHORITARIAN TRADITIONS WEIGH HEAVILY ON THIS

SECRET

NNNNPTQ3217

SECRET　　PTQ3217

PAGE 01　　　MOSCOW 00883 04 OF 04 111658Z
ACTION SS-00

INFO LOG-00 OASY-00 ADS-00　/000W
　　　　　　　　　—————9ABC78　111658Z /38
O 111652Z JAN 95
FM AMEMBASSY MOSCOW
TO SECSTATE WASHDC IMMEDIATE 9785
MOSCOW POLITICAL COLLECTIVE
INFO AMEMBASSY TALLINN
AMEMBASSY VILNIUS
AMEMBASSY RIGA
CIS COLLECTIVE

S E C R E T SECTION 04 OF 04 MOSCOW 000883

EXDIS

E.O.12356: DECL:OADR
TAGS: PREL, RS
SUBJECT: SIFTING THROUGH THE WRECKAGE: CHECHNYA AND
RUSSIA'S FUTURE

PROCESS, BUT THERE ARE ALSO UNMISTAKABLE SIGNS THAT
POLITICAL PLURALISM (THE INDEPENDENCE OF THE MEDIA IN
THE CHECHEN CRISIS, FOR EXAMPLE) AND ECONOMIC REFORM
(THE EMERGENCE OF A DYNAMIC PRIVATE SECTOR) ARE AT
LEAST BEGINNING TO TAKE ROOT. THOSE SYSTEMIC CHANGES
WERE NOT PRODUCED BY A SINGLE POLITICAL PERSONALITY,
NOR ARE THEY LIKELY TO BE EASILY ERASED.
　　　　　　　　SECRET

SECRET

SECRET

PAGE 02   MOSCOW 00883 04 OF 04 111658Z

19. SECOND, WE MUST CONTINUE TO EMPHASIZE OUR SUPPORT
FOR SUSTAINABLE REFORM POLICIES, NOT PARTICULAR
PERSONALITIES. WE REMAIN IN CONTACT WITH A BROAD
RANGE OF RUSSIAN LEADERS, AND WE WILL CONTINUE TO CAST
A WIDE NET. THAT DOES NOT MEAN THAT WE SHOULD RUSH TO
DISTANCE OURSELVES FROM YELTSIN. YELTSIN AS CATALYST
FOR REFORM HAS BEEN SEVERELY WOUNDED, MOST LIKELY
FATALLY SO; BUT HE IS STILL THE ELECTED PRESIDENT OF
RUSSIA. THE BROADER POINT IS THAT WE SHOULD AVOID THE
TEMPTATION TO OVER IDENTIFY WITH, OR OVERREACT TO, ANY
PARTICULAR POLITICAL FIGURE.

20. THIRD, FAR FROM ABANDONING HOPE IN POLITICAL
REFORM IN RUSSIA, WE SHOULD REDOUBLE OUR EFFORTS IN
THOSE AREAS IN WHICH POTENTIAL COUNTERBALANCES TO
AUTHORITARIAN TRENDS ARE MOST LIKELY TO EMERGE.
ACTIVE SUPPORT FOR AN INDEPENDENT MEDIA IS ONE CLEAR
EXAMPLE. SO ARE STEPS -- ESPECIALLY THE CREATIVE USE
OF EXCHANGE VISITS -- TO BOLSTER THE LEGISLATIVE AND
JUDICIAL BRANCHES OF GOVERNMENT AT ALL LEVELS, AND TO
CULTIVATE REGIONAL ELITES WHO MAY INCREASINGLY HOLD
THE KEY TO THE RUSSIAN POLITICAL BALANCE. A FOCUSED
MILITARY-TO-MILITARY CONTACT PROGRAM IS ANOTHER
VALUABLE TOOL.

21. FOURTH, WE NEED TO RECOGNIZE THAT ASSERTIVENESS
AND NATIONALIST THEMES WILL CONTINUE TO FIGURE HEAVILY
IN RUSSIAN FOREIGN POLICY, BUT THAT DOES NOT
NECESSARILY MEAN THAT COLLISIONS WITH CORE U.S.
INTERESTS ARE UNAVOIDABLE. YELTSIN'S RECENT POLICIES,
                    SECRET

SECRET

PAGE 03   MOSCOW 00883 04 OF 04 111658Z
STRONG NATIONALIST RHETORIC NOTWITHSTANDING, HAVE BEEN
BROADLY CONSISTENT WITH OUR GOALS IN KEY AREAS LIKE
UKRAINE -- BY FAR OUR GREATEST CONCERN IN THE NEAR
ABROAD. AND WHATEVER THE INTENTIONS OF YELTSIN'S
SUCCESSORS, RUSSIAN MILITARY AND ECONOMIC CAPABILITIES
WILL LIKELY BE SHARPLY CONSTRAINED FOR YEARS TO COME.

22. FINALLY, AND PERHAPS MOST IMPORTANTLY, WE NEED TO
PRIORITIZE BETTER AMONG THE MANY CONCERNS ON OUR
AGENDA WITH THE RUSSIANS. TWO YEARS AGO, WE COULD
PRETTY MUCH HAVE IT OUR WAY ON A WHOLE RANGE OF
ISSUES, SO LONG AS WE PAID SOME MINIMAL DEFERENCE TO
RUSSIAN SENSIBILITIES. THAT IS NO LONGER THE CASE.

SECRET

WE CAN'T SUCCEED IF WE DEFINE ALL OUR CONCERNS AS HIGH PRIORITY; AND WE CAN'T INSIST ON MAKING EVERY PROBLEM A TEST OF THE RELATIONSHIP.

23. STEADINESS AND CONSISTENCY OF PURPOSE WILL BE HARD TO MAINTAIN AMIDST DEEPENING DOMESTIC PRESSURES IN BOTH RUSSIA AND THE UNITED STATES. THERE ARE DANGERS ON BOTH SIDES OF CONTRIBUTING TO SELF-FULFILLING PROPHECIES; RUSSIANS IN PARTICULAR HAVE TENDED SINCE NOVEMBER 8 TO SEE GREATER FRICTIONS WITH THE U.S. AS INEVITABLE, AND HAVE PROBABLY BEEN MORE PRONE TO TAKE RISKS IN RELATIONS WITH US AS A RESULT. THERE ARE ROUGH WATERS AHEAD, FOR RUSSIA AND FOR U.S. POLICY, BUT WE NEED TO TRY AS BEST WE CAN TO KEEP OUR COURSE PLOTTED ON LONG-TERM POSSIBILITIES FOR CHANGE IN RUSSIA WHICH REMAIN PROFOUNDLY IN OUR INTEREST. PICKERING

SECRET

SECRET

PAGE 04   MOSCOW 00883 04 OF 04 111658Z

1999 Amman 1059, February 7, 1999,
"King Hussein's Legacy and Jordan's Future"

The death of King Hussein—the Middle East's longest-serving ruler—was a traumatic event for Jordan and a pivotal moment for the country's relationship with the United States. This cable outlined the challenges facing King Abdullah II as he took the throne, and it argued for doing everything we could to support a critical partner during a time of tumultuous transition.

C06323486 ED U.S. Department of State Case No. MP-2015-07420 Doc No. C06323486 Date: 06/27/2017

DECLASSIFIED

~~CONFIDENTIAL~~ PTO8362

RELEASE IN PART
1.4(D)

PAGE 01   AMMAN 01059 01 OF 02 071239Z
ACTION NODS-00

INFO LOG-00 CCOE-00 SAS-00   /000W
----------------A006D8 071239Z /38
O 071242Z FEB 99
FM AMEMBASSY AMMAN
TO SECSTATE WASHDC IMMEDIATE 1223

~~CONFIDENTIAL~~ SECTION 01 OF 02 AMMAN 001059

NODIS   DECAPTIONED
FOR THE PRESIDENT AND SECRETARY ALBRIGHT FROM AMBASSADOR

E.O. 12958: DECL: 2/7/19
TAGS: PREL, JO
SUBJECT: KING HUSSEIN'S LEGACY AND JORDAN'S FUTURE

CLASSIFIED BY AMBASSADOR WILLIAM J. BURNS FOR REASON 1.5 (B) AND (D)

1. (C) MR. PRESIDENT: JOHN FOSTER DULLES REPORTEDLY SAID SOME FORTY-FIVE YEARS AGO THAT KING HUSSEIN WAS "AN IMPRESSIVE YOUNG FELLOW. IT'S A SHAME NEITHER HE NOR HIS COUNTRY WILL LAST VERY LONG." HUSSEIN PROVED FAR MORE RESOURCEFUL THAN DULLES AND MANY OTHERS COULD IMAGINE. HE TOOK AN IMPOVERISHED, BARELY LITERATE SOCIETY AND TURNED IT INTO A RELATIVELY STABLE, MODERN STATE. IN A REGION HARDLY NOTED FOR SUCH TRAITS, HUSSEIN BUILT A COUNTRY WITH A REPUTATION FOR TOLERANCE AND OPENNESS, AND A COMMITMENT TO LIVING IN PEACE WITH ITS NEIGHBORS. WHILE HE MADE HIS SHARE OF MISTAKES ALONG THE WAY, HE TOUCHED US ALL DEEPLY WITH HIS COURAGE AND

~~CONFIDENTIAL~~

PAGE 02   AMMAN 01059 01 OF 02 071239Z
DECENCY -- NEVER MORE SO THAN IN HIS LAST HEROIC BATTLE WITH THE CANCER THAT KILLED HIM.

THE CHALLENGES AHEAD
----

2. (C) KING HUSSEIN LEAVES BEHIND A JORDAN INFINITELY BETTER OFF THAN WHAT HE INHERITED NEARLY HALF A CENTURY AGO, BUT STILL BURDENED WITH ENORMOUS CHALLENGES. CHIEF AMONG THEM IS AN ECONOMY IN DEEP TROUBLE. IF YOU WERE TO ASK MOST JORDANIANS IF THEY WERE BETTER OFF NOW THAN WHEN YOU LAST VISITED JORDAN FOUR YEARS AGO, THE ANSWER WOULD BE A RESOUNDING "NO." UNEMPLOYMENT IS TWENTY-FIVE PERCENT AND RISING; STANDARDS OF LIVING ARE FALLING; AND THE GAP BETWEEN THE CONSPICUOUSLY-CONSUMING ELITE OF WEST AMMAN AND THE REST OF THE COUNTRY IS GROWING. ECONOMIC WEAKNESS EXPOSES JORDAN TO REGIONAL PREDATORS, LIKE SYRIA AND IRAQ, AND MAKES IT MUCH HARDER TO DEAL WITH STRUCTURAL CHALLENGES LIKE BROADENING POLITICAL PARTICIPATION AND INTEGRATING JORDANIANS OF PALESTINIAN ORIGIN INTO

Declassification Authority: Geoffrey W. Chapman, OCA, Senior Reviewer, A/GIS/IPS

UNCLASSIFIED U.S. Department of State Case No. MP-2015-07420 Doc No. C06323486 Date: 06/27/2017

A POLITICAL SYSTEM FROM WHICH THEY HAVE BEEN LARGELY EXCLUDED FOR DECADES.

3. (C) HOW JORDAN RESPONDS TO ALL THOSE CHALLENGES MATTERS TO US FOR SOME VERY PRACTICAL, UNSENTIMENTAL REASONS. WITHOUT A STABLE PARTNER ON THE EAST BANK OF THE JORDAN RIVER, THE PALESTINIAN-ISRAELI PEACE PROCESS WOULD BECOME MUCH MORE PROBLEMATIC. WITHOUT JORDAN'S SUPPORT, OUR STRATEGY IN IRAQ WOULD BECOME HARD TO SUSTAIN. IF WE DIDN'T HAVE A FRIENDLY STATE AT THE POLITICAL AND GEOGRAPHICAL CENTER OF THE REGION, WE'D HAVE TO TRY TO INVENT ONE. FOR ALL THOSE REASONS, WE HAVE A POWERFUL STAKE IN HELPING THE JORDANIANS NAVIGATE THROUGH WHAT IS BOUND TO BE THE MOST TRAUMATIC
                                    CONFIDENTIAL

PAGE 03   AMMAN 01059 01 OF 02 071239Z
PERIOD IN THEIR HISTORY, AS THEY COPE WITH THE LOSS OF THE ONLY LEADER MOST OF THEM HAVE EVER KNOWN.

A TIME OF TESTING FOR ABDULLAH
----

4. (C) IT'S HARD TO IMAGINE A MUCH MORE INTIMIDATING SET OF CIRCUMSTANCES FOR A NEW HEAD OF STATE THAN THOSE FACING KING ABDULLAH. IN THE LAST TWO WEEKS, HE HAS GONE FROM SPECIAL FORCES COMMANDER TO CROWN PRINCE TO REGENT TO KING, SUCCEEDING ONE OF THE LAST TRULY LEGENDARY FIGURES ON THE WORLD STAGE. BUT ABDULLAH HASN'T BUCKLED UNDER THE PRESSURE YET, AND I DON'T THINK HE WILL. HE STILL HAS A LOT TO LEARN ABOUT NON-MILITARY ISSUES; HOWEVER, HE HAS THE SAME RESTLESS ENERGY AND TOUCH WITH PEOPLE THAT HUSSEIN ALWAYS HAD, AND HIS LOYALTY TO HIS FATHER AND TO JORDAN IS INTENSE. (AT ONE POINT IN THE 1980'S, WHEN HUSSEIN WAS FACING ONE OF HIS PERIODIC ROUNDS OF ASSASSINATION THREATS, ABDULLAH SLEPT OUTSIDE HIS FATHER'S BEDROOM DOOR WITH A PISTOL FOR NIGHT AFTER NIGHT.)

5. (C)
                                                                                            1.4(
                                                                    HASSAN IS NOT
HAVING AN EASY TIME ADJUSTING TO BEING DUMPED AFTER THIRTY-FOUR YEARS AS CROWN PRINCE, BUT HE HAS BEHAVED WITH DIGNITY AND IS READY TO TRY TO PLAY A CONSTRUCTIVE ROLE. ABDULLAH'S WIFE, RANIA, IS A PARTICULAR SOURCE OF STRENGTH AND COMMON SENSE. HER PALESTINIAN ORIGIN MAKES HER A NATURAL POLITICAL ASSET; EVEN MORE IMPORTANT HAS BEEN HER LEVELLING INFLUENCE ON ABDULLAH AND THE REST OF THE ROYAL FAMILY OVER THE PAST TWO DRAMATIC WEEKS. SHE HAS ALREADY
                                    CONFIDENTIAL

PAGE 04   AMMAN 01059 01 OF 02 071239Z
ENCOURAGED ABDULLAH TO REACH OUT AND BROADEN HIS CIRCLE OF ADVISERS, WHICH FITS BOTH HIS NATURAL INCLUSIVE BENT AND HIS NEED TO SHOW THAT HE IS MORE THAN JUST A MILITARY MAN.

OUR ROLE
----

6. (C) AS ABDULLAH COPES WITH A DIFFICULT TRANSITION, WE WILL NEED
TO TRY TO SUPPLY A STEADINESS AND SENSE OF PERSPECTIVE THAT THE
JORDANIANS MAY BE AT LEAST TEMPORARILY INCAPABLE OF PROVIDING
THEMSELVES. IT IS WORTH KEEPING IN MIND SEVERAL GENERAL POINTS:

-- FIRST, OUR SUPPORT WILL BE AT LEAST AS IMPORTANT SIX MONTHS OR
A YEAR DOWN THE ROAD AS IT IS NOW. JORDANIANS ARE LIKELY TO RALLY
AROUND ABDULLAH IN THE SHORT RUN, AND OUR EFFORTS AND THOSE OF
OTHERS TO STABILIZE THE DINAR AND SHORE UP JORDAN HAVE BEEN VERY
TIMELY. BUT THE REAL CHALLENGE TO ABDULLAH COULD COME SOME MONTHS

CONFIDENTIAL

CONFIDENTIAL   PTQ1033

PAGE 01   AMMAN 01059 02 OF 02 071239Z
ACTION NODS-00

INFO LOG-00 CCOE-00 SAS-00   /000W
              -----------------A006DD 071239Z /38
O 071242Z FEB 99
FM AMEMBASSY AMMAN
TO SECSTATE WASHDC IMMEDIATE 1224

C O N F I D E N T I A L SECTION 02 OF 02 AMMAN 001059

NODIS
FOR THE PRESIDENT AND SECRETARY ALBRIGHT FROM AMBASSADOR

E.O. 12958: DECL: 2/7/19
TAGS: PREL, JO
SUBJECT: KING HUSSEIN'S LEGACY AND JORDAN'S FUTURE

AHEAD, IF THE ECONOMY REMAINS STUCK IN THE MUD AND THE REGIONAL
PICTURE FAILS TO IMPROVE. OUR COMBINED ECONOMIC AND MILITARY
ASSISTANCE PROGRAM, WHICH INCLUDING SUPPLEMENTAL REQUESTS SHOULD
TOTAL $1 BILLION OVER THE NEXT THREE YEARS, PROVIDES AN EXCELLENT
BASIS FOR PROVIDING STRONG SUPPORT.

-- SECOND, WE WILL NEED TO BE CAREFUL NOT TO OVERLOAD THE CIRCUITS
WITH ABDULLAH, ESPECIALLY AT FIRST. HE IS GENUINELY COMMITTED TO
THE MAIN POLICY LINES LAID DOWN BY HIS FATHER, BUT WILL NEED A
LITTLE TIME TO FIND HIS FOOTING. WE SHOULD ALSO AVOID FEEDING ANY
PERCEPTION THAT WE ARE TRYING TO TAKE ADVANTAGE OF THE TRANSITION
TO BEND JORDANIAN POLICY IN OUR DIRECTION.

1.4(D

-- THIRD, THE TRANSITION IN JORDAN IS JUST THE FIRST IN A SERIES
OF SUCCESSIONS LIKELY TO OCCUR IN A REGION DOMINATED FOR DECADES BY

THE SAME LEADERS. CIRCUMSTANCES IN EACH SOCIETY WILL DIFFER --
WHETHER IT'S SYRIA OR SAUDI ARABIA OR THE PALESTINIAN AUTHORITY OR
ANY OF THE DOZEN MIDDLE EASTERN STATES FACING A LONG-AWAITED
TRANSITION. WHILE NO ONE SHOULD EXAGGERATE JORDAN'S ROLE AS A
TREND-SETTER, A SUCCESSFUL TRANSITION IN JORDAN WOULD AT LEAST
OFFER A POSITIVE EXAMPLE AND SUSTAIN THE KIND OF FRIENDLY, MODERATE
REGIME THAT BEST SERVES OUR INTERESTS. MOREOVER, GIVEN ABDULLAH'S
TIES TO THE YOUNGER GENERATION OF GULF LEADERS, HELPING HIM FIND
HIS FOOTING IN JORDAN MAY HELP INDIRECTLY TO CEMENT RELATIONS AMONG
STATES WHICH WILL BE IMPORTANT TO US FOR YEARS TO COME.

A FINAL NOTE
----

7. (C) IT'S HARD TO LOOK AHEAD WITHOUT REFLECTING ON THE
EXTRAORDINARY LIFE OF KING HUSSEIN. EVEN IN HIS FINAL DAYS, HE
SHOWED THE SAME STUBBORN COURAGE THAT HE HAD ALWAYS DISPLAYED. HIS
DOCTORS EXPECTED HIM TO DIE VERY SHORTLY AFTER HE RETURNED TO
JORDAN, UNCONSCIOUS AND WITH VITAL ORGANS SHUTTING DOWN, BUT HE
HUNG ON FOR SEVERAL MORE DAYS. IT WAS ALMOST AS IF, CONSCIOUS OR
UNCONSCIOUS, THE KING WAS DETERMINED TO SHOW THAT ONLY HE -- NOT
CNN OR ANXIOUS FOREIGN AUDIENCES OR MEDICAL EXPERTS OR ANYONE ELSE
-- WOULD DECIDE WHEN HE WOULD MAKE HIS EXIT. IN HIS OWN PROUD WAY,
HE HELD CENTER STAGE RIGHT UNTIL THE END.
                CONFIDENTIAL

PAGE 03   AMMAN 01059 02 OF 02 071239Z

8. (C) HUSSEIN LIVED A LIFE THAT ALWAYS RAN AGAINST THE ODDS. JOHN
FOSTER DULLES WAS JUST THE FIRST IN A LONG LINE OF PEOPLE TO
UNDERESTIMATE HIM, AND TO UNDERESTIMATE JORDAN. IT'S WORTH
REMEMBERING THAT AS JORDANIANS, AND ALL OF US, CONTEMPLATE A FUTURE
WITHOUT HUSSEIN. HIS SUCCESSOR AND THE JORDANIAN PEOPLE FACE
DAUNTING CHALLENGES, AND STEEP ODDS, BUT THEY HAVE THE CAPACITY TO
COPE WITH THEM. IT IS VERY MUCH IN OUR INTEREST, AND IT IS A VERY
FITTING TRIBUTE TO HUSSEIN, TO DO ALL WE CAN TO HELP THEM. BURNS

          CONFIDENTIAL

<< END OF DOCUMENT >>

2000 Amman 6760, December 5, 2000,
"Peace Process: Relaunching American Diplomacy"

From my perspective as the American ambassador in Amman, the collapse of the Camp David peace talks and the outbreak of the second Palestinian Intifada were ominous signs for Jordan and the broader Middle East. In a highly unusual move, I joined our ambassador to Egypt, Dan Kurtzer, in authoring a joint cable that shared our thoughts from the region on U.S. policy and made the case for the Clinton administration to articulate its own parameters for a peace deal.

C06323473IED U.S. Department of State Case No. MP-2015-07420 Doc No. C06323473 Date: 06/27/2017

DECLASSIFIED

RELEASE IN PART
1.4(B),1.4(D)

~~SECRET~~   PTQ1973

PAGE 01   AMMAN 06760 01 OF 03 051617Z
ACTION NODS-00

INFO LOG-00 CCOE-00 SAS-00 /000W
      ------------------A7C5A0 051617Z /38
O 051609Z DEC 00
FM AMEMBASSY AMMAN
TO SECSTATE WASHDC IMMEDIATE 7539
INFO AMEMBASSY CAIRO IMMEDIATE
AMEMBASSY TEL AVIV IMMEDIATE
AMCONSUL JERUSALEM IMMEDIATE
AMEMBASSY DAMASCUS IMMEDIATE
AMEMBASSY BEIRUT IMMEDIATE
AMEMBASSY RIYADH IMMEDIATE
WHITEHOUSE WASHDC IMMEDIATE

~~SECRET~~ SECTION 01 OF 03 AMMAN 006760

NODIS SIERRA   DECAPTIONED

DEPARTMENT FOR THE SECRETARY, A/S WALKER AND
SMEC/ROSS; WHITE HOUSE FOR NSA BERGER, RIEDEL AND
MALLEY

FROM AMBASSADOR KURTZER AND AMBASSADOR BURNS

E.O. 12958: DECL: 12/5/20
TAGS: PREL, EG, JO, XF
SUBJECT: PEACE PROCESS: RELAUNCHING AMERICAN
DIPLOMACY
       ~~SECRET~~

PAGE 02   AMMAN 06760 01 OF 03 051617Z

REFS: (A) CAIRO 7716 (B) CAIRO 7946

CLASSIFIED BY AMBASSADOR DAN KURTZER AND AMBASSADOR
BILL BURNS FOR REASON 1.5 (B,D)

1. (S) AS SEEN FROM CAIRO AND AMMAN, U.S. POLICY IN
THE PEACE PROCESS AND OUR OVERALL POSTURE IN THE
REGION ARE STILL HEADING IN EXACTLY THE WRONG
DIRECTION. WITH OUR INTERESTS UNDER INCREASING
SCRUTINY AND ATTACK, WE ARE ACTING PASSIVELY,
REACTIVELY AND DEFENSIVELY. THERE IS NO GUARANTEE
THAT A BOLDER, MORE ACTIVIST AMERICAN APPROACH WILL
STOP THE HEMORRHAGING -- BUT IT SEEMS CLEAR TO US THAT
THINGS COULD GET A LOT WORSE UNLESS WE REGAIN THE
INITIATIVE.

2. (S) OUR STAKE IN REVERSING THE DRIFT TOWARD MORE
VIOLENCE, REBUILDING AMERICAN CREDIBILITY, REFOCUSING
ATTENTION ON THE POSSIBILITIES OF A POLITICAL PROCESS,

Declassification Authority: Geoffrey W. Chapman, OCA, Senior Reviewer,
A/GIS/IPS

UNCLASSIFIED U.S. Department of State Case No. MP-2015-07420 Doc No. C06323473 Date: 06/27/2017

AND GETTING AS FAR AS WE CAN OVER THE NEXT SEVEN WEEKS
TOWARD A FRAMEWORK AGREEMENT IS SELF-EVIDENT. WHAT IS
LESS OBVIOUS IS HOW TO GET FROM HERE TO THERE. ONE
OPTION IS TO FOLLOW BARAK'S LEAD. THAT MAY SERVE WHAT
HE SEES TO BE HIS TACTICAL INTERESTS AT THIS POINT,
BUT IT'S HARD TO SEE HOW IT SERVES OURS.

1.4(I

AMMAN 06760 01 OF 03 051617Z
A SECOND OPTION IS TO SEE IF WE CAN EXTRACT
FROM THE PALESTINIANS A CLEARER SENSE OF HOW FAR
THEY'RE PREPARED TO GO RIGHT NOW, AND THEN USE THAT TO
CRAFT AN APPROACH TO BARAK. BUT IT'S UNLIKELY THAT
ARAFAT WILL LEVEL WITH US AT THIS POINT; AND WHILE
RECENT EGYPTIAN AND JORDANIAN EFFORTS WITH THE
PALESTINIANS HAVE BEEN HELPFUL, IT'S NOT AT ALL CLEAR
THAT THEY WILL PRODUCE A WORKABLE STARTING POINT.

3. (S) THAT LEAVES IT TO US TO LAY OUT THE HARD TRUTHS
-- FOR ALL PARTIES -- THAT MUST UNDERPIN ANY ENDURING
POLITICAL SOLUTION. AS WE HAVE TRIED TO EMPHASIZE IN
REFTELS, THAT WILL REQUIRE THE POLITICAL WILL TO STAND
UP FOR WHAT WE HAVE FOUGHT SO HARD FOR OVER THE PAST
EIGHT YEARS, AND A READINESS TO DECLARE THE
INDEPENDENCE OF OUR POLICY.

4. (S) THE CRITICAL ELEMENTS OF AN EFFECTIVE AMERICAN
APPROACH INCLUDE THE FOLLOWING:

-- ARTICULATE A "CLINTON VISION" FOR THE PEACE
PROCESS: WE HAVE A UNIQUE BUT WASTING OPPORTUNITY TO
TAKE ADVANTAGE OF A REMARKABLE ASSET: THE PERSONAL
REPUTATION AND DEMONSTRATED COMMITMENT OF PRESIDENT
CLINTON. HE HAS BUILT UP SUBSTANTIAL PERSONAL CREDIT
WITH THE PARTIES OVER THE YEARS, AND NOW IS THE TIME
TO USE IT. HE CAN SKETCH A VISION OF WHAT HE BELIEVES
A COMPREHENSIVE PEACE WILL REQUIRE OF ALL PARTIES --
PALESTINIANS, ISRAELIS, AND ARAB STATES ALIKE. HE
WILL HAVE TO BE WILLING TO SAY THINGS TO EACH PARTY
THAT THEY WILL NOT WANT TO HEAR, BUT THAT IS THE
SECRET

PAGE 04   AMMAN 06760 01 OF 03 051617Z
DEFINITION OF A BALANCED AND CREDIBLE APPROACH (OUR
IDEAS FOR SUCH A U.S. PACKAGE ARE CONTAINED IN REF A).

1.4(I

-- MAKE PUBLIC THE RESULTS OF CAMP DAVID II: THE
EGYPTIANS, JORDANIANS, AND MANY OTHERS IN THE REGION

BELIEVE THAT PRESIDENT CLINTON MADE ENORMOUS PROGRESS
WHEN HE BROUGHT THE PARTIES TOGETHER AT CAMP DAVID.
THEY BELIEVE THESE RESULTS SHOULD BE MEMORIALIZED AND
PURSUED VIGOROUSLY IN SUBSEQUENT NEGOTIATIONS. PART
OF LAYING OUT OUR VISION SHOULD BE TO MAKE SURE THAT
WE DO NOT LOSE WHAT WE HAD IN HAND IN CAMP DAVID.
THIS CAN BE DONE IN AN OP ED PIECE OR ARTICLE IN A
JOURNAL.

-- EMPOWER THE FACT-FINDING COMMISSION: WE OUGHT TO

SECRET

SECRET   PTQ1976

PAGE 01   AMMAN 06760 02 OF 03 051617Z
ACTION NODS-00

INFO LOG-00 CCOE-00 SAS-00   /000W
------------------A7C5B0 051617Z /38
O 051609Z DEC 00
FM AMEMBASSY AMMAN
TO SECSTATE WASHDC IMMEDIATE 7540
INFO AMEMBASSY CAIRO IMMEDIATE
AMEMBASSY TEL AVIV IMMEDIATE
AMCONSUL JERUSALEM IMMEDIATE
AMEMBASSY DAMASCUS IMMEDIATE
AMEMBASSY BEIRUT IMMEDIATE
AMEMBASSY RIYADH IMMEDIATE
WHITEHOUSE WASHDC IMMEDIATE

S E C R E T SECTION 02 OF 03 AMMAN 006760

NODIS SIERRA

DEPARTMENT FOR THE SECRETARY, A/S WALKER AND
SMEC/ROSS; WHITE HOUSE FOR NSA BERGER, RIEDEL AND
MALLEY

FROM AMBASSADOR KURTZER AND AMBASSADOR BURNS

E.O. 12958: DECL: 12/5/20
TAGS: PREL, EG, JO, XF
SUBJECT: PEACE PROCESS: RELAUNCHING AMERICAN
DIPLOMACY
                    SECRET

PAGE 02   AMMAN 06760 02 OF 03 051617Z

AVOID GETTING AMERICAN FINGERPRINTS ALL OVER THE FACT-
FINDING COMMISSION, AND AVOID GETTING CAUGHT IN THE
TRAP OF PRE-NEGOTIATING ALL OF ITS PROCEDURES WITH THE
ISRAELIS AND PALESTINIANS. WE HAVE NO ILLUSIONS ABOUT
THE SUBSTANTIVE VALUE OF THIS EXERCISE, BUT IF THE
COMMISSION'S FIRST TRIP IS PERFUNCTORY AND MAKES IT
LOOK AS IF WE'RE SIMPLY CHECKING A BOX, IT WILL HURT

OUR INTERESTS CONSIDERABLY THROUGHOUT THE REGION.

-- SHAPE AN "INTERNATIONAL OBSERVER PRESENCE" TO OUR
LIKING: WE DON'T UNDERSTAND WHY WE AND ISRAEL HAVE
TAKEN SUCH A DIM VIEW OF PROPOSALS FOR AN
INTERNATIONAL PRESENCE IN THE TERRITORIES. WHILE SOME
PALESTINIAN PROPOSALS MAKE LITTLE SENSE, THE GENERAL
IDEA OF INTERPOSING INTERNATIONAL OBSERVERS SEEMS WELL
WORTH EXAMINING. IF SHAPED CAREFULLY, IT COULD EVEN
BECOME A CATALYST FOR SUSTAINED IMPLEMENTATION OF THE
SHARM EL-SHEIKH UNDERSTANDINGS, IN WHICH BOTH SIDES
HAVE A STAKE. IF WE'RE NOT GOING TO BE ABLE TO MAKE
THIS ISSUE GO AWAY, WHY FIGHT THE PROBLEM ? WHY NOT
TRY TO TAKE THE LEAD IN MOLDING SUCH AN INTERNATIONAL
PRESENCE?

-- KEEP THE SUPPLEMENTAL ASSISTANCE PACKAGE INTACT OR

1.4(D

SECRET

PAGE 03   AMMAN 06760 02 OF 03 051617Z

1.4(D

-- SEEK URGENT CONGRESSIONAL APPROVAL OF THE JORDAN
FTA, IF POSSIBLE ALONGSIDE THE SUPPLEMENTAL PACKAGE:
THIS WOULD BE A BIG BOOST FOR ABDULLAH, AT A TIME WHEN
LITTLE ELSE IS GOING RIGHT FOR JORDAN. WE SHOULD ALSO
RESPOND TO MUBARAKQS SPECIFIC REQUEST TO THE PRESIDENT
TO START TALKS NOW WITH EGYPT ON A FTA.

-- TALK PEACE NOT WAR: HAVING DEVOTED MORE THAN TWO
DECADES TO ACTIVE PEACEMAKING IN THIS REGION, WE MUST
NOT YIELD TO CRITICS OR TO THOSE WHO EXULT IN THE
PROBLEMS WHICH THE OSLO PROCESS IS CONFRONTING. IT IS
ENTIRELY SENSIBLE TO WARN REGIONAL PARTIES PRIVATELY
AGAINST THE DANGERS OF ESCALATION AND REGIONAL
CONFLICT, BUT WE HAVE TO BE CAREFUL NOT TO RAISE FEARS
OF WAR IN OUR PUBLIC STATEMENTS. ON THE CONTRARY, WE
OUGHT TO BE ON A PUBLIC RELATIONS BLITZ, BOTH AT HOME
AND ABROAD, ON WHY IT IS ESSENTIAL TO KEEP GOING IN
THE SEARCH FOR COMPREHENSIVE PEACE, AND HOW MUCH
GROUND WAS COVERED IN THE CAMP DAVID SUMMIT LAST
SUMMER.

SECRET

PAGE 04   AMMAN 06760 02 OF 03 051617Z
-- ENGAGE, ENGAGE, ENGAGE: WE DO NOT SPEND ENOUGH
TIME JUST TALKING TO OUR FRIENDS IN THE REGION.
ESPECIALLY NOW, WHEN OUR INTERESTS ARE INCREASINGLY
THREATENED IN THIS REGION, WE NEED TO HAVE SENIOR
DIPLOMATS OUT HERE AS MUCH AS POSSIBLE. (EARLY
RESCHEDULING OF UNDERSECRETARY PICKERING'S TRIP TO
SEVERAL ARAB CAPITALS WOULD BE VERY USEFUL.) OUR
WILLINGNESS TO ENGAGE AND LISTEN IN WHAT WILL
ADMITTEDLY BE A VERY TOUGH DIALOGUE WILL BE AN
IMPORTANT ELEMENT IN RECONSTRUCTING OUR STRATEGIC
RELATIONSHIPS THROUGHOUT THIS REGION.

5. (S) AS WE HAVE EMPHASIZED BEFORE, WE KNOW THERE ARE
REAL RISKS IN THE APPROACH WE HAVE OUTLINED, AND NO
GUARANTEES THAT IT WILL PRODUCE ANY FORMAL AGREEMENTS
(LET ALONE A FAPS) WITHIN THE NEXT SEVEN WEEKS. BUT
WE ARE ALSO CONVINCED THAT THE COSTS AND RISKS OF
INACTION ARE MUCH GREATER. PRESIDENT CLINTON HAS MADE

SECRET

SECRET   PTQ1978

PAGE 01   AMMAN 06760 03 OF 03 051617Z
ACTION NODS-00

INFO LOG-00   CCOE-00 SAS-00   /000W
------------------A7C5B5 051617Z /38
O 051609Z DEC 00
FM AMEMBASSY AMMAN
TO SECSTATE WASHDC IMMEDIATE 7541
INFO AMEMBASSY CAIRO IMMEDIATE
AMEMBASSY TEL AVIV IMMEDIATE
AMCONSUL JERUSALEM IMMEDIATE
AMEMBASSY DAMASCUS IMMEDIATE
AMEMBASSY BEIRUT IMMEDIATE
AMEMBASSY RIYADH IMMEDIATE
WHITEHOUSE WASHDC IMMEDIATE

S E C R E T SECTION 03 OF 03 AMMAN 006760

NODIS SIERRA

DEPARTMENT FOR THE SECRETARY, A/S WALKER AND
SMEC/ROSS; WHITE HOUSE FOR NSA BERGER, RIEDEL AND
MALLEY

FROM AMBASSADOR KURTZER AND AMBASSADOR BURNS

E.O. 12958: DECL: 12/5/20
TAGS: PREL, EG, JO, XF
SUBJECT: PEACE PROCESS: RELAUNCHING AMERICAN

C06323473¦ED U.S. Department of State Case No. MP-2015-07420 Doc No. C06323473 Date: 06/27/2017

DIPLOMACY
                    SECRET

PAGE 02   AMMAN 06760 03 OF 03 051617Z

ENORMOUS CONTRIBUTIONS TO PEACE IN THIS TROUBLED
REGION OVER THE PAST EIGHT YEARS. WE SHOULDN'T LET
THEM WASTE AWAY WITHOUT A FIGHT.

BURNS

                    SECRET

<< END OF DOCUMENT >>

Email to Secretary of State Condoleezza Rice,
February 8, 2008, "Russia Strategy"

As the George W. Bush administration reached the end of its second term, looming policy "trainwrecks" threatened to push U.S.-Russia relations to a new post–Cold War nadir. In this email to Secretary Rice from Moscow, I made plain the risks of a collision and tried to offer my best advice on how to avoid a collapse in bilateral ties.

C06394587⁻IED U.S. Department of State Case No. MP-2015-07420 Doc No. C06394587 Date: 09/15/2017

REVIEW AUTHORITY: Paul Hilburn, Senior Reviewer

RELEASE IN FULL

From: Burns, William J (AMB-Moscow) (Moscow)
Sent: Friday, February 08, 2008 9:22 AM
To: Beecroft, Robert S
Cc: S_SpecialAssistants; Negroponte, John D; Burns, Nicholas R; Fried, Daniel
Subject: Russia Strategy

SECRET

February 8, 2008

Madam Secretary,

I know you are wrestling with a number of very difficult issues involving my ever-congenial hosts, ranging from Kosovo to Bucharest to the next 2x2 meeting. Following are some personal thoughts on what's at stake with the Russians, what's driving them, and what may be possible over the next few months. I still think it's possible to make a big, strategic play with Putin in the Kremlin; it will get harder after he leaves in May, because Medvedev will be too weak initially to make bold choices, and Putin won't want to be seen to be making them for him. By that point, moreover, the Russian inclination will be simply to wait for the next Administration.

1. The next couple months will be among the most consequential in recent U.S.-Russian relations. We face three potential trainwrecks: Kosovo, MAP for Ukraine/Georgia, and missile defense. We've got a high-priority problem with Iran that (post-NIE) will be extremely hard to address without the Russians. We've got a chance to do something enduring with the Russians on nuclear cooperation, with a 123 agreement almost signed and more to be done on GNEP and counter-proliferation. And we've got an opportunity to get off on a better foot with a reconfigured Russian leadership after

1

Medvedev's likely election, and to help get the Russians across the finish line into WTO this year, which is among the most practical things we can do to promote the long-term prospects for political and economic modernization in this proud, prickly, complicated society.

2. My view is that we can only manage one of those three trainwrecks without doing real damage to a relationship we don't have the luxury of ignoring. From my admittedly parochial perspective here, it's hard to see how we could get the key Europeans to support us on all three at the same time. I'd opt for plowing ahead resolutely on Kosovo; deferring MAP for Ukraine or Georgia until a stronger foundation is laid; and going to Putin directly while he's still in the Presidency to try and cut a deal on missile defense, as part of a broader security framework.

3. I fully understand how difficult a decision to hold off on MAP will be. But it's equally hard to overstate the strategic consequences of a premature MAP offer, especially to Ukraine. Ukrainian entry into NATO is the brightest of all redlines for the Russian elite (not just Putin). In my more than two and a half years of conversations with key Russian players, from knuckle-draggers in the dark recesses of the Kremlin to Putin's sharpest liberal critics, I have yet to find anyone who views Ukraine in NATO as anything other than a direct challenge to Russian interests. At this stage, a MAP offer would be seen not as a technical step along a long road toward membership, but as throwing down the strategic gauntlet. Today's Russia will respond. Russian-Ukrainian relations will go into a deep freeze, with Moscow likely to contemplate economic measures ranging from an immediate increase in gas prices to world market levels, to a clampdown on Ukrainian workers coming to Russia. It will create fertile soil for Russian meddling in Crimea and eastern Ukraine. There'd be much chest-thumping about repositioning military assets closer to the Ukrainian border, and threats of nuclear retargeting. The NATO-Russia Council would go on life support, or expire altogether. On Georgia, the combination of Kosovo independence and a MAP offer would likely lead to recognition of Abkhazia, however counterproductive that might be to Russia's own long-term interests in the Caucasus. The prospects of subsequent Russian-Georgian armed conflict would be high.

4. If, in the end, MAP offers are made to Ukraine and Georgia, you can probably stop reading here. I can conceive of no grand package that would allow the Russians to swallow this pill quietly. If we opt to defer MAP, while making clear that it is coming eventually, we have a chance to explore a strategically ambitious package with Russia, which could help anchor our relationship and some of our most significant global interests for some time to come. I do not mean to suggest that Putin and company would view a deferral of MAP as a great strategic concession and leap enthusiastically to greater moderation on other questions; they are not an especially sentimental bunch. But the way would at least be clear to probe for accommodations that would suit our most vital needs, and to find a way to agree to disagree on Kosovo without huge collateral damage.

5. I'd see two parts to a bold package of understandings to pursue with Putin. The first would be a security framework, and the second would be a renewed commitment to economic cooperation. The first would be a lasting contribution from both Presidents to a safer world and a reflection of the unique capabilities – and unique responsibilities – that the United States and Russia continue to have in the nuclear field. The second would be, over the medium and longer-term, the most effective means of advancing the President's freedom agenda, and a way to help lock Russia into global economic organizations and rule of law. That won't change the reality that Russia is a deeply authoritarian and overcentralized state today, whose dismal record on human rights and political freedoms deserves our criticism. But it will reinforce over time the instincts for private property and market-driven opportunity, and the vastly increased connections that young Russians have to the rest of the world through foreign travel and the Internet, that are slowly but unmistakably transforming this society.

6. A security framework might include several ingredients. Completion of a 123 agreement, progress on GNEP, and a common diplomatic approach on DPRK and Iran (following a third UNSCR) would be the starting point. A second component would revolve upon how we manage our own remaining nuclear arsenals. That means meeting Bratislava commitments on Nunn-Lugar upgrades by the end of 2008, and a Russian commitment to sustain them. It also means seeking an agreement in principle on post-START, involving a legally-binding text whose level of detail and shape would fall somewhere between the Moscow Treaty and START-I. (We might also consider support for Putin's global INF treaty, however slim the chances for success.) A third feature could be a reinvigoration of counterterrorism cooperation, including the new Global Initiative against Nuclear Terrorism, and greater Russian contributions in Afghanistan. And fourth, and most challenging, would be missile defense.

7. I don't know if Putin can be persuaded at this stage to do a deal on regional missile defense cooperation that would allow us to move ahead on Polish and Czech deployments. But it's still worth a try, if only as a way to show the Allies that we've exhausted every avenue. To make a dent in Putin's thinking, and overcome the objections that he's likely to hear from a deeply skeptical Russian bureaucracy, you and Secretary Gates would probably have to convey to Putin directly a revised U.S. paper, indicating a willingness to make a maximum effort to reach an understanding with the Russians before formalizing agreements with the Poles and Czechs (it wouldn't work to announce a deal during the Tusk visit to

2

Washington on March 10 and then try to reach an accommodation with Putin). We'd also have to go further in indicating a readiness to link operationalization of sites to concrete evidence of long-range missile capability (via flight testing), and in finding a formula for continuous mutual presence at each other's sites.

8. An economic basket would include a hard push on WTO, built around Kudrin's visit to Washington in April. It would also feature the launching of a new government to government economic dialogue in the spring, led by Reuben Jeffery and his Russian counterpart, and possible visits to Russia by Secretary Paulson and Secretary Gutierrez (with a renewed business to business dialogue emerging from the latter). The possible appointment of a new, high-level energy envoy for Eurasia could be another opportunity (especially if it was someone like Don Evans, whom the Russians know and trust).

9. Tactically, it would be essential to roll all this out as a really significant strategic play, conveyed at least in broad terms from the President to Putin. A piecemeal approach won't succeed. A first step might be a call to Putin from the President in the second half of February, maybe after the Africa trip but well before the March 2 Russian Presidential election. Then there could be a 2x2 meeting in Moscow, shortly after the election, to allow a detailed, direct engagement with Putin, Medvedev and others. To focus Putin's interest, the President might keep open the possibility of a brief stop in Moscow after Bucharest, if/if sufficient progress had been made. While the odds of success would be long, it's at least conceivable that the two Presidents could ultimately point to a security framework, including a missile defense understanding; a coordinated approach on Iran, following passage of a third UNSCR and the Majles elections; agreement to disagree on Kosovo; and significant movement on WTO. All that would protect our core interests, play to Putin's sense of legacy, and get relations with Medvedev off to a promising start. At worst, we'd have built up capital with the Allies for making such an effort, which we'd no doubt have to drawn on to manage the fallout from Kosovo and missile defense.

10. I fully recognize that all this is much, much easier said than done. But even partial success would help cushion some of the trainwrecks that lie ahead, and help create an atmosphere in which eventual decisions on MAP might go down easier.

Best regards,

Bill Burns

3

Memo to Secretary of State Condoleezza Rice, May 27, 2008, "Regaining the Strategic Initiative on Iran"

In 2008, the Iranian nuclear program was accelerating and American diplomatic efforts were stalling. In this memo to Secretary Rice, I laid out a new approach for strengthening U.S. leverage on the nuclear issue and advocated joining the negotiations between Europe, Russia, China, and Iran.

UNCLASSIFIED U.S. Department of State Case No. ~~SECRET~~ of 120 Doc No. C06419958 Date:

UNDER SECRETARY OF STATE
FOR POLITICAL AFFAIRS
WASHINGTON

RELEASE IN FULL

Copy

May 27, 2008

~~SECRET/Eyes Only~~
DECL: 5/27/2018

NOTE FOR THE SECRETARY

Seen by

NOV 2 1 2008

FROM: P – Bill Burns

P

SUBJECT: Regaining the Strategic Initiative on Iran

Madam Secretary,

1. Our Iran policy is drifting dangerously between the current muddle of P5+1 diplomacy and more forceful options, with all of their huge downsides. Following are some preliminary thoughts on how we might use the remaining months of this Administration to regain the strategic initiative, revive leverage over Iran, and frame a sustainable, long-term approach to the Iranian challenge on which the next Administration might build.

The Iranian Challenge

2. The Iranian regime today is simultaneously cocky and insecure. Awash in $130/barrel oil, Tehran is defiantly continuing to enrich uranium, and pugnaciously pressing its hand in Lebanon and Iraq. But oil revenues can only partially compensate for Ahmadinejad's economic incompetence and 30% inflation, aggravated by financial sanctions. Iran has no natural regional allies, and remains suspicious that erstwhile partners like Syria ultimately have higher priorities (like the Golan). Having possibly overplayed its hand in Basra, the Iranian regime has been reminded that Iraqi nationalism can trump Shia bonds. And the regime is still beset by fundamental contradictions, caught between its own retrogressive traditionalism and popular pressures for modernization.

~~SECRET~~
Classified by: P, Bill Burns
E.O. 12958 Reasons: 1.4(b) and (d)

RELEASE AUTHORITY: Paul Hilburn, Senior Reviewer

~~SECRET~~
-2-

3. The basic dilemma we face is that the most dangerous dimension of Iranian behavior -- its nuclear program -- is both broadly popular in Iran as a symbol of national modernization and self-assertiveness, and likely to outpace the internal contradictions which will eventually cause either the implosion of the current regime or the mellowing of its behavior. This is a race that we, and the rest of the international community, are still losing.

4. Part of the problem is also that the Iranian regime has been largely successful in camouflaging its vulnerabilities. That is not just a product of $130/barrel oil, although that certainly doesn't hurt. The regime has constructed a narrative which portrays Iran as the victim of implacable American hostility, increasingly gaining the diplomatic upper hand regionally and globally, with the American administration -- not Iran -- increasingly the isolated party.

5. Reviving significant pressure against Iran's nuclear program requires us to puncture that narrative. That means calculating every step we take not only with a view toward the immediate impact on the regime, but also toward the international, regional and domestic Iranian audiences that are so critical to Tehran's inflated self-confidence. A successful strategy will require calculated risk-taking on our part, applying pressure at as many points as we can, while simultaneously exploring creatively subversive ways to accentuate the gap between the regime's deeply conservative instincts and popular Iranian desire for normalization with the rest of the world, including the U.S.

Elements of a New, Long-Term Strategy

6. I can think of no safer prediction today than that Iran will not agree to suspension of enrichment and reprocessing in response to the P5+1's refreshed incentives package. We have neither enough sticks nor enough carrots in play right now to fundamentally alter Iran's calculus. Anticipating that the current P5+1 process is going to run out of steam during the summer, we ought to craft a bolder and more systematic approach that might help us rebuild momentum through the rest of the year.

7. Tempting as each might seem, I'd be very careful at this stage about the two bookend options before us, either the use of force against Iranian nuclear sites to set back their program, or a unilateral, unconditional offer of direct, bilateral

~~SECRET~~

-3-

dialogue on all subjects. I'm deeply opposed to the first, which would in any case only make sense as a genuine last resort; the truth today is that we are nowhere near exhausting all our other possibilities. The second is intriguing, and may have made sense in 2003, when our leverage was significantly greater, but leaping to that conclusion under current circumstances could only feed Iranian hubris.

8. Conceptually, our renewed approach ought to borrow from classic containment theory, based on Kennan's original notion of how you deal with a profoundly hostile adversary beset by its own serious, and ultimately fatal, internal contradictions. Iran is not the Soviet Union, and it does not pose an existential threat to us (although it could to Israel). But our overall strategy should employ the same combination of multiple pressure points, diplomatic coalition-building, wedge-driving among Iran and its uneasy partners, and selected contacts with the regime that animated much of Kennan's concept.

9. **First**, we should shore up international pressure against Iran's nuclear ambitions. The Iranians hate UNSC resolutions not so much because of the practical impact of sanctions, but because of their political symbolism in underscoring Iran's isolation. A fourth sanctions resolution in early fall, with as much teeth as we can put in it, really does have diplomatic value. (Even talking about sanctions against refined petroleum products and gasoline would have an impact on Tehran.) Another resolution would provide cover for other, more biting, financial sanctions outside the formal bounds of UNSC actions.

10. **Second**, we should continue to look vigorously at ways we can unilaterally (and in partnership with other key players) disrupt the nuclear program and squeeze Iran's financial system. There is still more room for tougher enforcement of existing sanctions, and creative application in areas like insurance coverage that would slowly undermine the Iranian economy.

11. **Third**, we should be more active in disrupting Iran's regional position. Direct Iraqi expressions of discontent with Iranian meddling are quite effective. Kinetic responses in Iraq to Qods Force and Special Group threats, without public fanfare, is a language the Iranian regime understands. More broadly, we can pursue tighter cooperation with the GCC+3, perhaps including discussion of security assurances

-4-

against Iran -- even as we keep the door open for Iran's participation in regional security dialogue. On Afghanistan, we should also push back hard when Iranian behavior crosses coalition interests, but consider revived dialogue on practical issues like counter-narcotics, perhaps on the margins of an UNGA 6+2 meeting.

-- Deepening consultations with Turkey on Iran also helps get Tehran's attention, even if the Turks are reluctant to actually do much; the Iranian regime seems far more wary about Turkey, a big Moslem society whose modernization in the last three decades dwarfs their own feeble economic accomplishments, than it does about the Gulf Arabs, about whom the Iranians love to be dismissive and patronizing.

-- Syria's flirtation with peace talks with Israel, via the Turks, also presents an opportunity. The Iranians don't trust the Syrians, but depend on them heavily to sustain their connection to Hizballah and influence in Lebanon. Any contacts that we have with the Syrians in the current environment will help unnerve the Iranians, and that is not a bad thing.

12. **Fourth**, we should consider how we might use carefully-structured contacts with Iran to turn the tables on Tehran diplomatically, put them back on their heels tactically, and exploit the disconnect between the regime's need to paint the U.S. as the enemy at the gates and the Iranian population's thirst for access to American society and the rest of the world. Such contacts should include Parliamentary exchanges, more sports and cultural visits, and more innovative broadcasting and outreach, including use of Farsi-speaking U.S. officials on Iranian programs.

-- More ambitiously, I'd strongly recommend a well-orchestrated proposal to set up a U.S. visa office or interests section in Tehran. There are a number of variants, the simplest of which would involve sending 3 or 4 American diplomats to work under our current protecting power (for which the Iranians would no doubt insist on reciprocity in Washington). The default position of the Iranian regime will be to reject such an offer, but we can make it very awkward for them to do so, especially if we package it with 1000 scholarships for Iranian students and a willingness to talk directly with Iranian officials about how to set up an office.

~~SECRET~~

-5-

-- We might combine a visa office proposal with a parallel offer to have the American political director (me) join our P5+1 colleagues in a second round of talks in Tehran, if /if the Iranians agree to the "freeze for freeze" idea that Solana will explore with them as a limited duration step to facilitate pre-negotiations. (The Iranians would have to cap their nuclear program for six weeks, and we would agree not to pursue new sanctions during that period -- which we probably couldn't do anyway.) We would not change our stance on Ministerial-level participation; that would still depend on Iranian suspension.

Plan of Action

13. All of this is, of course, much easier said than done. The trick would be to implement the visa office idea and limited direct contacts in a way that significantly enhances our diplomatic leverage, and gets us something in return -- if not from the Iranians, then in terms of better cooperation from the P5+1 and wedge-driving between the regime and the Iranian people. Like Ronald Reagan and George Shultz in opening the U.S.-PLO dialogue in late 1988, we would also be breaking a taboo in a way that would strengthen the hand of the next Administration.

14. There are a number of options for introducing the ideas of a visa office and limited participation in P5+1 talks. On the visa office, you could use a trusted private intermediary, perhaps via the Iranian PermRep in New York. You could use the British. Or you could use the Russians -- which probably carries both the biggest risks and the biggest payoff.

-- What I would suggest is that you meet privately with Lavrov and try to trade the visa office and limited P5+1 participation offers for Russian agreement -- if the Iranians turn us down -- to a fourth resolution, with as much teeth as we can get, and an informal commitment to continue to slow-roll implementation of past missile contracts. Buying the Russians into this approach is key to sustaining international consensus through the end of the year.

~~SECRET~~

~~SECRET~~
-6-

-- If the Russians agreed, we could use them to convey our offers. On the visa office or interests section, we'd also insist that the Iranians designate someone with whom we could follow up directly, and who we could be confident represented the Supreme Leader. It's possible that that channel could be used for other subjects in the future, but the initial conversation would be about the visa office.

15. We'd still retain the cards that matter most to Tehran, including security guarantees and limited enrichment programs. There are strong arguments against playing those now. We need to rebuild leverage first, and regain the initiative. But by launching the limited steps that I've suggested here, we'd have a chance to upset Iranian calculations, and set in motion a workable, long-term strategy -- whether the Iranians accepted our offer or not. That would be a valuable contribution to the next Administration, and to American interests for years to come.

~~SECRET~~

Email to Secretary of State Hillary Clinton, February 22, 2011, "Note for the Secretary from Bill Burns: Cairo, February 21-22"

Written less than two weeks after the ouster of President Hosni Mubarak, this dispatch from Cairo tried to capture both the exuberant mood in Egypt's streets as well as the depth of the challenges facing the country's new leadership. Throughout my tenure as undersecretary and deputy secretary, I frequently sent such first-person notes to capture my impressions and offer recommendations.

<table>
<tr><td></td><td colspan="2" align="right">RELEASE IN FULL</td></tr>
<tr><td>From:</td><td>Doyle, Robert F</td></tr>
<tr><td>To:</td><td>Macmanus, Joseph E; S SpecialAssistants; Sullivan, Jacob J</td></tr>
<tr><td>Cc:</td><td>Steinberg, James B; Feltman, Jeffrey D; Wells, Alice G; "mspence@nsc.eop.sgov.gov"; Nides, Thomas R</td></tr>
<tr><td>Subject:</td><td>Note for the Secretary from Bill Burns: Cairo, February 21-22</td></tr>
<tr><td>Date:</td><td>Tuesday, February 22, 2011 4:21:28 PM</td></tr>
</table>

SECRET

February 22, 2011
Cairo

Madam Secretary,

Amidst the bloody chaos next door and continued tumult elsewhere in the region, Egypt's ten day old transition is taking on more and more significance. My impression after two very full days of meetings in Cairo is that Egyptians are pointed in a positive direction, with no shortage of potential political and economic pitfalls ahead. The mood here remains generally optimistic. The Supreme Council of the Armed Forces has so far managed its unaccustomed role with more finesse than most would have suspected. Soldiers are still being treated like celebrities, with mothers perching their kids on the sides of tanks for souvenir photos. Walking along the corniche yesterday to the MFA, we went past piles of barbed wire and dozens of armored vehicles in front of the State TV building, with demonstrators, families and sidewalk vendors combining to create the street party atmosphere of this still incomplete revolution. Banks have reopened without disaster, and the fundamentals of the economy are not in bad shape. Youth leaders are deeply proud of the historic role that they've played. The political class is filled with genuine enthusiasts for change, as well as ex post facto revolutionaries, eager to declare their heretofore well-concealed antipathy for the Mubarak regime and claim that they were really with the revolutionaries in Tahrir Square all along. There is a powerful sense that what has happened is irreversible, and a feeling of new possibility and promise. That's the good news.

The not-so-good news is that expectations are unrealistically high. The military leadership is struggling with transparency, a concept which doesn't come naturally. Their evident determination to hand off to civilian rule in six months is raising doubts on the part of both youth leaders and political figures like Amr Mousa and Mohamed el-Baradei, both of whom worry that trying to cram Constitutional revisions, Parliamentary and Presidential elections into the next half year will benefit only the Muslim Brotherhood and the remnants of the NDP – the only organized parties on the playing field for early Parliamentary elections. The business community is spooked both by political uncertainty and what appear to be an open-ended series of prosecutions against ex-Ministers and the business elite that prospered under Mubarak. The current government, reshuffled this evening to add a few more opposition leaders, is weak and increasingly criticized by youth activists. The emergency law is still in place, and state security has not gone away. None of this should be all that surprising less than two weeks after the end of the Mubarak era, but it would be a mistake to underestimate the challenges that lie ahead.

RELEASE AUTHORITY: Paul Hilburn, Senior Reviewer

I found Field Marshal Tantawi self-assured and more engaging than I remember him in our previous meetings. He will never be accused of being voluble, but he clearly is proud of the role that he and the senior military leadership are playing, and of the trust with which they are regarded today by most Egyptians. Always risk averse in the past, and a stubborn defender of the military's business empire against economic reform, Tantawi nevertheless appeared determined to carry out a crisp political transition. He was very appreciative of the President's letter, and stressed his firm commitment to strong U.S.-Egyptian relations. Margaret Scobey and I praised the military's role, and emphasized the wider significance of Egypt's transition for a region in the midst of its own profound set of transitions. I pressed for more openness and inclusiveness, urging, for example, that the SCAF ensure that the committee preparing draft constitutional amendments go on television and get around the country in the weeks ahead to explain their efforts, and solicit public and expert reaction. I also raised the value of asking the UN to quietly send technical electoral experts to Cairo to help navigate the very complicated terrain of preparing for both Parliamentary and Presidential elections. I probed him on the wisdom of trying to do Parliamentary elections in only a few months, before Presidential elections, noting the difficulty of organizing new parties and ensuring a level playing field. He was unmoved on that issue, but agreed on the importance of engaging with people more broadly on the proposed constitutional amendments (which may be ready as early as this weekend), and kept the door open on a potential role for UN technical experts. (I subsequently followed up with U/SYG Lyn Pascoe, who confirmed that he will be coming to Cairo next week with a team of experts.) Tantawi also asked in general terms for short-term economic help, citing in particular the collapse of tourism revenue. He said he would appreciate our continuing informal advice on the transition, indicating that he had seen the paper we had sent him on other transition experiences, and found the Indonesia example to be especially relevant.

PM Shafiq came off as well-intentioned but uncertain of his role. He complained openly of his lack of connection to the SCAF, noting that he continued to argue for putting Presidential elections first and preparing more carefully for Parliamentary elections. He was clearly preoccupied with the Cabinet reshuffle, although he engaged in a useful conversation with David Lipton on the need to address both short-term economic recovery problems and medium-term modernization. In a separate conversation, the Minister of Finance offered a sensible overview of Egypt's economic challenges, arguing for debt relief from the U.S. as part of an effort to provide "fiscal space" during the crucial first few months of the political transition, and stressing his interest in creating private sector jobs and encouraging small and medium sized enterprises.

FM Aboul Gheit was less argumentative than usual, although he argued vehemently against EU and Australian ideas about "Friends of Democratic Egypt" or donors conferences, maintaining that "Egypt is not Pakistan or Somalia." He and the Minister of International Cooperation laid out their case for writing off the roughly $350 million in bilateral debt payments that Egypt owes the U.S. this year, and also urged an increase in bilateral ESF. David pointed out that debt relief is very complicated, and might undercut Egypt's message to investors that its economy is fundamentally sound. We explained the reprogramming of $150 million in ESF for immediate job creation and other potential short-term economic programs. We also made clear our intent to support a range of civil society groups, registered as well as non-registered. Aboul Gheit pushed back, not surprisingly, but we were equally insistent, and his resistance was a little half-hearted. (I doubt that this is the last word on this issue. Although it did not come up in the Tantawi meeting, Aboul Gheit indicated that the SCAF is also very sensitive about any change in the pattern of democracy assistance.) We also spent some time discussing the mess in Libya and changes elsewhere in the region. Aboul Gheit was matter of fact in his conclusion that "Qadhafi's days are numbered, and that's good."

We also saw Amr Mousa, who was pretty upbeat about the transition so far and clearly intent on becoming a Presidential candidate. His interest in his role at the Arab League is obviously fading fast, and he made only a passing reference to our UNSC veto. Mohamed el-Baradei was sharply critical of the SCAF's lack of transparency and rushed timetable, but he expressed his determination to work with youth leaders to create a new political party and compete in Parliamentary elections. He was a little coy about his own potential Presidential candidacy. We met with several groups of political party leaders, human rights activists and civil society figures, as well as U.S.-based NGO's. All stressed familiar concerns about the pace of the transition and the need to prepare more carefully and transparently. Perhaps the most interesting of our conversations was with several youth leaders, who had driven events in Tahrir Square and remained intent upon achieving sweeping political change. They were adamant about replacing the Shafiq government, and generally impatient and suspicious of the agenda of the SCAF. They may overestimate their ability to keep filling Tahrir Square in the short-run, to keep up pressure on the current leadership, but there's no mistaking their commitment and energy.

I'll talk later tonight to Cathy Ashton, with whom I am overlapping in Cairo, and will have some further ideas for you on how we might work with the EU, the UN and all the various Egyptian players to continue to urge careful preparation for elections. On economic issues, David will be developing his own thoughts, but we agree that Egypt has two main economic challenges. The first is to maintain financial stability in the face of uncertainty around the political transition. Economic disruptions during the period of protest, as well as wage and subsidy demands in the wake of Mubarak's departure, are significant problems. We will want to help Egypt avoid financial instability, which would likely take the form of inflation and currency depreciation, in order to create an environment of economic calm in which political dialogue can take place. Our help can include bilateral support from the U.S. and EU, loans from the IFIs, and possibly financial support from Egypt's regional partners.

In the longer term, Egypt's most pressing need is economic modernization. Economic growth needs to be restored, but in a way that provides opportunity to the young, the unemployed and those who have not been part of the formal economy. We and other donors can provide assistance aimed at building human capital, promoting the private sector, and strengthening credit programs to broaden access to finance. But aid alone is not sufficient. Egypt's economy grew rapidly in the past decade, with several years of seven percent growth, attracting more than ten billion dollars per year in foreign investment. Too much of the fruits of that growth went to the privileged and the connected, who obtained special protections and advantages from the government. That created widespread resentment. The challenge ahead is to restore growth while breaking down the web of privilege and protection. Egypt will need a program for economic modernization, elimination of the many controls that restrict private entrepreneurship, and an opening up to trade and competition. We and the Europeans should explore how we can support such a program, including by offering enhanced market access, either by expanding existing programs such as Qualified Industrial Zones, or, over time, pursuing new and improved trade agreements.

I also had a chance to do a townhall meeting with American and Egyptian embassy employees, and conveyed your appreciation. They are an extraordinary group, very well-led by Margaret.

All in all, Egypt's transition, for all its obvious challenges, offers remarkable opportunities. Getting it right matters enormously at this moment of sweeping changes across the region.

I fly to tomorrow morning to Tunis, where another tricky transition is already underway.

Best regards,

Bill

Sensitivity: Sensitive
Classification: ~~SECRET//NOFORN~~
Classified by: bill burns, u/s, p, state
Reason: 1.4(d)
Declassify On: 2036/02/22

Bibliography

Abdullah II, King of Jordan. *Our Last Best Chance: The Pursuit of Peace in a Time of Peril.* New York: Viking, 2011.

Albright, Madeleine. *Madam Secretary: A Memoir.* New York: Miramax, 2003.

Allison, Graham T. *Destined for War: Can America and China Escape Thucydides's Trap?* Boston: Houghton Mifflin Harcourt, 2017.

Art, Robert. *A Grand Strategy for America.* Ithaca, N.Y.: Cornell University Press, 2013.

Bacevich, Andrew. *American Empire: The Realities and Consequences of U.S. Diplomacy.* Cambridge, Mass.: Harvard University Press, 2002.

Baker, James A., with Thomas M. DeFrank. *The Politics of Diplomacy: Revolution, War, and Peace, 1989–1992.* New York: G. P. Putnam's Sons, 1995.

Baker, Peter, and Susan Glasser. *Kremlin Rising: Vladimir Putin's Russia and the End of Revolution.* New York: Scribner, 2005.

Beschloss, Michael, and Strobe Talbott. *At the Highest Levels: The Inside Story of the End of the Cold War.* Boston: Little, Brown, 1993.

Bohlen, Charles. *Witness to History: 1929–1969.* New York: W. W. Norton, 1973.

Brands, Hal. *Making the Unipolar Moment: U.S. Foreign Policy and the Rise of the Post–Cold War Order.* Ithaca, N.Y.: Cornell University Press, 2016.

Brooks, Stephen, and William Wohlforth. *America Abroad: The United States' Global Role in the 21st Century.* New York: Oxford University Press, 2016.

Brzezinski, Zbigniew. *Second Chance: Three Presidents and the Crisis of American Superpower.* New York: Basic Books, 2008.

———. *The Grand Chessboard: American Primacy and Its Geostrategic Imperatives.* 2nd ed. New York: Basic Books, 2016.

Bull, Hedley. *The Anarchical Society: A Study of Order in World Politics.* 4th ed. New York: Columbia University Press, 2012.

Bush, George H. W., and Brent Scowcroft. *A World Transformed.* New York: Random House, 1998.

Campbell, Kurt. *The Pivot: The Future of American Statecraft in Asia.* New York: Twelve, 2016.

Chandrasekaran, Rajiv. *Imperial Life in the Emerald City: Inside Iraq's Green Zone.* New York: Knopf, 2006.

Chollet, Derek. *The Long Game: How Obama Defied Washington and Redefined America's Role in the World.* New York: PublicAffairs, 2016.

Chollet, Derek, and Ben Fishman. "Who Lost Libya?" Response to Alan Kuperman. *Foreign Affairs,* May/June 2015.

Christopher, Warren. *In the Stream of History: Shaping Foreign Policy for a New Era.* Stanford, Calif.: Stanford University Press, 1998.

Clinton, Hillary. "Leading Through Civilian Power." *Foreign Affairs,* November/December 2010.

———. *Hard Choices.* New York: Simon & Schuster, 2014.

Cohen, Eliot. *The Big Stick: The Limits of Soft Power and the Necessity of Military Force.* New York: Basic Books, 2017.

Coll, Steve. "The Back Channel." *New Yorker,* March 2, 2009.

———. *Directorate S: The C.I.A. and America's Secret Wars in Afghanistan and Pakistan.* New York: Penguin Press, 2018.

Colton, Timothy J. *Yeltsin: A Life.* New York: Basic Books, 2008.

DeYoung, Karen. *Soldier: The Life of Colin Powell.* New York: Vintage, 2007.

Engel, Jeffrey A. *When the World Seemed New: George H. W. Bush and the End of the Cold War.* New York: Houghton Mifflin Harcourt, 2017.

Feith, Douglas J. *War and Decision: Inside the Pentagon at the Dawn of the War on Terrorism.* New York: HarperCollins, 2008.

Freedman, Lawrence. *A Choice of Enemies: America Confronts the Middle East.* New York: PublicAffairs, 2008.

Freeman, Chas. W., Jr. *Arts of Power: Statecraft and Diplomacy.* Washington, D.C.: United States Institute of Peace Press, 1997.

———. *The Diplomat's Dictionary.* Washington, D.C.: United States Institute of Peace Press, 1997.

Friedman, Thomas. "Foreign Affairs; A Dangerous Peace." *New York Times,* January 12, 1999.

Fukuyama, Francis. *America at the Crossroads: Democracy, Power, and the Neoconservative Legacy.* New Haven, Conn.: Yale University Press, 2007.

Gaddis, John Lewis. *The Cold War: A New History*. New York: Penguin Press, 2005.

——. *Strategies of Containment: A Critical Appraisal of American National Security Policy During the Cold War*. New York: Oxford University Press, 2005.

——. *George F. Kennan: An American Life*. New York: Penguin Press, 2011.

Gall, Carlotta, and Thomas De Waal. *Chechnya: Calamity in the Caucasus*. New York: New York University Press, 1998.

Gates, Robert. *Duty*. New York: Knopf, 2014.

Gellman, Barton. *Contending with Kennan: Toward a Philosophy of American Power*. New York: Praeger, 1984.

Ghattas, Kim. *The Secretary: A Journey with Hillary Clinton from Beirut to the Heart of American Power*. London: Picador, 2014.

Goldberg, Jeffrey. "The Obama Doctrine." *Atlantic*, April 2016.

Green, Michael. *By More Than Providence: Grand Strategy and American Power in the Asia Pacific Since 1783*. New York: Columbia University Press, 2017.

Haass, Richard. *Foreign Policy Begins at Home: The Case for Putting America's House in Order*. New York: Basic Books, 2013.

——. *A World in Disarray: American Foreign Policy and the Crisis of the Old Order*. New York: Penguin Press, 2017.

Hill, Fiona, and Clifford Gaddy. *Mr. Putin: Operative in the Kremlin*. Washington, D.C.: Brookings Institution Press, 2013.

Hoffman, David E. *The Oligarchs: Wealth and Power in the New Russia*. New York: PublicAffairs, 2002.

Hoffmann, Stanley. *Chaos and Violence: What Globalization, Failed States, and Terrorism Mean for U.S. Foreign Policy*. Lanham, Md.: Rowman & Littlefield, 2006.

Holbrooke, Richard. *To End a War*. New York: Random House, 1998.

Ikenberry, G. John. *Liberal Leviathan: The Origins, Crisis, and Transformation of the American World Order*. Princeton, N.J.: Princeton University Press, 2011.

Jentleson, Bruce W., and Christopher A. Whytock. "Who 'Won' Libya? The Force Diplomacy Debate and Its Implications for Theory and Policy." *International Security* 30, no. 3 (2006): 47–86.

Jervis, Robert. *American Foreign Policy in a New Era*. Abingdon, UK: Routledge, 2005.

Kagan, Robert. *Dangerous Nation: America's Foreign Policy from Its Earliest Days to the Dawn of the Twentieth Century*. New York: Knopf, 2006.

——. *The Jungle Grows Back: America and Our Imperiled World*. New York: Knopf, 2018.

Kaplan, Robert. *The Revenge of Geography: What the Map Tells Us About*

Coming Conflicts and the Battle Against Fate. New York: Random House, 2012.

———. *The Return of Marco Polo's World: War, Strategy, and American Interests in the Twenty-First Century*. New York: Random House, 2018.

Kennan, George. *Memoirs, 1925–1950*. Boston: Atlantic–Little, Brown, 1967.

———. *Memoirs, 1950–1963*. Boston: Atlantic–Little, Brown, 1972.

Kerry, John. *Every Day Is Extra*. New York: Simon & Schuster, 2018.

Kessler, Glenn. *The Confidante: Condoleezza Rice and the Creation of the Bush Legacy*. New York: St. Martin's, 2007.

Kirkpatrick, David. *Into the Hands of the Soldiers: Freedom and Chaos in Egypt and the Middle East*. New York: Viking, 2018.

Kissinger, Henry. *Diplomacy*. New York: Simon & Schuster, 1994.

———. *World Order*. New York: Penguin Press, 2014.

Leigh, David, and Luke Harding. *WikiLeaks: Inside Julian Assange's War on Secrecy*. London: Guardian Books, 2011.

Lieven, Anatol, and John Hulsman. *Ethical Realism: A Vision for America's Role in the World*. New York: Pantheon, 2006.

Lippman, Thomas. *Madeleine Albright and the New American Diplomacy*. New York: Basic Books, 2000.

Lynch, Marc. *The New Arab Wars: Uprisings and Anarchy in the Middle East*. New York: PublicAffairs, 2016.

Matlock, Jack. *Reagan and Gorbachev: How the Cold War Ended*. New York: Random House, 2004.

McDougall, Walter A. *Promised Land, Crusader State: The American Encounter with the World Since 1776*. Boston: Houghton Mifflin, 1997.

McFaul, Michael. *From Cold War to Hot Peace: An Ambassador in Putin's Russia*. New York: Houghton Mifflin Harcourt, 2018.

Mead, Walter Russell. *Special Providence: American Foreign Policy and How It Changed the World*. New York: Routledge, 2002.

Menon, Shivshankar. *Choices: Inside the Making of India's Foreign Policy*. Washington, D.C.: Brookings Institution Press, 2016.

Miller, Aaron David. *The Much Too Promised Land: America's Elusive Search for Arab-Israeli Peace*. New York: Bantam, 2008.

Morgan, Dan. *Merchants of Grain: The Power and Profits of the Five Giant Companies at the Center of the World's Food Supply*. New York: Viking, 1979.

Muasher, Marwan. *The Arab Center: The Promise of Moderation*. New Haven, Conn.: Yale University Press, 2009.

———. *The Second Arab Awakening: And the Battle for Pluralism*. New Haven, Conn.: Yale University Press, 2014.

Norris, John. "How to Balance Safety and Openness for America's Diplomats." *Atlantic*, November 4, 2013.

Obama, Barack. *The Audacity of Hope: Thoughts on Reclaiming the American Dream.* New York: Crown, 2006.

O'Hanlon, Michael E. *Beyond NATO: A New Security Architecture for Eastern Europe.* Washington, D.C.: Brookings Institution Press, 2017.

Ostrovsky, Arkady. *The Invention of Russia: From Gorbachev's Freedom to Putin's War.* New York: Viking, 2015.

Packer, George. *The Assassins' Gate: America in Iraq.* New York: Farrar, Straus & Giroux, 2005.

Parsi, Trita. *Losing an Enemy: Obama, Iran, and the Triumph of Diplomacy.* New Haven, Conn.: Yale University Press, 2017.

Pickering, Thomas. Oral History Interview. Association for Diplomatic Studies and Training, April 18, 2003.

Pope, Lawrence. *The Demilitarization of American Diplomacy: Two Cheers for Striped Pants.* Basingstoke, UK: Palgrave Macmillan, 2014.

Powell, Colin L. *My American Journey.* New York: Random House, 1995.

———. *It Worked for Me: In Life and Leadership.* New York: Harper, 2012.

Rhodes, Ben. *The World As It Is: A Memoir of the Obama White House.* New York: Random House, 2018.

Rice, Condoleezza. *No Higher Honor: A Memoir of My Years in Washington.* New York: Crown, 2011.

Ross, Dennis. *The Missing Peace: The Inside Story of the Fight for Middle East Peace.* New York: Farrar, Straus & Giroux, 2004.

Sakwa, Richard. *Chechnya: From Past to Future.* London: Anthem Press, 2005.

Sanger, David E. *The Inheritance: The World Obama Confronts and the Challenges to American Power.* New York: Harmony Books, 2009.

———. *Confront and Conceal: Obama's Secret Wars and Surprising Use of American Power.* New York: Crown, 2012.

Sargent, Daniel J. *A Superpower Transformed: The Remaking of American Foreign Relations in the 1970s.* New York: Oxford University Press, 2015.

Sestanovich, Stephen. *Maximalist: America in the World from Truman to Obama.* New York: Knopf, 2014.

Sherman, Wendy. *Not for the Faint of Heart: Lessons in Courage, Power, and Persistence.* New York: PublicAffairs, 2018.

Shevtsova, Lilia. *Yeltsin's Russia: Myths and Reality.* Washington, D.C.: Carnegie Endowment for International Peace, 1999.

———. *Putin's Russia.* Washington, D.C.: Carnegie Endowment for International Peace, 2005.

Shifrinson, Joshua R. "Deal or No Deal? The End of the Cold War and the U.S. Offer to Limit NATO Expansion." *International Security* 40, no. 4 (2016): 7–44.

Shultz, George P. *Turmoil and Triumph: My Years as Secretary of State.* New York: Scribner's, 1993.

Slaughter, Anne-Marie. *A New World Order*. Princeton, N.J.: Princeton University Press, 2009.

Smith, Charles. *Palestine and the Arab-Israeli Conflict*. New York: St. Martin's, 1992.

Stent, Angela E. *The Limits of Partnership: U.S.-Russian Relations in the Twenty-First Century*. Princeton, N.J.: Princeton University Press, 2014.

Talbott, Strobe. *The Russia Hand: A Memoir of Presidential Diplomacy*. New York: Random House, 2002.

Taubman, William. *Gorbachev: His Life and Times*. New York: Simon & Schuster, 2017.

Telhami, Shibley. *The World Through Arab Eyes: Arab Public Opinion and the Reshaping of the Middle East*. New York: Basic Books, 2013.

Wehrey, Frederic. *The Burning Shores: Inside the Battle for the New Libya*. New York: Farrar, Straus & Giroux, 2018.

Woodward, Bob. *Plan of Attack: The Definitive Account of the Decision to Invade Iraq*. New York: Simon & Schuster, 2004.

———. *Obama's Wars*. New York: Simon & Schuster, 2010.

Worth, Robert Forsyth. *A Rage for Order: The Middle East in Turmoil, from Tahrir Square to ISIS*. New York: Farrar, Straus & Giroux, 2016.

Wright, Thomas. *All Measures Short of War: The Contest for the Twenty-First Century and the Future of American Power*. New Haven, Conn.: Yale University Press, 2017.

Zakaria, Fareed. *The Post-American World: Release 2.0*. New York: W. W. Norton, 2012.

Zeleny, Jeff. "A Foreign Classroom for a Junior Senator." *Chicago Tribune*, September 23, 2005.

Zelikow, Philip, and Condoleezza Rice. *Germany Unified and Europe Transformed: A Study in Statecraft*. Cambridge, Mass.: Harvard University Press, 1995.

Notes

PROLOGUE

1. Memo to Secretary of State–Designate Christopher, January 5, 1993, "Parting Thoughts: U.S. Foreign Policy in the Years Ahead."
2. Henry Kissinger, *Diplomacy* (New York: Simon & Schuster, 1994), 836.

CHAPTER 1: APPRENTICESHIP: THE EDUCATION OF A DIPLOMAT

1. 1984 Amman 6594, July 16, 1984, "The Changing Face of Jordanian Politics."

CHAPTER 2: THE BAKER YEARS: SHAPING ORDER

1. George Kennan, *Memoirs, 1925–1950* (Boston: Atlantic–Little, Brown, 1967), 326–27.
2. Thomas Friedman, "Washington at Work; In Quest of a Post–Cold War Plan," *New York Times*, November 17, 1989.
3. Quoted in Michael Beschloss and Strobe Talbott, *At the Highest Levels: The Inside Story of the End of the Cold War* (Boston: Little, Brown, 1993), 25.
4. George H. W. Bush and Brent Scowcroft, *A World Transformed* (New York: Random House, 1998), 12.
5. Memo to Deputy Secretary Eagleburger, April 10, 1990, "Deepening U.S.–East European Relations."
6. Quoted in John Lewis Gaddis, *The Cold War: A New History* (New York: Penguin Press, 2005), 248.

7. David Hoffman, "U.S. Envoy Conciliatory to Saddam," *Washington Post*, July 12, 1991.

8. Memo to Under Secretary Kimmitt, August 4, 1990, "Kuwait: The First Post–Cold War Crisis."

9. Memo to Kimmitt, August 20, 1990, "Containing Saddam: Diplomatic Options."

10. 1990 Riyadh 2457, November 20, 1990, "Reflections on Post-Crisis Security Arrangements in the Persian Gulf."

11. Memo to Secretary Baker, April 30, 1992, "Foreign Policy in the Second Bush Administration: An Overview."

12. Memo to Secretary of State–Designate Christopher, January 5, 1993, "Parting Thoughts: U.S. Foreign Policy in the Years Ahead."

Chapter 3: Yeltsin's Russia: The Limits of Agency

1. 1994 Moscow 35565, December 9, 1994, "Russia on the Eve of the Vice President's Visit."

2. William Jefferson Clinton, "Remarks to the American Society of Newspaper Editors," Annapolis, Maryland, April 1, 1993.

3. Strobe Talbott, *The Russia Hand: A Memoir of Presidential Diplomacy* (New York: Random House, 2002), 5.

4. 1994 Moscow 27483, September 22, 1994, "Yeltsin and Russia on the Eve of the Summit."

5. Tom De Waal, "Chechnya: The Breaking Point," in *Chechnya: From Past to Future*, ed. Richard Sakwa (London: Anthem Press, 2005), 187.

6. 1995 Moscow 883, January 11, 1995, "Sifting Through the Wreckage: Chechnya and Russia's Future."

7. Interview with Secretary Christopher, *MacNeil/Lehrer NewsHour*, PBS, November 13, 1994.

8. Thomas Pickering, Oral History Interview, Association for Diplomatic Studies and Training, April 18, 2003.

9. 1995 Moscow 5788, February 22, 1995, "Yeltsin and Russia Totter On."

10. 1995 Moscow 19971, June 26, 1995, "Coping with Uncertainty: Russia on the Eve of the Vice President's Visit."

11. 1995 Moscow 6176, February 24, 1995, "Ambassador's Meeting on Chechnya with Disaster Relief Expert."

12. 1995 Moscow 19896, June 26, 1995, "Ingush and Chechen Views on the Fred Cuny Case."

13. Ibid.

14. 1995 Moscow 26910, August 23, 1995, "Cuny Case."

15. 1995 Moscow 19971.

16. Richard Holbrooke, *To End a War* (New York: Random House, 1998), 117.

17. 1995 Moscow 32066, October 5, 1995, "Thoughts on the Eve of the VP's Meeting."
18. Memo of Conversation Between Presidents Clinton and Yeltsin, May 10, 1995, National Security Council and NSC Records Management System, "Declassified Documents Concerning Russian President Boris Yeltsin," Clinton Digital Library.
19. 1994 Moscow 35186, December 6, 1994, "Russia and NATO."
20. 1995 Moscow 32066.

Chapter 4: Jordan's Moment of Transition: The Power of Partnership

1. 1999 Amman 615, January 26, 1999, "A Poignant Farewell."
2. Jeremy Konyndyk, "Clinton and Helms Nearly Ruined State. Tillerson Wants to Finish the Job," *Politico*, May 4, 2017.
3. 1999 Amman 1059, February 7, 1999, "King Hussein's Legacy and Jordan's Future."
4. "Jordan's Hussein Says His Cancer Is Curable," CNN, July 28, 1998.
5. Hourani letter to author, April 1984.
6. Dana Priest, "CIA Taps Richer for Operations Post," *Washington Post*, November 30, 2004.
7. 1998 Amman 9928, November 5, 1998, "Your Visit to Jordan."
8. 1998 Amman 9517, October 20, 1998, "Staying Ahead of Events in Jordan."
9. 1999 Amman 1059.
10. 1999 Amman 3867, May 10, 1999, "A Young Man in a Hurry."
11. 2000 Amman 698, February 8, 2000, "Keeping a Sense of Perspective About King Abdullah's First Year."
12. 2000 Amman 1909, April 12, 2000, "Political Drift in Jordan."
13. 1999 Amman 1588, February 26, 1999, "Jordan in Transition."
14. 2000 Amman 5743, October 15, 2000, "The Tragedy Across the River and Jordan's Uncertain Future."
15. Ibid.
16. 2000 Amman 6760, December 5, 2000, "Peace Process: Relaunching American Diplomacy."
17. 2001 Amman 336, January 22, 2001, "Abdullah Faces a Troubled New Year."
18. 2001 Amman 1658, April 2, 2001, "King Abdullah's Visit to Washington."

Chapter 5: Age of Terror: The Inversion of Force and Diplomacy

1. "CIA Beirut Station Chief Is Among the Dead," *Washington Post*, December 25, 1988.

2. Email to Secretary Powell, March 24, 2004, "Note from Bill Burns: Libya, March 23."
3. "Remarks to the Senate Foreign Relations Committee," April 17, 2001.
4. Memo to Powell, February 15, 2002, "Moving to Tenet Implementation."
5. Paper for Powell from Bureau of Near Eastern Affairs and the Policy Planning Staff, August 30, 2001, "Strategies for Preserving U.S. Political Capital in the Middle East."
6. 2002 Riyadh 06674, October 21, 2002, "Talks in Egypt and Jordan."
7. Memo to Deputy Secretary Armitage, November 19, 2001, "Deputies Committee Meeting on Iraq."
8. Interview with Richard Armitage, "Bush's War," *Frontline*, PBS, December 18, 2007.
9. 2003 Amman 00467, January 22, 2003, "Meetings in Bahrain and UAE, January 21–22."
10. Memo to Powell, February 14, 2002, "Regional Concerns Regarding Regime Change in Iraq."
11. Email to Powell, April 1, 2002, "Next Steps on Middle East."
12. Memo to Powell, July 29, 2002, "Iraq: The Perfect Storm."
13. Email to Powell, August 16, 2002, "Iraq and the President's UNGA Speech."
14. Memo to Powell, January 16, 2003, "Today's Iraq PC."
15. Memo to Powell, July 22, 2002, "Role of the External Iraqi Opposition."
16. Email to Powell, July 11, 2003, "Rethinking Our Iraq Strategy."
17. Email to Powell, March 22, 2003, "Middle East: Update, 3/22 (1500)."
18. Ibid.
19. Memo to Powell, June 11, 2002, "Principals Meeting on Middle East."
20. Email to Powell, June 13, 2002, "Rice Meeting with Israelis, June 13."
21. Ibid.
22. Memo to Powell, June 25, 2002, "President's Speech: Short-Term Follow-Up."
23. Quoted in Aaron David Miller, *The Much Too Promised Land: America's Elusive Search for Arab-Israeli Peace* (New York: Bantam, 2008), 352.
24. Quoted in Charles Smith, *Palestine and the Arab-Israeli Conflict* (New York: St. Martin's, 1992), 513.
25. Memo to Powell, March 11, 2003, "Read-Out of Libya Meetings."
26. Email to Powell, February 6, 2004, "Libya Talks, February 6."
27. Memo to Secretary of State–Designate Rice, December 6, 2004, "Policy Paper for the Bureau of Near Eastern Affairs."

Chapter 6: Putin's Disruptions: Managing Great Power Trainwrecks

1. Memo for the Record, October 22, 2006, "A Birthday Dinner with Putin's Politburo."

2. 2006 Moscow 6759, June 26, 2006, "Your Visit to Moscow."
3. Ibid.
4. 2006 Moscow 1925, February 28, 2006, "Lavrov's Visit and Strategic Engagement with Russia."
5. 2008 Moscow 886, April 1, 2008, "Your Visit to Sochi."
6. Email to Secretary Rice, April 11, 2006, "Note for the Secretary from Bill Burns."
7. 2006 Moscow 6759.
8. 2006 Moscow 1925.
9. 2006 Moscow 11939, October 25, 2006, "Your Visit to Moscow."
10. Ibid.
11. Angela E. Stent, *The Limits of Partnership: U.S.-Russian Relations in the Twenty-First Century* (Princeton, N.J.: Princeton University Press, 2014), 147.
12. Email to Rice, February 16, 2007, "Thoughts on Munich and Russian Government Reshuffle."
13. Email to Rice, January 31, 2007, "Thoughts on Lavrov Visit."
14. Ibid.
15. Ibid.
16. Email to Rice, February 16, 2007.
17. 2007 Moscow 2776, June 11, 2007, "June 9–10 Conversations with Putin and His Senior Advisors."
18. 2007 Moscow 2588, June 1, 2007, "Your Meeting with Putin at G-8."
19. Email to Rice, February 8, 2008, "Russia Strategy."
20. Stent, *The Limits of Partnership*, 167.
21. 2008 Moscow 886.
22. Ibid.

CHAPTER 7: OBAMA'S LONG GAME: BETS, PIVOTS, AND RESETS IN A POST-PRIMACY WORLD

1. In 1982, Walter J. Stoessel, Jr., became the first active foreign service officer appointed deputy secretary of state. Lawrence Eagleburger (1989–92) and John Negroponte (2007–9) were both retired from the Foreign Service when they were appointed deputy secretary by George H. W. Bush and George W. Bush respectively.
2. Memo to Secretary Rice, August 27, 2008, "Indian Civil Nuclear Initiative."
3. Memo to Secretary Clinton, March 20, 2009, "A New Partnership with India."
4. The best account of the back-channel talks is Steve Coll, "The Back Channel," *New Yorker*, March 2, 2009. The Pakistan discussions are also addressed in Memo to Clinton, June 12, 2009, "Seizing the Moment with India."

5. Hillary Clinton, *Hard Choices* (New York: Simon & Schuster, 2014), 83–100.

6. Contemporaneous personal notes.

7. Memo to Clinton, February 13, 2009, "February 11–12 Meetings in Moscow."

8. Ibid.

9. Email to Clinton, September 7, 2009, "Note for the Secretary: Missile Defense."

10. Memo to Clinton, December 5, 2011, "Monday Update."

11. Michael McFaul, *From Cold War to Hot Peace: An American Ambassador in Putin's Russia* (New York: Houghton Mifflin Harcourt, 2018), 254.

CHAPTER 8: THE ARAB SPRING: WHEN THE SHORT GAME INTERCEDES

1. Email to Secretary Clinton, February 23, 2011, "Note for the Secretary from Bill Burns: Tunis, February 23."

2. Hillary Clinton, "Remarks with Spanish Foreign Minister Trinidad Jimenez," January 25, 2011, and Joe Biden, *PBS NewsHour*, January 27, 2011.

3. Robert Gates, *Duty* (New York: Knopf, 2014), 504.

4. Email to Clinton, February 22, 2011, "Note for the Secretary from Bill Burns: Cairo, February 21–22."

5. Ibid.

6. Email to Clinton, June 30, 2011, "Note for the Secretary from Bill Burns: Tunis and Cairo, June 27–30."

7. Email to Clinton, January 12, 2012, "Note for the Secretary from Bill Burns: Egypt, January 10–12."

8. "WikiLeaks Cables Reveal Personal Details on World Leaders," *Washington Post*, November 28, 2010.

9. Muammar al-Qaddafi, radio address, March 17, 2011.

10. Email to Secretary Kerry, April 25, 2014, "Tripoli, April 23–24."

11. Email to Clinton, February 17, 2010, "Note for the Secretary from Bill Burns: Meetings in Damascus, February 17."

12. Ernesto Londono and Greg Miller, "CIA Begins Weapons Delivery to Syrian Rebels," *Washington Post*, September 11, 2013.

CHAPTER 9: IRAN AND THE BOMB: THE SECRET TALKS

1. Memo to Secretary Rice, May 27, 2008, "Regaining the Strategic Initiative on Iran."

2. Ibid.

3. Memo to Rice, July 19, 2008, "Meeting with Iranians, July 19."

4. Memo to Secretary Clinton, January 24, 2009, "A New Strategy Toward Iran."

5. Ibid.

6. "A Nowruz Message from President Obama," March 19, 2009.

7. Philip Rucker, "Hillary Clinton Defends Her 'Hard Choices' at State Department," *Washington Post*, May 14, 2014.

CHAPTER 10: PIVOTAL POWER: RESTORING AMERICA'S TOOL OF FIRST RESORT

1. Memo to Secretary of State–Designate Christopher, January 5, 1993, "Parting Thoughts: U.S. Foreign Policy in the Years Ahead."

2. From a 1946 lecture at the National War College, quoted in Barton Gellman, *Contending with Kennan: Toward a Philosophy of American Power* (New York: Praeger, 1984), 126–27.

3. "Remarks by President Trump and President Putin of the Russia Federation in Joint Press Conference," Helsinki, Finland, July 16, 2018.

4. Alexis de Tocqueville, *Democracy in America*, volume 1, chapter XIII (1835).

5. John Lewis Gaddis, *Strategies of Containment: A Critical Appraisal of American National Security Policy During the Cold War* (New York: Oxford University Press, 2005).

6. Michael E. O'Hanlon, *Beyond NATO: A New Security Architecture for Eastern Europe* (Washington, D.C.: Brookings Institution Press, 2017).

7. James Goldgeier and Elizabeth N. Saunders, "Good Foreign Policy Is Invisible," ForeignAffairs.com, February 28, 2017.

8. Charles W. Freeman, Jr., *The Diplomat's Dictionary* (Washington, D.C.: Institute of Peace Press, 1997), 84.

9. Charles Freeman, Lecture Series at Watson Institute of International and Public Affairs, Brown University, 2017–18.

10. Memo to Christopher, January 5, 1993.

11. Ibid.

12. John Norris, "How to Balance Safety and Openness for America's Diplomats," *Atlantic*, November 4, 2013.

13. Memo to Christopher, January 5, 1993.

14. Quoted in Dan Morgan, *Merchants of Grain: The Power and Profits of the Five Giant Companies at the Center of the World's Food Supply* (New York: Viking, 1979), 301.

Index

About the Author

William J. Burns is president of the Carnegie Endowment for International Peace. He retired from the U.S. Foreign Service in 2014 after a thirty-three-year diplomatic career. He holds the highest rank in the Foreign Service, career ambassador, and is only the second serving career diplomat in history to become deputy secretary of state. Prior to his tenure as deputy secretary, Ambassador Burns served from 2008 to 2011 as undersecretary for political affairs. He was ambassador to Russia from 2005 to 2008, assistant secretary of state for near eastern affairs from 2001 to 2005, and ambassador to Jordan from 1998 to 2001. Ambassador Burns earned a bachelor's degree in history from La Salle University and master's and doctoral degrees in international relations from Oxford University, where he studied as a Marshall Scholar. He and his wife, Lisa, have two daughters.

burnsbackchannel.com

To inquire about booking William J. Burns for a speaking engagement, please contact the Penguin Random House Speakers Bureau at speakers@penguinrandomhouse.com.